Mary Queen of Scots

Examining visual, musical and literary works from the late Tudor period to the First World War, *Mary Queen of Scots* traces a nation's long romance with the queen it once rejected.

Considering both mainstream works (from Edmund Spenser to Sir Walter Scott) and the attachments to Mary that have been formed and sustained by certain subaltern groups, particularly women, Jayne Lewis explores both Mary's life and the myth that formed about her and shows how Mary's prevailing image as a sexualized mother has made her a complicated object of political and personal desire. Lewis demonstrates how this desire emerged at a formative moment in the history of modern Britain and, over time, subliminally shaped that very history.

Jayne Elizabeth Lewis is Associate Professor of English at the University of California, Los Angeles.

Frontispiece *Mary Queen of Scots in White Mourning*, unknown artist, after François Clouet. Courtesy of the Scottish National Portrait Gallery. © National Galleries of Scotland

Mary Queen of Scots
Romance and nation

Jayne Elizabeth Lewis

London and New York

First published 1998
by Routledge
11 New Fetter Lane, London EC4P 4EE

Simultaneously published in the USA and Canada
by Routledge
29 West 35th Street, New York NY 10001

© 1998 Jayne Elizabeth Lewis

Typeset in Garamond by M Rules
Printed and bound in Great Britain by Biddles Ltd,
Guildford and King's Lynn

British Library Cataloguing in Publication Data
A catalogue record for this book is available from the British Library

Library of Congress Cataloging in Publication Data
Lewis, Jayne Elizabeth.
    Mary Queen of Scots : romance and nation / Jayne Lewis.
        p.   cm.
    Includes bibliographical references and index.
    ISBN 0–415–11480–2. — ISBN 0–415–11481–0 (pbk.)
    1. Mary, Queen of Scots, 1542–1587.   2. Scotland—History—
Mary Stuart, 1542–1567.   3. Queens—Scotland—Biography.   I.
Title.
    DA787.A1L62   1998
    941.105′092—dc21
    [B]   98–17140
                                                                        CIP

ISBN 0–415–11480–2 (hbk)
ISBN 0–415–11481–0 (pbk)

What is it that makes History? Well, bodies.
And Art? – A body that has lost its head.

> Joseph Brodsky, "Twenty Sonnets to
> Mary Queen of Scots"

Your mother lives, but not for you.

> Sophia Lee, *The Recess; or,*
> *A Tale of Other Times*

Contents

Plates

Acknowledgments

Mary Stuart's famous motto, "in my end is my beginning," offers an irresistible epigraph for the process of writing this book – a book which exists only because of the boundless generosity, both intellectual and personal, of many people other than its author. In writing it, I have accumulated debts almost beyond calculation. The earliest are owed to Claire L'Enfant and Stella Tillyard, both of whom from the beginning demonstrated their belief in the myth of Mary, as I hoped to tell it. I also thank those who read or commented on parts of the manuscript as it emerged over the years – Helen Deutsch, Dianne Dugaw, Lowell Gallagher, Andy Kelly, Richard Kroll, Claire McEachern, Max Novak, Amanda Powell, Yopie Prins, Debora Shuger, and the members of the Southern California Eighteenth-Century Group, the University of Oregon Research Interest Group, and participants in the University of Pennsylvania's Conference on Jacobitism and English Literature in May 1997. I owe special thanks to Louise Bishop, Hilary Schor and Victoria Silver, all of whose witty and frequently exuberant engagements with the manuscript have been of inestimable value.

The UCLA Center for the Study of Women funded a crucial research trip, and I could not have completed the book without a grant from the National Endowment for the Humanities, or without generous research funding from the UCLA Academic Senate. The Henry E. Huntington Library, the William Andrews Clark Memorial Library, the Beinecke Library, the British Library, the National Library of Scotland and the Yale Center for British Art, and their staffs, all nurtured the quest for the Queen of Scots. My research assistants at UCLA – Lisa Hernandez, Norman Jones, Johanna Schwartz and Matt Titolo – have saved me countless hours of toil, while my meticulous readers for Routledge have given me more than they will ever know. Heather McCallum has been an exemplary editor – tactful, exacting and insightful throughout; Ruth Jeavons, Gillian Kay, Catherine Turnbull, Katherine Hodkinson and Zeb Korycinska have shepherded the book through the final stages of production with extreme agility.

Almost from the moment of this book's inception, I have benefited from the enormous kindness of Paul Korshin; and I am grateful to Margaret Anne Doody, Bob Folkenflik and James Turner for supporting this project without reserve. Several bibliographical and iconographic mysteries were amiably solved by Michael Dobson, Julia Douthwaite, Anne Mellor, Ronald Paulson, Judith Rosen, John Sutton and Nicola Watson. Vivian Folkenflik offered critical insight and fellow feeling throughout, and made my work less lonely.

Several people have contributed to this work in the deepest – and least expressible – of ways. Maryclaire Moroney exhibited a near saintly devotion to its cause early on. Doris McIlwain saw Mary when and as I did; that shared and steadfast gaze guided me through much of the writing. Nancy Glazener remains the most heroic reader I have ever had . . . and the most treasured. I thank Brook Thomas for his perpetual gift of faith and foundation, and my parents, Eldon and Stella Lewis. To Geneva Phillips, I offer my most affectionate gratitude, especially in memory of James E. Phillips. All of these people, no less than the resilient specter of Mary Queen of Scots herself, surely prove the motto: *in my end is my beginning*.

Introduction

Touring Scotland in the spring of 1856, the American novelist Nathaniel Hawthorne naturally made a pilgrimage to Abbotsford, once the home of Sir Walter Scott. Several paintings graced the walls, and Hawthorne admired them all. But, he later confessed,

> the one that struck me the most — and very much indeed — was the head of Mary Queen of Scots, literally the head cut off and lying on a dish: the hair curls or flows all about it; the face is of a death-like hue, but has an expression of quiet, after much pain and trouble — very beautiful, very sweet and sad; and it affected me strongly with the horror and strangeness of such a head being separated from its body. Methinks I should not like to have it always in the room with me.[1]

This book is about what it is like to have the severed head of Mary Queen of Scots always in the room with one. It is written partly from experience. But at its heart lies a more general observation, one akin to Hawthorne's: for all the "horror and strangeness" of Mary's beheading in 1587, people ever since — especially British people — have gone to considerable trouble to keep her in the room with them. Why?

The riddle is especially perplexing because it is the British — or at least their English ancestors — who did away with her in the first place. Devoutly Roman Catholic, half-French and briefly Queen of France, the Queen of Scots in life also pressed a formidable claim to the English throne that her Protestant cousin once-removed, Elizabeth Tudor, so splendidly occupied for much of the sixteenth century. From her birth in 1542 to her death at the scaffold in 1587, Mary Stuart seemed only to revolt the English Protestants whose tastes would come to dominate modern British history, politics and culture. That dominion begins with Mary's end. Indeed, it seems to have exacted it.

Yet if in the flesh the Queen of Scots was a compulsory sacrifice to a nascent fiction of collective identity, her ghost has since captivated many a private imagination. Indeed, Mary's cryptic motto, *en ma fin est mon commencement* ("in my end is my beginning"), eerily foretells her ironic sovereignty in the affective lives of the people who might have been her subjects. Centuries of drama, art and literature attest to that sovereignty, and to this day no one can venture into England without stumbling across some monument to her memory, be it the veritable shrine of her tomb in Westminster Abbey or the ubiquitous bookshop pyramid built from copies of Antonia Fraser's romantic biography, *Mary Queen of Scots*. Just so, in Scotland, the corridors of Edinburgh's Holyrood House all seem to lead to Mary's bedroom, and curators yearly touch up the "bloodstain" that marks the spot where her Italian secretary was stabbed to death at her feet. Motorboats ferry tourists across Lochleven to the gaunt ruins of the island castle where the queen was once held captive by her own subjects, while a memorial house in the border town of Jedburgh bursts at the seams with plaintive, if apocryphal, relics of her life.

Here, I offer an account of Mary Stuart's stubborn hold over the people who once repudiated her. Though it travels across time and makes liberal use of historical materials, my account is not itself a history in any strict sense. Indeed, its anxiety to respect the enigma and perdurability of its subject better classifies it as a critical romance. When recently the poet Joseph Brodsky addressed a full twenty sonnets to Mary Stuart, he pointed out that while human "History" is obviously made by human bodies, "a body that has lost its head" is best approached through the avenues of art and desire.[2] It is with that moral in mind that I tell the story of the long and often mysterious love affair between Mary Queen of Scots and what I will call the fiction of Britain.

The reader will understand that by "Mary Queen of Scots" I refer as much to an image, or an idea, as to a historical woman. By "the fiction of Britain" I likewise mean two things. First, I mean the admittedly slippery and dynamic political entity that was born in England and that eventually incorporated Mary's native Scotland along with Wales and Northern Ireland. This entity may be regarded as a fundamentally Protestant one, and is of course the creation (if also the creator) of individuals who have called themselves British. Second, by "the fiction of Britain," I mean the imaginative forms produced by some of those individuals over time – their poems, plays, novels and assorted other works of art. Whether we understand it as a sociopolitical formation or as a body of imaginative expression, the fiction of modern Britain turns out to have been shaped by its authors' romance with the image and idea of Mary Queen of Scots.

Mary Queen of Scots: Romance and Nation traces that romance through the vast body of literature that has been written about Mary since her birth in 1542. My focus, however, is on the years between the accession of Elizabeth I in 1558 and the death of Victoria in 1901 – years when the modern fiction of Britain was forged, challenged and (to its own mind anyway) briefly perfected. During that time, Mary Queen of Scots often stood for what had to be repressed, selectively, if that fiction was to achieve plausibility and coherence. At the same time, for individual Britons in search of psychological unity and artistic affirmation, Mary also played an extraordinary range of roles. Some of those roles were polemical and others aesthetic; some were congratulatory and others subversive. But the most consistent and compelling of them was often akin to that of the mother in a family romance of epic proportions. It is to this essentially erotic role that my own narrative will always return.

Everyone already knows something about the heroine of the romance at hand: her life was, after all, among the most catastrophic and complicated in European history. Born in 1542 to the Stuart King of Scotland, James V, and his French wife, Mary of Guise, Mary Stuart was crowned Queen of Scotland in earliest infancy. She was reared in France, whose language, aesthetic, and prevailing, Roman Catholic religion became her own, and whose sickly Crown Prince, François II, she married at fifteen. She ruled with him until his death in 1560, whereupon her life unravelled into a tangle of sexual misalliances and political disasters. Resuming her throne in the country of her birth, Mary suffered much at the hands of her own ambitious and unscrupulous Protestant nobles; her desperate marriage to the English Catholic Henry Lennox, Lord Darnley, only dragged the reins of political authority further from her hands. When Darnley was murdered in 1567, the queen was suspected of conspiracy in his untimely end, and she herself only seemed to confirm the worst rumors when she either eloped or was forced into marriage with James Hepburn, Earl of Bothwell, the believed mastermind of Darnley's murder. After compelling Mary to relinquish the crown to her baby son James VI, her erstwhile subjects defeated Bothwell and drove him from the country; she herself eventually fled to England, where the threat posed by her Roman Catholic and continental alliances, not to mention her famously seductive person, induced Elizabeth Tudor to keep her in captivity for nineteen years. Finally, at the insistence of Elizabeth's ministers, Mary was brought to trial and found guilty of treason against the English queen. Pressured by her overwhelmingly Protestant parliament, Elizabeth reluctantly sentenced the Queen of Scots to die on the scaffold in the winter of 1587.[3]

These, anyway, are the reasonably certain features of Mary Stuart's life. But all of them were molded as both Scotland and England struggled to establish modern political and religious identity, often through their relationship to the Queen of Scots.[4] As James Emerson Phillips richly demonstrated a generation ago, most of the facts of Mary's life are thus so clouded by contemporary political propaganda and the passions that fired it that it is almost impossible to speak with confidence of the woman behind them.[5] It is indeed impossible to decide how much of Mary's tragedy stemmed from personal guilt, how much from blind sexual passion, how much from religious persecution, how much from weakness of character, and how much from simple bad luck. Our heroine, however familiar her story feels to us, is always also a mystery.

This mystery transcends the question of what Mary did or did not do and why. Why, for instance, has she in Britain almost always been called Mary Queen of Scots? The name is an archaism and a misnomer. For one thing, Mary herself spoke and wrote in French, and always signed her name "Marie." At the very least, the English determination to call her "Mary" tells us how much the heroine of our romance is also the creation of the English-speaking individuals who could not help involving themselves imaginatively and emotionally with her memory. Yet even as the name "Mary" betrays those individuals' desire to claim her as one of them, the tendency to denominate her Queen "of Scots" seems to distance her. At the same time, "Mary Queen of Scots" is an essentially tribal designation, one which identifies its referent not with a place but with a people. Together with the push and pull already built into her name, that identification is where we should begin if we seek the heart of Mary Queen of Scots's relationship to the fiction of Britain. It suggests that to the extent that she is a queen – commanding subjection – Mary rules over no land (the modern touchstone of national identity), but rather over something at once more nebulous and heritable, something that coheres more generationally than geographically, and something which is internal and intangible rather than visible and readily demarcated. By consigning Mary Queen of Scots to nowhere, her popular name actually acknowledges her potential presence everywhere.

Historically speaking, Mary menaced so many of her own contemporaries because together her blood and faith did indeed seem to put her everywhere, or at least at the intersection of several places which included England, Scotland, France and, more remotely, the Catholic powers of Spain and Italy. Mary's extremely significant claim to the English throne meant that for as long as she lived so too lived the danger that the British Isles might be engulfed by continental and Catholic interests. What's more, since there were in fact many within both Scotland and England who shared their continental contemporaries' love of the Queen of Scots, she also ignited fears that this gulf might open from within.

From the perspective of the non-Catholic Englishmen who were to carry the day, such fears bespeak a psychological dilemma as well as a political one, mirroring the ego's early struggles for differentiation against the double threat of self-division and of absorption into another. It is striking that the first agitation over Mary Queen of Scots coincided with the infancy of the entity that came to know itself as modern Britain. From this point of view, too, it is especially fitting that, alone among female claimants to the sixteenth-century English throne, Mary should, literally as well as metaphorically, have been a mother – the background against which, ontogenetically, differentiation first takes place, and the figure whose rejection is frequently theorized as essential to the formation of a coherent ego identity.[6]

A comparison with Mary Stuart's perennial rival, the unmarried Elizabeth Tudor, illuminates the case. In contrast to Mary, Elizabeth was consciously and generally wanted by her English subjects, particularly by the Protestants. In practical terms, Elizabeth's lack of husband or children conveniently detached her from the invasive interests of other kingdoms. More important, even in her very earliest addresses to her subjects, Elizabeth exploited her unmarried and childless state to reify the image of herself as their figurative, and hence ideal, "mother" and "spouse."[7] Free of precisely the biological entanglements and stain of sexual guilt that often made women who actually gave birth threatening, Elizabeth was able to gratify her subjects' conscious desire for self-determination. She thus offered a mythic point of origin by which they need not feel complicated or corrupted.[8]

Elizabeth's reign marks the genesis of the modern nation state that would eventually be Great Britain. But, throughout Britain's modern history, Mary Stuart's memory would counter and complicate the figures and formations that inherited Elizabeth's function of reflecting a people's singularity, autonomy and unity back to it. The Queen of Scots provided a mirror of a far different sort, one which demonstrated the porousness and indeterminacy of that people's own identity, both as individual men and women and as constituents of a larger sociopolitical whole. Over time, and for a variety of reasons, many furtively sought themselves in this mirror, even as a virtually national commitment to certain myths of self-authorship and psychological coherence obliged them to turn around and shatter it. This ambivalence, I suggest, is the essence of romance, and in the case of Mary Queen of Scots it generated a tension that lies at the heart of the fiction of Britain.

We might say that Britain's romance with Mary began with the Queen of Scots's own desire to rule. It was a desire that brought her from France to Scotland when she was only eighteen years old and it sent her to the scaffold at the age of forty-four. By every account, Mary's longing to be queen was unwavering: she claimed England's arms as a girl and in her mid-twenties led an army to reclaim the Scottish crown that had been wrested from her; she kept her cloth of state even though she lost that crown for good, and she died convinced that she belonged on England's throne, if not in Elizabeth's stead, then at least once she was gone. But Mary's real and potential subjects' desires concerning *her* were vastly more ambivalent. This ambivalence's characteristic expression was of course the Queen of Scots's beheading, an event memorable not only for the fact that it occurred, but also for the thoroughness with which it was actually botched. The death sentence itself was shrouded in the ambiguities of delay, retraction and denial, and finally three awkward strokes of the axe were required to carry it out, in a fiasco that betrays something in excess of mere incompetence.

We should not be shocked by the anxiety and hesitation made visible in Mary's beheading, or by the division within her accusers that found its macabre emblem in the far from neat partition of the queen's own body. For, in the contemporary terms that both Mary and Elizabeth invoked, to kill a queen was to kill a political mother. Just so, it is finally desire for a lost and indeed repudiated mother that is here seen to inform England's — then Britain's — subsequent romance with Mary Queen of Scots. Notably unlike Elizabeth, Mary bore at least one child, and her Roman Catholic supporters construed her as their own "most careful and tender mother."[9] Contemporary representations of her, like those of her son James VI/I, reverted obsessively to the subject of her maternity, and rumors flew around the twin babies who were apparently stillborn to her at Lochleven.[10] To the extent that Mary stood in the

Elizabethan imagination as one, very un-Elizabethan kind of mother – prolific, erotically compelling, choosing and unchosen – her rejection by the reciprocal means of fictionalization and physical violence was necessary if England was, in the minds of certain Protestant Englishmen, to believe the image of its own unity. Though individuals living at different moments in time obviously forge their own conceptions of motherhood, the many novels, poems and plays written about Mary since her death relapse inexhaustibly to the matter of her maternity, often giving her new children erstwhile "unknown to history," and in a variety of ways enacting a strikingly infantile attachment to her. "Your mother lives, but not for you," their nurse informs Mary's long-lost twins in *The Recess*, Sophia Lee's riveting historical novel of the mid-1780s.[11] She could have been speaking to anybody British.

England's initial repudiation of Mary Queen of Scots is of course perfectly legible in ideological terms: Mary was a Catholic in an increasingly Protestant country; she was a sexualized woman in an era which could barely stomach female rule; she had blood ties to the continent at a time when many English subjects were determined to distinguish themselves from other Europeans; she held to a medieval model of sovereignty as political power began to pass out of the hands of kings and queens. Historians, to whom this book is deeply indebted, have taken up all of these issues and the forms of political desire that they reflect.[12] But because my evidence comes from art and literature – and so from a nation's dream work – I spotlight an involvement with the Queen of Scots that seems to exceed – if not to precede – ideology. This involvement's persistence over time, in very different individuals, and across a range of political and religious situations, bears witness to the force of a different kind of desire.

As it mimics the one between mother and child, that desire is visible in the kind of wishes that Britons have always entertained with respect to Mary – wishes to rewrite her life, to rehearse her death, to know exactly what she was like, to bring her back, even to be her. A pair of Victorian women called it "a passionate desire of access," and it is one that is in essence narcissistic, regressive and infantile.[13] Although its object is often reunion with Mary, just as often it has been the rejection or destruction of her, and to trace it is to stumble upon one point at which history – consequential, directly recorded and scarcely inevitable – crosses the path of desire, which cannot be described that way at all. To trace modern Britain's desire for Mary Queen of Scots is also to grasp an important element in its relationship both to its own past and to its inherent difference from itself. Above all, though, it is to create at least the illusion of understanding Mary in a way that I do not believe she has, consciously, been understood before.

As I suggested earlier, such an understanding is built upon the notion that Britain's history is comparable to that of a family, and has from that point of view been as much a romance (a drama of compulsion and desire) as a history (a sequence of rationally analyzable events). The rejection of parental love in the quest for autonomous and coherent identity is of course the essence of the family romance, and one theory as to how it unfolds collectively and over time is outlined in Freud's classic study *Totem and Taboo* (1913). Freud's totemism begins with the murder of a ruler, who becomes, symbolically, an object of a fear and guilty fascination that organize both individual and collective psychic life. According to Freud, totemism is a feature of "savage" life, one that has left "only the slightest traces behind it in the religions, manners and customs of the civilized peoples of today." Freud detects some of these "traces" in Catholic ritual, in the obsessive compulsive neuroses of individuals and, perhaps most intriguingly, in the pseudo-magical repetitions of childhood.[14]

Scott's horrifying, yet enthralling, head of Mary Queen of Scots is only one thread in the tapestry of evidence that one of the most indelible "traces" of totemism in western civilization is the institutionalized, if scarcely universal, British obsession with a Catholic queen. Freud's totemic narrative even expands to include Mary's grandson, Charles I, who also lost his head, and who like her has enjoyed a number of covert revivals. Indeed, in many ways Charles fits the totemic paradigm far better than Mary ever did, for Freud himself is very clear that this paradigm is oedipal, requiring the murder of the father to trigger the mechanisms of guilt and expiation that bind individuals (implicitly, the father's sons) together into groups. On the other hand, Mary's willed demise, coming earlier than Charles's, was that of a mother. And to apply Freud's totemic theory to a queenly mother rather than to a kingly father who actually died after her is to understand the ties that bound generations of modern Britons less along oedipal lines than within what we might see as a preoedipal matrix. It is, that is, to presume the totemic object's literal and indissoluble – its presymbolic and unsymbolizable – connection with the living subject of guilt and desire. Such continuity guarantees both the imperfection and the necessity of its own disavowal. In turn, because desire for Mary so often reflects the ambivalent, essential one between mother and child, her death carries a different valence from that of a father-king. It stands not only as the primal murder that provides the basis of social order but also as an image of division *within* the individuals who inflicted it – individuals who consciously wanted, instigated and witnessed Mary's death, but who at the same time could not help but feel themselves to be a part of her. The accompanying schism of desire, I suggest, passed from the Elizabethans to their children and grandchildren to become, for many, a paradoxical condition of their shared fictions of integrated collective and personal identity.

Mary, of course, never actually made it to the English throne; moreover, she outlived her life as Scotland's queen. But if, as a classic totemic figure, she remains partial and subjunctive, these qualities have, I suggest, actually contributed to her persistence in a modernity that is itself finally atomistic in sensibility and design. Mary's own fractures are compounded by the aura of visible fictionality that surrounded her even in her own time – an aura that I argue was in part produced by her Protestant enemies in defense against the compulsion to be incorporated by her. Her image thus remains one of the most fragmented in history. Unlike Elizabeth Tudor, for example, Mary left no recognizable iconography behind her beyond, perhaps, the widow's veil she assumed upon the death of the first of her three husbands, François II, and which she wore off and on for most of the rest of her life. Nor have we inherited many consistent and reliable visual clues as to her physical appearance, the one exception being her extraordinary height of five feet, ten inches. Not one of the portraits for which she actually sat much resembles any of the others, and together these disparate images spawned so many imitations and outright forgeries that historians have long since given up the struggle to ascertain exactly what the Queen of Scots looked like.[15]

The intrinsic incompleteness of Mary's image has three consequences for anyone involved imaginatively with her. For one thing, it builds a narcissistic element into any attachment to her, guaranteeing that imaginary resurrections of the Queen of Scots will always be exercises in the possibility of both individual and collective self love. For another, that incompleteness instills a visible fictionality in even the most fervent revivals of her memory – a fictionality that has often fostered a subversive understanding of cultural order in a range of British subalterns, most especially women. Third, my critical romance is partly governed by the notion that Mary's image remained an erotic object to British imaginations ironically *because* of the deficiencies built into it – because of an inherent openness to misconstruction that over time permitted the influx of specific, variable and always earthly passions.

This paradox has roots in one of Britain's oldest notions of sovereignty, one that at the time of Mary's birth had for centuries accorded kings two bodies, one spiritual and political, the other temporal and corporeal.[16] Constance Jordan and Marie Axton have both shown how this idea was brought to crisis not only by the rise of Protestant skepticism in the sixteenth century, but also by the "problem" of female rule, uniquely vexatious in the sixteenth century, thanks to the unprecedented number of female claimants to various thrones, combined with the popular assumption that women's bodies were too thickly mixed with matter to sustain the medieval myth of their duality. Elizabeth, Axton suggested, solved this problem by metaphorically disengaging herself from her own body, a strategy that subsequent scholars have shown to be fraught with contest and peril, but one which on the whole succeeded well enough for Elizabeth to become a veritable icon of English – and eventually British – unity, integrity and superiority.[17]

A wife and mother, Mary Stuart had no such luxury. Her beheading marked a different resolution to the problem of the queen's two bodies, for it literalized that concept (not to mention Elizabeth's solution of disengagement) and brought all of the forms of reference attached to it down to earth. At the same time, the cultural use of the notion of a ruler's two bodies was to create the socially securing possibility that one of those bodies would last infinitely over time, even as the other died and was replaced by that of a new king. Mary Stuart's fate over time actually sustains this notion in an ironic register. After her own death, her image survived in the mess and ambiguity of bodily desire to counter the idealized vision of continuity that Elizabeth had managed to foster. This congenital immersion in the partiality of emotion and the fantasies that splinter off it is what so uniquely suits the Queen of Scots to the modern era.

My account of Britons' uncannily self-renewing desire to keep Mary Queen of Scots always in the room with them might best be described as a romance rather than a history, but like many a romance, it does not at all disregard history, or the cultural variants that history produces. For instance, to spotlight Britain is in no way to imply that Mary has only captivated the British. Far from it. "Marie Stuart" has enjoyed an almost saintly status in the French imagination, and today the largest collection of works about her is housed in the Bibliothèque Nationale. Those who, even casually, cock an ear toward the continent will catch strains of Gaetano Donizetti's *Maria Stuarda* (1835) and Robert Schumann's poignant lieder, *Gedichte der Könige Maria Stuart* (1852). Friedrich Schiller's *Maria Stuart* (1800) remains the best-known dramatization of the end of Mary's life. And in the twentieth century, it has often been American stage and cinema that have revived her in productions like Maxwell Anderson's *Mary of Scotland* (1934). The Broadway play's 1938 film version, with Katharine Hepburn, was improbably directed by someone (John Ford) known for his Hollywood westerns, and owed many of its more surreal camera techniques to the silent costume drama *Dorothy Vernon of Haddon Hall*, wherein America's sweetheart Mary Pickford disguises herself as Mary Queen of Scots so that the "real" queen can escape her castellated prison.

But while many a country has laid its own claims to Mary Stuart, British attachment to the Queen of Scots is uniquely intimate and conflicted. It is also uniquely instructive if we seek to understand how, as Jacqueline Rose puts it, the history of groups, like that of individuals, "unfolds in the deepest recesses of the mind" – so much so that the psychological meaning of the word "state" grounds our modern sense of polity.[18] My own critical romance is thus limited to the intertwining histories of England and Scotland – two countries significantly separate in Mary Stuart's lifetime but united monarchically with the English accession of her son James in 1603 and legally with the Act of Union in 1707. That their marriage has not always been a happy or egalitarian one is a given, though it is worth noting that Mary was in life as loathed and repudiated by Protestant Scots as she was by their English counterparts, and so cannot be made to flesh out some sentimental image of Scotland as England's battered *femme couverte*. For better or for worse, Scotland and England's intertwining histories provide a chronological order for my critical romance.

I do not mean to imply that this order is teleological. One lesson of Mary's own conflict with Elizabeth is, for example, that England's future either as part of the larger entity of Great Britain or as a Protestant state was far from certain. But the story told here does have a developmental slant, in the sense that Elizabeth's reign is seen to signal a modern sense of national coherence, one

fundamentally Protestant in the priority it gives to the coherence and autonomy of the private mind. Likewise, while in no way directly responsible for it,
Victoria's death eventually came to symbolize the beginning of Britain's
decline from a certain summit of imperial power and perceived internal unity.
Hence this study is framed by her reign on one end and Elizabeth's on the
other.

Elizabeth and Victoria stand as brackets for another reason: they, like Mary,
were obviously women. In turn, all of the historical moments under scrutiny
here can be seen to have revolved around particular figures of femininity.
Ranging from Stuart women like Mary II and Queen Anne to bourgeois
abstractions like the eighteenth-century woman of sensibility to wayward ral-
lying points like Caroline of Brunswick, such figures helped to shape popular
images of Mary Stuart at any given moment in time. And, as we might expect,
British women's visions of the Queen of Scots have often diverged radically
from those of British men. This difference naturally raises an array of questions:
does women's habitual identification with a ruined queen reflect their own
sense of cultural dispossession and exile from history? How to explain the
explicit bonds that British women of vastly different eras, classes and faiths
have forged through Mary Queen of Scots, often with recourse to the story of
an adolescent girl who learns that Mary is her mother? Without claiming
that all British women have always felt the same way about Mary, I have
made the shared investments of queens and working women the subplot of the
present story – its counter romance, we might say.

This book's most obvious precedent, meanwhile, is *Images of a Queen*, James
Emerson Phillips's nuanced and convincing study of sixteenth-century representations of Mary. I depart from Phillips most noticeably in my concern to
move beyond Mary's own historical moment to take into account her claims on
trans-generational fantasy. What is more, while invaluably showing how Mary
was essentially invented by sixteenth-century political propaganda, Phillips
also divided the resulting iconography of the queen between two opposing
sides, one Catholic, one Protestant. This binarism does not absolutely structure
my own account, partly because I see competing political passions as intertwining, if not outrightly conspiratorial, and partly because I see the most
relevant and persistent divisions in Britain's mental life as existing within and
between individuals.

As Phillips did, however, I focus on written material instead of on the visual
arts. For one thing, an excellent account of Mary's place in British art already
exists in Helen Smailes and Duncan Thomson's *The Queen's Image*, the *catalogue
raisonné* for the Scottish National Portrait Gallery exhibition of 1987.[19] More
pertinently, though, I have understood the fictions of both integrated collective and unified individual subjectivity as founded on writing, and especially
on certain text-based conceptions of authorship and its prerogative that came
in time to describe consciousness, if they did not deliver it outright. I stress
always that Mary has compelled the English language and its characteristic
texts to admit a relationship to the primary claims of affective life – to bonds

that cannot be symbolized or sequentially expressed, despite (or perhaps because of) their centrality to a symbolic and historical understanding of the world and one's place in it.

In short: as of the moment of her death, Mary Queen of Scots could be understood – indeed, could hardly *not* be understood, whatever one thought of her guilt or innocence – as a sacrifice to the imagined coherence of the nation-state and its representative Elizabeth. She thereby became the perfect figure for what had to be repressed in order for both individuals and the collective they formed to believe the fiction of their own unity and integrity. At the same time, Mary's prevailing image as a sexualized mother not only distinguished her radically from the maidenly Elizabeth; it also made her – or at least the lure of attachment to her – a special problem for the self seeking unity. This problem persisted over time as England and Scotland became the primary constituents of the modern nation-state of Great Britain. It remained in some ways generic – approximately the same for male and female subjects – but in other ways turned out to be quite different for men and women. Likewise, in the centuries after Mary's death, different problems were more or less prominent and took slightly different forms, according to the urgencies created by the nation's history, its monarchy and its social life.

This, in essence, is the argument of *Mary Queen of Scots: Romance and Nation*, which otherwise unfolds in four parts, each linked to a particular dynastic interval in Britain's history. Beginning with Elizabeth's reign and moving through the monarchical indeterminacy of the Stuart period to the rise of constitutional monarchy under the four Georges, my story really ends in the imperial splendor of Victorian Britain. Though in each of these periods, the riven myth of Mary Queen of Scots betrays a duality within those who resurrect it, my own aim is not to "expose" the incoherence of the fiction of Britain. Nor is it really to spotlight the gap at that fiction's heart that for centuries, if ironically, ensured both its survival and Mary's subliminal charisma as the object of its desire. In the end, *Mary Queen of Scots: Romance and Nation* is rooted in certain historical and literate individuals' involvement with something that exceeds, even precedes, history – with the finally nonhistorical force of their own desire.

It seems especially fitting that upon seeing Walter Scott's image of Mary's severed head Hawthorne himself was put in mind of another portrait of the queen, this one in youth: "I thought of the lovely picture of Mary that I had seen at Edinburgh Castle," he remembered, "and thought what a symbol it would be, if that beautiful young Queen were painted as carrying this vessel, containing her own woeful head, and perhaps turning a curious and pitiful glance down upon it, as if it were not her own."[20] Hawthorne was of course an American – of English descent, but at last divided from Britain by time, space and sensibility. These qualities, however, may be what allowed him to appreciate the self-division that the subjects of modern Britain had long projected into the woman who might once have been their queen. Perhaps those she might have ruled suspected that they were not their own either. This is why, when we explore their enduring romance with Mary Queen of Scots, we are less likely to catch a glimpse of her than to sense the shadow of a more common quest for self-love – a quest that the flickering image of a long lost mother both frustrated and ever promised to fulfill.

Part I

Elizabethan Mary

> . . . then her dressing of lawn fell from her head, which appeared as if she had
> been seventy years old, polled very short, her face being in a moment so much
> altered from its form when she was alive, as few could remember her by her
> dead face. Her lips stirred up and down almost a quarter of an hour after her
> head was cut off.
>
> Robert Wyngfield, *An Account of the Execution of Mary,*
> *the Late Queen of Scots* (1587)

Few beheadings end in an incident more gruesome or arresting than the stroke
of death itself. But in this, as in much else, the execution of Mary Queen of
Scots proved exceptional. Robert Wyngfield was a meticulous witness to the
events that took place at Fotheringay Castle on the morning of 8 February
1587. Accused of having plotted to kill England's Protestant queen, Elizabeth
Tudor, Roman Catholic Mary had done everything in her power to turn the
scene of punishment into a stage for her own martyrdom. Dressed to the teeth
and poignantly veiled, she murmured psalms in Latin, forgave the headsman,
comforted her weeping women in waiting, and calmly declined to part with
her crucifix. Wyngfield watched. Skeptically. Then he wrote a long report to
Elizabeth, one which captured – and inverted – every detail of Mary's dress and
deportment, from her "borrowed hair" under its "dressing of lawn" to her
"boots of Spanish leather." The Protestant Englishman omitted neither the
Queen of Scots's flirtatious asides to those charged with removing her sumptuous black, green and crimson costume nor the showy rosary that rattled at
her waist.[1]

As he neared the end of his litany of impostures, Wyngfield naturally tab-
ulated the "two strokes" of the executioner's axe that "left a gristle behind,"
presumably necessitating a third application of the hatchet. But in a rare display of compunction he neglected to mention this final stroke. The climax of
his account comes, thus, not at the moment when Mary's head left her neck –
strictly speaking, that moment never arrives – but rather at the one subsequent
to it, when, he tells us, her fetching headdress slipped to reveal that the formidable figure of a few seconds before not only was no more but, in a sense,

had never been, "her face being in a moment so much altered from its form when she was alive, as few could remember her by her dead face." Wyngfield's failure to register the decisive moment when Mary's head left her neck is of a piece with his insistence that the wizened woman at the scaffold was not the same queen, "of stature tall, of body corpulent," who had so recently made her way toward it. Along with the decidedly fantastic claim that Mary's "lips stirred up and down almost a quarter of an hour after her head was cut off," these peculiarities conspire to deny that the Queen of Scots actually died at the time she was beheaded.

It seems odd indeed to detect such a denial in the words of someone who, like many a loyal English subject of his day, obviously and urgently wanted Elizabeth's chief female enemy dead. Most of Wyngfield's account reflects this more admissible desire: "of face fat and broad," freighted with all the paraphernalia of popery, the doomed queen it paints is a gaudy *grande dame* whose charade of pious serenity cries out to be seized and vengefully degraded into farce. Yet if Wyngfield's report of her telltale "dressing of lawn" and chattering jaws presents Mary Stuart as a garish fraud, the same details also keep her in motion. Indeed, those details' extravagance, unto incredibility, suggest that the dead queen actually unleashed a flood of desire in our hostile Protestant author – for symbolic mastery of the situation she herself dominated, true, but also for continued contact with her, for the moment of her death never to arrive, or end.

Both its eagerness to lay her faintly lascivious artistry bare and its bent toward caricature make Wyngfield's text a classic example of the propaganda against Mary Stuart that engulfed the British Isles during the reign of her cousin once-removed Elizabeth Tudor. Between the year of Elizabeth's coronation (1558) and 1603 (the year of Elizabeth's death) countless pamphlets, plays, ballads, sermons, poems, letters and parliamentary orations all called for Mary's blood, or justified its shedding. To counter the image of martyred majesty that Mary and her supporters tried to create, their fierce and twisted eloquence forged a notoriously deplorable picture of the Queen of Scots. But that eloquence's very urgency also testifies to Mary's extraordinary hold on Anglo-Scottish imaginations at a formative moment in their shared history. What we might term the libidinal subtext of Wyngfield's "True Declaration" – its author's unspoken craving to keep the Queen of Scots alive and dominant – also drives any number of contemporary diatribes against her, not to mention the works of fantasy that sprang from them.

The pressure of longing that harasses even words as resolute as Wyngfield's and threatens to unseat their conscious aims may well unlock the mystery of just what the Catholic Queen of Scots meant to many in the second half of the sixteenth century. That mystery asks to be approached in two steps. The following chapter explores Mary's effect on several, mostly Protestant men during her personal rule in Scotland, which began in 1560 and ended, ignominiously, with her forced abdication in 1568. The one after it charts her long captivity in England, her trial for treason, her death and above all her afterlife in the twilight years of Elizabeth Tudor's own reign. Like the first, it finds what we might call the "Queen of Scots effect" an internally schismatic one, breeding an array of literary texts as deeply and yet imperfectly divided as Mary's own body ended up being. Indeed, whereas in England the wish to be ruled by Elizabeth proved compatible with a mounting desire for political and psychological self-government, both for many English people and for the Protestants who gained political ascendancy in the Scotland of her own day, Mary Stuart came to stand for a profound affliction of the will, one at last insupportable in conscious life.

Mary and Elizabeth never met, and it is of course Elizabeth who became the epitome of English – and, retrospectively, of British – majesty. Nonetheless, England's conscious attachment to Elizabeth and all she represented went hand-in-hand with a much more ambiguous and ungovernable devotion to the Queen of Scots. Exemplified in Wyngfield's *Account*, the voluminous body of Protestant literature against Mary is shaped by twinned yet warring impulses – to detach Mary from her own physical body and its unseemly arts but also to be absorbed into those very arts. Far more than simple adoration of Elizabeth, or unadulterated revulsion against Mary, it is this contradiction and the inner rift that it created which at last sponsored both a singularly durable form of private subjectivity and a voucher for the Queen of Scots's eerie persistence through generations of collective psychological life.

1 "The finest she that ever was"

Scotland, 1558–1568

Practically everyone who attempts to decipher Mary Queen of Scots in her own day ends up resorting to dichotomy. If Mary's conspicuous differences from England's reigning queen, Elizabeth Tudor, do not come to the fore, then the radical, religiously inflected divide that opened between contemporary representations of the Queen of Scots will take center stage. These are just and powerful distinctions: politically maladroit and sexually active, a stranger in her own country and a captive in the one she felt she should have ruled, Mary Stuart was indeed everything that her famously chaste and indomitable cousin once-removed was not. At the same time, our own dependence upon the verbal records of her life makes it impossible to know exactly what Mary was. Drawing on the political controversy and persistent theme of erotic transgression that ravaged her personal rule in Scotland, Protestant writers painted the Queen of Scots as a scheming seductress and bloodthirsty "competitor" for Elizabeth's crown. But the woman they described bears little resemblance to the one who appears in Mary's own letters, and still less to the saintly victim of a barbarous state who was virtually canonized by her Catholic supporters.[1] The tendentious, contentious character of contemporary writing about the Queen of Scots confirms little more than Elizabeth Tudor's own slippery epitome of her cousin as "the daughter of debate, that eke discord doth sow."[2]

Since the standard oppositions – Mary *versus* Elizabeth, Mary *versus* Mary – tend to cancel each other out, it might be more fruitful to begin from a less strictly bifurcated point of view. Long before she came to the scaffold, or even to England, Mary Stuart was after all very widely regarded as the most attractive woman in Europe – "the finest she that ever was," Elizabeth's ambassador to her court admitted in 1563.[3] She was a "goodly personage" who "hath withal an alluring grace," confirmed another Englishman, Nicholas White, when he visited Mary in England at the beginning of her nineteen-year captivity there. Such "alluring grace" could, evidently, ignite chain reactions of feeling, fantasy and action in all who came into contact with the Queen of Scots, regardless of political allegiance or religious belief. Though steeled against her, White could not help but speculate that the queen's "pretty Scotch speech" and "searching wit, clouded with mildness," might easily "move some to deliver her" from captivity. Whereupon "glory joined to gain might stir others to adventure much for her sake; then joy is a lively impetuous passion, and carrieth persuasions to the heart, which moveth all the rest."[4]

Bound to undermine both individual autonomy and conscious intent, and liable even to erode already often frail distinctions between Catholic and non-Catholic, it was just this uncontainable erotic power that made Mary so dangerous. For as it brought those who felt it together, it threatened to shatter the fragile community of feeling that English Protestants had already built around another woman by the time the Queen of Scots arrived in their midst, in the spring of 1568. In 1579, the eleventh year of Mary's English captivity, the printer John Stubbs warned that woman, "Elizabeth of England," that her cousin "hath already cost us enough of our English blood, and cares not though she make havoc of nobility and people."[5] Stubbs was referring, directly enough, to the many conspiracies against Elizabeth which had been traced to Mary since her arrival in England, and he lost his right hand for naming the "gaping gulph" of animosity to the Tudor queen that yawned just under the surface of her own superficially quiescent kingdom. But in order truly to appreciate the sort of "havoc" that Mary could unleash within both "nobility and people," we ourselves need to look beneath the strictly political threat that she posed. We should begin instead with the way in which sex, power and the possibility of collective unity first chanced to converge, imaginatively, in the figure of "Elizabeth of England."

THE REGIMENT OF WOMEN

Elizabeth's rocky road to England's throne, which she ascended in 1558, is well known. She was the second child and second daughter of Henry VIII, whose frustrated wish for a son had led him to divorce his first wife, the devoutly Roman Catholic Catherine of Aragon, for a homegrown Protestant, Anne Boleyn. In spurning Catherine, Henry perforce forsook the Roman Catholic faith, replacing it with an independent Church of England. Catherine's personal replacement, Anne, however, produced only a single daughter – Elizabeth – and shortly thereafter lost her head under confused charges of treason and adultery. Henry went on to collect the son he wanted from his third wife, Jane Seymour. For her part, Elizabeth was declared a bastard and went on to wait in the wings while first her half-brother, Edward VI, and then her Roman Catholic half-sister, Mary Tudor, inherited the throne.

Married to the Catholic Philip II of Spain and fired with religious zeal, Mary Tudor's persecutions of her own Protestant subjects bred a lasting enmity between them and their Catholic counterparts. England of course lacked the Salic Law which kept women from the throne in many other countries. But under Bloody Mary its vast Protestant population certainly marked the convergence of Catholic and female rule. Numerous political tracts jumped to identify both with unlawful domination, but none more nimbly – or bitterly –

than the Scottish Presbyterian John Knox's *First Blast of the Trumpet Against the Monstrous Regiment of Women* (1558).

In Knox's heated opinion, both holy writ and natural law dictate that woman is subordinate to man; all female "regiment" is thus by definition "monstrous." Its horrors are compounded by woman's emotional frailty, not to mention her unique enslavement to the unpredictable physical world of birth and death, traceable in great part to the past crime of Eve's fall and the enduring chains of maternity. "The authority of a woman is a corrupted fountain," Knox declared, so that "whosoever receiveth of a woman office or authority, are adulterous and bastard officers before God."[6] Furthermore, because "God hath dejected Woman from rule, dominion, empire and authority above man" (p. 417), every godly man is bound "to vindicate the liberty of his country, and to suppress the monstrous empire of Women." Indeed, "for that Woman reigneth above man, she hath obtained it by treason and conspiracy committed against God" (p. 415).

Knox's *First Blast* equated sex and subjugation, mixing the Protestant ideal of self rule with a potent misogyny at the same time that it acknowledged the "adulterous" thrill of submission to a queen regnant. His was only the most insistent voice on one side of the fierce debate over the attractions of female sovereignty that outlived Mary Tudor to imperil her sister Elizabeth's path to the throne. Then too, Elizabeth's official illegitimacy harnessed her to her mother's headless, whorish ghost. The conjunction only fueled contagious fantasies like Knox's, in which political and sexual insubordination joined forces with erotic domination to threaten the "liberty" of individual men and the stalwart, singular "country" they might together form.[7]

Still, even amid such fearful delusions, Elizabeth uniquely promised unity to a political and religious community exhausted by conflict. As is well known, she delivered at least the illusion of this unity in two interlocking ways: by restoring the English church to Protestantism and by declining to marry. A virginity strategically displayed could, and did, permit Elizabeth to transcend the supposed mixture of properties that allegedly made women inferior rulers.[8] At the same time, by postponing the choice of a husband, the Tudor queen created a pool of endlessly deferred desire around herself; she thereby wooed diverse aspirants into an ironically shared commitment to a single object. Though indebted to Petrarchan idealism, these strategies reflected one, fundamentally Protestant, assumption. Both, that is, presumed that signs (in this case that of the queen's body, charged with the responsibility of uniting England into one political and symbolic entity) can be detached from their natural referents (in this case, the living Elizabeth). The resulting disjunction authorized the queen's disparate and independent "readers" in a way that ultimately brought them together.[9] It was by manipulating this form of self-representation – really a matrix of desire – that Elizabeth managed to win the political and psychological consent of groups of powerful and formerly factionalized men: noble members of Parliament, the emerging commercial classes in London, poets and lawyers in the Inns of Court.[10]

At her coronation, Elizabeth accepted a copy of the Bible in English to signify her allegiance to a Protestant faith itself built upon the schism between substance and sign which grants individuals interpretive liberty. Henceforth England's political and imaginative coherence would depend on her adroit but inconspicuous manipulations and evasions of men who, behaving more or less as her readers, might establish both the corporate integrity and the individual authority they sought through her. Indeed, such readers often became authors, devoted ones like Sir Philip Sidney and Edmund Spenser, whose literary works made the queen's ultimately intangible image a confirming mirror for her accordingly adoring English subjects.[11] Nor could Elizabeth's lack of close relations, husband or child help but foster the nascent fictions of both England and the self-authorizing English subject. It is not hard to see how these fictions were virtually independent of the queen's physical reality.[12] Elizabeth got her subjects to want her to rule, or at least to agree to believe that they did, by refusing to do more than flirt with the possibility that the sign and the substance – the fiction and flesh – of their queen might ever converge.[13]

Elizabeth's accession, though, was marred by controversy not only over how sex and power should coincide but also over her specific right to the English crown. It is here that the problem of Mary Stuart first surfaced.[14] In 1558 Mary was fifteen years old. No scrappy *parvenue* of Elizabeth's stripe, she had been queen of neighboring Scotland from the first week of her life. Half-French through her mother, Marie de Guise, Mary had lived in Catholic France for ten years, and had wholly absorbed its language, culture and religion. She had also just married François II, the French Dauphin. More to the point, Mary's grandmother, Margaret Tudor, had been Henry VIII's sister, and to many (usually Catholic) minds, the Queen of Scots's sterling pedigree, untainted by the stain of bastardy, put her before Elizabeth in the line to the English crown. Mary's ambitious French uncles, the Duke and Cardinal of Guise, had taught their niece herself to take this view, even persuading her to quarter the arms of England with her own.

Spurred by fears of Mary's Catholic faith and ties to France, an increasingly influential aggregate of English Protestants ardently opposed her accession. Some of them cited a codicil in Henry VIII's will which prevented anyone of foreign birth from ascending to England's throne.[15] Born in Scotland, which of course bordered England and whose kings had intermittently acknowledged fealty to it, Mary may or may not have counted as an alien. Like her ties to France, her ambiguous status as at once England's intimate and a stranger to it mirrored the disturbing indefiniteness of a country then keen to realize its own religious, linguistic and territorial boundaries.[16] Other arguments against Mary's accession seemed equally embarrassing: for example, some held that since women could not inherit property in England, they were surely unfit to inherit the country itself. This was a dangerous point to make, for it implicitly undermined Elizabeth's own claims to the crown. As long as Mary's sex disqualified her from the English succession, the myth that all of England wanted Elizabeth Tudor to rule it was also held in check.

Once we have identified the major threat that Mary Stuart posed as a symbolic and erotic one – as a matter of uncertain boundaries and diverted desire – we can begin to see just why "Elizabeth of England," no less than the male subjects who had begun to establish corporate and individual identity through her, had, in John Stubbs's words, to "beware of Scottish Mary." First, and most simply, Mary stood for an England ominously other than the one Elizabeth mirrored back to it, its borders dangerously open rather than tidily closed, its texture of religious faith oppressively Catholic instead of autonomously Protestant. Second, there was the kind of woman that Mary, even at fifteen, appeared to be. In contrast to the chaste singularity that made Elizabeth metaphorically available at once to all and none of her subjects, Mary Stuart's marriage, not to mention her blood ties to one of the most powerful houses in Catholic Europe, the Guise, grounded her in a set of sexual and genetic relationships which would only multiply and deepen as she went on to marry twice more and, most importantly, to bear a child.

To contemporary minds, such importunate bonds and their attendant entanglements found analogues in Mary's Frenchness, in the pleasures she took, and even in her Catholic faith. For instance, the Valois court of Mary's girlhood was the most decadent and sophisticated in Europe, and it was notoriously dominated by decadent women like Catherine de'Medici and Diane de Poitiers. Wives, mothers and mistresses of their ilk influenced affairs of state from behind the scenes, through the invisible but imperious bonds of sexual and familial love.[17] Marie Stuart, "la reine dauphine" whose marriage to François had tied Scotland to France in just this way, was one of the French court's principal darlings, the subject of numerous luminous portraits and the object of countless adulatory verses by the tight-knit circle of court poets known as the Pléiade.

Exerted, then, through a vast and usually sexualized web of attractions and affinities, Mary's personal power was considerable, but it was not of Elizabeth's kind. Elizabeth could, and did from the start, freely exploit the ultimately ungrounded metaphor that England was her child, her lover, even her spouse. Mary really did participate in many such relationships; just so, even before she returned to Scotland, upon François's death in 1560, she seemed to enjoy far less influence over the way in which she was herself defined. While this ought to have disabled her, Mary actually seemed to take pleasure in the compensatory privileges of bodily connection, and even in the convergence of her metaphorical and literal lives. An artist whose favorite medium became in time the entirely tactile one of thread and fabric, she was famed also for her affecting poetry and poignant letters. In contrast to Elizabeth's of self-segregation and sublimation, all of Mary's arts seemed to extend the reckoning, exemplified in the Roman Catholic doctrine of transubstantiation, that even the most seemingly abstracted of signs can actually fuse with the matter they represent.[18] Her 1560 "Chanson" on François's death, for example, substituted her (living) visage for his painted one.[19] Later, during her English captivity, tapestries took shape under her own fingers, brilliant with acronyms and emblems

of the physical and even moral plight which gave rise to them. During her captivity too, Mary's many letters to Elizabeth would address the Tudor queen
variably as sister, "natural cousin," mother and spouse.[20] So might Elizabeth's
literal relationship to Mary – that of slightly removed cousin – bleed into a full
spectrum of imagined connections, depriving Elizabeth herself of the power to
fix Mary's difference and distance from her. In short, even as Elizabethan
England's integrity as a psychopolitical and symbolic whole came to rest upon
a foundation of marked differences, and distances, between individuals, the
Queen of nearby Scotland seemed to practice a counter art – an impure art –
of fleshly identification.

Because it recognized that even the most disjunct of physical and psychological entities, including Mary and Elizabeth themselves, are potentially one,
this counter-art naturally troubled imaginations in high places. Not long
before Mary's execution, Elizabeth's lady-in-waiting Lady Stafford was
rumored to have dreamed "she saw the Queen of Scots's head cut off, then her
mistress's head also." Upon which "the Queen then told her the like vision in
her sleep had troubled herself."[21] Long before Mary's ill-fated flight into
England, her ambassador to the English court, James Melville, observed
Elizabeth's inordinate attachment to a miniature portrait of Scotland's queen.
Kissing, fondling and "appear[ing] with great delight to look upon it,"
Elizabeth then interrogated Melville as to "whether my Queen's hair or hers
was best, and which of the two was fairest."[22] Upon learning that Mary's
favorite pastimes (ironically enough) included playing the virginals, Elizabeth
arranged for Melville next to come upon her seated at that instrument. During
the last months of Mary's life, Elizabeth would almost compulsively ground
her speeches to a bloodthirsty Parliament in her identification with "one not
differing from me in sex, of like rank and degree, of the same stock, most
nearly allied unto me in blood."[23]

The dangerous lure of not differing – of a similarity unto shared identity –
held two possible meanings for the cult of Elizabeth, which is to say for the
fundamentally autoerotic paradigm through which her subjects had begun to
differentiate themselves both individually and collectively. On the one hand,
it could be convenient to have Mary around. Thanks to lurid formulations like
Knox's, Elizabeth, as a female ruler, could all too easily look like a vulgar contradiction.[24] As long as Mary Stuart stayed in the picture, any animosity or
even ambivalence that Elizabeth excited could be deflected onto her increasingly wayward cousin. At the same time, though, precisely because Mary's sex
and blood made her such a convincing symbolic substitute for Elizabeth, she
remained in political reality an all too likely replacement for the Tudor queen,
one who moreover carried the unappealing certainty of attachment to continental Europe and a Catholic ascendancy. Then too, who was not to say that
anyone who scratched Elizabeth's skin – the skin, after all of the daughter of
a traitorous whore and a virtual autocrat – would not find another Mary Queen
of Scots beneath it?

Mary's inherent borderlessness and resulting infringement upon what their queen was believed to be naturally bred different desires in Elizabeth's own Protestant subjects – for Mary to stay and for her to go, for her to be Elizabeth in one way but not in another – that would prove incompatible in the long run. But in the beginning the tension between conflicting wishes fueled the rampant and remarkably consistent myth of the Stuart queen's erotic artistry. Designed expressly to deprive Mary of her natural and encroaching claims upon the affections of Scottish and English Protestants alike, that myth was forged in the torrent of literature against the Queen of Scots to which we now turn, and which began the moment Mary, widowed, left France to resume her Scottish throne. This writing is deeply ironic, for despite the *animus* that motivated them, its Protestant authors were frequently forced to find the sources of their own political and literary authority in unconscious identification with the art of female sovereignty that the Queen of Scots practiced. Finally maternal in its associations, that was an art charged with the *frisson* of boundaries disavowed, one which threatened to upend familiar categories of subjectivity and objectivity, domination and submission. But its greatest power, and therefore its greatest terror, lay in the quality it shared with mother love. The power of Mary's art lay in its evident priority to writing, the notoriously disembodied system of symbolic differences through which Elizabethan Englishmen and their Protestant counterparts in Scotland now intended to demarcate both themselves and their others.

THE RETURN OF THE MOTHER

After the death of her first husband, the childlike François II, Mary Stuart could easily have remained in France, a dowager queen with no political authority but considerable charisma. Instead, she returned to her native Scotland, and to the people, born her subjects, whom she herself had been born to rule. But her return, at the age of eighteen, contrasts dramatically with Elizabeth's largely triumphant accession two years before. Though she was not without a sizeable Catholic following, the Presbyterian demagogue John Knox was there, and allowed as how he had "never seen a more dolorous face of the heaven."[25] Clad in the white veil of mourning that was to become her trademark, the freshly widowed queen spoke a language – French – different from that of her own subjects. Worse, she practiced a religion to which many of them had grown hostile as they came to embrace the more severe and radically anti-monarchical tenets of the Protestant faith. In Mary's absence, furthermore, political power had fallen into the hands of a cadre of such reformers, led by the queen's own regent and bastard half-brother, James, Earl of Murray. The entertainments commemorating Mary's return to her native land thus projected only conflict: dragons standing for the Catholic Church went up in flames; at the last minute, the effigy of a priest elevating the host narrowly escaped the same fate.[26]

This inauspicious beginning was nonetheless representative of the days to come, for however adept Mary Stuart might have been in the finer points of court culture, she remained utterly inexperienced in actual affairs of state. Religiously tolerant but personally devout, and softened by her many years in France, the Queen of Scots found her personal powers largely limited to bodily ones – to affecting tears and a melodious voice, to a winning face, a regal carriage and vast personal charm. Intuitively, she sought support from an ever-shifting troupe of foreign secretaries and advisors, of whom the most notorious was her Italian secretary David Rizzio. Rizzio's alien blood and Catholic faith, not to mention his musicality and aptitude for the elegant court poetry that pleased the queen, were bound to ignite suspicion, animosity and envy in her dour Protestant nobles.

Desperate to shore up her tottering power base, and anxious to reinforce the ties to England that she hoped would sustain her in a country torn apart by religious antipathy, Mary finally wed the English Catholic Henry Lennox, Lord Darnley. "Handsome, bearded, and lady-faced" though he evidently was, Darnley made the queen's life miserable almost from the start.[27] As power-hungry as he was petulant and effete, Darnley demanded to be considered the queen's consort and equal. Mary's refusal to recognize him as such merely flaunted the sexual insubordination implicit in female rule. In fact, the only English spouse Mary might have taken without sowing similar discord was an impossible one: Elizabeth herself. Elizabeth's own secretary, William Cecil, openly flirted with this fantasy, musing that "God could not have blessed these two kingdoms with greater felicity, than, if one of the two queens had been a king."[28]

But God instead had doomed the two queens, and their people, to a kind of erotic frustration. The conspicuousness of Mary's own desires only made matters worse. To Scottish and English eyes, her apprenticeship in the licentious courts of the Valois kings made her queenly wishes, too visible in the first place, all look sexual in essence. While Scottish poets dutifully celebrated a marriage that "the race of Fergus and of Stuart joined,"[29] many saw Mary's choice of Darnley as the unbridled and disruptive indulgence of a gallic and entirely female libido. Even her own diplomat, Melville, reckoned that "without the restraint of a sensual bit" Mary had merely wed "such one as [she] deemed would serve [her] lust."[30]

Jealous of Mary's intimacy with her Italian secretary Rizzio, Darnley and Murray conspired to have him stabbed to death, as it happens at the feet of a queen seven-months pregnant with the future James VI. Shortly after James's birth, Mary began to seek counsel, and perhaps more, from an exceptionally ambitious Scottish noble, the Earl of Bothwell. Even the queen's supporters would eventually confess that Bothwell was "audacious, proud, inconstant,"[31] and by involving herself with him, Mary quickly opened herself to charges of adultery. Rumor only bred rumors more vicious when during one of Darnley's probably venereal illnesses the Edinburgh house where he was convalescing, Kirk o'Field, was blown to bits.

The minute Darnley's strangled corpse, unscorched, turned up in the garden, suspicion of murder landed on Bothwell, with Mary his supposed accomplice. Although her defenders maintained that the mastermind was Murray, Mary did little to salvage her own tarnished reputation when she almost immediately eloped with Bothwell. Their flight spawned a host of handbills and broadside ballads that painted the Queen of Scots as the sexually voracious avatar of all the most depraved women in ancient myth and history – Clytemnestra, Delilah, Jezebel. But at the same time, other ballads like the anonymous "Rhime in Defence of the Queen of Scots" cast Bothwell as Mary's ravisher, her hasty third marriage as rape. In these songs, Mary came across as a "good and vertuous Queen," one whose only fault lay in her political innocence: "This simple Queen each way/Was wrapt in wore and care," swore one sympathetic balladeer. "For they that have not skill and craft/Are soonest caught in snare."[32]

Both "this simple queen" and the tyrant overruled by her own passions are primarily powerless: both images strip Mary of volition and personal authority, just as both, like all propaganda, demand the same abdication of interpretive authority from their readers. Metaphorical loss soon became lived reality, for in 1567, not long after her ambiguous "ravishment" by Bothwell, Mary's rebel lords imprisoned her in a lonely castle in the middle of Scotland's desolate Lochleven. Here, following a miscarriage, evidently of twins, Mary was compelled by Murray and his henchmen, the Earls of Ruthven and Lindesey, to resign her crown to her year-old child. Apparently by captivating the young son of her own captor, Mary managed to escape Lochleven, and even mounted a briefly successful charge to regain her title. But in the end defeat drove her south, to England; she fled there in 1568, never to return.

Shot through with the theme of volition's loss and boundary's violation, this is the plot of Mary's personal rule in Scotland. There is no denying its disastrous cast. But in the end the eight years that Mary spent in her own country were shaped less by what she herself did or did not do than by the chimeras of desire that twisted themselves around her and may in the end be said to have created her fully as much as she inspired them. Part of Mary's emotional impact stems of course from the countervailing forces of Catholic affection and Protestant hostility, each of which produced its own polemical version of the Queen of Scots. Within the specifically Protestant genres of response to Mary, however, we find that both her own subjects and the diplomats who came to Edinburgh from Elizabeth's court developed a nuanced and strikingly narcissistic attachment to her. In retrospect, their often involuntary imaginative investment in "the finest she that ever was" does not look so very different from the infantile love of which they deliberately deprived her blood child, James, at exactly the moment they rid themselves of their own political mother.

JEZEBEL'S LETTER

What was it like to live with Mary? Sent there upon the Queen of Scots's return from France, Elizabeth's wary diplomat, Sir Thomas Randolph, was both mesmerized and repelled by her Scottish court, a carnival aglow with illusion and sensuality. Here, he confided to Cecil, "devilish devises are imagined upon" and entertainments "continued with joy and mirth, marvellous sights and shows, singular devices; nothing left undone either to fill our bellies, feed our eyes, or content our minds."[33] Such bewitching repletion was easily interpreted as wretched excess: George Buchanan, a Protestant Scot who had nonetheless addressed some adoring poetry to Mary while she lived in France, turned coat to opine that once she arrived in Scotland "scarce anything could satisfy" the queen.[34] The omnipresent John Knox even more grimly marked the "excessive expenses, and superfluous apparel" that attended "farces," "masking," and "other prodigalities" by which "fain would fools have counterfeited France."[35] To Knox's wary eye, Scotland under Mary threatened to become France. But that was not even the worst of it, for no boundary seemed sacred as long as "Jezebel's letter and wicked will [were] obeyed as law."[36] Transvestite pageants were imported from Paris, and the English guests were asked to don "Highland Apparell," while Mary often dressed her ladies-in-waiting (most of whom happened to share her first name) "as herself;" on Twelfth Night Mary's lady-in-waiting "Marie Flemynge was Queen."[37]

Mary Stuart presided over this undifferentiated farrago of inversion, imitation and disguise as both its insatiable artificer and its erotic center: "seized with love in ferventer passions than is comely for any mean personage," Randolph reported, she never "giveth care to any then such as follow her fantasy."[38] Scorning both the "placebo boys" who "affirm[ed]" her every whim "with like countenance" and the courtly spectacles that "proceeded from [Mary's] own womanly fantasy" (II: 240), Knox also perceived that all the signs contrived in Mary's court pointed back to their origin in the queen, mirroring the pleasure she derived from herself until no distinction survived.

Knox's censures went far beyond a Protestant reformer's recoil from voluptuous indulgence and a high sense of style. He saw Mary's self-absorbed and self-absorbing artistry – the fact that she "gladly beheld anything that would set forth her glory" – as a threat to the distinct differences which he felt should prevail between individuals.[39] In the end, Mary even seemed to menace the grid of discriminations, conferring identity, that was language itself. Contaminated by the queen's excesses, even words waxed foreign and too copious: Mary had been "brought up in joyousitie; so termed she her dancing, and other things thereto belonging" (II: 240). Her misdemeanors thus tempted Knox's own vocabulary into circumlocution: "Though we call her not a whore, she was brought up in the company of the wildest whoremasters." The queen, for her part, wept so often and profusely that tears became a kind of court vernacular that distorted and usurped the prerogatives of articulate utterance: "Howling, besides womanly weeping stayed her speech" (II: 387). And when it did not, Mary preferred to speak in French, or in a manner so ambiguous that she seemed not to have spoken at all. Randolph complained that "sometimes I seem willing to take some of her words as answer, but I see them drawn back again from me as though they had not been spoken."[40]

There was, of course, another name to give Mary's alternately teasing and enveloping style of queenship. Grounding their assessment in the queen's blood-bond to her son James, her supporters would later describe her original relationship to her Scottish subjects as an expression, indeed extension, of maternal solicitude. Unlike Elizabeth Tudor's oft-repeated rhetorical conceit that she was England's mother, this was in Mary's case an erotic expression, seldom verbal and often seeming to render the queen the object of her own liberal affections. In the approving view of the Catholic Bishop of Ross, Mary "tendered her subjects so lovingly, as that she would use herself toward them as a natural mother toward her children."[41] And, as she indeed seems to have played out a political version of a mother's preverbal – her sensual, fanciful and encompassing – involvement with her own infant, Mary often opened herself to the judgments of her Protestant audience, inviting them deeper and deeper into a certain vertiginous intimacy with her. She pronounced even the English Randolph "judge of my mind, that know my mind, that know my doings so much." Randolph in turn supposed that Knox "knew the secrets of her heart."[42] And Knox usually did conclude that "if there be not in her [. . .] a proud mind, a crafty wit, and an indureth heart [. . .] my judgement faileth me" (II: 287).

The Presbyterian demogogue could not convert the queen from her degenerate faith; nor could he change her sex. But he could use the curiously intimate spectacle of Mary's "joyousitie" and the scandal of her "letter" – of her wish made law – to fulfill his own apparent longing to know her deeply. Translated into Knox's peculiar idiom of moral judgment, that knowledge promised to ground Knox's own authority, thereby staking his precious purity in a space apart from the queen and all she embodied. When Mary staged the "mask and dancing of Orleans," Knox converted the festivities into a "witness" to a fantasia of degenerate oneness in which even "virgins and men's wives were made as common harlots, of the bordello" (II: 318). Similarly, when Mary addressed her parliament with what she presented as the meditations of her heart, Knox recoiled to cast her "painted orison[s]" as mere testaments to her "deep craft" (II: 381). One by one, Knox purloined Mary's engrossing performances and parlayed them into degenerate spectacles that in turn showcased his own powers of penetration, and ultimately reinforced the grille of words through which he was pleased to "let the world see how deeply Marie, Queen of Scotland, can dissemble" (II: 376).

Knox sneered at the "nobility" who continued to be "addicted to [Mary's] affections," (II: 388) but his fascination with how deeply she dissembled suggests that in their own way her Protestant detractors were no less enthralled. The fantastic "prodigalities" that held them captive were exceptionally involving dramas of deception. When an elderly Buchanan looked back upon his years in Mary's Scottish court, he found that he could not separate the queen's subterfuges from her physical appeal: "Her excellent beauty and transcendent parts, by her being bred at court, were set off to the best advantage; though that inclined her too much to insincerity."[43] Protestant memoirs of Mary's personal rule like Knox's and Buchanan's are preoccupied with the sensuous pleasure that Mary seemed to take as she made everything extend and resemble her. But they are driven just as hard by a frenzy to detect the queen's damning failure to resemble herself.

How to resolve this apparent contradiction within an otherwise single obsession with making out the Queen of Scots? One way would be to recall that Mary's return to Scotland produced something akin to developmental crisis in a group of subjects anxious to formulate themselves according to the almost obsessively individualistic premises of the Protestant Reformation. In essence, Mary's return compelled her newly Protestant subjects to take her in – physically into their state and psychologically into themselves, which is to say into their personal states of affection and reflection, of mind. Perceptions like Buchanan's, Knox's, and even Randolph's, that Mary was somehow not real – that she dissembled, was "insincere" – may be seen as symbolic protests, even defenses, against the pressure of introjection, which is to say against the compulsion to be part of their original ruler even as she showed herself to be part of them.

Such perceptions were meant, at least symbolically, to detach Mary from her own flesh, with its peremptory claims in the boundless and finally wordless domains of sexual charm, of pathos, even of blood. By refusing to see their "natural mother" as anything more real than a seductive sum of "devilish devices," and by refusing to understand the language she spoke as anything other than a deceptive aberration of the tongue, her Scottish subjects rehearsed the stroke of the axe with which their English counterparts were to end her corporeal life. As England's axe would try to do, they aimed, often by means of their own first words about her, to separate Mary from her overwhelming libidinal ground.

But that axe was to blunder, and so too in Mary's own Scottish court the acts of exposure meant to forestall the dissolution of personal, verbal and collective boundaries could not altogether outweigh the deliciousness of that dissolution – the fact that, as Randolph put it, the queen's "sights and shows" could nonetheless also "fill our bellies and our eyes." Like any mother worth her salt, Mary filled and Mary fed, and in one way or another – even through their very efforts at penetration and through the aggressive words which communicated the fruit and process of those efforts – her male subjects were also trying to enter and rejoin her. Even Knox "knocked so hastily upon her heart, that he made her weep."[44] Itself perhaps the only acceptable source of pleasure, this peculiar oscillation – between critical abstraction and emotional union, differentiation and coalescence – would, for the Scots, pause only once Mary was made to resign her crown to the son that she would never see again.

Achieved, appropriately enough, in the middle of an island, that particular *coup* revealed much. From a psychological point of view, compelling Mary to give up her crown separated the queen from her infant son, sundering a primal bond akin to the all-absorbing, if also highly imaginary, one that Mary had achieved with them. Politically, because Mary was forced to concede her throne to a baby, her forced abdication devolved rule upon the queen's own subjects, her political "sons." The self-sovereignty that they had so long sought in the form of freedom from Mary's seductive "joyousitie" became a reality. At the same time, however, as she herself would later point out, Mary did not literally and physically put her crown on James's head: she only signed her title away. Ironically, then, the medium through which the Scots became their own subjects proved to be the most *de*realized imaginable: Mary relinquished her shockingly bodily authority only through writing – through the least convincing, most sublimely disembodied and radically denatured of all symbolic forms.

Long before Lochleven, the queen had had to confront the deposing force of the written word, its power to usurp her own physical reality. After her elopement with Bothwell, "tickets and writings" had proliferated throughout Scotland, forcing her to swear publicly "that if she were the woman whom the placards named she was not only unworthy to reign over so ancient a people, but was also unworthy to live on the face of the earth."[45] Though, as Knox reported, Mary tried to outlaw all "defamatory writs" and even decreed that "those who shall read and publish such writing" should be "condemned and punished as criminals guilty of treason," she had trouble integrating her own body with the reviled "woman whom the placards named." As that woman took her place to become at once the object and the apparent catalyst of her people's passion, Mary held up a dark and fractured mirror to the face that Elizabeth Tudor had so carefully composed, precisely by absenting herself from her own subjects and the signs of their affection. The detachment from the marks of her own subjects' emotions that was life to Elizabeth promised death to Mary.

As if to turn the mirror to the wall, Elizabeth soon issued her own formal edict prohibiting all "blasphemous treatises and pamphlets" pertaining to the Queen of Scots, both pro and con. Elizabeth's action has been read skeptically, as an empty gesture meant to palliate Mary's powerful continental allies.[46] But it was also apotropaic, for Mary's scary vulnerability to the readerly cravings of both Protestant Scots and their English counterparts proved female sovereignty's own frailty before its political children's words and the eyes that devoured them. Why should Elizabeth wish to be reminded of that?

Peter Frarin, author of a 1565 "Oration against the Unlawefull Insurrection of the Protestants," pointed the moral. Berating "the traitorous Gospellers of England" for their cruelty to "their most virtuous lady Quen Marie, the rare treasure, peerless jewel, that most perfect pattern and example of our days," Frarin found Mary's Protestant enemies, English and Scottish alike, most abusive when they were most literary – when they "printed seditious books against her, [. . .] and named her traitorous Marie, mischievous Marie." The authors of the book of Protestant ire had degraded Mary into a "poor private woman in her own Realme," forced "to obey her own Subjects, and to do no more then they gave her leave." But they also aimed to reduce her to a peculiarly modern kind of literary figure – the kind wholly subject to readerly and authorial wishes only because there is, really, no one there at all.[47]

"FOUL MATTER AND ABOMINABLE": THE CASKET LETTERS

Except they did not quite succeed. And the actual paradoxes of desire that divide so many of the Protestant words written against Mary are nowhere more palpable than in the unsolved mystery to which we now turn. So far, that is, we have seen that the extent to which Mary renounced and resisted the words and highly publishable discernments of her own subjects was precisely the extent to which they remained almost slavishly involved with her. It was, indeed, the extent to which she animated an incipient language of self and state.

The queen's power to do so should have ended the minute she set foot in England in mid-May 1568. Humiliated, she came seeking harbor and the redress of grievances from her cousin Elizabeth. What she received was an almost comically attenuated trial, for a commission of Scottish noblemen immediately followed her across the border to charge her with adultery, conspiracy and treason against their late and suddenly beloved king, Darnley. When Mary and her accusers converged at York, an English council was appointed to pass sentence, but the resulting trial only vaguely resembled due process of accusation and defense. Its outcome was predictably ambiguous. Mary was found neither guilty nor innocent, the evidence against her inconclusive.[48] More significant, her trial generated a body of writing about the Queen of Scots that would become the foundation of her meaning for English Protestants. That writing turned out to be divided far more deeply than anything that had been written about her before. Read today, it seems to record an unfinished dream work, one whose contradictions were bound to impinge upon future figments of Mary Stuart. Its own uncanny foundation lies in the evidence that was actually summoned against Mary during her trial at York.

All of it written, this evidence fell into two groups. First, there was first a gilt casket bearing the initial of Mary's first husband, François II. Reportedly confiscated from Bothwell, the casket held eight love letters and twelve poems, which Mary had supposedly written to Bothwell during the last months of her marriage to Darnley. As one English onlooker, the Duke of Norfolk, informed Elizabeth, the casket correspondence included "ane long and horrible letter of her own hand, as they say, containing foul matter and abominable to be either thought of or to be written by a prince, with diverse fond ballads of her own hand."[49]

While officially they were used as evidence of crime, the *billets doux* and "diverse fond ballads" known collectively as the casket letters also projected a definite image of Mary as an author, one whose lascivious literary style confirmed her sexual reputation as a bloodthirsty adulteress even as she attempted to play that very role with her own reader. Consequently, the ascendant Protestant impression that Mary was a craven dissembler of the most wanton passions actually took root in the erotically charged act of reading an emotionally invasive female author. When practiced aright – which is to say defensively – this act might prove a reader's integrity, in every sense of that word. Norfolk put it best, remarking that "the said letters and ballads do discover such inordinate love between her and Bothwell, her loathsomeness and abhorring of her husband [. . .] as every good and godly man cannot but detest and abhor the same."[50]

If the first body of evidence against Mary was allegedly authored by her and seen as a test of the reader's self-defining power to resist it, the second was principally the work of a male writer, Buchanan. Already the author of two flagrantly "anti-monarchical" plays, this longtime Protestant denizen of Mary's court was only too happy to provide the English commission with an eyewitness account of her years in Scotland.[51] Buchanan's *Detectio sive de Maria* was attached to an incriminating "collection of presumptions and circumstances" relating to Mary's unhappy marriage to Darnley. The document known collectively as the *Book of Articles* bore witness to "the alteration of the said Queen's affection" from Darnley and her "inordinate affection" for Bothwell. It exposed "the conspiracy, device and execution" of Darnley's "horrible murder by the said Queen, his wife, and Bothwell" as well as "the sequel of the said murder," Mary's elopement with Bothwell.[52] With its many scandalous "sequels" and feverish prose, the *Book of Articles* reads more like a gripping tale of lust and intrigue than a chaste "collection of presumptions and circumstances." Its narrative self-consciousness is striking; in fact, Buchanan later polished and published his contributions to it. We might, therefore, take the *Book of Articles* not only as a kind of evidentiary portrait of the Queen of Scots but also as a bid to establish authorial expertise. It was at first perhaps only mildly embarrassing that the symbol of that expertise had to erect itself upon the torrid and presumably female-authored text of the casket letters themselves.

During her trial, Mary insisted that the casket letters were forgeries and demanded to be allowed to read them for herself. Elizabeth, always from afar, refused to let her until Mary promised to answer to charges against her, but Mary refused to answer until she should be permitted to view the incriminating evidence. The stalemate was never resolved. Nor was the casket itself publicly opened until after the trial moved to Westminster, leaving the defendant herself and all of her representatives behind in York. Shortly thereafter, the casket and its questionable cargo vanished into thin air. Mary's accusers were allowed to return to Scotland. She herself, though convicted of no crime, found herself Elizabeth's effectual prisoner. The ghostly letters hovering forever just beyond her grasp, Mary remained England's unwilling guest until a second trial sent her to the scaffold in 1587.

Long before then, however, the casket letters resurfaced – not in actuality, of course, but as a printed text published in 1571.[53] The original letters still lacked any foundation in the material world, but they were now convincingly printed in Scots, French and Latin, and to them had been added a revised version of Buchanan's *Detection*, translated into Scots by one of Elizabeth's diplomats, Thomas Wilson, and henceforth known in the vernacular as *Ane Detectioun of the Douings of Marie*. The revamped text was stylistically much more crafted, integrated and vivid than the *Book of Articles* had ever been. Like its cruder predecessor, however, the *Detection* solicits its own reader's credence by presenting itself as a reading of the queen's own passionate writing. So the specter of Mary as (illicit) author always shadows our impression of Buchanan as (morally outraged) author. Indeed, if Mary's supporters were right to suspect that Buchanan himself wrote the casket letters, his authority *is* Mary's. But even if he did not forge the letters, Buchanan's pose as discerning reader turned judicious narrator is justified, and secured, only by the precedent of Mary's sensuous artistry.

And what of the casket letters themselves? None actually plots the killing of the king; the letters bear no superscriptions or dates, and, as friends to the Queen of Scots would insist for centuries, their style and imagery are remarkably raw to have issued from the pen of a woman raised in the cultural refinement of the Valois court, who was already the acknowledged author of several graceful lyrics. Their literary properties aside, the themes of the casket letters range from sexual debasement to the fragility of reputation to the desire to compel their reader's belief. As these themes converge, they bring the casket letters into eerie harmony with Buchanan's own concerns as an author who becomes something more than a nebulous and unreliable projection of another's desire only by fashioning himself the discerning reader of an altogether too enticing queen.

The author of the casket letters places "herself" in utter submission to her reader and lover: "I have put in hazard for him both fame and conscience," one sonnet begins. "I will for his sake renounce the world,/I will die to set him forward."[54] In another the speaker feels "punished for making my God of you" (p. 129). With the reader her god, "she" naturally seeks self-confirmation by forcing him into belief in her own passionate existence: she vows to "give of my truth such proof/That he shall know my constancy without fiction" (p. 120) and protests that "my thoughts are so willingly subdued unto yours, that I suppose all that cometh of you [. . .] is] such as I desire myself." Hoping to "testifie unto you how lowly I submit me under your commandments," an especially wistful letter tenders "in sign of homage [. . .] one sepulture of hard stone coloured with black, sawin with tears and bones [which] I compare to my heart" (pp. 139–140).

In their abject quest for a non-verbal, hence credible, language of self-affirmation, the casket letters inevitably displace authority – the authority to assign and assess reality – from a sensuous, embodied author to a distant reader. Buchanan's own authority as Mary's plausible portraitist must therefore have depended on how dexterously he could disengage himself from the compromised and vulnerable – even empty – figure of an author who nonetheless, incessantly, requested reunion with him. In turn, because Buchanan was compelled to identify himself as the dissociated interpreter of signs rather than as their guilty female origin – their mother, in a manner of speaking – the *Detection* proper presented itself as an eyewitness account of Mary's personal rule in Scotland. Buchanan procured his mainly English readers many glimpses of Mary's savage cruelty to the hapless Darnley, and of her capricious passion for her own subjects, Bothwell especially. In the *Detection* the queen's "unnaturalness, hatred, barbarous fierceness [and] outragious cruelty" find expression in crimes "beyond all bounds and measure." "A woman raging without measure and modesty," she is "determined by force to remove all that stood in her way" (p. 57). The Protestants' Mary, as at once crafted and perceived by Buchanan, is quite literally an outlaw, "a woman greedily coveting untempered authority, who esteemed the laws her prison, and the bridle of justice her bondage" (p. 58).

This Mary even thwarts the boundaries of proper femininity. She does so implicitly just by occupying a throne that should, *pace* Knox, be out of bounds for women. But she is also a horrible wife. Whereas "other Women do chiefly comfort themselves in the lovingness of their Husbands, and confess that they find some ease of pain by sight of them," Buchanan's Mary "driveth her Husband away" (p. 44), and even when Darnley lies dying she fails to do "the other kind duties of honest matrons" (p. 63). She amounts at last to "a sister, [who] hath butcherly slaughtered her brother, a wife her husband, a Queen her King" (p. 89), a bad woman in part because she is too many women in one. This slaughtering queen's worst transgressions, however, turn out to be crimes of artistry. She is never altogether real. Sweeping through her personal reign like "some God out of a ginn in a tragedy" (p. 55), she stages her life with Darnley as a "tragedy" for which she herself appoints both the "lookers on" and "part players." At the same time, she usurps the role of the spectator, shamelessly "glutting herself with the sight of [Darnley's] miseries and torments." Indeed, Mary's "barbarous" arts are designed to provide their author and actor with a visceral pleasure in her own handiwork, the suffering of others. Visiting Darnley's body, Buchanan maintains that "as she had satisfied her heart with his slaughter, so she would needs feed her eyes with the sight of his body slain. For she long beheld, [. . .] with greedy eyes, his dead corps, the goodliest corps of any Gentleman that ever lived in this age" (p. 27).

Like her other crimes, Mary's savage artistry contaminates sign with substance, metaphorical satisfaction with literal satiety. As her barbarous and narcissistic productions collapse author, actor and onlooker, they also make Mary an author in the text – an author whose very willingness to relinquish her authority helps her to rival and at last impinge upon the readerly author *of* the text, Buchanan. Buchanan strives to anchor his own reality – his separateness and integrity of being – by denying Mary's. Yet his craft resembles no one's more than hers. Both hunger after a supremely convincing language. Mary finds her vocabulary in the sentient world, where she sheds copious tears "to move credit" for her many claims that she has been abused. As if to parody Buchanan's own efforts to expose her transparent deceptions to public view, she "gapingly fought for every small breath of suspicion against her Husband, and where true causes were not to be found, she invented such as were manifestly false" (p. 41). Buchanan, likewise, steadfastly denies "that I tell wonders" (p. 56), and beseeches his reader to see his words as if they were "things thus lying open before your eyes, thus palpable with hands, thus fast imprinted in mens ears and knowledge" (p. 79). Conversely, just as Mary's visceral efforts to "confirm suspicion against her Husband" prove to be nothing more than an illusion that she herself has wrought, so Elizabethans were inclined to read the *Detection* as art, not evidence. Buchanan's contemporary Gabriel Harvey formally pronounced "the tragical pamphlets of the Queen of Scots worth the reading over and over, both for the style and the matter."[55]

Buchanan's detection starts out as a bid to depose and derealize the Queen of Scots with her own subject's equally penetrating and self-affirming gaze. "Exhibited as Matter," though, and aesthetically enjoyable "for the style and the matter," his sensational words bleed back into what Norfolk called Mary's own abominable art of "foul Matter." If Mary's visceral and phantasmic art at first beckons, even rewards, the chastening language of detection, in the end it only mocks and seduces that language. At least in Buchanan's fantasy about her – the fantasy of a Protestant subject bent on divesting himself of subjection to female rule – the Catholic Queen of Scots recovers the idioms of interpretive privilege as a dialect of her own all-absorbing tongue. Spurious or not, the casket letters themselves epitomize this irony. On the surface, they seem mainly to have helped to create the wanton, wily queen that an entire generation of Protestants could happily imagine killing. Read in tandem with the *Detection*, however, they also remind us that Buchanan's own authority as the detective, portraitist and dreamer of that same queen begins and ends in the scandal that he himself is part of her.

"A MOST CAREFUL TENDER MOTHER WITH ALL": THE CATHOLIC IRONY

Several Catholic defenses of the Queen of Scots followed hot on the heels of the casket letters. In obvious contrast to Protestant documents of revulsion, these works openly presented themselves as professions of love. As such, they sought foremost to protect the object of their affection – an object they half-created by replacing Buchanan's "poisoning witch" with a princess akin to Frarin's "peerless jewel." In his widely (if illegally) circulated *Defence of the Honour of . . . Marie* (1569), the Queen of Scots's most ardent and prolific advocate, John Leslie, the Catholic Bishop of Ross, openly declared that her "person [. . .] and the whole trade of all her godly and virtuous life past, do far repel and drive away all [. . .] suspicion and conjectural presumptions" that her life had ever, even for a moment, been otherwise.[56] Like the first draft of Buchanan's *Detection*, Leslie's *Defence* was "made, for the most part, at the Queen's first coming into England [. . .] and augmented when all the commissioners were at Westminster and Hampton Court." But its determination to take note of Mary's whole life reflects a set of conventions, both perceptual and discursive, entirely foreign to those which governed Protestant response to the Queen of Scots. Leslie's way of looking at Mary was textured and contextual, favoring a panoramic view of long *durée* over discrete and mobile pieces of evidence.

Insofar as written words are individual entities that can be wrested from the world of lived customs and nonverbal conjunctions that originally gives them meaning, Leslie swore himself their enemy. He seems to have realized that he could never compel belief in Mary's innocence unless he turned his readers against writing's own authority. Inverting the Protestant claim that it was Mary who was the fraud, Leslie held that the queen was the victim of "feigned and forged reports and opprobious slanders," the casket letters themselves nothing more than "tricks and cunning illusions" intended to "face out and countenance their enemies' crafts and jugglings" (p. 13).[57] The only true signs of authority, he held, are non-linguistic ones; even "costly apparel and jewels," continuous as they are with the unbroken history of the flesh, supersede the empty designations of the written word. At Lochleven it was when Mary's "rebellious and traitorous subjects" substituted denatured signs for the queen's birthright trappings of inherited power that they had "bereaved her of her princely and Royal authority" (p. iii). They thereby "sequestrated" her within a set of disjunctions that can only come into existence by brutally "spoil[ing]" its own libidinal ground (*Defence*, p. 25). In the Catholic view Protestant propaganda against Mary, like the written articles of demission that she was forced to sign, not only abetted treason but actually constituted it.

It was, to Leslie's mind, treason against a fundamentally matriarchal vision of sovereignty, one that also applied to Mary's relationship to Elizabeth and entitled her to the latter's throne. For, Leslie held, Mary "is as it were, [Elizabeth's] daughter, both by daughterly reverence [. . .] and by reason she is by God called to the daughter's place in the succession of the crown" (*Defence*, p. vi). This is of course precisely the maternal logic of overlapping interests and mutual substitution that had so needled Mary's ambitious lords and dogmatic Protestant onlookers, and that once she fled to England would begin to make Elizabeth's own subjects nervous as well. Herself "a most careful tender mother with all" (p. 6), the Mary of Leslie's Catholic dreams provided the matrix of an intricate web of relationships between women, one that extended through lived experience across time and space.

So far, Leslie would seem to have plunged gladly into precisely that gulf of motherly love which we have seen Mary's potential and actual subjects all repudiated, the better to gratify their own wish to differentiate themselves and their historical moment. Yet if the Protestant authors who rejected Mary also conveyed their own craving for her continued presence, the Catholic case is also less straightforward than it might first appear to be. Certainly, like Buchanan in particular, Leslie finally sought to gratify his own desire for personal and political authority.

Openly adoring Mary would, on the surface, seem to have guaranteed that authority's loss: Leslie was thrown into prison for his literary efforts to repair her tattered reputation. One of the last of these efforts, however – a *Historie of Scotland* (1578) contemporary with Buchanan's own work of the same title – exploits the likeness between Leslie's own plight and that of his by now long-captive queen. First, Leslie dedicated his *Historie* to Mary, reminding her that "many [. . .] knew by me in how great misery was your grace, how fraudfully ye were invaded and closed with calamity on every side." Such readers, Leslie was sure, had been "surely, sorely moved" by his earlier *Defence*.[58] In other words, like Buchanan, Leslie forged his own authority (that proud "by me") on the anvil of Mary's shockingly direct appeal to her own readers, though in his case it is "calamity," not scandal, which solicits a reader's engagement and promises to gratify his every wish for the truth of the matter, or "mater," as the word was suggestively spelled.

For his own part, precisely because he cast the Queen of Scots as his reader, Leslie even today remains a remarkably pervasive presence in his own writing, a presence whose coordinates are difficult to distinguish from the queen's own. Like the francophone Mary, who in captivity would correspond in short-hand with her supporters in the outside world, Leslie wrote from beyond the pale of prevailing conventions of representation; denied paper and ink, he had to compose in pencil, between the lines of printed books. He wrote awk-wardly, for although he was a master of Latin, a London physician had to help him with the English. To make matters worse, Leslie complained that he was "close and straightly kept," and incessantly "vexed" by the "infirmities" bred by "close and corrupted air" (*Discourse*, II: 228). Ailing, fragmented, and by his own deficiencies rendered almost physically immanent in the words he wrote, Leslie identified with his royal subject so deeply that she seems to haunt those words as a physical presence indistinguishable from his own.

This merging with Mary would appear to be exactly what the queen herself wanted, at least in anxious Protestant fantasies about her. Leslie's loving portrait of his "most careful tender mother" virtually embodied one way in which the queen might infiltrate her own subjects until they became sympathetic extensions of her. Certainly this possibility informs Leslie's conception of the way in which the mother whose political life could not be separated from her biological one should be read as well as written. If Buchanan made reading an act of detection, bound up with the usurpation of Mary's female authority, Leslie's *Defence* makes it a mode of extenuation, of pity and pardon. Even if Mary did turn out to have written the casket letters, there were ways of reading them which would preserve an ultimately identificatory love for her. Advocating "pity" over penetration, for example, Leslie held that "the like estate of princes" would "turn all honest-hearted men to commiseration" (p. 3). His ideal reader exercises this pity, and likewise attends to increments and consistencies in Mary's story, assuming that no "man or woman fall[s] to extreme lewdness all at once" (p. 4). The same reader would concede that a web of circumstances can conspire against an individual trapped in them. Thus, rather than having *chosen* Bothwell as her third husband, Mary must have been pushed into his arms by "the distress, the discomfort, and desolation wherein she was presentlie bewrapped" (p. 16).

Leslie's adorable "Marie" persists within an extravagant web of involvements and continuities, one that encompasses her readers and her authors alike to deprive all of them of narrative control. Just so, the queen's rightful, if not sovereign, place in this web is visible and convincing only as long as Mary herself is vulnerable – as long indeed as she hovers on the verge of disappearance. In Leslie's scheme, one place to which she disappears is into the author; another is into the sympathetic reader. One place from which she disappears is from the pages of any history understood as a series of distinct choices and discontinuous events. No less than Mary's Protestant enemies, then, it would seem that her Catholic supporters had to balance the need for her to vanish against desire for her addicting, affecting presence. In future, the Catholic attachment to Mary would at once mirror its Protestant counterpart and underlie it, shadowing the phantoms of the Queen of Scots bound to appear and reappear in an increasingly Protestant tradition of imagining modern Britain's beginnings, and so its present state. Writers such as Buchanan and Knox might well have been driven by the passionate identifications with Mary that they would repudiate. But openly adoring writers like Leslie had to summon the specter of her majesty's death in order to keep loving it.

2 "The treason of pity"
England, 1568–1603

The paradoxes of desire that drove so many early Anglo-Scottish involvements with the Queen of Scots were both exaggerated and transformed during her long, unchosen sojourn in Elizabethan England. Throughout the nineteen years that she lived under lock and key, and even more dramatically after her beheading, Mary naturally inspired imprudent passions in many an English Catholic. But even the erstwhile wary Duke of Norfolk found himself wishing to take her part. Such diversions of desire certainly justified the widespread impression that Mary posed the direst of threats to the erotic and familial order of the Elizabethan state. Over time, that threat proved bitterly ironic, since it was the Queen of Scots's woeful predicament itself which came to arouse the most forbidden longings – for her liberty, even regnancy, and for Elizabeth's demise.

Norfolk was eventually beheaded for the rebellious sympathy that Mary awakened in him.[1] Stubborn rumors that he had secretly married her first show just how smoothly the libidinous glow that had suffused the Queen of Scots throughout her personal rule in Scotland could shade into the charisma of distress. Elizabethan imaginations continued to translate Mary into a scheming and seductive witch, one well equipped to deprive of their own will those who consciously wanted a Tudor queen. But after her arrival in England in 1568 it was most often Mary's tears and conspicuously captive graces, not to mention the pity they provoked, that jeopardized Protestant affection for Elizabeth Tudor.

As we gauge that jeopardy and the defenses contrived against it, we need to take account not just of the tears that could deflect Protestant affection for Elizabeth into a sense of fellowship with her "most nigh cousin" but also of the fears of treason that Mary ignited throughout her long stay south of the Scottish border. Elizabeth's subjects had always been prone to uncover plots against their queen. They spied them in every corner with a zeal that has been read as paranoia, and accordingly as a warped, but perversely efficient, psychological means of defending an illusion of collective integrity.[2] Once the half-French, entirely Catholic Queen of Scots entered England she naturally became paranoia's catalyst, even as fear of what she might do once she had left the country pushed Elizabeth to deny her freedom. Nor was anxiety about

Mary always unfounded, for conspiracies against Elizabeth's life and throne were indeed often concocted in her name; frequently the Queen of Scots even knew who was, as her English enemies liked to put it, "imagining" Elizabeth's death.

As it happens, loyal Elizabethans' fear of pity is almost impossible to separate from their fear of treason. Most obviously, of course, the one – pity – could be the condition of the other: English Roman Catholics' pity for a captive queen clearly put the non-Catholic state at risk, and more sinister still was the possibility that the Queen of Scots might win the sympathies of her own blood – her son James VI of Scotland, or, worse, Elizabeth herself. But in psychological terms, pity *is* treason, for it too undermines a seemingly integrated being from within, bespeaking that being's confusing affinity with something outside and other than itself. When Elizabethan authors represented Mary to themselves – and they did so obsessively both in the last years of her life and in the first following her death – it's therefore fitting that they should have dwelt, almost interchangeably, upon her own trial for treason and the piteousness of her plight. It is, in fact, the texts most preoccupied with the link between treason and pity – Edmund Spenser's *The Faerie Queene*, John Lyly's *Endimion*, and even John Pikeryng's over-the-top update of the *Oresteia* – that were slated to transport Mary's memory to a posterity largely Protestant in sensibility.

Borrowing the Elizabethans' revealing synonym for treason, we might regard these texts as 'imaginings' in their own right, literary dreams of love for Elizabeth which nonetheless bear treacherous marks of sympathy with the very woman "most bloodily infected" to the queen their authors had bound themselves to adore [3] Ironically essential to the records of disgust that they appear to mar, those marks possess extraordinary force and vitality. This is because their roots lie in Mary's own creative hostility to the conventional determinations and abstractions of the written word – a hostility wrought to an art over the time that she was locked away and perfected during the trial that began her own life's ending.

CORRESPONDENCE AND CAPTIVITY

Mary's long captivity was in fact a series of briefer confinements, each cut short by fear – on the part of both Elizabeth and her Protestant ministers – that the Stuart queen's piteous plight would join forces with her seductive person to move even her sternest keepers to treacherous pity. But what did it mean to pity the Queen of Scots? Leslie had already dramatized pity's peculiar origin in a kind of internal absence, in the recognition that, within, one is at once different from oneself and like another. What is more, for one of Elizabeth's subjects to succumb to pity was for passion to overthrow the rule of a more self-serving affection: those accused of having plotted against Elizabeth for Mary's sake were believed literally to have lost their "own motion."[4] In experiential terms, therefore, to pity Mary was to enter a psychological relationship akin to the erotic one that her Protestant subjects and Elizabeth's diplomats had resisted long ago in Scotland. It was to want, once again, the self-abdicating and thence peculiarly female version of sovereignty which the Queen of Scots alone embodied and whose psychological counterpart she seemed to create in others.

Through her sojourns in seven different castles – the longest under the care of the Earl of Shrewsbury and his hard-bitten wife, Bess of Hardwicke – Mary had clung to the trappings of monarchy. She canopied her chair of state with a cloth in which her riddling motto, *en ma fin est mon commencement*, had been stitched. She imported a fashionable continental wardrobe and a menagerie of exotic small animals, and she kept an almost worshipful retinue, the bulk of it female. Though she was unceremoniously trundled from prison to prison, each more cramped and malodorous than the one before, even the crippling illnesses that ensued became an unexpected source of ascendancy as the Queen of Scots used her own physical suffering to fashion herself as a Roman Catholic martyr. She wrote doleful poetry and one notable "Essay on Adversity" which looked piously for a better world to come. She stitched anagrams of her royal name and cryptic emblems of her plight into great lengths of silk.

Above all, however, Mary wrote letters. Most of her massive correspondence was in French, and a good part of it was in ciphers, a number of which the queen apparently invented herself. Some of it was written in her own huge, slanting hand, with many words obliterated, often by tears.[5] Much of it was addressed to Elizabeth in lieu of the personal meeting that Mary wanted but that the Tudor queen avoided with tragic success. Because they had to substitute for her mythically provocative and emotionally tyrannical physical presence, Mary's tear-stained letters to Elizabeth often tendered rhetorical self-portraits as detailed as the Queen of Scots could make them – wrenching images of bodily affliction and plaintive testaments to "the integrity of my deportment."[6] Though Mary sought many favors from Elizabeth over the years – liberty, assistance in regaining her own throne, even to be placed officially next in line for Elizabeth's – her favorite theme was that she herself was fundamentally part of Elizabeth: her letters invoked, incessantly, "the proximity of our blood." Begging Elizabeth always to "think what you would do in my place" (*Cal. State Papers, Scot.*, IV: 70–71), Mary's letters offered themselves to her "dearest sister" as tangible "proof of our thankful mind and sincere good will borne towards her" (VI: 413). They quoted verses that Elizabeth herself had scratched into a windowpane during her own short captivity under Mary Tudor.[7] Even their occasional tone of condescension echoed the one that Elizabeth might have been expected to assume, planting the seeds of likeness from which pity and eventually deliverance might grow.

English readers, Elizabeth among them, considered Mary's letters "written in a very strange sort," (IV: 75). To be sure, even those "filled with uncomely, passionate, ireful and vindictive speeches" (IV: 106) strove to take the place of the Stuart queen's own person – to recreate that person in the bodily imagination of their recipient and so to affect, even invade, that recipient as the sight of Mary's long-suffering body would have done. Unfortunately, a like illusion of corporeality also encroached upon the signs which made up Mary's correspondence with Elizabeth's enemies. Perpetually suspected of "pernicious practices" (IV: 1), she had by 1586 been twice accused of inspiring, if not actively devising, plots against Elizabeth. Virtually all of this seditious activity took place in letters; it was with reference to his written correspondence with Mary that the Duke of Norfolk confessed himself "entangl[ed . . .] to her" (IV: 40). If her addresses to Elizabeth were so "beautiful" and "lamentable" that the English queen avoided her in person, Mary's writing to her sympathizers was doubly feared for its collusion with the moving body which had produced it and which, precisely by relinquishing itself, threatened to move others out of their conscious and distinctive selves.

Mary for her part delighted in invisible inks and shorthands – in all forms of "secret writing," as she called it. She urged her correspondents to reply on white taffeta, in invisible ink, and to mark key words with a special symbol that she herself had devised. The fanciful and seductive materiality of Mary's letters defied the written word's normal pretensions to abstraction; they were even smuggled back and forth in beer caskets (bathetic versions of the fabled gilt casket), or in the toes of imported shoes. Despite elaborate trappings of secrecy, Mary's captors frequently knew about the letters, as Mary herself often knew. Her letters became shameless teases, inviting all manner of scandalous speculation about the author who seemed to infuse them with her physical presence. Even Mary's orthographic experiments made the written word far more than a set of marks untroubled by its own referents. In her hands, these very marks became animate, voluble, concrete, testimonial – the belongings of an authorial body always in intimate, if riddling, contact with them.

After seventeen years of illicit epistolarity, Mary apparently entered upon the most fateful of her many correspondences, with an English Catholic close to her own son's age. Throughout early 1586, letters between Mary and Anthony Babington, in cipher of course, passed in and out of the queen's current lodging, Chartley Castle, hidden in a beer casket. Each one was intercepted by Elizabeth Tudor's own secretary, Francis Walsingham, and copied before it was sent on. Babington's letters were crazed with ardor. Written in French, they mixed the idiom of Catholic zeal with personal passion for "my dread sovereign lady and queen, unto whom I owe all fidelity and obedience."[8] Of most interest to his Elizabethan readers, Babington almost immediately announced his intention to rescue Mary and do away with Elizabeth, replacing her with England's rightful Catholic queen.

Mary's responses to Babington's epistolary hyperventilations were mainly requests for more information. Nonetheless, led by Walsingham, Elizabeth's most influential ministers now found themselves in a position to brandish the letters as proof "that [Mary] knew of [the Babington Conspiracy], approved it, assented unto it, promised her assistance, and shewed the way and means" – that she had, in short, actively "plotted the destruction of the queen."

Babington was easily brought to admit his part in this almost comically maladroit conspiracy. Soon he had been drawn and quartered, in the company of the several co-conspirators in whose company he had imprudently had himself painted several months before.

An undercurrent of sexual excitement rippled through the charges that there had been "intercourse by letters" between Mary and Babington. Many a popular ballad traced the young English Catholic's crime to "Circe's charm," which had "bewicht [his] wretched senseless mind" with "words most fair and loving terms."[9] While Babington seemed to have lost his conscious will to a woman old enough to be his mother, Mary's letters were seen as the veritable documents of her own insatiable and yet self-destructive longings. One of the many English Protestants to call for her blood, the aptly named George Whetstone, declared that "her own hand writings be witness" that she was most "bloodily infected to Queen Elizabeth." In Mary's letters, Whetstone pursued, "there is nothing more manifest, then that her malice thirsteth to death of her own life."[10] Immanent in "her own hand writings," the Queen of Scots's imagined desire to annihilate herself mirrored the desire she was supposed to have raised in Babington when her legendary charms deprived him of his sensible mind. Mary's letters both wrought and represented just this troublesome fusion of the subjects and objects of desire.

To Elizabethan imaginations, Mary's writing was in any event so intimately, even materially, linked to its author's sexual and political appetites that she virtually existed within it. From one perspective, this made her all the more vulnerable to forms of detection not unlike those that Buchanan had brought to bear upon the casket letters. From another point of view, however, Mary's determination to transfuse her own personal claims into the impersonal and artificial systems of meaning that writing exemplifies would eventually hang the jury of collective feeling about her.

She was accosted at Chartley and carried to the bleak Northamptonshire castle of Fotheringay, where Elizabeth's Protestant envoys told her that she must stand trial for treason. As the anointed queen of another country and Elizabeth's peer, Mary did not see how she could possibly be viewed as a traitor, and a large part of her defense was simply to stake this claim, over and over again. The trial itself took two days, spanning the 15th and 16th of October, 1586. On the surface it looks very different from her first at York. Once charged with adultery and connivance at her husband's murder, Mary now stood accused of crimes against another queen. Rather than on those of an appointed commission, the burden of defense fell squarely on her own shoulders, although almost two decades of confinement had aged their owner to a gray and ailing version of her former self. "Destitute of counsellors," Mary, unlike before, eventually faced a verdict so far from ambiguity that Elizabeth subsequently, albeit reluctantly, signed the warrant for her execution.[11]

But there were also eerie echoes of the proceedings at York and Westminster. Cuckolding and conspiring against the man who was after all Scotland's king could be construed as acts of treason, even as Mary's supposed treason against

Elizabeth sounded echoes of infidelity to the woman who cast herself as Mary's protector. What is more, like the first, Mary's second trial mobilized an entire battalion of conflicted fantasies about her. Indeed, English Protestant poets, dramatists and polemicists would continue to rehearse Mary's crimes, captivity and conviction up until Elizabeth's own mute and lonely death in 1603. In part, of course, these Protestant writers were merely moved to refute Catholic claims that the trial had been a savage travesty of law. But as they wrested Mary into forms whose essence was absence, later Elizabethan representations of the Queen of Scots also attempted to allay a threat she had long posed, not just to Elizabeth but more gravely – through the treason of pity – to certain fledgling fictions of collective and individual independence and integrity. These fictions had been built in something utterly different from the maternal atmosphere of contact and continuity that radiated from the Queen of Scots. Their foundation was the abstracted and self-sustaining love of a virgin queen whose subjects stood no chance of touching her.

THE BONDS OF DISSOCIATION

Mary's trial for treason is easily read as a grotesque fiction plotted by Elizabeth's most devoted – and self-serving – ministers, chiefly Cecil and Walsingham. In the Stuart queen's own estimation, these Protestant peers of the realm and their cohorts were hard put to prove that they "proceed[ed] according to equity and right, and not by any cunning point of law, and extraordinary course."[12] The summer before Mary was formally charged with treason against Elizabeth, Walsingham had indeed staged and then pretended to detect a minor Catholic conspiracy, one he could later meld with the more damning particulars of the Babington case. Elizabeth's ministers also added at least a few incriminating lines to one of Mary's letters to Babington, and deceived her secretaries into testifying against her. These manipulations achieved a curious effect, for besides making the proceedings against the Queen of Scots look decidedly contrived, they allowed Elizabeth's loyal Protestant subjects, albeit in imagination and temporarily, to conspire against Elizabeth herself. Though the end was to trap Mary Stuart, the means allowed the trappers to sustain a long and lurid fantasy of their beloved queen's own death.

That fantasy had already been indulged legally, under the guise of at once protecting Elizabeth and addressing the unique threat that Mary posed as a seductive element, at once foreign and familiar, lodged within England's own borders. A number of Elizabeth's Protestant nobles had long wanted Mary dead and her claims on Elizabeth expunged. To this end, several years before the Babington conspiracy surfaced, some of them had joined forces with certain members of the House of Commons to draft a document that they called the Bond of Association. The Bond officially defined England as a body of men who, being "natural born subjects of this realm of England," had "engag[ed] and oblig[ed] themselves to each other." As they vowed to preserve the "life of our gracious sovereign Queen," they also vowed to preserve themselves as an integrated, coherent body, against "divers others."[13] Tens of thousands of signatories came forward throughout England and the Bond easily passed into a parliamentary Act of Association. This act, in effect, authorized the corporate body of Elizabeth's subjects to take justice into their own hands should anyone – including foreign monarchs, crowned and uncrowned – plot or even inspire plot against her. All such acts were henceforth classified as treason.

While the Act of Association was obviously devised with the Queen of Scots in mind, it was also intended to create a special bond among Protestant Englishmen. This bond was only metaphorical, and as such it needed to identify a "divers other" if it was to be seen as coherent, cohesive, and, above all, believable. Mary Stuart certainly counted as a "divers other." But at least as important as the establishment of her otherness was the fact that the Act of Association translated Elizabeth's own vulnerable flesh into the mere sign under which her (male) subjects might associate themselves with one another. Mary's true enemy thereby became a corporate and imaginary body rather than an individual and living one.

This transformation had actually been under way for several years. As early as 1572, a treatise listing the "Inconveniences Produced by Elizabeth's Delays" in expunging Mary Stuart (that "irritated tyrant," "traitoress and pestilence of Christendom") had contended that to execute Mary would be to "save [Elizabeth's] own blood, and her dearest councillors' blood, and infinite blood of a whole realm."[14] That is, Elizabeth's symbolic bond to England – the ties of figurative blood – had to be made to seem more "real" than her true blood tie to Mary before Mary's own blood could justly be spilled. That spilling – even the fantasy of it – would be in turn a further means of reifying Elizabeth's symbolic ties to her English subjects. From this perspective, the living Elizabeth was as much a casualty of an emerging configuration of self and state as Mary was. The irony could be disguised only when Mary's own blood-based and absolute appeals to all her readers were classified as treacherous fictions.

In many Elizabethan subjects, an archaic need to heed Mary's appeal to ties of blood and pity did battle with a need for autonomous personal and political identity to come from a fictional corporation sealed by recent words. But that conflict is nowhere more urgent than in the imaginative work of one of the authors of the Act of Association, one John Pikeryng. Pikeryng would eventually become the most vociferous member of Elizabeth's Parliament to call for Mary's head. In 1567, his "Newe Enterlude of Vice," *Horestes*, made that request thinkable by pitting a husband-murdering Clytemnestra against her own son. In Pikeryng's updated version of Euripides's *Orestes*, the protagonist Horestes is torn between the "pity" that "Dame Nature" dictates he should feel for his "natural mother,"[15] and the male counsellors, usually abstracted into allegorical figures, who spur him to "imitate the flower of Grecian land" (l. 128) and, like a "manly knight" (l. 293), avenge "King Agamemnon's death" (l. 186). Like the Mary of Buchanan's *Detection* and virulent Scottish balladry, which also compared the queen to "Clytemnestra fell [. . .] which slew her spouse,"[16] Pikeryng's Clytemnestra is an "adulterous dame," a monster of excess who "on whoredome murder vile/Hath heaped up, not content her spousal bed to fill" (ll. 175–176). As they encroach even upon the identity of her son, her excesses demand her elimination.

Pikeryng's play thus stages a conflict between two different systems of meaning. In one Clytemnestra is innocent, or at least easily absolved; in the other she is guilty and deserves to die. As modern readers have noticed, Horestes chooses to embrace the abstract cultural code – troped as imitation of masculine cultural authorities – which licenses him to kill his mother.[17] Yet Clytemnestra herself appeals to a different bond, one that in turn urges a different course of action that would generate different meanings. This kind of psychological and symbolic action can be neither distanced nor coolly imitative. After it all springs from the "spark of mother's blood [. . .] within [Horestes's] breast" (l. 730), from the fact that, as Clytemnestra reminds him, "in me thou hast they human shape compos'd" (l. 801). When he kills Clytemnestra, Horestes (whose name bears permanent traces of his mother's "whoredom") does not simply sever the ties that bind him to his mother's body. He also tries to destroy an alternative form of art and authority, one in which one "shape" is materially "compos'd" with, and within, another. The classic Elizabethan subject, Horestes chooses to compose himself alone, in sterile imitation of invented heroes.

The end of Pikeryng's morality play has Horestes triumphantly crowned by Truth and Duty once he has slain his mother. Duty then invites the audience to "pray/for Elizabeth our Queen" (ll. 1192–1193). His words effectively separate Elizabeth from the maternal – the feminine and "natural" – order that Clytemnestra once embodied. It makes sense, then, that our last prayers are asked not for Elizabeth but for the lord Mayor "and for all his brethren, with the commonality" (ll. 1202–1203). Clearly Horestes's authority – and by implication Elizabeth's – is now subject to the "minds" of the "Lordes and Commons" that, by the play's end, he is desperately struggling to "know," only to be tersely informed that "the state of this our Commonwealth need not to be inquired" (ll. 1150–1151). So it would seem that Clytemnestra's killing does not finally resolve a crisis of authority. Instead, it precipitates a new one – a depleted regime of isolation, abstraction and fear. Epitomized in the Bond of Association, that regime can cohere only as long as the threat of Clytemnestra – including the seductive piteousness of her maternal plea – is obsessively recalled. The unconscious aim of *Horestes* was, in the end, to recall it.

"WITHAL SHE SHED PLENTY OF TEARS": THE TREASON TRIAL

As Pikeryng's *Horestes* had done well in advance, Mary's 1586 trial for treason tested the premises of the Act of Association: although forced to define herself within a fiction obviously authored by her English Protestant enemies, the queen held herself to exist outside and prior to the manmade premises of her trial, and the spurious laws of collective identity that they were meant to uphold. Steadfastly maintaining that the proceedings against her could boast nothing more than the "shew and colour of just and legal proceeding," she proceeded to arouse pity by making an "extraordinary course" even more so.[18]

At first Mary refused outright to appear at her trial. Unswayed when informed that "neither her imprisonment, nor her prerogative of royal majesty could exempt her from answering in this kingdom," she was persuaded to "lay aside the bootless privilege of royal dignity" only when apprised that the trial "could and would proceed against her, though she were absent" – only, that is, when her prosecutors acknowledged that they had indeed orchestrated a gross travesty of justice. Fearful she would, if she remained silent, "draw upon [her]self suspicion and lay upon [her] reputation an eternal blot and aspersion" (Cobbett, p. 1169), Mary submitted to examination "with an ill will," all the more disgruntled since she was forced to defend herself in a foreign tongue, without notes, and according to laws unintelligible to her.

The Queen of Scots did not lack impressive acquaintance with canon or with Roman civil law. But of course the "laws and statutes" she was accused of having violated were of very recent vintage and entirely specific to England – "by me most unknown," as she herself would observe (p. 1169). Carefully diagrammed by Elizabeth's secretary, Cecil, the trial's very *mise-en-scène*, Fotheringay's great hall, only flaunted Mary's grievous disadvantage. Elizabeth herself was not even there. Her person was signified only "at the upper end of the chamber" by a "chair of estate," draped with the "cloth of estate" meant to represent her. Forced to appear in the flesh, Mary was assigned a place "below and more remote."

Such details make it very easy to see the proceedings at Fotheringay as little more than the spectacle of Mary's eradication. Though the Stuart queen's spoken defense turned out to be intricate and moving, it certainly did not save her from conviction, and less than four months after she delivered it she was dead. Yet if we interpret the trial in the terms that Mary herself introduced into it, we find, if not a symbolic victory, then at least a genuine challenge to the legal fictions on which the trial depended, to the novel fiction of collective integrity that the trial was meant to protect and, finally, to the self-serving and ultimately bloodless fiction of love for Elizabeth Tudor herself.

In her defense, Mary first addressed the sheer lack of logic in the treason charge, maintaining that (Lochleven notwithstanding) she remained an "absolute queen." She was "no subject," she declared, "and rather would she die a thousand deaths than acknowledge herself one." If she was "no subject," then she was inherently incapable of treason against one above her. In refusing to "prejudice the height of regal majesty and withal confess herself to be bound by all the laws of England" (p. 1170), Mary invoked reverence for the royal blood she shared with Elizabeth. Like the Act of Association, however, Mary's trial was built upon the pitiless abstractions of the written word. It began with the reading of a letter from Elizabeth which called Mary "as a subject [to . . .]

appear personally in judgment" and Mary's own treacherous epistles were soon produced against her.

Mary's reaction to the fundamentally literary character of her trial was to return these damning letters from their present state as coldly expository marks to their origins as volatile and performative signs. Her first line of defense was to deny, vehemently, that she had ever written to Babington. She also denied that, even if she had written them, the letters convicted her of treason. She was Elizabeth's sovereign equal; only subjects could commit treason. These two claims mirrored one another, for in both Mary resisted subordination, first to readers, then to another ruler. By linking these two modes of subjugation, she unveiled the covert tyranny of the reading subject – his nascent sovereignty and the service of an autonomous self which guided both hatred of her and love for Elizabeth. At the same time, however, she practiced a different form of submission, one whose end seemed to have been somehow to induce her beholders to submit to their own feeling for and with her.

Mary did all she could to locate herself outside writing, though she insisted that she did so perforce, for "all my papers are taken from me." "With a countenance composed to royal dignity and with a mind untroubled" (p. 1168), she also disavowed all connection with the "word and writing" that had been produced against her, holding first that the "Packet of Letters" (p. 1170) to Babington, written in cipher, "proceeded not from her but from the Alphabet of Ciphers in France," it being "an easy matter to counterfeit the Ciphers and Characters of Others." Typically, Mary next decided to disown only the incriminating passages, claiming that these contained "such things as she had not dictated" but had been interjected by untrustworthy secretaries. Finally, she denied that she had received letters from Babington, weeping upon word that others had confessed to the contrary. Mary used the Babington letters to present herself as writing's victim rather than as its author, and while from the perspective of the prosecution, Mary's inconsistencies merely exaggerated the appearance of guilt, they also destabilized the writing's own authority. Not only did the Queen of Scots manage to present herself as the piteous victim of her own imputed letters, but in her hands the Babington correspondence swung as wildly as a weathervane in a high wind, pointing first toward one kind of relationship to its authors, then to another.

Mary also cast the written word as itself a traitor of sorts because it deprived her of her rightful sovereignty. While planning her own defense, she informed her accusers, she had "taken note of [Elizabeth's] scruples in a manner confusedly, and by snatches, severally by themselves, but would not deliver them written out, for it stood not, said she, with her royal dignity, to play the scrivener." By rejecting the role of the "scrivener," Mary at once accepted and exploited the part that she *had* been given. She conducted the rest of her defense in contempt of the fundamentally literary fiction of the trial scene, interrupting the reading of the letters, and using her voice and body to disrupt what amounted to an interrogation of written signs. She "fell into speeches" again and again, and "wandered far in these digressions," often meandering into the subject of the "offices of kindness which she had tendered [Elizabeth] these twenty years." "Called back again and prayed [. . .] to speak plainly," she was more likely to weep: "tears burst forth" from her incessantly; "withal she shed plenty of tears."

Mary's tears, her interruptions, her "digressions," and her insistence upon innate and interpersonal identity all dramatically altered the symbolic structure of her own trial. As affecting as the image of traduced innocence and besieged rightful sovereignty that she cultivated might have been, the passionate devices she used to create it proved even harder to forget. They permeate the written records of her trial to tease the yoked authority of a makeshift English law and manmade signs, whose restrictions and petty sublimations she scorned. As the lawyer and Catholic apologist Adam Blackwood would put it the next year, "there was no thing but Paper that could speak" against a queen who truly did speak. And as Mary's "speeches" foregrounded the merely metaphorical nature of any authority that had to fall back on something as artificial as the written word, they exposed the spuriousness and fragility of the forms of corporate identity that are established solely through writing.

Practically, of course, Mary's defense had almost no effect. Elizabeth's Protestant commissioners trooped back to Westminster to pronounce her guilty of treason. Days of hysterical parliamentary discussion followed, none of it contentious, since virtually everyone who spoke on the subject wanted Elizabeth to sentence Mary to death. The declaimers ranged from a young Sir Francis Bacon to one Job Throckmorton, whose need to brand Mary "the daughter of sedition, the mother of rebellion, the nurse of impiety" harked back to John Knox's less than humble opinion that, despite our original dependence on the maternal body, any woman who "reigneth above man" does so only "by treason and conspiracy committed against God."[19]

Parliament twice petitioned a reluctant Elizabeth to sentence Mary to death. *Horestes*'s author, John Pikeryng, was most ruthless, explicitly pitting the Tudor queen's debts to her own subjects against anything that she might have owed Mary by virtue of blood. Whereas Mary was nothing more than "a cousin to you in remote degree," he reminded Elizabeth, he and his fellow Englishmen "be the sons and children of this land, whereof you be not only the natural mother, but also the wedded spouse." This being so, "it would exceedingly grieve and wound the hearts of your loving subjects" were Mary permitted to live. "To spare her is to spill us."[20]

Unlike Mary, Elizabeth was of course no "natural mother" at all, and she certainly felt the chasm between fiction and blood that structured every metaphor that Pikeryng exploited. She temporized and equivocated, agonizing above all over the extent to which to put Mary to death would be to cripple the myth of maidenly grace that had long underpinned her own authority. "What is it which they will not write now," she demanded of Parliament, "when they shall hear that I have given consent, that the executioner's hands shall be imbrued with the blood of my nearest kinswoman?"[21] The real fear that girds this question is of course the fear that, precisely by denying kinship with her cousin, Elizabeth would become another Mary, a bad mother at once blood-thirsty and vulnerable to her own subjects' words. Had not Mary herself agreed to appear at trial because she feared she might otherwise "lay upon [her] reputation an eternal blot and aspersion"? To protect her own reputation, Elizabeth blamed the "Act of Parliament" that "brought me to a narrow Streight, that I must give order for her death, which is a princess most nearly allied unto me in blood."[22] For a time she even avoided giving such an order, salving her inflamed ministers and the peers of the realm with nothing more than an infamous and entirely inconclusive "answer without an answer" to the question of whether or not Mary should be put to death.[23]

But even this answer had the effect of exposing Elizabeth's true likeness to – even her identity with – Mary. Presenting her own words for Parliament to interpret as it would, Elizabeth's need to appear feeling and not ruthless forced her to describe the Queen of Scots as one "not differing from me" in any material point – "sex," "rank," even "blood." Indeed, in the weeks following the Queen of Scots's trial, Elizabeth seemed to become Mary, at once incalculable and exposed, forced to action by her own subordinates and at last unable to detach herself from what was "spread" about her. No longer a "maiden" tantalizingly closed to her thus doubly ardent suitors, Elizabeth stood before Parliament as the open, indeed gaping, "mother" of her own guilt, and theirs. Unsurprisingly, the libels that came down from Scotland after Mary's beheading denounced Elizabeth in the imagery once reserved for the Queen of Scots, as "Jezebel that English whore."[24]

It is difficult then, to conclude that Mary Stuart's second trial was an unconditional defeat. We could also see it as the moment of likeness's unleashing, the split but definitive second in which Elizabeth was at last compelled to become one with her. It was also a moment in which the tie of forbidden love and dangerous pity that bound Mary to her potential subjects was erased only imperfectly from the official text of English identity. At the very least, the parliamentary record of Mary's trial and its aftermath registers a fiction of corporate and individual identity's less than secure or innocent beginning. We discover instead this fiction's conspiracy with anti-royalist, anti-Catholic and even misogynist forms of literary, political and personal authority. Instead of portraying a guilty queen safely expunged, the record of Mary's trial, like that of its aftermath in the Houses of Parliament, remains haunted by its own victim. The self-splitting, self-subverting, even self-emptying impulses to a childlike identification which Mary nurtured persist within it, and make it the traitor of itself.

"LADIE OF GREAT COUNTENANCE": SPENSER'S DUESSA

Though Mary's trial ended in mid-October of 1586, Elizabeth could not be brought to issue the proclamation of death until early December, and it was not until well after the new year that she finally signed the death warrant, harried into this conclusive act of writing only by rumors of civil unrest. Even then, Elizabeth later claimed, the actual warrant was dispatched without her knowledge or "pleasure" by an understudy for an ailing Walsingham, one William Davison. Davison went to the Tower, albeit briefly, for his zealous haste. But by that time Mary's keeper at Fotheringay, the grim and unsusceptible Puritan Sir Amyas Paulet, had long since read Elizabeth's decree and performed it to the letter.

Having recognized the fact of "like blood" only to betray it, Elizabeth appears to have been, quite literally, beside herself when word arrived that Mary had been put to death. Her guilt naturally mingled with fears of Scottish, French or even Spanish retaliation. But most wracking of all was the anxiety that she might inherit the Queen of Scots' old reputation for vindictive cruelty. Such a reputation threatened to destroy Elizabeth's own subjects' love, and even to deflect it onto the specter of Mary – not the reprobate queen of Scottish days, but rather the tragic victim that Mary seemed to have become in the final, and most pitiable, phase of her life.

As the words of her cryptic motto (*en ma fin est mon commencement*) had predicted, Mary's departure from the corporeal world alone gave her an edge over Elizabeth. Not only had she faced death like a true queen – and a martyred Catholic one at that – but, as Elizabeth herself had recognized even before her own coronation, desire most ardently seeks what it does not have close to hand.[25] In leaving the world of human cravings and illicit sympathies under such literally incoherent circumstances, Mary actually improved her own chances of absorption into the affections of the living.

Her resurrection in Catholic hearts was of course predictable. Within months of her death, the Queen of Scots was stirring again in Roman Catholic martyrologies like Richard Verstegan's *Theatrum Crudelitatum*.[26] Her "cruel murder" also moved writers like Blackwood, whose graphic and distraught rendering of that deed used its gruesome minutiae, right down to the "pierced [. . .] strings within her head," to make readers "plainly and manifestly understand" that "the savage English" are "more brutish and savage than the most savage beast," their sovereign Elizabeth a "monster of all woman kind."[27]

The dead queen bred new and surprisingly vital meanings in the visual arts as well. As if their subject still lived, elaborate and flattering new portraits of Mary began to appear, almost for the first time since her adolescence in France. Framed with inset plates that featured the closing scene at Fotheringay and based on the only portrait of her in captivity (Plate 1), they too revived everything that the authors of her execution had labored to erase. Meanwhile, popular martyrologies printed their own moving pictures of the queen's demise. Forged on the continent for smuggling over England's border, these images showed the headsman's axe poised to deliver a second blow while the gash from the first, misguided one glared at the base of Mary's skull (Plate 2). As it suspended the Queen of Scots at some tantalizing point between life and death, the portraiture of martyrdom kept her body a catalyst for the very political and religious passions that decapitation was meant to extinguish.

Plate 1 Mary Queen of Scots, possibly by Rowland Lockey, from Hardwick Hall. Courtesy of the National Trust Photographic Library/Hawkley Studios.

Plate 2 Theatrum Crudelitatum, from Richard Verstegan. Courtesy of the Huntington Library and Art Collections.

Far more audacious than the Catholic reanimation of the Queen of Scots, however, was its unintentional counterpart in the artifacts of Protestant fantasy. We saw at the outset that even hostile accounts of her beheading like Robert Wyngfield's harbored a latent impulse to remain in intimate, even slavish contact with Mary. Precisely because they recognized how powerful this impulse could be, Elizabeth's Protestant ministers sought to muzzle all posthumous representations of the Stuart queen. Their object was in part to prevent the "blemish" of Elizabeth's "good renown." More generally, though, they hoped to guarantee that "sinister opinion" concerning the Stuart queen would not "sink deeply and be imprinted, especially in the ruder minds." Officially, all sympathetic impressions of the Queen of Scots were to be "speedily suppressed" with "the very weapons of truth."[28] But when such weapons could not be summoned, then poetic fancy might suffice. So it was that nine years after Mary knelt at the scaffold, Elizabeth's very devoted subject Edmund Spenser translated the trial that took her there into the language of Protestant allegory.

This was an undertaking that betrays its own difficulty, and even its inherent violence, in the uncharacteristic turbulence, unto incoherence, of the poetry that resulted.[29] Spenser's herculean task was to pare away the wretched excess of meaning provided by history and thereby to render a neatly bounded allegory in that history's place.[30] In an alchemy at least equally arduous, he was to make his readers see, and believe, that Elizabeth Tudor was a merciful and virtuous queen, as different from her wayward cousin (once-removed) as day from night.

In Book V of Spenser's unfinished epic, *The Faerie Queene* (1596), "a Ladie of great countenance and place," Duessa, is thus "brought as prisoner to the barre," there to be charged as the author of "many haynous crymes, by her enured."[31] As Duessa's chief prosecutor, one Zele, puts it, the most "haynous" of these crimes is that she "to pitie had allured" two knights, who then internalized Duessa's own desire to kill their queen, Mercilla, and usurp her throne. This pitiable defendant, co-author of so many dangerous desires, now faces judgment by "the dread *Mercilla*" herself, one of *The Faerie Queene's* several stand-ins for Elizabeth Tudor. Duessa, of course, is an obvious apparition of Mary Stuart, although she has by this point in *The Faerie Queene* already appeared in various guises and disguises which have had nothing to do with the Queen of Scots.

Duessa's multiplicity makes her both like and unlike Mercilla, whom we meet in Book V but who shares a single referent – Elizabeth – with many other women in the poem. In other words, Mercilla belongs to a fixed system of meaning in which many signs have just one significance, while Duessa herself only sometimes stands for the Queen of Scots: the system of meaning that supports *her* promiscuously allows many signifiers to have many signifieds, and to claim equal authority with them. In Book V Duessa is therefore on trial partly for the threat she poses to Spenser's allegorical structure. A form of literary love meant in this instance to exalt "the most high, mighty and magnificent

Elizabeth," allegory by definition depends on a stable one-to-one correspondence – and chaste distance – between signs and their already idealized
referents. Much as pity denies the difference between its subject and its object,
so does Duessa taunt the symbolic fixity of Spenser's allegory, not to mention
its sustaining economy of desire. She thus reprises the essence of Mary Stuart's
threat to the erotic and symbolic order of the Elizabethan state.

Just as Elizabeth's subjects needed to perceive an acute difference between
the queen they consciously wanted and her captive and captivating cousin, so
did Spenser's allegory need Duessa to be entirely different from Mercilla if it
was to protect an idealized vision of the good queen, Elizabeth. But what
Spenser actually wrought was no gallant exoneration of a merciful Elizabeth.
He tendered instead a conflicted document of desire, one troubled not least by
its own failures of detachment, both from its origins in a felt history and from
the self-emptying claims of identificatory love.

All, at first, is well. Clothed in a mysterious "cloth of state," Spenser's "gracious Queene" Mercilla sits secure "on high, that she might all men see,/And
might of all men royally be seene" (5.9.27). The cloth of state that conceals
Mercilla shines "like a cloud, as likest may be held," while the blinding beams
of light around her skirt are "glistring like gold." She herself is "angel-like."
So many "likes" weave a subliming veil of analogy that defends Mercilla's
ideality, literally by shielding her from sight. Analogy's omnipresence in
Spenser's poetic language also signals the presence of a stable symbolic con-
vention, one that reliably links two entities through their similarity but also
makes it clear that they are not and can never be the same. Likewise, it is by
virtue of analogy's veil that Mercilla is "honour'd of all," just as Elizabeth's vir-
ginal sequestration from her own subjects had in the past given them a single,
exalted form of desire to share.

But once the "great and weightie case" of Duessa is underway, the polite rec-
iprocity between symbol and wish disintegrates. For one thing, in terms of
Spenser's poem, the "weigh[t]" of historical reference – of Mary's case, still
fresh in Elizabethan memory – forces itself upon the transcendent fiction of
Protestant allegory. Then too, Duessa disrupts all of the firm agreements that
keep Mercilla's authority intact. Her case is "on both sides, [. . .] debating
hard" (5.9.36) and, as in Pikeryng's *Horestes*, two commissions come forward to
lodge competing claims about her. First, cold abstractions – Authority, the
Law of Nations, Religion and "Iustice" charge Duessa with a will to "peremp-
torie Power" and with "breach of lawes" (5.9.44). "On the contrarie part,"
though, Duessa has "many advocates" – "Pittie with full tender heart,"
"Regard," "Daunger," "Nobilitie of birth" and tearful "Greife" (5.9.45).
Drawing its persuasive power from the present image of suffering beauty, this
little contingent's appeal to sympathy – the ties that bind feeling bodies – vies
with bloodless principle for mastery over the official and unofficial judges of
the scene.

The official judge is of course Mercilla. The unofficial ones are a "Briton
prince," Arthur, and his knight Artegall, who have happened by just in time

to watch the trial. Readers in the text, these manly observers also stand in for Elizabeth's own male subjects, ever the inquisitive witnesses to her relationship with Mary. Duessa's direct, even visceral, appeals to these two onlookers forces Spenser's poem with its airy title and gossamer cast of characters to absorb not just a narratable history of events but also an inchoate one of feeling – of rage, of pity and of desire.

"The sad terror of so dreadfull fate;/And wretched ruine of so high estate" indeed moves Arthur to such "great ruth" that he is at last dissolved by the "nere touch" of "Pitie with full tender heart" (5.9.46). And Mercilla in the end lets fall a "few perling drops from her fair lampes of light" (5.9.50). Spenser's poem bravely labors to wrest the affective history that threatens to absorb both Arthur and Elizabeth into conformity with his own expressed desire to perpetuate and rehabilitate Elizabeth's image, to "consecrate" that image with his book. To this end, he aims to detach his narrative from its experiential and libidinal ground. Mary and Elizabeth meet as they never did in life, and Duessa improves upon the historical Mary Stuart in two ways. Whereas Mary spoke at length throughout her trial, Duessa says nothing.[32] And while Mary was seldom without her trademark veil of mourning, here only Mercilla is veiled; Duessa's "great countenance" stands open to view.

Spenser's narrator studies this countenance at such length that we might do well to look at it too:

> Yet did appeare rare beautie in her face,
> But blotted with condition vile and base,
> That all her other honour did obscure,
> And titles of nobilitie deface.
>
> (5.9.38)

Duessa's face counts as evidence of her own guilt; it is Exhibit A in the prosecution of the many "haynous crymes by her enured." As readers have readily noticed, however, Duessa's face resembles nothing so much as a written text, one whose blots and superimpositions betray its roots in the material, affective world. Duessa's features obscure the boundary between carnal realities and pure symbols, exactly as both Mary's spoken defense and her earlier adventures in epistolarity had once done. Her defacement brings the historical Mary – Mary as she had created, and destroyed, herself in order to create fellow feeling in others – across *The Faerie Queene*'s monitored boundaries straight into the heart of Spenser's text. With her come two undesirable guests: the possibility of identification unto pity, and the impossibility of maintaining a credible distinction between Mercilla and Duessa.

We can take the second impossibility first. Duessa's face, we recall, is bare, whereas the historical Mary wore a veil. That accessory has migrated to Mercilla and provides her and Duessa a shared foundation in the Queen of Scots. But even without the specter of the veil, Duessa's countenance betrays an initially hidden alliance with Mercilla's. It is full of contradiction, to be sure, and in it "beautie" couples with the marks of "foule abuse" to counter the coherent analogies that project Mercilla. Yet the source of its contradictions lies in its layers; its surface is "blotted" and its "titles of nobilitie deface[d]." This palimpsestic quality subliminally identifies Duessa's "great countenance" with Mercilla's strategically veiled one. For like Mercilla's, Duessa's face is finally inscrutable, the graffiti of "abuse" no more legible than the "beautie" and "nobilitie" it deface[s]." In the end, Duessa's stripped yet "blotted" face parodies the idealized signs that at once produce Mercilla and hide her from view.

Spenser's effort to distinguish Duessa from his affection's proper object, Mercilla, founders most dramatically when it becomes clear that Duessa's wretched face can still stir the pity that Spenser would reserve for the anguished and eventually tearful Mercilla. Duessa's crime is reiterated as, precisely, that of provoking pity: "In that wretched semblant, she did sure/The peoples great compassion vnto her allure" (5.19.38). Like Mary's own Protestant subjects of old, Spenser seeks to escape her sentimental orbit by falsifying her, reducing her to a "semblant" and enchantress. "Compassion" demands that all observers absorb Duessa's cause, but its demands need not be met if her wretchedness is not real.

Spenser's Duessa stands as a maddeningly reflexive counter-text within the officially exculpatory text of *The Faerie Queene*. She thwarts the poem's narrator from his goal of sublimating Elizabeth by embodying the internal contradictions which stem from a chaste allegory's embarrassing affinity with what lies outside itself, in the uncertainties of emotional experience and the inevitably mottled pages that attempt to record it. What both botches and enables all efforts to turn life into words is of course finally feeling, life's only, but indelible, trace. And *The Faerie Queene* – or at least the segment of it compelled to incorporate the Queen of Scots – is finally driven by the self-defacing need to arouse readerly pity. As with all propaganda, this is also a need to deprive that reader of interpretive choice – to tyrannize precisely through self-abdication. It is, in other words, to be like the Mary so often imagined from Buchanan on.

On the surface, Spenser's trial of Duessa revives Mary Queen of Scots in order to kill her again in the seemingly pure space of poetic language. That purity *is* only seeming, though, and Spenser would seem to know it. Many Elizabeth-centered readings of *The Faerie Queene* are afloat in the world today, and they acknowledge at once that Spenser's effort to rewrite a controversial trial invariably mars the smooth figural surface of his poem, so that it is only through rhetorical violence that he translates Elizabeth's harsh justice into mercy. But a Mary-centered reading finds Spenser, oddly enough, protecting Mary too. In spite of himself, he at last compelled his readers to sense, if not to see, that to go on loving Elizabeth perfectly and in concert would be to sacrifice a capacity that has little to do with the prettiness of allegory, or poetry's sculpted form – the capacity to feel, limitlessly, with and for another.

"TELLUS, WHO IS MADE ALL OF LOVE":
JOHN LYLY'S *ENDIMION*

Spenser's *Faerie Queene* frankly rewrites history: it puts Mary into the physical contact with Elizabeth that she never had and it does not explicitly send her to the scaffold. It replaces "what really happened" with a dream, one like all dreams driven by conflicting wishes and so presenting itself to its interpreter riddled with the most involving gaps and inconsistencies. Nor was Spenser's the only such dream to betray itself in England in the decade after Mary's death. In 1588, Elizabeth's learned courtier John Lyly's lyrical court entertainment *Endimion, or the Man in the Moon* revived the Queen of Scots in the seductive and pathetic figure of Tellus, terrestrial foil to Lyly's celestial heroine Cynthia. Classified by its author as "neither comedy, nor tragedy, nor story, nor anything," *Endimion* was performed before Elizabeth on Candlemas Night, almost a year after Mary's execution.[33] That Elizabeth should have watched and even enjoyed it suggests that Lyly was fulfilling more desires than his own. In any case, *Endimion* was published three years later, and its plot speaks volumes.

The soulful young poet Endimion loves Cynthia, Queen of the Moon. This is only as it should be, since Lyly's play is both the repetition of an ancient myth and an allegory of the proper Elizabethan subject position. The rub lies in Cynthia's lady-in-waiting, Tellus, whose decidedly sublunary "body is decked with fair flowers;" even her "veins are vines" (p. 151). Tellus, "who is made all of love," is so smitten with Endimion that she plots to "entangle him in such a sweet net that he shall neither find the means to come out, nor desire it" (p. 157). So "deluded with love" that she can obey "neither rule nor reason" (p. 152), she contrives numerous ways to enchant him, all of which make him something rather other than his conscious self: "All his virtues will I shadow with vices," she resolves. "His person [. . .] shall he deck with such rich robes as he shall forget it is his own person" (p. 152). She fails, however, as she does also to convince him that the unadulterated Cynthia is not unlike Tellus herself – that she is "but a woman" and "shall have an end;" "her beauty is but subject to time" (p. 158).

As a last resort, Tellus sends Endimion into a deep sleep, then goes to prison for having meanwhile seditiously employed her "long tongue" against Cynthia. Her official punishment is to "weave the stories and poetries, wherein were showed both examples and punishments of tattling tongues" (p. 175). Tellus takes up the work both of Mary's own needle and of her tongue. And, like Mary, she is driven to create images of her own submission. So instead of cautionary tales, she compulsively "embroider[s] the sweet face of Endimion" (p. 73). Meanwhile, Tellus's pitying jailor, Corsites, falls from pity into downright love with her. As many of Mary's Elizabethan "hosts" had done, he confesses that her plaintive "beauty in the same moment took my heart captive that I undertook to carry her body prisoner" (p. 180). Lyly's seductress foments "combats" in Corsites, pitched battles between piteous love and letter-perfect duty, between obligatory reverence and genuine affection. If Endimion was the ideal Elizabeth subject, the ambivalent Corsites is the real one.

Tellus both mirrors and creates this divided self. As Mary's did, her "fairness" seems to mask inner corruption, but her passions also divide her, rendering her, she insists, her own victim: "My heart, too tender to withstand such a divine fury [. . .] yielded to love" (p. 189). The same passions also make her Endimion's victim, depriving her of self-sovereignty: He "so ravished my heart with love that to obtain my desires I could not find means" (p. 189). It is of course this loss of self-government, Tellus's helplessness even before herself, that holds such sway over Corsites, and seduces him into relinquishing his own volition, joining his lot to hers instead. Endimion, by contrast, is restored to an intending consciousness by Cynthia, who then marries him and pardons Tellus. The latter, now mute, makes her final exit as Corsites's unblushing bride.

The dreamscape of Lyly's play feels even more like wish-fulfillment than Spenser's poem did, especially since, while Spenser's Mercilla at last succumbs to "strong constraint" and sentences Duessa to death, Lyly's Cynthia finally forgives Tellus, if not for her delusion that she is Cynthia's "equal," then at least for the seductive "fairness" that inspires pity, "pinching the heart" (p. 193) of her worst enemies. In *Endimion* Mary, in the guise of silenced Tellus, is finally absorbed into the world that Cynthia, or more accurately the love of her, rules. As one of the play's recent critics suggests, Cynthia and Tellus can be seen to stand for two "different modes of enchantment" that are two different modes of "subjugation to the feminine."[34] Endimion is enthralled by Tellus's spells but he willingly submits to Cynthia's attractions. This means that Cynthia's triumph is that of the active Endimion over the passive one. It is the victory of one version of subjectivity, its autonomy guaranteed by a remote and pure female figure, over another that is locked in struggle with the active and present woman whose amorous fantasies perpetually recreate it as *her* object, not its own subject.

But the creative power of Tellus' own active fantasies persists, transposed into the texture of the play about her. As was true of *The Faerie Queene*, that is, there is one layer of *Endimion* that perpetuates the very reflexive arts Mary seems to have practiced in reality. Those arts, we saw, incorporated the bonds of identificatory love, and thus had to be sacrificed if certain forms and fictions of subjectivity were ever to seem real. From this point of view, Lyly's story of Tellus's survival is not a story at all. Rather, with singular immediacy, it registers "what really happened" during Mary's brutal subordination to reciprocal fictions of political and psychological identity.

When Cynthia forgives Tellus her trespasses and declines to punish her, Lyly at first seems to sublimate what went between the Tudor and Stuart queens into gossamer myth. Aside from marriage to the imbecile Corsites, Tellus's only punishment is that she must only "so much of Endimion as his picture cometh to, possess" (p. 193). Tellus accepts her sentence in silence. She does not speak again, and Lyly's epilogue retells the fable of the sun and wind who "strive for sovereignty" by trying to make a traveller give up his coat. Lyly applies the fable implicitly to the superiority of Cynthia's power to that of the blustery Tellus, then explicitly to Elizabeth's fortitude against "the malicious that seek to overthrow us with threats." Such enemies, Lyly assures his own "dread sovereign," "but stiffen our thoughts and make them sturdier in storms" (p. 194). Suddenly, Elizabeth is the vulnerable traveller, not the sun. So what Lyly's play confirms in the end is less Elizabeth/Cynthia's resistance to assaults on her integrity as an "incomparable" sign than her male subject's influence on the queen he seems merely to revere, his capacity to create her and thereby prove he has created himself. This is the reading we get anyway when we approach *Endimion* with the Protestant interpretive devices that Mary's Elizabethan readers forged upon her, that they might spare Elizabeth.

But what if we were to read according to the Marian poetics that is figured in Tellus's ensnaring, and yet self-ensnaring, love? From this perspective, sub-lunary signs claim authority equal to that of celestial significances, and the mastery of their meanings is not always detectably different from submission to those same meanings. Such a perspective would confirm what Tellus (like Mary) insisted all along: her difference from Cynthia (or Elizabeth) is actually negligible, at best a fiction through which the authority of the modern English subject can be forged and even, if artificially, reproduced. Second, we might find that to retain Elizabeth/Cynthia as a sign of that authority also requires keeping Mary/Tellus alive and, above all, loving. In Lyly's play, Tellus's fate is to possess "only the picture" of what she loves, the male subject. But Cynthia herself is mindful that Tellus has "wrought" that very picture. Always partly made by Tellus, Endimion will never wholly coincide with himself as long as he denies it.

In converting the death of Mary Queen of Scots into an almost mystical extension of her life, Lyly confirmed that that life had meant the birth of modern forms of personal and political psychology. Like Spenser, he struggled against a system of meaning, maternally embodied in Mary, which is prior to and responsible for that psychology, and bound to haunt it ever after. Like many other Elizabethans, Lyly and Spenser both saw "Scottish Mary" as an author and an artist. They detected her guilty, longing and yet curiously yielding body's presence in their own words in order to claim Elizabeth as their true mirror – or at least as the one in which they could recognize themselves as subjects of a credible fiction of personal coherence and collective identity. To be convincing, such a *méconnaissance* requires separation first, and subliminal discord ever after. But to represent this discord and its birth was not just to kill Mary again and again in order to protect a fledgling fiction of personal and collective unity. It was also to concede the Queen of Scots a measure of the very authority she herself had claimed as the "most careful tender mother" of her political children, their real and rightful queen.

Part II

Stuart Mary

A new and unexampled Kind of Tomb is here extant, wherein the Living are enclosed with the Dead.

> Epitaph on the first grave of Mary Queen of Scots (removed)

What haunts are not the dead, but the gaps left within us by the secrets of others.

> Nicolas Abraham, "Notes on the Phantom" (1975)

By official count, Mary Queen of Scots was buried twice: once at Peterborough Cathedral in 1587 and then a second time, in Westminster Abbey, in 1612. Yet over the course of the seventeenth century, as Mary's own descendants came and went from the English throne, apparitions of the dead queen resurfaced so often as to suggest that she had in fact to be laid to rest many times over. How might we account for Stuart Britain's failure to bury – in psychological terms, to forget – the mother of its (usually) ruling dynasty?

It is tempting to conclude that the Elizabethans made it impossible for their children to do otherwise. The contradictions that divided various outspoken Protestants' attachment to Mary meant that the verbal images of her that they left behind strained always against themselves, across a widening void. From flagrant prose caricatures like Buchanan's *Detection* to well-wrought allegories like Spenser's *Faerie Queene*, the longing to surrender to the libidinal realm in which Mary prevailed never quite made peace with the more savage, if self-satisfying, wish to wrest her from that same enveloping tapestry of pity and desire. To the extent that Mary Stuart may be said to have become one with both her real and her potential subjects' unresolved affections toward her – and to the extent that it is through the fictive artifacts of those affections that future generations made contact with the Queen of Scots – we can hardly expect her either wholly to have died or altogether to have lived on. As her own motto had so eerily foretold, her end was her beginning.

Perhaps more to the point, however, in the bodily life that did end Mary had been a mother. And as things turned out it was her conveniently Protestant son James who inherited Elizabeth Tudor's crown when that queen died, in 1603.

Until the death of James's great-granddaughter Anne in 1714 Mary thus hovered in the background as the matriarch of Britain's ruling dynasty; even after that dynasty went into exile, it was her unhappy story, not Elizabeth's triumphant one, that provided the true matrix of the Stuart family romance. Though dead, Mary thus posed a dilemma of maternal influence and filial desire even more immediate than the metaphorical one that had cloven the earliest representations of her in Scotland and England.

For the Stuarts' subjects, this dilemma was exacerbated by the conflictual nature of collective life at that time. James's accession of course united the crowns of Scotland and England, and in 1707 the Act of Union, under Anne, sealed the entity of Great Britain politically and economically. But despite such convincing signs of coherence, Stuart Britain was almost always locked in some form of opposition to itself: Puritan revolution led to the civil wars of the 1640s and eventually to the regicide of James's son, Charles I, in 1649. A decade without monarchy followed before the precarious restoration of Charles II in 1660. And though the Stuart period lasted somewhat longer in name, the warrant for its execution was signed in 1688 when Charles's autocratic Roman Catholic brother James II was asked to leave the throne. The second James's ignominious replacement by his own daughter, the second Mary Stuart, and her consort William of Orange, dismantled the last trappings of true sovereign authority in Britain. William and Mary were constitutionally answerable to Parliament, and when Mary's sister Anne came to the throne in 1702, she succumbed almost entirely to the wishes of her ministers.

All of this makes for a fundamentally ironic historical moment. It is one in which, even as Britain's ruling family was engaged in being overruled, its subjects were engaged, often at once, in being and not being ruled by the Stuarts – indeed, in being and not being ruled by any monarch at all. Such a predicament sustained and even magnified the old Elizabethan strife between the desire for absolute personal authority and the seductions of its loss. In turn, as for the Elizabethans, for both the Stuarts and their subjects Mary's memory linked contemporary crises of authority to an even more primal struggle to establish individual, impervious identity in relation to a maternal body, archaic and enticing, which both models and demands the loss of a historically specific self. Accordingly, throughout the seventeenth century the motherly figure of the Queen of Scots refused to distance herself in time, while a powerful sense of Mary's continued physical presence kept almost everyone, royal or otherwise, from coming to terms with her paradoxically enthralling legacy of failure and loss.

The following chapter first sets out to describe Mary's distinctive style of persistence through the reigns of the Stuarts; it does so largely with reference to her children and their children, whose public images and private dreams she haunted. A look at the new histories of the British Isles which began to cast themselves as the registers of collective memory, though, suggests that many Stuart Englishmen were also "haunted," if not by Mary herself then by certain gaps within the Elizabethans' recorded experience of her. These gaps provided receptacles for the new recognition that, regardless of what the Queen of Scots might have been – and regardless of how she might have failed – the Stuarts still owed physical existence and royal prerogative to her. Indeed, they owed something more – a model for achieving influence through emptiness, emotional impact through radical inconsistency. As historians cast about for an authority of their own, they hoped to adapt this model to the written language of collective memory. So for a time the Queen of Scots took up a most revealing residence in their words, transformed there from the Elizabethans' motherly seductress of the will into the ambiguous object of an uneasy love.

Yet despite their perpetual equivocations, Stuart era romances with the royal family's stubbornly undead mother did manage to change over time. To see how they did, we turn in Chapter 4 to John Banks's 1684 stage tragedy, *The Island Queens*. Banks's dramatic rendering of the end of Mary's life was banned before it could be performed, but in 1704 it reappeared, much changed, as the wildly popular *The Albion Queens*. At the time of its birth, *The Island Queens* vividly re-enacted the conflicts and equivocations that had gripped England and Scotland for nearly a hundred years. But by the early eighteenth century, Banks had successfully revamped the royal mother who had so pervaded Stuart memory. By the reign of the last Stuart, Anne, a new culture of sensibility had begun to repress the many contradictions of authority and desire that had been the essence of the Stuart age. In Banks's hands, Mary Queen of Scots became that culture's heroine.

3 "A new and unexampled kind of tomb"
1603–1714

Separated from the Queen of Scots in infancy, Mary's son James could not possibly have remembered his mother. Yet he often seemed haunted by her memory. The Venetian diplomat Giovanni Scaramelli observed that after his accession to the English throne James never "le[t] a day pass without lamenting that his mother's head fell, at the third stroke, by a villainous deed, till those who, even by relationship, are stained with that blood grow fearful [. . .] lest their end be a bloody one."[1] Scaramelli's English contemporary Sir John Harington concurred that "the Queen his mother was not forgotten."[2] While such reports no doubt gratified their authors' own desire for James's mother to remain alive to him, the king certainly contributed to the impression that she had by ordering the most ostentatious representation of the Queen of Scots that survives from the seventeenth century – her monument at Westminster Abbey.

Immediately after her beheading, Mary's body had been hastily rolled in a cloth torn from a nearby billiard table. At length, however, propriety triumphed, and the queen's remains were "wrapped and soldered in lead;" six months after her death they were finally buried – not without ceremony – at Peterborough Cathedral. For a time, Mary's nearby grave bore an eerie epitaph that pronounced hers "a new and unexampled Kind of Tomb, wherein the Living are enclosed with the Dead." Predicting that "the same wicked sentence" that "doomed [Mary] to a natural Death" guaranteed that "all surviving kings, being made as Common people, are subjected to a civill Death," the epitaph was, for obvious reasons, soon spirited away; the queen's body remained for another 25 years.[3]

After Elizabeth had died and grudgingly left him king, James's Roman Catholic subjects were "grieved [. . .] when they saw no memory at all made of so memorable a mother either in word or in work; she lying [. . .] obscurely in that place where her enemies cast her after cutting off her head."[4] So in 1606 James launched a campaign to revive and rehabilitate the memory of the mother whose sometimes shady life he had done nothing in particular to save. At a cost of nearly £1100, he commissioned Cornelius Clure to sculpt a monument for Mary. James Maury would do the painting and gilding. Their joint handiwork was to stand in Westminster Abbey opposite Elizabeth's "plainer and less sumptuous" tomb. Six years in the making, the monument was majestic indeed; 75 years later it was still easy to admire Mary's "Image in her Royal Habiliments, painted, and gilt with Gold," as it graced "a noble Pedestal of curious wrought Alabaster, overshadowed by an arched Canopy, supported by eight Corinthian pillars of black Marble, the Capitals and Pedestals gilt, the Architrave adorned with Arms, and the whole of an admirable composure."[5]

For all its "admirable composure," this artificial body in its gaudy showcase seems not to have been sufficient to satisfy James's newfound desire for some version of maternal presence. Deciding that it was "inconvenient that the monument and her body should be in several places," the king ordered "the corpse of our said dearest mother" carried from Peterborough to Westminster, "the same being taken up in as decent and respectful a manner as is fitting."[6] Nonetheless, the Queen of Scots's reburial was far more subdued, even covert, than her funeral at Peterborough had been. Her body was brought to Westminster under cover of darkness – "to avoid a concourse," explained James's Roman Catholic favorite, the Earl of Northampton. As if to compensate for a general repression of pageantry in "the place whence she had been expelled with tyranny," Northampton gave Mary a poetic re-interment in his own language. "She is buried with honour," he proclaimed, "as dead rose-leaves are preserved, whence the liquor that makes the kingdom sweet hath been distilled."[7]

For all that Mary's burial would seem to mark her incorporation into England's body politic, James himself apparently did not care to witness it. At once ardent and detached, his conflicted solicitude for his mother's body kept that body above ground as surely as the physical act of her exhumation had done, and guaranteed that, psychologically, it would remain unburied for much longer. It is, in turn, this lack of settlement, far more than the queenly body's actual removal to Westminster, which seems to have been the object of desire.[8] And James's obvious wish both to have Mary's body and to keep it at a distance finds many an analogue in the visual commemorations of Mary that proliferated in England during his reign. Catholic observers reported with satisfaction that the minute Elizabeth was dead her picture was "hidden everywhere, and Mary Stuart's shown instead with declaration that she suffered for no cause other than her religion."[9] Northampton himself amassed as many as five portraits of the dead Queen of Scots, one of which hung in his bedchamber opposite a depiction of the Passion of Christ.[10]

Of course, not everyone was happy to trade an exemplary chaste political mother like Elizabeth for the more controversial one who had actually given birth to the present sovereign; and individual responses to Mary's memory were themselves divided. William Drummond, for example, sent his friend Ben Jonson copies of the emblems ("worthy your remembrance") that the Queen of Scots had once embroidered into her bed of state. They included "a *Phoenix* in flames," "the Sun in Eclipse" and "two women upon the Wheels of Fortune [. . .] which *Impressa* seemeth to glance at Queen *Elizabeth* and her self." But Drummond tempered their passion and urgency into a decidedly detached aesthetic judgment, coolly concluding that "the workmanship is curiously done, and above all value, and truly it may be of this Piece said *Materiam superbat.*"[11]

Drummond fled from direct evidence of Mary's suffering into the chilled idiom of connoisseurship. Mary's onetime lady-in-waiting, Elizabeth Curle, tussled with the bloody memory of the Queen of Scots in a different way. Curle had been present at Fotheringay, and in the early seventeenth century she commissioned a memorial portrait (Plate 3) based on the only image of Mary that had been made during her captivity (Plate 1). The memorial portrait reverses its "original," softening the queen's angular features and shifting the crafty slant of her eyes so that they look in the same direction she faces. Gone is the distraction of the perspectively incorrect Persian carpet, and Mary's Catholic faith is more evident, in the enlarged crucifix she carries and in the missal she holds. Such details are borrowed from the continental martyrologies that appeared immediately after her death, as is the inset tableau depicting her execution in miniature; Latin inscriptions confirm the Queen of Scots as, among other things, a "true daughter" of the Roman Church.

Unlike a martyrological woodcut, however, Curle's memorial portrait is not meant, at least primarily, to freeze Mary into the mold of a Roman Catholic heroine. Its details instead are often fraught with the burden of passing time and personal grief. So the diminutive figures of Mary's weeping women-in-waiting become part of the scene, and one reaches out, improbably, to touch the Stuart queen's comparatively gigantic dress. Mary's face, moreover, has been aged from the time of the original portrait, the better to resemble her as she must have appeared at the hour of her death. Meanwhile, the inset image of her execution introduces yet a different moment in time to make the canvas, in effect, an uneasy collaboration between the memory of the execution that Curle carried in her own body and the transpersonal iconography in place long before either Curle or Mary had ever drawn breath. Ungainly though the result might be, Curle's canvas offers not just a memorial image, but an image *of* volatile and self-contradictory feeling interfering with long-established forms of recollection in order, finally, to perpetuate itself through its own object.

The anachronisms and incongruities that give Curle's memorial portrait its arresting openness recall James I's ambivalent gestures toward the memory of his mother. As they fuse reflexive distance and furtive intimacy – and as they betray Mary's visceral intrusion upon a present reluctant to include her – these early memorials weave the inconstant desires of the living into the fixed visage of the dead. Both in their disregard for historical distance and in the variable boundaries that they establish between a feeling subject and the object of its passion, such incoherent images capture exactly the undecidable Mary Queen of Scots who would with consequent and eerie vitality reappear again and again throughout the reigns of James VI/I and his descendants.

Plate 3 Mary Queen of Scots Memorial Portrait. By permission of the Blair Museum
Trustees, Aberdeen.

"THE FACT OF THE MOTHER": JAMES VI/I

James himself is often remembered for his conviction of personal omnipotence.[12] Yet the fact is that James's political authority was radically compromised as long as his mother lived. The crown of Scotland had not come to him in any inevitable or irreversible way. As one court historian, Robert Johnston, euphemistically put it, "the Diadem of Scotland adorned King *James* the sixth, ere his head was well out of its cradle, his Mother consenting thereto." Then too, after Roman Catholic Mary had "divested her self of Majestical robes" and fled to England, never to see her eleven-month-old son again, James was educated as a Protestant, his tutor none other than Mary's voluble detractor, George Buchanan. Johnston vividly described the chasms that opened thereafter: not only did "the disparity betwixt [James's] age and rule cause him to govern by proxy," but "the knife of envy [. . .] parted the kingdom into two unnaturall factions of Son and Mother, King and captivated Queen."[13] James seems to have internalized his subjects' schismatic desires, for any love for Mary that he may have harbored rivalled the self-affirming bond he had formed with "his" own people. He was certainly inclined to figure his situation in the terms of an unresolvable erotic conflict, confiding to the Earl of Leicester "how fond and inconstant I were if I were to prefer my mother to the title."[14]

While James floundered halfway between the involuntary ties of nature ("my mother") and a political and symbolic order now demonstrably subject to human mastery ("the title"), Mary denied that she had ever voluntarily relinquished her crown; in her own mind, she remained Queen of Scots until her death. As the Stuart memoirist David Moysie would put it, even in captivity the queen programmatically refused to "nam[e James] king." Treating the conjunction of title with man as mere coincidence, all communication from "his majesty's mother, then in England, nam[ed] the King only prince on the back of his letters."[15]

An imaginary portrait of 1583 (Plate 4) commemorates the interminable conflict between identification and antipathy – and thus the irresolution of desire – that shaped James's relationship not just to Mary but equally to his own title and the kingly prerogative that it conferred. The image of mother and son assigns identical expressions, garments, and even hand positions, to the unhappy couple. Indeed, it distinguishes its two royal subjects only through the objects they touch (Mary's necklace, James's sword handle) and their hair ornaments (Mary's widow's cap and James's feathers). The Scottish crown hovers diplomatically between them, as if to suggest that the signs of their difference are only signs – that the two, though different, may yet be seen as one and the same.

Beholders of our own day have reckoned that this portrait presents James as the "mirror of his mother," the better to imply that his own "power derived from re-production, literally and figuratively."[16] But we can also see Mary as the mirror of her son, and in any case, James's authority looks to be challenged, not corroborated, by the maternal bond. The portrait itself obviously refuses to

Plate 4   Mary Queen of Scots and James VI/I. From the Blair Castle Collection, Perthshire.

choose between mother and son; in this it mirrors James himself, who was "said not to have lost all affection to his mother," yet "had rather have her as she is than himself to give her place."[17] Mary's very failure gave her the power to make James unreal – a mere reflection of authority – even as it made *her*, like a reflection, at once unreal and real to *him*. It was perhaps to defend the integrity of his kingly title without entirely denying its impure source in Mary that the king spoke of his mother as dead while she was still alive, and as living when she was dead. To his cronies he confided that Mary's "death was visible in Scotland before it did really happen, being, as he said, spoken of in secret by those whose power of sight presented to them a bloody head dancing in the air."[18] Yet the news that Mary had passed from life to death struck him as a fiction: "He suspended his judgment" at report of her demise, "and thought the matter almost incredible."[19]

Before her execution, James had resisted his mother's advances – including her suit for a joint crown – even as he maintained at least the illusion of desire for her survival. "To manifest his natural affection towards his dearest mother, whose preservation he always earnestly wished," Moysie recalled, he "required the ministers to pray for her at all preachings and common prayers," and threatened revenge "in case of her execution."[20] And his first homosexual encounter was apparently with Esmé Stuart, an emissary from the Duke of Guise. In both familial and political terms, Esmé Stuart was closely tied to James's half-Guisean mother; as a male rather than a female, however, he also supplied a way to repudiate her. While obviously James's manifest ambivalence toward his mother can be explained in terms of political expediency, it also suggests an internal compromise with the desire to destroy her, or, at the very least, with the wish that she would cease to be.

The compromise was delicate because, his reign having begun so very long before her death, James, in some sense, *was* Mary. To want her end was to hope for his own. The double portrait hints as much, casting one of the king's great challenges as that of differentiation from the Queen of Scots, especially in the eyes of his people. Edward Peyton's virulently anti-Stuart *Rise, Reign and Ruin of the House of Stuart* (1652) saw the first Stuart king's determination "to settle to himself and his successors an unbridled power of Dominion" prefigured in Mary's desire for "Viripotency." Just so, James's political craving for "the Power of Law" to be "enclosed in his sole Arbitrary breast" seemed of a piece with his mother's "inclination to be more absolute in her passion and Love to choose without control a Paramour suitable, when, how long and who she pleased."[21] To Stuart detractors throughout the century, James merely translated his mother's alleged longing for sexual dominion into political terms. He thereby sustained the Marian paradox of will pursued only through submission to one's own most despotic longings.

Often James even appeared to be an organic transcription of Mary's physical and psychological selves, and thereby a living sign of the past's haunting of the present. For one thing, James was continually depicted in terms of what had happened to him before he was born. He was known as the Scottish (later British) Solomon, an epithet more likely to invoke his mother than his own wisdom and probity: one funeral sermon pointed out that, like James, "King *Solomon* is said to be *Vgentius Coram Matriae Sua*, the only son of his mother" and that, just as "*Solomon* began his Reign in the Life of a Predecessor, [. . .] so by the Force and Compulsion of that state did our late Sovereign *James*."[22] On the less flattering side, there was the joke, allegedly put into circulation by Henri IV, that James was the new Solomon because he was actually "the Son of David," or, in Scottish parlance, "son of seigneur Davie."[23] "Davie" in this case was David Rizzio, the Italian secretary who had, in Peyton's words, so "inchant[ed] the Queen with his voice," that her jealous husband Darnley was provoked to order him stabbed to death in the pregnant queen's presence.[24]

The Rizzio episode spawned another, more telling characterization of James, one likewise derived from the time when his body and Mary's were essentially one. Anthony Weldon's classically hostile portrait of the king recalled that his "legs were very weak, having had, as some thought, some foul play in his youth, or rather before he was born."[25] More frequently noted was the tremor of James's hand, and his agitation around swords. The Roman Catholic virtuoso Sir Kenelm Digby sadistically regaled a pregnant relation with the cautionary tale of:

> the strange antipathy which the late King *James* had to a naked sword, whereof the cause was ascribed, in regard some *Scotch* Lords had entered once violently into the bed-chamber of the Queen his mother, while she

was with child of him, where her Secretary, an *Italian*, was dispatching some letters for her, whom they hacked and killed with naked swords before her face, and threw him at her feet; and they grew so barbarous, that there wanted but little but that they had hurt the Queen her self, who endeavouring to save her Secretary, by interposing herself, had her skin rased in divers places. [. . .] Hence it came that her son King *James* had such an aversion all his life-time after to a naked sword, that he could not see one without a great emotion of his spirits; although otherwise couragous enough, yet he could never overmaster his passions in this particular.[26]

Such conceptions of the power of the "mother's fancy" were rife in the seventeenth century. They aimed to identify some gateway between the imaginary and the given worlds, and to many they also betrayed the aberrant craft of a maternal artist.[27] In Digby's account, a physical impression on the mother's flesh (the "ras[ing] of her skin in divers places") supposedly molds the child's mind, "the emotion of his spirits." Doubting that the sword had actually touched Mary, others held that James's physical tremors had been molded by Mary's fear.

In either case, what mattered was the yielding of the boundary between past and present, matter and spirit, mother and child. And in the end, precisely because it seems to have been so dangerously desirable, the yielding itself was the most disturbing point. The theme carries through in the notion that what James inherited from a Mary overwhelmed by her own "Scotch Lords" was an inability to "overmaster his passions." More even than that of transmigration, it is the romance of capitulation which seems to have given Mary's memory its peculiarly corporeal force. Meanwhile, possessed by Mary's, the king's body seemed a point of transition between inner and outer worlds, and even between present and past. A vulnerable James became his mother's own ghost, even as her vulnerability seemed to have produced the very essence of both his political and his physical selves.

As we might expect, Mary became most visible in James only after he had safely gained the English throne. Before then, poems commemorating his accession represented him as the offspring of everyone but his own mother – as "Successor of a Maide," "Gods Sonne," and "Vertues Sonne." Succession treatises were careful to trace his bloodline back through his English father, Darnley, for they "would not have the fact of the Mother, [. . .] by whatever means to prejudice her son."[28] But once James was settled under Elizabeth's old crown, "the fact of the Mother" needed to be erased no more. On the contrary, Mary limned a dangerously alluring myth in which humiliation and failure actually promise to triumph over the most apparently intransigent of boundaries – those which divide fact and fantasy, person and person, life and death.

Written sometime around 1601, Thomas Wenman's *Legend of Mary Queen of Scots* gave that myth precocious shape and voice. In Wenman's degenerate rime royal, Mary speaks from beyond the grave, ghostlike, inviting us to behold her "like my self in Royal robe, . . ./A lady faire; a Queen whose wounds do bleed;/To see Despite on my Reproach to fear,/Who being dead may not be clear forgot." Wenman's Mary is at present "a senseless Corpse by overhastened Death,/In shrouding's sheet in grave's deformed disguise." But her reproductive powers persist less in spite of the "grave's deformed disguise" than through the dissolution it harbors.[29]

Mary's tomb at Westminster Abbey sustained this paradox most faithfully, as some nineteenth-century adventurers were later to discover. Seeking James's own body, whose exact location had been somehow forgotten over the years, they opened the vault beneath Mary's still resplendent monument to find it crammed with the coffins of over twenty of her "minor" descendants. At the very bottom of this macabre cache rested a casket:

> saturated with pitch, [. . .] of a more solid and stately character, and [. . .] shaped to meet the form of a body [. . .] which would exactly agree with the age and rank of Mary Stuart. The difficulty of removing the whole weight of the chest would of itself have proved a bar to any closer examination. But, in fact, it was felt not to be needed for any purpose of historical verification, and the presence of the fatal coffin which had received the headless corpse at Fotheringay was sufficiently affecting, without endeavouring to penetrate further into its mournful contents. It cannot be questioned that this, and this alone, must be the coffin of the Queen of Scots.[30]

Mary's womblike tomb marks the eerie intersection of presence and absence, emotional penetration and bodily impenetrability, certainty and mystery. It stands as a most telling legacy of the time when the Queen of Scots was laid to rest there. Just as her massive casket would seem somehow to have produced the Stuarts piled on top of it, so that casket's unknowability and even its emptiness creates an emotional effect that, even at over two centuries' remove, yields its own dense certainty, a tearful conviction "that this, and this alone", must be Mary.

For the Victorians who lowered themselves into her crypt, Mary's overburdened casket made the "wreck and ruin of the Stuart dynasty" available to the senses, a present reality to draw them into the past. At the very least, "the remains of the younger generations" were piled on top of those of their ancestors in a way that fulfilled the prediction of Mary's first epitaph – "the Living" were indeed eventually "inclosed with the Dead." That early epitaph turned out to be more than a political warning, more than a tribute to "the Ornament of our Age and a Light truly Royall," more even than a reproach to the "barbarous and tyrannical Cruelty" alleged to have taken Mary's life.[31] In a gruesome parody of generation, it marked the perverse fecundity of surrender to incoherence and decay. The early Stuart historian William Camden assured his readers that the offending lines were "soon after taken away." But, reprinted three times by the end of Charles I's reign, the pages of his *Annals* continued to reproduce them, even as the future became the past and the Stuart monarchy headed for its grave. Mary's persistence in James predicted that that monarchy would rise again – as indeed it did.

THE OTHER STUARTS

James VI/I was of course only the first of Mary's progeny to occupy the English throne. And the Stuarts are, notoriously, the most affecting and troubled family to have ruled in England. They often managed to command sympathetic identification even as they provoked in many of their subjects a bitter determination to undermine the absolute authority that they too often claimed. This is no mean feat. Even in their own day the Stuarts after James won the power to cause others to lose themselves in sympathy only *by* losing – their lives, their crowns and, upon occasion even their integrity. Even now their old portraits retain a charisma that has been attributed to a force of character that wasn't there. It would seem that a certain lack of self-consistency has endowed their images with a coherence and interest that those of other, more politically successful persons have often failed to achieve.[32]

It may be precisely this interesting vacancy which made it seem that Mary's turbulent, self-emptying life recapitulated itself in those of her children and grandchildren. We certainly see her most vividly in the precariousness of their political claims, and in the *mythos* of troubled sexuality that enveloped them. The mother also returns in the radical split in public opinion about her offspring, in their notorious craving for things French, and in the fear of Catholic sympathy that they provoked.

What is more, from Mary on the Stuart line suffered from an almost womanly weakness, a persistent vulnerability that flew in the face of the potent metaphors of patriarchal authority that the Stuart kings frequently summoned to their side. Gilbert Burnet recalled James's "saying, that by ruining his mother, and setting him in her room while a year old, they had ruined monarchy, and made that crown subject, and precarious; and had put him in a very unnatural posture."[33] One influential genealogy of the Stuart family saw the family line as "beginning [. . .] and [. . .] terminating in a *female*," meaning the Queen of Scots and Queen Anne respectively.[34] In retrospect, indeed, it appears that over the course of the seventeenth century the Stuarts were emasculated first figuratively, in the 1649 decapitation of Charles I and the 1688 deposition of James II, then literally, as the crown passed to two Stuart women, Mary and Anne, leaving the male heir to the crown, James III, only the shadow status of Pretender.

Beginning with the illicit demission of Mary's crown, guilty, incomplete and apocryphal inheritance became a Stuart signature. With it came a conspicuous vulnerability to history's contingencies. The Stuarts learned to ground their own mythology in the resulting pathos, which in turn became that mythology's genetic code, the key to its replication over time.[35] This makes for a very unusual contract between "fact" and figure, one in which many members of the family (especially those called Charles) seemed capable of reproducing themselves as much in the nervous systems of others as in the insentient images that were meant to work the heart into a frenzy of pity and desire for them. The Stuarts' progressive loss of political authority was compensated for by a new absolutism in sympathy's half bodily and half imaginary realm.

What role did Mary play in her family's perverse ascendancy? Most of her descendants' attempts at biological reproduction met with frustration – a situation doubly galling given the emphasis that they placed on blood rights of inheritance. The birth of James II's son was publicly doubted; James I's paternity was frequently questioned; Mary II not only inherited the throne before her father's own death but bore no children, and though her younger sister Anne was pregnant at least seventeen times, none of her children survived more than eleven years. But the Queen of Scots multiplied with impressive regularity in *representations* of descendants whose lives did seem to repeat hers. And to the extent that it was the felt passions of their subjects, both affectionate and aggressive, which shaped and sustained those representations, we must again acknowledge that she persisted through a kind of living death.

Charles I's demise at the scaffold in 1649 (on which occasion he was distinctly heard to inquire, "Is my hair well?") obviously recapitulated his grandmother's in a much more public setting. James II's Catholicism and his eventual expulsion from his own throne reprised Mary's misfortunes in Reformation-minded Scotland. The fog-shrouded boat that had carried Mary from France to Scotland as a young widow turned into a popular figure for the fortunes of Charles II. Four English ships happened to be leaving when he arrived in Scotland in 1650, but as his ship drew near Garmouth, a mist rose to shroud him from sight. Loyalists recalled that a "like Providence" had preserved Mary 90 years before, and "pray[ed] God [Charles] prove more fortunate."[36] A more sinister description of the same boat trip appeared in the anti-royalist gossip sheet *Mercurius Politicus*, which described the storms that had kept Charles from embarking for Scotland a few days before as signs of the wind's desire to have "blown away the *Shuttlecock* of Monarchy." It was a desire first visible in the fate of "old *Mary* Queen of *Scots*," who "never crossed the sea but in a *Storm*," her grandson Charles I had likewise "gone a-wooing to *Spain* in a *Storm*, and so returned back again."[37]

If Mary's troubled sea crossing offered a mythic prototype for her male descendants' misadventures, the female heirs to the Stuart crown differently invoked their great-great-grandmother. The second Mary Stuart's dexterity with the embroidery needle, "softness," "charming Behaviour" and "genuine Sweetness" of temper all recalled the first. Mary II was also regarded as the Catholic Queen of Scots's Protestant corrector, one whose demure piety made amends for her namesake's indiscretions and in the process justified "female Government" itself. Thus Gilbert Burnet's loving memorial recalled that:

two *Mary*'s in this Island shewed a greatness of Genius, that has seldom appeared to the World. But the Superstition and Cruelty of the one, and the Conduct and Misfortunes of the other, did so lessen them, that their Sex had been much sunk by their means, if it had not been at the same time as powerfully supported by the happiest and most renowned of all Sovereign Queens. I know I need not name her.[38]

As Burnet blended a sinking and lessened – and very Catholic – Mary Queen of Scots with the Protestant Mary II (herself so recently deceased), he accidentally reminded his readers that the "II" after the latter's royal name was ambiguous. Mary II was (after Mary Tudor) the second Queen Mary of England, but she was also the second Queen Mary of Scotland. No wonder Burnet felt he could "not name her."

When Anne Stuart followed Mary II's widower, William, to the throne in 1702, she consciously patterned herself on Elizabeth Tudor rather than on her much more direct ancestor, Mary Stuart.[39] But it was Mary who shadowed most contemporary portraits of the last Stuart queen. Anne's reign (1702–1714) marks the last phase of Britain's long transition from a monarchy bolstered by its blood claims to a two-party system dominated by manipulative ministers.[40] After her death, Britain's crown passed from the Stuarts to the German house of Hanover. Before it did, Anne's struggles in many ways repeated Mary's, and even her sympathizers tended to recall the Marian features of her unhappy life – the "various Changes of Fortune which never forsook her till she resign'd her Life" and "the Infirmities of a broken Constitution" stemming from continual pregnancy that eventually killed her.[41]

As they awakened memories of the mother of their dynasty, Mary's lineal descendants could be seen as fleshly representations of her, their stories new enactments of hers on a historical stage whose changefulness was retarded by her refusal to go away. Mary's phantasmic persistence made successive moments in Stuart history feel contemporary, all rooted alike in the experientially timeless realms of feeling and its fantasies. Particularly through their disasters, the Stuarts supplied human occasions for Mary's recollection, and representations of them became indirect and yet immediately affecting reflections of the almost-first Stuart queen, their undead original. At once oblique and corporeal, sensible and fantastic, these living images marked Mary's repeated trespasses upon the land of the living – a land that the memory of her could make feel empty and dead.

This stayed true even after the Stuarts lost Great Britain's throne for good. Forced into exile in favor of the more securely Protestant, if German, house of Hanover, the Stuarts remained a serious threat to Britain's political stability until the middle of the eighteenth century, and long thereafter they continued to draw forth tears and inspire romantic imagination. The banished claimants to the British crown, James Francis Stuart and his son Charles Edward, reminded their would-be subjects of their presence by means of pathetic portraits, through secret references buried deep in superficially innocent texts, and via mythic appeals to the possibility of a past returned through them. But Mary's memory threaded its way steadily through each of theirs; she was their antique original. And after Charles Edward met his decisive defeat at Culloden in 1745, it was her image which regained ascendancy, until it seemed along with the now wholly poignant one of "Bonnie Prince Charlie" to capture the full poignancy of the lost Stuart cause.

The ballad "Queen Marie" then passed out of the Jacobite song repertoire into a more broadly Scottish one, while miniature copies of Mary's portrait were treasured by Jacobite families long after the '45, along with certain personal items believed to have been hers, such as missals, slippers and pieces of jewelry.[42] The exiled Stuarts themselves felt the fascination of such secular relics. In June of 1747 Charles Edward sent his father "a Curious present, [. . .] it being the Cross that Queen Mary of Scotland wore when she was beheaded."[43] Among the Stuarts' latter-day sympathizers, one, the Earl of Buchan, had himself painted with his hand resting on a bust of Mary. Another looked for the day when "it would be treason to talk of Queen Mary but as a saint and martyr," while his Jacobite friends praised yet another for a mind that faithfully "revolv'd the various misfortunes of the beautiful and unhappy Mary."[44]

Except to the extent that it colored the last vestiges of the Stuart myth, Mary's fate in eighteenth-century Britain lies beyond us just at present. But it is worth asking why she should have enjoyed such a vivid afterlife during the ill-starred personal reigns of the Stuarts. Of course, it is possible to interpret Mary's perceived resurgence in her offspring as part of a mourning ritual – as their, and their subjects', effort to recover, at least symbolically, the dynastic mother lost to a savage Elizabethan blade. Yet the figments of the Queen of Scots that were so easy to discern in the fates and faces of her descendants are too ambiguous to sustain this notion, the contemporary responses encoded in them too ambivalent. It might be more productive to remember the mixed legacy of repudiation and desire bequeathed by Anglo-Scottish Protestants of Mary's own day. At the very least, Mary's almost palpable return by means of the deficiencies built into the lives and bodies of her children, their children and grandchildren gives a new and strikingly bodily quality to certain Elizabethan versions of her, particularly those deliberate fictions which betrayed their roots in a pitched conflict of desire.

In 1673 the late Stuart historian Francis Osborn noticed how stubbornly Mary lingered in British imaginations. In search of the reason why, Osborn turned to her beheading, botched as it had been, and tersely observed that "because no body either would or durst do it alone, the reproach was entailed upon the whole nation, by the apparition of an inimical and counterfeit justice."[45] Osborn attributed Mary's extraordinary afterlife to shared guilt and common cowardice, it's true, but he also pointed to a decisive rift between an "apparition" and an actuality – one the Elizabethans had built into Mary's memory from the start. It was the counterfeiting of the Queen of Scots, and especially the forging of the final chapter of her story, which had left her both unknowable and oddly available, the flickering source of a nonetheless perpetual emotion.

Accounting for the psychological phenomenon in which children seem to suffer from traumas that only their parents have experienced, and indeed often re-enact them, the psychoanalysts Nicolas Abraham and Maria Torok also point to a gap within the parents' own language, one created by a defensive need to distance raw emotional experience from its representations. Those born into a parental language thus distracted by its own fictions shape themselves within its hollow symbols, at once filling and perpetuating those symbols with their own wishes and dilemmas. As the child adopts his or her parents' secrets, the frustration of certain knowledge becomes the object of his or her own perverse desire.[46]

Could something of this sort have been happening when Stuart Britons seemed to see Mary Queen of Scots before their very eyes? In order to imagine how or that this might be true, we need to turn away from the Stuarts themselves to the many literary treatments of the queen's own life which began to appear early in James's reign. In general, Stuart historians consciously conceived their work as a simulacrum of collective memory. And to the extent that a group's memory identifies it as a being with a life, their depictions of the Queen of Scots may also yield a clue concerning her role in the formation of something like a shared – and eventually British – identity. At the same time, however, endless political commotion over what that identity and its authorities should be made the task of establishing collective memory a vexatious, even dangerous one. It may then be that the most common purpose Mary's vivid memory served was simply that of deferring resolution. Attachment to her, as to any maternal figure, postponed commitment to a distinct and formal structure of self-representation even as it guaranteed the involving pleasure of just wondering – the pleasure of continued life.

"THE LIFE OF MEMORY"

In a telling phrase, one of Mary's first Stuart biographers, William Udall, designated the emerging art of British historiography the very "Life of Memory."[47] This organic image, which can seem so odd to us, did not look that way at all to Udall's contemporaries. When they pictured personal memory they saw not the fixed engraving we often do but rather flights of animal spirits scurrying nimbly between the tangible and intangible worlds. Likewise, encouraged by the atmosphere of political uncertainty in which they wrote, the seventeenth-century historians who cast themselves as the first voices of Britain's collective memory were prone to see themselves less as faithful transcribers of a firmly distanced past than as mediators between competing desires and instincts of belief. In this capacity, they felt caught, both physically and mentally, in time's headlong streams and unexpected eddies.

Memories of the dead were nowhere livelier than when it came to Mary

Queen of Scots. The frontispiece of William Sanderson's *Compleat History* (1656) of her life and reign offered a typically cadaverous image of the queen whom the following pages proceeded to remember back to life. Sanderson's prose played tricks of its own. Seldom sticking to a single tense, he eschewed linear plot progression in favor of continual digressions back in time. Others, like the author of the preface to a 1651 reprint of Buchanan's *Detection*, altered well-known chronologies with impunity, so that Mary was said to have been left Queen of Scotland when she was four years (not a few days) old, to have married François II at twelve (not fifteen), and on returning to Scotland to have "found her Mother" – actually long dead – "well trying in her cruelties, [. . .] wasting and gathering with all her might."[48] Whether these false memories were deliberate lies is anyone's guess: possibly the *Detection*'s new editor was as reliable as anyone else if he, like Sanderson, valued the dynamic revival of Mary's life over the slavishly linear transcription of it.

By the end of the seventeenth century this irrepressibly organic sense of what historical discourse might be had begun to die out, taking with it historians' willingness to embrace the loops of desire and uncertainty – the suspense, in every sense of that word – that all narrative flow creates. It is tempting to think of the fluid way of talking about the past that thrived till then as content in search of a form, indeed as the profligate father of the frugal discourse of consensus that would eventually count as the truer history of nations.[49] Yet the language that conveyed Mary Queen of Scots to readers in the Stuart age seems to have sought something more interesting than a straight path to its true and higher form. Instead of establishing certain truths about Mary, her Stuart biographers shamelessly revived her in the unpredictable, unfinished, and thus altogether enticing shape that she had taken in her incoherent life. For a very long time Mary's story stood as the best and least abashed example of written history's ability to lead the "life of memory" – a life inextricable from that of readerly curiosity and desire.

Thus Udall held that reading of Mary was like "drawing neere unto [. . .] the Sepultures of our Ancestors," there to reanimate them with the pleasure that we ourselves take from reading about them. In his joint history of Mary and James (1656), Sanderson likewise sought "to enliven their Memories with their *Lives* and *Actions*" and his own words became a dynamic means of refusing to "leave [. . .] Sovereigns buried in the *Graves* of *Oblivion*."[50] As we might expect, these memoirists of the Queen of Scots wrote – or said they did – in intense, even physical, consciousness of their readers. Sanderson designed "barely to represent the Narrative, and to leave the censure to the Readers sentence." Updates of John Stow's *Annales* (1631) addressed themselves to "the honest and understanding reader" and promised him that their goal was "to give thee good content, and to delight thy successors."[51] Over the course of a turbulent and ever more cynical century, readers of Mary's story became collaborators with it, responsible for realizing its ghostly traces in themselves.

On occasion, this process of involvement and excitation might well interest a reader in the Stuarts' ever-embattled cause. Sanderson's *Compleat History* of

Mary's life and reign appeared in the waning hours of the Interregnum, and Udall's *Historie* and revisions of Stow's *Annales* in the 1630s, just as Charles I was beginning to confront the first direct challenges to his majesty. But what the historians had to say about Mary, like the relationship they were forced to have with her, usually lacked the rhetorical confidence that would allow us to interpret them strictly or even primarily as Stuart propaganda.

Rather, the very excess of material pertaining to Mary thrust the historian who would retrieve her into a morass of exceedingly human difficulties. Even those who wanted to bleach the queen's scarlet reputation saw perfectly well that the documents pertaining to her life were a quagmire of error, confusion and outright lies, and that many more had been prematurely suppressed as "contain[ing] things fit to be corrected and blotted out of memorie." Camden recorded his own frustration in the face of "great Piles and Heaps of Papers and Writings of all sorts, [. . .] in regard of Variety of the Arguments very much confused." He "labored over [them] till I sweat, [. . .] covered all over with Dust, to fit matter together."[52]

The narratives that emerged from this "intricate Difficulty" were bound to be of precarious authority, and well aware of their own vulnerability to the deforming passage of time. Likewise, in writing Mary's story down, Sanderson hoped "only to set down such particular *Actions Memorative* as may hereafter enlighten abler Pens to consecrate."[53] Mary's inherently uncertain image could *only* be perpetuated in these fluctuating forms; instead of supporting royalist conviction, she vindicated hesitation and deferral as valid vehicles of understanding, even as they, God knew, tended to vindicate her too often dubious story.

To admit that story's dependence upon the erratic dance of memory, or upon the defective evidence of the past, was really to root it in the physical world, the universe of changing bodies incessantly exposed to the vicissitudes of time. It was to supply the unavoidable artifices involved in writing about a time gone by with an unpredictable – but in its own right convincing – foundation in a corporeal present.[54] Mary lent herself to this unusually animate style of writing about the past in part because so much of what had happened to her bears witness to the vulnerability of human being – the manner of her death, her hopeless love affairs, the loss of her child, her pathetic letters, even her extravagant attention to her personal appearance.

By dwelling on just such details, biographers like Camden and Udall kept the queen's volatile passions and manifold physical predicaments in the foreground. Whenever they could, they even incorporated fragments of her indisputably moving epistolary petitions to Elizabeth into their own prose. They hacked out a hasty stenography of the letters Mary herself had written while "vexed and troubled in mind, oppressed with misfortunes and pining away with the calamitie of her longlasting imprisonment." Taking "the originals written with her own hand," Udall "abbreviate[d] them," then made them physically part of his own text. Camden had also assimilated excerpts from letters in which Mary sought, by her own words, to "imprint" her "woful

Complaints" on Elizabeth's "conscience, that some Innocency may appear to posterity."[55]

In contrast to their Elizabethan forerunners and Georgian successors, Mary's latter-day biographers were unique not only in the buoyant, almost freakishly immediate brand of history that they produced but also in their historical position *vis-à-vis* the Queen of Scots herself. For one thing, while Mary's story was for the first time complete, this was also the last time she would be a living memory for anyone. Historians like Camden could, for instance, still consult those who were eyewitnesses to the events of her own day, but they did so only to find them in contradiction. Then too, several sixteenth-century texts written by participants in the drama of Mary's life were printed for the first time: Francis Walsingham's letters pertaining to the Duke of Norfolk's trial (1681), Mary's diplomat James Melville's memoirs (1683), and her French admirer the Abbe de Brantôme's *Vies des dames illustrees* (1665). Many of the queen's own letters were still in active circulation, especially among members of the emigré circle that surrounded Charles II during his exile in France. John Evelyn, for instance, was in possession of several of them, which he lent to Gilbert Burnet as the latter set about writing his *History of the Reformation*. Yet the reassurance that should have come from so much evidence tended to evaporate. Evelyn's letters mysteriously disappeared – "pretended," he complained, "to have been lost at the press." A quarrel with Burnet ensued, but Evelyn in the end had to accept the loss of "originals which had been now as safe records as any you can find in that history." To make matters worse, Evelyn was later defrauded of other letters of Mary's by the Duke of Lauderdale.[56] When it came to Mary, matter could not but give up its own ghost.

Crucial as it was to the transmission of Mary's memory to future generations, Stuart historiography on the Queen of Scots is thus both unprecedentedly stable (the past of concern *is* past) and uniquely fluid (it still survives as physical traces in some individual memories). It presses on the senses only to disappear from their purview. It suffers almost physically from what the Elizabethans only half-said or simply did not say about Mary, but it also tantalizes thanks to its own disability. From this perspective, it can only seem that the historians who whipped up readerly desire for more contact with the first Mary Stuart were re-activating the emotional legacy bequeathed by "the finest she that ever was." As their sentences sometimes split upon her riddling case, and sometimes clustered there like so many greedy bees, they leave us with the impression of a feverish dream. But if the point was not always, or even usually, to shape readerly belief about the Stuart dynasty, what wish – and whose – was this dream seeking to fulfill?

THE USES OF AMBIVALENCE

Stuart histories generally, and those of Mary in particular, have their prototype in Camden's *Annals*. Those rambling volumes were actually meant to memorialize Elizabeth Tudor; Camden had been appointed, by James I, to guarantee that "her happy and renowned Memory still liveth, and shall for ever live in the Minds of men to all posterity."[57] This was easier said than done, for James had also asked the celebrated antiquary to vindicate his own mother's memory after the skeptical French historian Jean-Auguste de Thou had painted a most unflattering portrait of Mary in his *History of His Own Times*. Camden undertook his task reluctantly, partly because of the sheer labor involved, and partly out of secret sympathy with de Thou's more skeptical view of Mary. The resulting portrait of the Queen of Scots, as many commentators have observed, is highly equivocal. It is also inevitably wedded to the riddling ambivalence of its sources – an ambivalence that Camden could only pass on to his successors.

The works of those successors had several overt aims. The most obvious was to substantiate Stuart authority by artfully memorializing Britain's past. New versions of Mary's story that painted her as a "sad and most illustrious pattern of all Misfortune" and hoped to prove her mournful innocence also confirmed her descendants' own entitlements and virtues, including their exemplary piety toward their own wronged dynastic mother.[58] Sometimes, too, seventeenth-century historians sought to cultivate the Stuarts themselves as readers. Udall's *Historie*, largely redacted from Camden, directly appeals to Charles I's "desire and disposition," bred by "Nature," to be "delighted with the relations and story of his own Ancestors and Predecessors."[59] And Mary's life could also be used to comment critically on present-day politics. In order to justify James II's 1688 deposition, Thomas Morgan reprinted an obscure Elizabethan document which had argued for Mary Stuart's right of succession and thus for a step away from "the usual strict Grounds" of succession.[60] Earlier, in the aftermath of the Popish Plot, one anti-Catholic tract held that "that *great Princess*" had been brought "to Ruine" because she had the misfortune to be misled by "Popish *Priests*."[61] The memory of the Queen of Scots could also justify the recent Puritan revolt against the Stuarts, as it did in a new address to George Buchanan's venomous *Detection*.[62]

Clearly, Mary's story might be brought to life in the service of the most opposite ends. What animated it could thus not have been the ends themselves but rather the story's own capacity to involve its readers in history's emotional texture, in the enduring fears and fascinations of a past whose very vividness proved it not altogether past. These qualities are oddly unhistorical and anti-teleological by nature, for they exploit recurrent feelings, purposeless actions, rhetorical ends capsized by the means used to achieve them. A history bound to them might well invoke the Stuart *mythos*, but can scarcely be said to have endorsed it.

Similarly, an argument in favor of Mary's entitlement to the English crown could easily show up in a text meant to justify the deposition of her Catholic great-grandson. Works as ideologically opposed as reprints of Buchanan's blistering *Detection* and Udall's adulatory *Historie* bore the same crude woodcut image of Mary on their title pages. And printed narratives sympathetic to

Mary's plight were on occasion bound together with handwritten continuations of Drummond's *Historie of Scotland* (1655) that maligned Mary as a conniving fraud.[63] If the new historiography sought some way to arbitrate rationally among competing evidences, then Mary's notoriously pleated, ever-contested image only thwarted that desire.[64] If it wanted to work as political propaganda, frustration again lay in store.

But what if we saw a certain irresolution as an object of desire in its own right? What if the one interest common to all sides in the free-for-all of the day was to remain ambivalent and unknowing as far as the Queen of Scots was concerned? Surely the Stuarts themselves had something to gain by doing so; possibly the historians of their day did too. At the very least, Sanderson only complained about the "counterfeit Materials" of earlier histories that made it so arduous to "pick out [the] truth" about Mary.[65] He did not say he had managed to do so – quite the opposite, and yet neither did he reckon that he had failed in what he set out to do. Likewise, Johnston, whose *Historie of Scotland* (1646) considers Mary Queen of Scots at length, declared that in writing this work "my end was not glory but desire of truth," not truth itself.[66]

Mary's story seems above all to have fostered a desire for desire – not to know the "truth" but certainly to want it, and to keep wanting it, and in always wanting it never to have it. Volatile and often downright false memories of Mary allowed multiple feelings, repulsive and receptive, to coexist, all unclaimed and all promiscuous, all sustaining a form of fantasy about the Queen of Scots whose practical effect was to keep her, in her unknowability, available to anyone who happened to run into her. The greater goal may therefore not have been to fortify Stuart authority *per se*, or, for that matter, to challenge it. More often, it seems simply to have been to secure readerly involvement in the Queen of Scots, an indeterminate but always lively investment in her mischiefs and mishaps. As it made this investment possible, the pages of British history mirrored the irresolution of the political sphere, and thereby withstood many of the upheavals to which contemporary government was subject. If that page can be seen as the mirror of collective memory, it was above all a revivified and hence unresolvable Mary who kept it from cracking.

From this point of view, Stuart histories of Mary's life naturally went hand in hand with literary romance. Indeed, the Mary who appears in Madame de Lafayette's "most famed Romance," *La princesse de Clèves* (1678), possesses the same openness – the same restless and affecting personal charm – that we find in countless English histories of her life. Lafayette's novel was twice translated into English (in 1679 and 1688) and it was even dramatized by Nathaniel Lee in 1689. Its setting is the Valois court of Mary's youth, which Lafayette presents as a royal hive of "ambitious Humour," intrigue and passion.[67] The court's "Soul" is "Ambition and Gallantry" (p. 22), and the repository and embodiment of these desires would seem to be "the Lady Mary Steward," whose lively attractions threaten to usurp the official reigning queen, Catherine de Medici, not to mention the other French princesses. We learn that she "had taken up an Ambition from her Infancy, that (in despite of her green years) she was resolved not only to love, but to understand all such things as might contribute to her Improvement" (pp. 3–4). Especially once she was translated into a rambunctious English, Lafayette's infinitely desirous "Dauphin Queen" incarnated all of the appetites of the court. Linked as much to its shapely artifices as to its renegade passions, Mary was romance itself, a fantastic vortex of colliding, conspiring secrets and wishes whose exact center could never quite be reached. Indeed, in Lafayette's novel, her ardors and affectations work to turn the Valois court into the very nursery of romance, especially as she gossips avidly and doles out highly confidential love stories from her bed.

Historical accounts of Mary's life shared romance's seductive multiplicity of meaning, its tendency to tweak its readers' wishes, leading them to discover the object of desire in their own desire for more of her. Hence, for example, Mary's relationship to Elizabeth I frequently took center stage. Some works, like Edmund Bohun's 1693 *Character of Queen Elizabeth*, chastised the Tudor queen for her "uneasie and cruel Restraint" of Mary, and for the "spirit of Jealousie and Revenge" – the "Personal and Selfish Humour" – that led her to "a detestable piece of wickedness" against "a poor Captive Queen."[68] But more often it was Elizabeth's conflicts over Mary that came to mind. "Never did *Clemency* and Good *Nature* more bravely resist the charms of Interest and threat of danger, than in the noble breast of our Queen," asserted one Stuart writer, convinced of "how extreamly loth she was to consent to the death of the Queen of *Scots*."[69] Sanderson was also arrested by Elizabeth's quandary over Mary: "She was in distraction what to do, but whilest she doubted, the Councel did it for her. And so had her head taken off by the axe."[70] Fittingly, the subject of Sanderson's sentence shifts from Elizabeth's figurative head to Mary's literal one until at last the two queens seem to merge. Camden likewise leaves the minds of both Mary and Elizabeth to "wave[r] in uncertain cogitations."[71] Elizabeth's dilemma and the uncertain bond to Mary that it exemplified made her a perfect prototype for seventeenth-century readers as enthralled by Mary's memory as they were skeptical of it.

Revealing new stories also grew up around Mary's long-ago beheading, the most popular having to do with the "remarkable [. . .] accident" in which the "little shag-dog, that always followed her Person, even to her footsteps, [. . .] crept under her Garments" as she passed to the scaffold. Once the death blow fell, the poor creature, Sanderson reported:

> would not remove but by force, snarling and biting, nor would afterwards depart, but laid between her head and shoulders. [. . .] The commissioners gave way to the humour of the dog, who imbrued himself in her blood, snarling and casting up his eyes as if to quarrel with them all, and bit at them who washed him, as they did all things else that were bloody.[72]

Details like these can only turn history into romantic myth – not because they make it less true but rather because they subordinate the question of whether or not a thing "really" happened to a desire, even a need, to endow certain personalities with perpetual volubility, their injured bodies with continuing life.

In turn, the longing to keep Mary's meaning multiple and the queen herself the indirect object of the desire to be knowing and experiencing undermined efforts to make her story fit the simple plot of providence. For Udall, Mary, "tossed and turmoiled with infinite misfortunes," proved the maxim that "there is nothing eternal"; those who "seem to be created of the most pure Substance of the Elements [. . .] yield themselves to the triumph of Death," usually under the "violence and precipitation of the most tumultuous circumstances."[73] Sanderson also concluded that a life so very "sad and troublesom to so excellent a Lady" was meant:

> to shadow out unto us, that Eternity is not on Earth; that Kings and Princes, seeming the best substance of Elements and if possible incorruptible, as being the fairest Seals of Natures Impression, yet these yield to the triumph of Death: not calmly neither, but by death dis-seasoned, in several conditions of their life, as well as in Youth, as after Age; and so it fell out upon this Queen.[74]

For the Stuarts and their subjects, the effort to give Mary's life a certain meaning was, not altogether unhappily, destined to fail. When it came to the lost mother of the Stuart line, even Providence had to consort with unpredictability, just as dominion met its match in vulnerability, and the edges of fact dissolved into the mists of fiction.

Mary's own permanence in seventeenth-century British minds finally had little to do with the exact political convictions of those who revived her. She was never a very handy ideological tool in the campaign to restore or retain the Stuarts; nor was she a reliable weapon against them. What she was was the ineradicable mother of the Stuart dynasty, and as such she bore witness to the ways in which loss can sustain life. In reviving her story and pressing upon those elements of it that made Mary at last the most intimate of mysteries, Stuart historians may not have done a good job of passing judgment on the nuts and bolts of Stuart rule. But they did allow uncertainty – a perpetual forgetting-within-memory – to live on as a species of belief. Like the Stuarts themselves, they allowed, we might say, love.

4 "False kindred"

The Island Queens and The Albion Queens

Like most Stuart representations of Mary Queen of Scots, John Banks's 1684 tragedy about her, *The Island Queens*, revolves around the imagery of inheritance. One particularly memorable turn is taken at the end of the play by Elizabeth Tudor, just after Mary has lost her head: "Falsehood from *Eve* on all her race descends," Banks's Elizabeth concludes, bitterly. "False Kindred all, false Subjects and false Friends."[1] The words are eminently fitting, since throughout the play Banks's winsome Mary has been suspected for a fraud. But at the moment Elizabeth is more concerned with the prevarications of her own male "Subjects," who by painting Mary as a scheming and deceitful usurper turn out to have tricked Elizabeth into signing her death warrant. It is not women's lies but the lies about them which "descend" through their very bodies – a truth Elizabeth grasps only, if ironically, upon hearing the story of Mary's death.

Banks's dramatization of the last days of her life marks Mary Stuart's migration from the pages of collective memory to the English stage . . . or would have done, had the play not been banned before it could be performed. Banks vaguely explained its suppression in a prefatory epistle dedicated to the fortuitously named Mary, Duchess of Norfolk: though the restored Stuart king, Charles II, liked the tragedy and "was pleas'd to consent to the Acting of it," certain unnamed "evil Spirits" at the last minute "incens'd the King with a wrong Interpretation of the Scenes, or of the Story" (sig. A2v).

What this "Interpretation" might have been, and how it differed from the one Banks sought, is anybody's guess: the playwright's friend, Gerard Langbaine, ventured only that "some mistaken Censures occasioned its being prohibited on the Stage," and an early nineteenth-century critic could go no further when he proposed that *The Island Queens* suffered from "the profound penetration of the master of the Revels, who saw political spectres in it."[2] Such "spectres" might have been raised by the Popish Plot (1678), a scandal recent enough to cast a shadow upon a Catholic heroine whom later illustrations for Banks's play would even endow with a massive crucifix pointed, dagger-like, at her own breast.[3] Or perhaps *The Island Queens*, whose subtitle was *The Death of Mary of Scotland*, charted the undermining of sovereign authority at too critical a juncture in the ever precarious history of the Stuart monarchy.

But be its "political spectres" what they may, twenty years later Banks's tragedy rose from the dead, in somewhat altered form, to take the stage as *The Albion Queens*. In this guise it was revived again and again throughout the eighteenth century.

The lovable "Queen of Scotland" whose "Death" supplies the centerpiece, subtitle and *raison d'être* of Banks's play visibly descends from the pages of Camden, Udall and Sanderson. And Banks indulges a longstanding obsession with her final hours, thereby also endorsing the characteristic perception of his day that no real line divides Mary's life from her death. Indeed, Elizabeth's bitter lament about "Falsehood" bequeathed through female flesh reminds us that throughout the seventeenth century Mary Queen of Scots stood for a form of reproduction in which fiction, fantasy and blood all participate. In a pivotal scene, Banks's Queen of Scots actually confronts her own reflection, whose unexpected beauty drives her to repudiate it as a "false" image of her true mental and physical suffering. When Mary dashes her mirror to the floor because it refuses to show her forehead "graven with the Darts/Of eighteen years of sharpest Miseries" (p. 23), the illusion of fidelity among image and body splinters as well. None replicates the others accurately, yet all are bound together.

These are themselves scattered observations on *The Island Queens*. But they are meant to suggest that the quandaries over their undead mother which beset the Stuart line and its sometime subjects converged in the work of one extraordinarily popular playwright. If the point of these quandaries – and the vivid attachment to a seemingly present Mary that they supported – was to sustain a vital present, how can we account for the fact that the way Mary was seen began to narrow toward the end of the troubled Stuart period? *The Island Queens*'s metamorphosis into *The Albion Queens* might tell us; but it can only do so if we appreciate the first version of the play in its own right.

THE FINEST "SHE-TRAGEDY" THAT EVER WAS

Like a dream, *The Island Queens* condenses episodes from different moments in Mary's life. Actually twenty when Mary went to the scaffold, her son James is a "Cradle Prince" and "Infant King" in Banks's play; Mary's English suitor Norfolk was beheaded in 1572 for his enigmatic involvement with her, but here he perishes just before she does. George Dowglas, who assisted in Mary's escape from Lochleven, is, unexpectedly, on hand to report her death, and, in *The Albion Queens*, to die of grief in the telling. Like a dream too, *The Island Queens* fantasizes not one but two meetings between Mary and Elizabeth, thereby twice tearing the veil that customarily divides fact from fantasy, wish from fulfillment. Banks's characters encounter one another as apparitions that drift back and forth between the "real" and phantom worlds of imagination, guilty memory, sleep and even death. We're thus tempted to read *The Island Queens* as the work not just of a flourishing playwright, but of his society's unconscious mind as its members clung to their own equivocal mirror, the lost mother of the Stuart dynasty.

The Island Queens was not the first tragedy Mary Stuart had ever inspired. Banks's dramatic model seems to have been the French neoclassical tragedian Antoine de Montchréstien's *L'Escossaise, ou la Désastre* (1601), which dramatizes both Mary's misery and Elizabeth's dilemmas over her to testify to the fated woes of kings ("Leur Estat n'a rien seur que son incertitude").[4] Though shattered by "un, deus, trois, quatre coups sur son col" (p. 135), Montchréstien's Mary – ever "féconde en artifice et façonde en discours" (p. 107) – is at last assimilated to a coherent moral about the sad but inevitable lot of kings. Banks's tragedy lacks such sources of coherence, as well as the French dramatist's respect for the fact that Mary and Elizabeth never met. Banks's queens, moreover, meet in an atmosphere of exorbitant passion that so twists, inflames and distresses Banks's own language that one eighteenth-century commentator called that language "barbarous."[5] Despite a greater historical distance from the matters Banks depicts, the differences between his tragedy and Montchréstien's betray a much less resolved relationship to the Queen of Scots, one peculiar to Stuart art.

Banks was once a lawyer, accustomed to problems of vindicating innocence and weighing evidence. He had turned to the stage in the early 1680s to become, with Thomas Otway and Nathaniel Lee, one of the architects of a new dramatic form, the "she-tragedy." The vogue of the she-tragedy coincides with the fatal softening of sovereignty itself, as Mary's restored great-grandson Charles II's notoriously dissolute reign drew to a close. The genre's popularity also reflects the growing presence of women in the theater audience. Through the suffering female victims at their centers, she-tragedies explored predicaments of feeling in ways that had not been possible in the ranting heroic tragedies popular earlier in the Restoration, and they marked also a new interest in the heroic possibilities of helplessness. Their heroines were often borrowed from the pages of English history, especially in the case of Banks, whose *Vertue Betray'd* (1681) and *The Innocent Usurper* (1683) dramatized the sad fates of Anne Boleyn and Lady Jane Grey respectively. That the she-tragedies should have overlapped with imaginary renditions of recent English history suggests that history itself had become the semi-mythic template of emotional life and self-definition.

As the Stuarts themselves were fated to be, the she-tragedies were known by and through their fixation upon vulnerability. Fulfilling Lee's prediction that "women shall rule the stage," a she-tragedy heroine was likely to "rule" less through the assertion of her own will than through a moving demonstration of her own distress and vulnerability. And although it dominated the London theater for at least a dozen years, the she-tragedy has for this reason usually been disparaged as a dramatic form: critics of our own century have chided plays of this genre for possessing "rarely an atom of tragic greatness, although some of them are affecting, [and] all are pathetic and touching." For one such critic in particular, the she-tragedies' "insistence on the feminine, and, along

with the feminine, the pathetic," debilitated which would have done well to
"be made hard, approaching the masculine in quality, or else be relegated to a
position of minor importance in the development of the plot."[6] More recently,
however, the she-tragedies are recognized as having fulfilled Restoration audiences's characteristic craving for an almost embarrassing immediacy – for an
"instrumental" language that might overmaster them as it "forces sensibility
to evaluate and respond" to onstage objects of emotion.[7] Even more than other
she-tragedies, Banks's master their audiences by subordinating themselves to
those audiences's emotion. Thematically, it is often the overwhelming and
explicitly female helplessness of all his protagonists that erodes all boundaries
between a representation and its human witnesses.

Just so, Banks's contemporaries were quick to see him as a woman's playwright: his first biographer Gerard Langbaine expressly noted that he "had had
the fortune to please the fair sex."[8] Not only did most of the tragedies in which
"his Genius lay wholly" focus on women – and on real ones at that – but he
seems to have liked picturing himself as a woman, particularly where his own
inadequacies were concerned. Although *The Island Queens* was banned, Banks
did publish it, dedicating it to a woman with the apology that "tho' it be
mean, 'tis like the poor Womans Mite, It is my All" (sig. A2r).

Twenty years later, the advertisement for *The Albion Queens* would disavow
its published predecessor as "wholly incorrect and imperfect."[9] But the "feminine" inadequacy that bridges most chasms between image and viewer
sustains the very erotic mystique that Mary Stuart's descendants had inherited
from her, and that would in 1688 begin its permanent alienation from the
seats of acknowledged power. In the survivor of his two island queens,
Elizabeth, Banks brings to view the fundamentally split and self-alienated
mind that this alienation brought to birth. In his Mary, he exonerated the
interlocking empires of political and personal meaning that would be lost with
the Stuarts, at last absorbing the Queen of Scots's maternal address to the
body's imaginings into his own theatrical practice.

"REVENGE AND MALICE BURY'D BE"

Set in the last days of Mary's life, *The Island Queens* first sets its spotlight on
Mary's English devotée, the Duke of Norfolk. By the end of the first act,
Norfolk's infatuation with the Queen of Scots has made him the dupe of her
enemies, who include two power-hungry nobles (Morton and Cecil) and
Elizabeth's overreaching secretary, Davison. Norfolk is Mary's lover, but his
heart is not the most significant in Banks's play: Elizabeth's is. And it is
Elizabeth's doomed love affair with Mary, not Norfolk's, that transforms
Banks's play from a schematic depiction of court intrigue and traduced innocence into a complex – if histrionic – exploration of the human bonds whose
disavowal ironically creates an illusion of psychic and symbolic order. Initially
frightened and envious of Mary, Elizabeth is moved to pity when Norfolk,

bearing letters from the Queen of Scots, delivers an affecting description of the captive queen whom she has never met. Elizabeth eventually agrees to a meeting, whereupon her enmity dissolves and she gives way to her own love for Mary. Begging the Queen of Scots to "throw thy lov'd Arms as I do mine about thee," the English queen succumbs to an "unspeakable" joy – a rapture so intense that she calls for her subjects' trumpets to "sound *Mary* and *Elizabeth* your Queens" (p. 38).

Cecil and Davison, however, persuade a "tortur'd" Elizabeth of the threat Mary poses; brandishing false evidence of her conspiracy with Elizabeth's enemies, they trick and intimidate the English queen into signing the warrant for Mary's execution. Mary goes to her death after holding a last supper for her supporters, during the course of which she asks that "all Revenge and Malice bury'd be/In this kind Bowl, as is this Wine in me" (p. 67). But the wish for oblivion is never fulfilled. On the contrary, the play ends with Elizabeth's recognition that her own "Head no more shall sleep,/But cover'd oe'r with Dust, for ever weep" (p. 70). Its last lines are her lament that "Falshood from *Eve* on all her Race descends" (p. 70). Far from "bury'd," the past and its conflicts have been absorbed into a consciousness – Elizabeth's – that grapples for a mythopoetic language to communicate its own torment. It is this consciousness which extends, bleakly and indefinitely, into a future that, we know, includes Banks's own play. That play in turn reaches back to its point of origin and seeks to recover what was lost.

What is left out of this plot sketch is of course exactly what had been lost: Mary herself. And indeed, though very much a presence in it, Mary is also in other ways virtually absent from Banks's tragedy. She does not appear until the end of the second act. Yet she has been invoked from the first minutes of it, when we are told of her longstanding competition with Elizabeth, the "Virgin Constellation" against whom "*Scotlands* Queen, that Northern Star [. . .] darts her Rival Light" (p. 2). Mary is conjured repeatedly as the object of Norfolk's amorous pity. And she is the subject of his speeches to Elizabeth, to whom he feels he must "count her miserable Plaints" (p. 7) and to whom he offers a wrenching verbal portrait of Mary "asleep [. . .] upon the Floor, [. . .] the sad Effigies of her self" (p. 12). Norfolk's picture of Mary as her own effigy captures the Stuart queen's strange place, half-in and half-outside the play – her standing, in Banks's own favorite phrases, between what is "Invention" and what is "real."

Though Banks's Mary is far from insentient, this quasi-fictive quality leaves her much more the object and catalyst of feeling than its subject. Strangers who share, or profess to share, the same sentiments about her embrace at the discovery; adoring crowds, we learn, have "hung like cluster'd Grapes,/And covered all her chariot like a Vine," even "swarmed like Bees upon her coaches side" (p. 19). When she "disperses" them with her "kind looks," "all harmony from discord seem'd to flow" (p. 18). Elizabeth is soon swept into this centrifuge of affection. The love that she immediately feels for Mary is presented as natural, and potentially self-unifying to the extent that it carries her out from the center of her isolated self and identifies her with others. Just so, Elizabeth's later decision against Mary creates almost unbearable conflict, and is presented as a violation of her natural self – a self which is finally indistinguishable, not to mention inseparable, from Mary. Recognizing this, at the news of Mary's death Elizabeth longs to experience what she did. She calls for "the Ax just reaking with my Sisters Veins," the better to "lop this hated member from my Body,/This bloody, cruel Hand that sign'd her Death" (p. 70).

Elizabeth's wish to be dismembered is more than a version of the Stuart era's desire to make the living body a replica of Mary's. In a throwback to the Elizabethans themselves, hers is also a revulsion from that part of the body which is able to create abstract signs, exemplified in words. As they mediate between human bodies, and even substitute for them, such signs always threaten to destroy those bodies' true bonds with one another. And it is precisely by manipulating Mary's letters and other symbolic "evidence" of her involvement in a conspiracy against Elizabeth that Mary's enemies are able to mutilate Elizabeth's faith in her. Throughout the play, all communication except through direct meeting is suspect. Mary's aristocratic enemy Morton sneers at Mary's reported "Plaints" as at "a Syrens Song," and until she herself actually appears on stage Norfolk's outspoken adulation of her must compete with Morton's equally articulate verdict that she is "wrapt in [. . .] a Cloud of Crimes" (p. 8), and Cecil's that she is a usurper who "hopes to snatch" the crown from Elizabeth's "rightful Head" (p. 5). At the very least, Mary seems unknowable on the word-level of the play. There the language of the heart is itself suspect, easily parroted by Mary's worst enemies as they convince the smitten and gullible Norfolk of their non-existent "Pity" for the Stuart queen.

In a world of verbal "Invention" run amok, Norfolk's credulousness – and Elizabeth's – keep questions of belief at center stage. These questions touch not only upon the security of historical knowledge (ours of the world that Banks depicts) but also upon that of what we might call pathetic knowledge, otherwise known as love. As in the Stuart biographies of Mary that cast their lot with romance, these two forms of knowledge overlap in *The Island Queens*. In the figure of Mary, especially, knowing and loving coincide. Fantasy thus gains such decisive purchase upon visceral experience that the word "real" and its cognates can only haunt Banks's play. Reality here is more something no character can be sure he or she is experiencing than it is a positive condition. Mary declares that "the World till now was but a Dream to me" (p. 24); and her response to Elizabeth is simply, "Can this be real?" (p. 37); Elizabeth's to Mary's apparent guilt: "If this be real, I had soon been dead" (p. 47). Mary's presence, in other words, makes the category of the "real" porous, permeable. Almost anything becomes "real" through her power to inspire an identificatory, even self-creating, love.

As the object and catalyst of everyone's fantastic love, Mary stands outside and even before conventional forms of mediation, including language. She herself seeks only the most immediate signs, and with them a form of symbolic authority increasingly scarce in the world of the play – as for that matter in the notoriously skeptical epistemological climate of late Stuart England. Upon her first meeting with Elizabeth, she begs that queen to "cleave to my Breast, for I want words to tell" the extent of her own love for her. And by her second she is calling for a knife to "unrip this Bosome," so that in the carnage Elizabeth "may see wrong'd Innocence inthron'd." "My Heart may be believed, though I am not" (p. 37). It's predictable, then, that Mary should define herself foremost as a mother: she often invokes her son and sees her supporters as her own offspring ("I have . . . no Children nigh but you" [p. 67]). In the course of the play her name and her story become identified with the pre-linguistic bonds that mothers and infants share: when Mary entered London, Elizabeth learns to her chagrin, that "Mothers, when they with joy her Face had seen,/Wou'd point, and to their Infants shew the Queen,/Whilst they (ne're learnt to talk) for her wou'd try,/And the first word they spoke wou'd *Mary* cry" (p. 19). Later Mary asks her faithful servant Dowglas "my story to relate/To men that now are Children in the womb" (p. 66).

In stressing Mary's maternity, Banks hits upon what linked Stuart versions of the Queen of Scots to their earliest Elizabethan prototypes. For him, Mary mothers in large part by returning language to its bodily source: whereas the historical Mary's Protestant detractors felt threatened by this effect of the way that she used words, Banks seems to have welcomed the fantasy that verbal signs can devolve from their task of formal mediation back into an earlier version of themselves – that they might become their own content, and thereby permit an unbroken bond between different sentient beings. The same ideal shapes Mary's political desire for England and Scotland to be one – to see "the White Cross with the Red thus ever joyn'd," like "two streams,/[. . .] making one Current as we make one Soul" (p. 39). Because this idea of fusion proves so seductive, Elizabeth's initial fear and envy of Mary slowly gives way to the conviction of a deeper similarity to her. She experiences a heightened susceptibility to her own softer passions, and a growing conviction that, as Mary had held, she and the Queen of Scots are one. If Mary is as guilty of deception as Elizabeth's ministers insist she is, she will, Elizabeth realizes, have "robb'd me of your Self" (p. 49). Such epiphanies show Elizabeth's temporary submission to an explicitly matriarchal system of meaning, one whose principles could only prove the Stuart queen's innocence of her alleged crimes. Mary's death, when at last it comes, is also the death of that vindicating system of meaning.

Much of *The Island Queens* is in fact devoted to proving Mary's innocence of crime against Elizabeth. From the beginning, Norfolk vows to "prove/That *Mary* Queen of *Scotland* is abus'd,/That she is Innocent, and all is forg'd." But as the tragedy unfolds, Norfolk's efforts to establish Mary's innocence by conventional means can only fail. Everything that Norfolk says about her – his recitals of her own words, his florid descriptions of her beauty – is open to the same charges of fraud as the words of Mary's enemies. The Queen of Scots's innocence simply can't be demonstrated in language.

It can, however, be proved in the vocabulary of flesh and blood, most especially when Mary's injuries put that vocabulary itself into disarray. The Queen of Scots herself is well aware of this. Midway through the play, she announces that "my own Innocence shall conquer all" (p. 36), and even when Elizabeth, turned "deaf and cruel" by her ministers' insidious hints, withstands her passionate petitions for life and fails to "pity" her, she insists that "when my Story's told/Good men inspir'd with pity of my Wrongs,/May say my Innocence was basely stain'd" (p. 51). Though she cannot actually "unrip [her] Bosome" to show Elizabeth "wrong'd Innocence inthron'd" (p. 51), Banks's Mary can recreate in all witnesses to her story the vindicating passion of pity. Her efforts to do so are part of her effort to return words to their origins in the body's imaginings – to restore their primary identity as passionate phantoms that claim their own unique powers of generation.

So when Davison insists that only "the Law must quit you," Mary places herself beyond its reach, choosing another system of meaning in which physical action, symbolic reaction and descent through time all become one:

> All the Courage and Divinity,
> Of my imperial Ancestors inspire
> This Breast, from *Fergus* first to *James* my Son
> Last of his Race that sway'd the *Scottish* Globe
> For fifteen hundred years, shine through my Face,
> Print on my Forehead ev'ry awful Grace,
> Defend your Royal Right, and for me plead,
> Shoot from my Eyes, and strike my Judges dead
>
> (p. 52)

While such spectacular vindication cannot, alas, come Mary's way, she can allow herself to be absorbed imaginatively into the bodies of the other characters in the play. To do so is to become manifestly innocent, for if she is part of the others, it is impossible for her to be guilty of crimes against them. Just after Mary calls for the pride and passion of her "Race" to be imprinted in her flesh, Elizabeth begins to imagine herself as a "distracted Mother," whose "Child a Wolf had from its Cradle bore" (p. 53) – precisely the same image that Mary, mother of James, will use at the end of the play to describe herself. And in the end, Elizabeth ingests the guilt that fell upon Mary, mourning the loss less of the Queen of Scots than of a crucial part of herself. She sees that "the long shining, fear'd and spotless Reign/Of fame's *Elizabeth* is set in Night;/That *England*'s stain'd, its Maiden Monarch stain'd,/Stain'd, stain'd, like banisht *Cain* for ever mark'd" (p. 70). These are of course the same stains that had fixed themselves on Scotland's queen earlier in the play. In adopting them, Elizabeth becomes a living approximation of Mary, and her own ghost.

Through Elizabeth's tragedy Banks's play does more than show what killing the "Queen of Scotland" could mean in his own day. It does more, too, than make reparation to Mary by restoring as much of her innocence as could be restored while yet admitting how uncertain the truth about her was, thanks to the Elizabethan fictions which had "entailed reproach" upon so many. In its own languages and actions, *The Island Queens* attempts to undo, then redo, the Elizabethan traducing of Mary. It thus aims to restore the only system of meaning – the pathetic one – in which Mary might be vindicated convincingly. This is obviously always part of the process of dramatization, but for Banks it became true in ways which transcend performance's unique ability to tap the human body's evocative and expressive power.

First, there is the oddly acted and yet unacted nature of the play, the fact that *The Island Queens* itself hovers, so strangely, between possibility and actuality. Because the play was never performed, it kept the palpable, physical shape of a text; and it was a text that Banks expected to be read by an influential woman – Mary, Duchess of Norfolk – whom he also expected to form an intense emotional bond to it. Moreover, not only did this female reader's name unite Mary with Norfolk; she was physically bound to someone whose blood tied him to the characters in the play – in Banks's words, she was "joyn'd by Heaven, to a Prince, who is the true Inheritor of [. . .] the Blood of that Illustrious Duke, the Hero in the Play" (sig. A2v). Banks's comparison of his playbook to "a poor Woman's Mite" because "it is my All" also reclaims the Mary deprived of life and credence as a presence within it. Bound by history, the plot of *The Island Queens* might have found its heroine's style of knowing and affecting the world doomed, but as a visibly depleted text it was able to bring that style to life again, reinvigorating it through reference to the living, feeling human beings involved with it.

As it happens, Banks's unique contributions to the English theater also recall the powers and properties he accorded Mary in *The Island Queens*. He was never "accounted a Poet of the first form,"[10] but one feature of his language was noted again and again in the century following the publication of *The Island Queens*. This was its peculiar immediacy, its ability to abandon its hollow symbolic function in favor of an effect so visceral, even licentious, that those who came across it were inclined to call it barbarous. The actor and sometime theater critic Colley Cibber, for instance, noted that Banks's works were "all written in the most barren, barbarous Stile," one that invariably "interested the Hearts of his Auditors." Cibber attributed Banks's "Success" to "the intrinsick and naked Value of the well-conduc'd Tale he has so simply told us," and to the way that "all his Chief Characters are thrown into such natural circumstances of Distress, that their Misery, or Affliction, wants very little of the Ornaments of Stile, or Words to speak them."[11]

As it conflates (emotional) surplus and (linguistic) scarcity, the economy of representation in Banks's work is uniquely rooted in the human body; meaning is conveyed most vividly through certain deficiencies of language. What words want is provided on the one hand by the actor's "bare plaintive Tone Voice, the Cast of Sorrow from his Eye, his slowly graceful Gesture, his humble Signs of Resignation under his Calamities," and on the other by "the attentive

Auditor," who "supplies from his own Heart, whatever the Poet's Language may fall short of, in Expression, and melts himself into every Pang of Humanity, which the like Misfortunes in real life cou'd have inspired."[12] A biographical notice of 1791 similarly admitted that Banks's talent for "the excitement of *feeling*" is rooted "in circumstances foreign both from his sentiment and his diction." So while *The Albion Queens* – not to mention its even rougher predecessor, *The Island Queens* – is "turgid and incorrect, [. . .] much of its exuberant bombast" seemed to be "retrenched in the representation."[13] Even in the nineteenth century, Banks's "story founded on the Scotch and English histories" was remarked for its "power of affecting the passions" in a way that "sometimes makes amends for want of poetry and language."[14]

THE ALBION QUEENS

All of which is to say that the finally redemptive force of *The Island Queens* lay in what finally was *not* there, in the English words. And it was precisely this enthralling deficiency that Banks intended to revive in the Queen of Scots, thereby rendering her innocently real for – and in – seventeenth-century spectators. Those spectators did not of course materialize, but through its metamorphosis into *The Albion Queens*, Banks's tragedy continued to rely on this paradox. The play that finally found its way to the stage in 1704 – with Fanny Knight as Elizabeth, Anne Oldfield as Mary, and Robert Wilks as Norfolk – was, however, far more temperate than its earlier incarnation had been. In expectation of a different breed of onlooker, the language of *The Island Queens* is in *The Albion Queens* simplified and condensed, and the actions of Mary and Elizabeth are less overtly political. Though in 1684 the two queens "by different Sides maintain each other's right," in 1704 they "by different Arts oppose each other's interest."

What recalled Banks's play to this more pallid life? The most detailed account of its belated arrival on the London stage tells us that the author:

> had [. . .] the good fortune to prevail with a nobleman to favour his petition to Queen Anne, for permission to have it acted. The Queen had the goodness to refer the merit of the play to the opinion of that noble person, tho' he was not Her Majesty's Lord Chamberlain, upon whose report of its being in every way an innocent piece, it was soon after acted with success.[15]

Banks's vindicated "innocen[ce]" again almost physically links his play with that of the heroine whose "Innocence" it too vindicates. Moreover, Anne's deference to a "noble person" in the matter of the play's licensing exemplifies the political shift, from sovereign as assertive agent to sovereign as manipulated object, which became official in 1688 but continued to be advertised throughout her reign.

Anne's presence on the English throne may tell us why *The Island Queens* finally found its way to the stage. As the first woman to reign alone since Elizabeth, Anne naturally made explorations of the dilemmas of female monarchy more interesting to her own subjects. Banks's play dramatizes rulers' domination by their own subjects and those subjects' fictions. In *The Island Queens* this is very obviously true of Mary. But in *The Albion Queens* it became true of Elizabeth too. While men were merely placed "about [Elizabeth's] Royal Person" in 1684, they are now "above [their] Royal Mistress," and Elizabeth's resemblances to the distressed Mary are even more exaggerated. She is given a mirror scene like defenseless Mary's and her proud recollection of the time she "led forth [her] Armies,/Arm'd like an Amazon" disappears altogether. Her virulent diatribes against Morton, denouncing him as a "Slave" and "Snake" and threatening to "bore him through/The tongue" are tempered to leave him nothing more than a "daring Insect."[16] The new Elizabeth is more interested in assuring her hangers-on that the throne is an "Altar with soft Mercy crown'd,/Where both yourselves and your Monarch may be blest" (*AQ*, p. 15). Indeed, both Elizabeth and Mary are more delicate and domesticated the second time around. Banks adds "Blushings" to "veil Mary's charming Face" (*AQ*, p. 77) as she anticipates the scaffold, and the Elizabeth of 1704 no longer calls for an axe to "lop" the "hated" hand that signed Mary's death warrant. After Mary's death the new Elizabeth refrains from lamenting that "England's stain'd, its Maiden Monarch's stain'd." As critics have suggested, the line became "tactless" with Anne on the throne.[17]

But the new and squeamish sentimentality of *The Albion Queens* moves less to elevate than to efface what it so clearly marks as feminine. At the end of *The Albion Queens* Dowglas now relays every detail of Mary's execution ("her snowy Neck, now on the Block is laid;/Tears in vast torrents flow from ev'ry Eye"), expiring onstage at the moment "the stroke is given" (*AQ*, p. 77). Elizabeth herself draws attention to the "dismal Object of his body," which she pronounces "dead to no other wound than Sorrow's Dart,/Or some unhappy Poison." Dowglas's death from grief puts him – a much less ambiguous object of compassion than Mary herself – at center stage. It also softens and sentimentalizes the end of Banks's play, smoothing its jagged edges while at the same time bringing the sensory details of Mary's death, now fused with their sentimental effects on the male onlooker who usurps her pathos, into the representation. In *The Albion Queens* the violent mourning that gave *The Island Queens* its riveting fervor and drew actors and audiences together in Mary's maternal body degenerates into hackneyed melancholia, the figment of one man's narcissism.

In fact, as *The Island Queens* had not, *The Albion Queens* begins with a prologue which modelled appropriate emotional reactions and made them a part of the play. The new prologue further shapes and contains – we might say cooks – the raw excesses and primitive ruthlessness of *The Island Queens*. A more transparent and uncomplicated vocabulary domesticates the audience's own responses. It also defends the audience from its own feelings, politely erasing (or at least masking) the more violent, savage ones, and leaving only a saccharine sorrow in their place.

Promising that here a *"Queen* Distress'd [. . .] dies" with "a *British Queen* lamenting [her] sad Fate,/And mourning over the Unfortunate," the new prologue demands to know "Who is there here, that cou'd so cruel be,/As not to mourn at their sad Tragedy?/To see such Honour and such Beauty fail,/And *England's Queen* mourn at their Funeral?" (*AQ*, sig. A3r). Ties of mourning that were once associated with Mary (the "mourning Goddess" and the "mourning Nightingale") are now also credited to the play's audience: they will be taught to absorb her sorrow, to make it the exclusive property of the subject (the audience), not something it shares with the lamented object (Mary). Tears of the sort *The Albion Queens* evokes translate the guilt and pain of immediate identification with Mary into a safer and more distanced simulacrum of feeling, one that ignores emotion's roots in violence and denies ambivalence's part in love.

These tears have a political application too. Banks's new prologue expects them to soften militant *"Britons"* who, "tho' for Arms renown'd,/Have for the Fair a tender Pity found: /And in the midst of Slaughter still took care,/Not to destroy but guard the tender Fair" (*AQ*, sig. A3r). Such an exercise could be thought of in national terms – in terms, that is, of the management of a kind of political affect, henceforth to be shared by *"Britons"* as a group. Just as its new title swallows Scotland into "Albion," Banks's play subordinates the emotional bond between Elizabeth and Mary to more watery affective ties between *"Albany* and *Albion,"* "the White Cross" and "the Red" (*AQ*, p. 39).

Historians like Sanderson had already long assumed that merely to tell Mary's story was to unite English and Scottish history – "to mold [the two countries] both into one body."[18] Such molding had a particular urgency in 1704, when agitations for the union of the crowns of Scotland and England had reached a fever pitch. Here sexual and national politics converged. Acquiescence to the wish for total union was widely seen as another instance of Anne's disempowerment at the hands of her own ministers; as one onlooker put it, "the Queen, indeed, for fashion sake, was sometimes addressed to; but such Application was made to these two Lords [Anne's ministers Marlborough and Godolphin], that it was obvious to all the world, how much the Scots Affairs depended on them."[19]

The Albion Queens, with its story of the tragedy of frustrated union, might easily be seen as a political allegory, a veiled argument for the kinds of unity, ultimately embodied in the new Great Britain, that had been equally desired and feared throughout the period of profound ambivalence that was the Stuart age.[20] Banks's play surpasses allegory, though. It retains enough traces of *The Island Queens* to be less a symbolic resolution than a symptom of the anxieties about incorporation and the death of a certain version of political love that accompanied the fiction of Union. Mary Queen of Scots, that is, had stayed both alive and dead in Stuart memory because (as in many cases of love) longing for her return went hand in hand with the ineradicable wish to destroy her. As Freud would put it somewhat later, the myths of a people, while under formation as they were in the nascent and conflicted Britain we have been considering, first require that collective memory eliminate all of its most "painful" motives.[21] In Mary's life, the motives of everyone from Queen Elizabeth down to the headsman who had botched his job and the Protestant underlings who watched had been nothing if not painfully mixed. In the next century the Stuarts and their subjects inherited this mixture and the complicated falsehoods that it wrought, keeping Mary alive – and themselves linked to her – by refusing either wholly to remember or entirely to repress the conflict she aroused. But, even against its will, *The Albion Queens* tolls the knell of Stuart authority. Repression gains the upper hand; and out of the ashes of a troublesome ghost a sentimental heroine is born.

Part III

Georgian Mary

In a few weeks, I had the *sorrow* of seeing the Queen, her two female domestics, [. . .] the executioner, the coffin, scaffold, &c. &c. all under a glass-case, and compleating a most affecting scenery.

The Gentleman's Magazine (1789)

She had been dead, of course, for more than two centuries. Even her Stuart progeny had lost their throne over seventy years before. But early in 1789 one of London's best known periodicals, *The Gentleman's Magazine*, printed a most interesting letter from one of its readers – a letter which proved that, if neither exactly alive nor altogether well, Mary Queen of Scots had nonetheless managed to keep her old hold on British imaginations.

The letter began by recommending "a most particular account," recently published, of "every circumstance which passed" at Mary's long-ago execution. Vowing that "those who can read it with a dry eye, if not a more affecting sensation [. . .] shall never moisten their mouth at my board" the letter's author, one "P.T.," expressed confidence that this moving chronicle of her many sufferings would at last "establis[h] the real character of Mary, [. . .] who fell a sacrifice to the *personal jealousy of our yellow-pated Bess.*" Even more remarkable was the account's stunning impact upon the modern heart. For, P.T. testified:

> it struck my family in so forcible and affecting a manner, that they immediately dressed up a beautiful figure, representing the unfortunate Queen, exactly according to her real dress on that fatal day, which was a very graceful one, and it induced me to prevail on them to execute the whole scene in the same manner; and in a few weeks I had the *sorrow* of seeing the Queen, her two female domesticks, [. . .] the executioner, the coffin, scaffold, &c. &c. all under a glass-case, and compleating a most affecting scenery. The head of her faithful servant Melville was modelled by myself, and, though it was my first and last attempt, it was agreed that I had depicted sorrow successfully.[1]

This ersatz "scene of sorrow" (as P.T.'s letter later put it) could only have been staged in eighteenth-century Britain. Only there, at some remove from the fierce political and religious animosities of the last centuries, could it have unleashed such a unanimous torrent of tears; and only there could its agreeable audience have spread beyond a private drawing room to include the comparatively vast readership of a fashionable magazine. All in all, P.T.'s sociable rendition of Mary's "sacrifice" feels like a far cry from her Protestant contemporary Robert Wyngfield's troubled, angry caricature of the queen's last minutes upon earth.

Our own quest for Mary's meaning to modern Britons began by acknowledging the conflicts of desire that she awakened in onlookers like Wyngfield – savage conflicts reborn in the Stuarts' (and their subjects') animating uncertainty about a complex and bewildering dynastic mother. But if until the beginning of the eighteenth century the Queen of Scots retained no inconsiderable degree of splendor, vigor, and indeed erotic power, by the end of it we find her dwindled to a waxwork figurine. Dwarfed by the immensity of the "affecting sensations" whose mere occasion she seems to have become, P.T.'s "unfortunate Queen" evidently bears the same relationship to the riddling, divisive, wonderfully seductive Mary Stuart of old that a mock epic bears to the *Iliad*.

What can have brought her to such a pass? A reasonable question, surely. On the other hand, it is so tempting to snicker at the diminutive doll at its center that we easily overlook the ways in which P.T.'s earnest letter to the editor actually sustains a lengthening tradition of involvement with the Queen of Scots. At the very least, we are reminded of the covert forms of immersion in Mary and her plight that threatened to turn the Elizabethans out of their bounded and determinate selves. Then too, as the "T" family dissolves in tears and then regroups long enough to build the "most affecting scenery" that will induce it to cry more, it also takes up the old seventeenth-century habit of discovering the mother of the Stuart line in the senses of the living. Perhaps this "scene of sorrow" is not so alien after all.

Who was the Georgian version of the Queen of Scots it featured? How far did she truly differ from earlier versions of herself? What unique psychological and symbolic service did she do Great Britain in the first century or so of its existence? To judge by the tearful spectacle at hand, Mary remained, as ever, an object of desire. But desire for what, exactly? Surely not for the queen herself, or at least not for her actually to have lived to some ripe and prosperous dotage. On the contrary, a certain morose pleasure and even a sense of group cohesion seem to have followed from collective re-enactments of her precipitous death. And we find such re-enactments everywhere, from P.T.'s letter to the "Representation of the Execution of Mary Queen of Scots in Four Views" that one Earl of Abingdon published in 1790, complete with "music composed for and adapted to each view." In different ways, the next three chapters all interpret a new Mary Stuart in light of the linked, and actually ruthless, wishes for self-approbation and affective concord that appear to have ruled England and Scotland from the accession of George I in 1714 to that of Victoria in 1837. Far more than to "the personal jealousy of our yellow-pated

Bess," it was to these entwined desires that the complex and dimensional Queen of Scots of old became, in P.T.'s term, "a sacrifice."

But never, by her nature, a very perfect one. We begin, in Chapter 5, with Mary's career as a sentimental heroine. The 1704 debut of Banks's *Albion Queens* secured her place in a culture of sensibility that, as it worked to produce an unprecedented sense of distinctly British community and history, served its moneyed male members remarkably well. Yet for all that they conceived of themselves very much as modern Britons too, Georgian women seem to have profited less from the so-called age of feeling, and Chapter 6 turns to the ruined Stuart queen's enormous significance for them. Especially women who took up the pen found, in Mary, a way to convey their shared predicament as artists in an essentially patriarchal society, their peculiar bonds and legacies. What is more, after 1789 anxiety provoked in part by revolution in Mary's cherished France began to remold the sentimental icon so dear to Georgian hearts. Especially in the wake of Regency-era scandals like the adultery trial of Caroline of Brunswick, the Georgian Mary Queen of Scots began to stretch the unifying sensibility that had (over)wrought her to its limits. By the time Victoria came to the throne, the antique queen whose spectacular pathos had helped to unite modern Britons in the flattering illusion of a single senti- mental community had grown inclined to expose that community's strifes and hypocrisies, the shallow barbarism of its most prized desires.

5 "The sorrow of seeing the queen"

1714–1789

The death of Anne and the accession of the German elector George I put an end to Stuart rule in England and Scotland. But while thoughts of the last Stuart queen seem to have been scarce under the house of Hanover, the notoriously sentimental subjects of eighteenth-century Britain shed more than their fair share of tears for the woman who might have been the first. Between 1714 and the outbreak of the French Revolution in 1789, Banks's *Albion Queens* made many a trip to the London stage, with frequent side-jaunts to provincial venues where, "at the desire of several Ladies of Quality," actors "dress'd in old English dress" recreated the last days of Mary Queen of Scots before the streaming eyes of the *beau monde*.[1] Popular new histories of the countries so recently joined to make Great Britain devoted hundreds of pages to Mary's "forlorn condition,"[2] while translations of her poignant, if apocryphal, "Chanson" on leaving France ("Farewell, sweet France!;" "Dear France, adieu;" "Adieu dear pleasant Land of France") inundated contemporary periodicals.[3] New in the eighteenth century, and viewed today as symptoms of an ascendant, middling public sphere that scorned affiliation with the court, these same magazines nonetheless brokered countless doleful queries as to the present whereabouts of the Queen of Scots' belongings – prayer books, rings, sewing boxes, letters and other relics.[4]

Compendia meant to exalt national accomplishment, like Thomas Birch's *Illustrious Heads of Great Britain* (1747) and George Ballard's *Memoirs of Several Ladies of Great Britain* (1752) meanwhile painted touching verbal portraits of Mary, and countless old English buildings became interesting primarily in relation to her melancholy fate. Throughout the eighteenth century, chivalrous historians revived the casket letters controversy with the idea of "rescu[ing] an unfortunate and injured princess, from [the] load of infamy that ha[d] been thrown upon her,"[5] and by the 1770s painters had begun to reconstruct the most lamentable episodes of Mary's life on canvas. During his famous trip to Scotland, the memory of her plight moved Samuel Johnson to chide his hosts for having "let your Queen remain twenty years in captivity and then be put to death."[6] And in the mid-1780s droves of British readers wept over Sophia Lee's gothic novel, *The Recess*, whose heroines learn that they are Mary's daughters and spend the rest of her days bemoaning her misfortunes, the rest of theirs reliving them.

From the evidence of so very many tears, we can only conclude that the Queen of Scots meant rather a lot to the Georgians. But their evident need to be convulsed by her sorrows is something of a puzzlement. It was after all under the Hanover family – especially the stolid, Germanic Georges I, II and III – that Britons forged a collective identity rooted both in a staunchly Protestant Church of England and in the secular doctrine of contempt for absolute sovereign authority that had been in the works since the days of Elizabeth at least.[7] Seven years after the Act of Union, the Hanoverians were welcomed to the British throne in part because they promised to drain it of any popish or autocratic glamour that may yet have clung to it; political and cultural authority were thereby at last secured in the hands of parties of privileged Protestant men.

Steadfastly convinced of her own right of rule and alluring in the extreme, the Catholic Queen of Scots had once promised a very different state of affairs. Indeed, in her own lifetime, Mary had often elicited precisely the desire not to be ruled from too far above which presumably now "united" the new British "kingdom." What is more, at least until their defeat at Culloden in 1745, her Stuart descendants posed the gravest of threats to a complacent sense of national identity. The sweep and sheer tenacity of the Jacobite movement proved that the people of Great Britain were most emphatically not all of one mind: at the very least, many of them still believed in right of blood and craved the aura of majesty.

On the other hand, it appears that most eighteenth-century Britons very much liked to have feelings. In the wake of the influential late seventeenth-century empiricist John Locke, it was hard not to hold the sentient and sympathetic body to be the wellspring of personal identity and human society, the condition of mutual understanding and the ground of any art. After the civil catastrophes of the seventeenth century, the cultivation of a shared and softer sensibility became, perforce, a national priority. Addicted to the cohesive fiction that we can actually feel one another's pain, Great Britain spent its first decades nurturing a literature – and theater – of sensibility. Foundling hospitals, humane societies and other public charities sprang up almost overnight, while the susceptible woman and effeminate man of feeling became cultural paragons, the affective family the fundamental unit of society.[8]

Whatever her own desires might have been, the misfortunes that befell her proclaimed that Mary Queen of Scots was born to be the heroine of such a world. In an exploding commodity culture whose plethora of tangible, possessible objects reinforced commitment to the *sensus communis*, she easily assumed the shape of a touching small thing – a doll, a piece of costume jewelry, a frontispiece. More to the point, as it announced her very human vulnerability, Mary's history of mishap made her compelling in a way which did not necessarily invoke the indomitable mystique that once enveloped the rejected kings of old. On the contrary, her endless, and endlessly disempowering, tribulations made her seem very much a creature of the present day. Her story summoned tears bound to display the moral authenticity and fellow feeling of those who shed them – tears that also reminded modern Scots and Englishmen, Protestants and Catholics, Jacobites and Hanoverian Whigs, of their ostensibly shared history. In short, Mary offered a common object of sympathy in a mercifully receding past. But since in reality that past had been bitterly divisive, with the Queen of Scots one conspicuous reason why, sentimental investment in her was always risky. It may have been in order to combat its possible groundlessness that the Georgians took a tip from the Elizabethans and found ways to falsify the Queen of Scots herself. Indeed, their most ostentatious efforts to regain a wholly pathetic Mary in material form often only thinly disguised the compulsion to make certain of her loss, and losses.

Of this there is no better example than P.T.'s letter to *The Gentleman's Magazine*. In that letter, recall, the "unfortunate Queen" of long ago recovered shape and substance in just the sort of sentimental enclave peculiar to Georgian Britain – in "a most affecting" domestic "scenery" and in the tearful bodies of the private family "struck" there "in so forcible and affecting a manner." The painstakingly crafted "scene of sorrow" was itself hopelessly cluttered, packed to the gills with "the Queen, her female domestics, [. . .] the executioner, the coffin, the scaffold, &c., &c." So much affecting paraphernalia cannot help but set modern nervous systems all aquiver. Who would not agree as to which emotions are appropriate in the circumstances? Who would not wish to show them?

And yet at the heart of so much mutually resounding matter we find something else – the nearly incantatory reiteration of the word "sorrow." P.T.'s "scene of sorrow," he tells us, gave him not only "the sorrow of seeing the Queen" but also the consolation that for his part he "had depicted sorrow successfully." And sorrow – the feeling Mary most often seemed to arouse – is an extraordinary thing. For one thing, it requires some damage done. For another, it is itself peculiar. Locke saw sorrow as an "uneasiness in the Mind, upon the Thought of a Good lost, or the Sense of a present Evil" and throughout the eighteenth century the word described, interchangeably, both an emotion (the quality of a subject, an effect) and the cause of that emotion (the quality of an object, a cause). Indeed, in Locke's own formulation, "Sorrow" hovers between the "presen[ce]" of an object ("Evil") and the depletion of the perceiving subject through its own "uneasiness" and eerie sense of the "lost."[9]

In Lockean terms, P.T.'s "scene of sorrow" both verified a modern family's sensibility (its physical existence in virtuous response to the world of things) and, together with the very object of its sorrow, emptied that family of a certain reality. Hence the waxwork replica of Queen Mary's execution is "a scene *of* sorrow," not a scene *invoking* sorrow; it absorbs those living beings who feel back into the very images that provoke their feeling. In turn, such images have a way of vanishing, and not just because they are wrought of something as evanescent as wax. As if to concede the inherent fragility of objects, P.T. informed "the curious" that if they "should ask under whose roof this scene of sorrow is at present, I cannot answer it. I left it, with many other things of value, when I went abroad, with a man who *called himself* a gentleman." The latter apparently made off with P.T.'s "unfortunate Queen," leaving the original owner "his detester" and us with a paradox: domesticated under a "glass case," Mary's darkest hours become present realities which can release reassuringly vast reserves of emotion in those who witness them. Such tearful effusions in turn render those witnesses visible, and virtuous, both to themselves and to each other. But these dividends follow only from some rehearsal of Mary's original degradation, her depletion into a vulnerable and at last fleeting image.

Down to the reflex of hollowness at its core, P.T.'s interest in Mary's execution sustained an increasingly venerable tradition. Long before he expressed it, for example, the enterprising Whig, Samuel Croxall, had published the sensational *Memoirs* (1727) of Mary's "Imprisonment and Death." Like P.T., the anonymous author of the *Memoirs* expected their reader to "have a Tear to shed for this disastrous Princess." To make sure that he or she did shed it, the author exaggerated the "Barbarity of those, who were the Promoters of her untimely Death,"[10] even speculating that because Mary's "Beauty continued for some Time after her Death," the Earl Marshal in attendance was "suspected, how truly we dare not venture to affirm, guilty of a Crime, too horrid to be imagin'd" (p. 374). By perversely eliciting a mental image of this apocryphal "Crime," the *Memoirs* reprised the "Barbarity" of Mary's executioners. In the name of compelling sympathy, fictitious details launched an assault of their own, not only on their reader's captive sensibility but also on the exceptional command that Mary actually exhibited on the scaffold.

The Queen of Scots who was resurrected in wax and words in the years between, say, the *Memoirs* and P.T.'s letter to the editor, all too often appeared to be this kind of helpless victim. As such she promised the unity of gentle sensibility that allowed eighteenth-century Britons to approve of themselves as uniformly and even unprecedentedly moral beings. Yet obsessive fondness for a Mary ever trembling on the verge of an undeserved scaffold finally betrays the deeper disregard that underwrote many Georgian forms of sympathy, eventually emptying them of their vaunted humanity. In turn, while she tended to look more innocent of certain unsavory crimes of passion than ever before, Mary became even harder to tell apart from the fabrications of others. Far from accidentally, it was in the eighteenth century that wholly imaginary scenes from her life first began to appear on British canvasses, their aim less to convey a sense of who the queen might have been than to unleash torrents of tears in their beholders. It would seem that the Queen of Scots was, for the sentimental, destined to remain an imposter of sorts, ever more the invention of the empty-hearted tearful than the dignified recipient of their understanding.

GEORGIAN FABRICATIONS

Poor "daughter of debate!" Part of Mary was visibly counterfeit from the start, a misfortune that has at least helped us to understand both her resonance at specific historical junctures and the amazing ease with which her story passed through time. Predictably, just as Mary's legacy of pathos took on a new timbre amid the fibrillating sympathies of so many modern Britons, so in the eighteenth century did her inherent fictionality achieve a different meaning from any it had possessed before.

For one thing, Mary's received, and duelling, reputations as adulteress and ravished captive, ambitious absolutist and pious victim of an envious cousin, made unadulterated affection itself a form of artistry bound to fabricate its feminine recipient. At the same time, in vivid contrast to their Stuart forebears, the Georgian historians now in charge of crafting national memory hoped to create consensus about the past by penetrating each object of historical knowledge and illuminating it indisputably from within. Even to the most eminent of them, Mary's "intricate and perplexed" life story could be a source of infinite frustration, clotted with logjams of propaganda, fantastic gaps and lapses that could only be filled with artful speculation.[11] Finally, to those francophobic, anti-Catholic, and anti-Stuart members of English society who were evidently bent on economic, political and affective unity, the half-French, devoutly Catholic mother of the disgraced and exiled Stuart dynasty threatened to expose collective self-approval as a convenient fantasy.

In each of these instances, the Queen of Scots's inherently illusory quality passed from her into those who now made her the object of their affection and interest. The prodigious volume of tears poured over her throughout the eighteenth century suggests a massive and remarkably successful denial of a certain emptiness within those who shed them. And deny it many did, for, in the words of one eminent biographer, empty-heartedness went hand in hand with a capacity for "perfidy, cruelty and bigotry" that had supposedly passed away with the Elizabethans.[12] It is not hard to recognize such progressive assumptions about British identity as the gist of the triumphalist history of the nation which began to write itself after the Revolution of 1688. As the eighteenth century wore on, more and more Britons began to subscribe to an altogether flattering story about who they were and where they had come from. As that story's supremely credible authors came to include even Scots like David Hume and William Robertson, the Jacobite threat ebbed apace. Now more visible as the victim of another woman than as a Stuart, Mary Queen of Scots supplied proof positive of Britain's climb out of moral darkness to a state in which no one, surely, would ever have injured her.

This is not to say that Mary did not also figure in the lingering Jacobite cause, whose own version of history owed more to tragedy than to the comic myth of a march toward perfection. The Queen of Scots's miniature portrait was even treasured by the exiled Stuart kings; but as the century wore on sympathy for them found increasingly comfortable accommodation with mainstream sentimental culture. Before long, cameo copies of the same miniature had been rehabilitated as fashionable accessories for the well-to-do. Still, the kinks in Mary's character remained: had she plotted against Protestant Elizabeth? Had she eloped with Bothwell or, Clarissa-like, been drugged and abducted by him? On the whole, Georgians were inclined to find Mary guilt-less, but such stubborn ambiguities, together with her continuing resonance for the Jacobites, help to account for the hugger-mugger aura that enveloped new editions of the "secret" letters she allegedly wrote, Eliza Haywood's popular 1725 "Secret History" of her life, and even the "recess" where Mary's daughters hide in Sophia Lee's novel of that name.

Enclaves of secrecy like these could only counterbalance the highly visible and very public-spirited cult of Elizabeth that thrived alongside the Georgians' newfound tenderness for Mary. Despite their disdain for the barbarous Elizabethans, the Georgians were also eager to find traditions behind what they deemed their own finer points, and there was no denying, for example, that Elizabeth had presided over the first great efflorescence of English trade, or that she had been a staunch Protestant, and had almost certainly preserved an admirable chastity. Indeed, had it not been for Mary, she would have reigned undisputed in the brighter regions of collective memory, but even Jane Austen remarked, severely, that to "pity" Elizabeth was "an injury to the memory of Mary."[13] With the gentler sentiments at such a premium, Elizabeth was thus forced to share British culture's main lobby with the supremely pitiable Mary, while the Stuart queen alone haunted the clandestine corridors that joined a wide range of cultural subalterns – diehard Jacobites, beleagured English Catholics, Protestant women. In spite of the religion she had so inconveniently embraced, Mary seems to have been even more popular among the Georgians than her Tudor rival of old.

But which Mary? Because eighteenth-century feeling for "Queen Mary" crossed so many boundaries of sex, politics and religion, it is impossible to see its object either, simply, as an "unfortunate and injured princess" now miraculously palatable to collective imagination, or as a transgressive totem that knitted together the members of diverse marginal groups. She was both of these things at once, and so she was never quite either. We risk eternal suspension between them unless we realize that what the Georgians ended up most truly sharing was a compounding investment in her actual absence from their world.

The revival of the casket letters controversy offers a case in point. When the incriminating epistles returned to popular attention, they did so under the banner of desire to win agreement at last about whether or not "Queen Mary" had actually written them; but what they in fact reflected was the extent to which she had become little more than a sentimental fiction. The apocryphal epistles and their accompanying sonnets were first reprinted in 1720 along with sections of Buchanan's scandalous *History of Scotland*. But in 1754, the Edinburgh librarian Walter Goodall published a meticulous *Examination of the Letters Said to be Written by Mary, Queen of Scots*, which concluded that the letters were forgeries: a queen who "so far excelled all other sovereign princes" could not possibly have written them.[14] For several decades, the letters were analyzed *ad infinitum*. Events surrounding the alleged correspondence were painstakingly reconstructed, and reams of new evidence for Mary's innocence were dredged up from obscure libraries to prove that she had been slander's victim, if not that of everyone from Murray to the Earl Marshal suspected of having ravished her after death.[15]

Once re-opened, the case of the casket letters attracted the most prominent British historians of the day, Hume and Robertson among them. Both swam against the tide of popular sentiment when they accepted that Mary had indeed written the letters. But they did so in a language so guarded and equivocal – and so bedevilled by pity for what she had suffered through her disastrous marriages, captivity and death – that it was clear the Queen of Scots put the truth status of material evidence itself in serious question; she herself must at last be seen as a figment of that evidence's own imagination. Meanwhile, to the ardent antiquarians who rushed in to champion Mary's innocence, the letters were a mythological machinery that had in the end but generated a phantom queen. For Mary's principal defender, William Tytler, the casket itself became a "fatal box, like Pandora's, full of every evil, [. . .] an instrument to dethrone an independent Queen [. . .] and to transmit to future ages, as infamous, a character hitherto unsullied and splendid."[16] Chivalry and evidence-mongering turned out to be reciprocal fictions, chimeras shaped by the wish to win consensus about her, and through her about British history itself.

Mary's usefulness to a new and generally agreeable sense of British history can, in fact, not be underestimated. The case of the casket letters would never have flourished except in a world suddenly glutted with antiquarians, connoisseurs and enterprising new historians. Each of these groups nursed Britain's mounting obsession with the national past; each likewise shaped the sentimental cult of the Queen of Scots. We turn to them now in order to see how, if not why, someone as slippery as Mary could have found herself at the center of a century-long project of collective self-creation, the manifestly phantasmic and yet irresistible key to almost everybody's sentimental quest for unity and self-approval.

STRANGE SATISFACTIONS

In 1775, the Scottish aristocrat and amateur antiquarian James Boswell paid a visit to Edinburgh Castle. There, he later confided to his journal, he felt a "strange satisfaction" in entering "the little room in which Queen Mary was delivered of King James VI."[17] Naturally one wonders what was so "strange" about this "satisfaction." Since Boswell liked to pose as the crony of George III, perhaps he alluded to the illicit stirrings of Jacobite sympathy that any vestige of the Queen of Scots seemed to arouse in him. Perhaps he was embarrassed that it could be so pleasurable to stand on the "little" site of so feminine an event. Or, perhaps what was "strange" was simply the fact that the past, though obviously gone, could still produce the plenitude of satisfaction in the present.

Whatever its logic, Boswell's strangely satisfying visit to Edinburgh Castle was not uncommon. On the contrary, it offers a rather fine example of what happened whenever Georgians with an antiquarian bent used the memory of Mary to bring old buildings to life before their minds' eyes. Such acts of imagination mattered in eighteenth-century Britain not least because, out of the often abstract or confusing mists of time, they could occasionally harvest evidence of improving continuity, evidence that might in its turn lend authority to a nation actually born in 1707. Conveniently, architectural relics of the "national" past littered the eighteenth-century landscape. Some, like Westminster Abbey or the castles and old country houses newly open to tours, had indeed been around in the days of the Tudors, the Bruces and the Plantagenets. Others – such as Boydell's Shakespeare Gallery, Cobham's Temple of Liberty and the Gothic Temple at Hawkwell Fields – had been built well after the Act of Union. But all of them nurtured a shared sense of history, evincing the proud tradition that, presumably, made modern Britain "great."[18]

This was, as we've seen, a highly selective tradition, one moreover uneasily entwined with the conviction that on the whole the present far surpassed the past. Mary supported both forms of historical self-approbation. For one thing, as we've seen, sympathy with her exceptionally "calamitous" sufferings could prove the gentleness and discipline of modern feelings, even as it gave those feelings a common focus in a shared history. At the same time, conjuring the Queen of Scots was also a way to re-enchant a present that conspicuously did not include her; it was a semi-mystical act which could reaffirm the majesty of modern Britain by signalling the absence of all the strife once linked to her – and so, in the end, of Mary herself. It would thus seem that the conflicts of old were merely transformed into a new, more private and invisible tension, one in which bemoaning Mary's misfortunes went hand-in-hand with making certain she was gone for good. This tension informed virtually every antiquarian effort to identify the Queen of Scots with Britain's ageing architecture.

The buildings particularly associated with Mary were invariably places where she had lost some title, blood or shred of dignity. Even the most obscure of them held an interest: in 1788, *The Gentleman's Magazine* bothered to print a diagram of the humble Edinburgh house where she was "confined" after her surrender at Carberry Hill, there to endure the "most despiteful language" of her own subjects.[19] A far more famous building in the same city, Holyrood House, was of course where Mary's Italian secretary David Rizzio had lost his life at her feet; Boswell accordingly pronounced its abbey the "most beloved object of all" and encouraged his friend John Johnston of Grange to "think on Queen Mary" there. "Be much of an Antiquarian."[20]

When one of Mary's prisons, Hardwick Hall, opened to the public, the poet Thomas Gray paid it a visit. He wrote to his doctor afterwards in a transport of melancholy pleasure: "one would think Mary Queen of Scots was but just walked down into the Park with her Guard for half-an-hour," Gray marvelled. Minutely noting that "her Gallery, her room of audience, her anti-chamber" still contained "the very canopies, chair of state, footstool, lit-de-repos, oratory, carpets, & hangings, just as she left them, [. . .] all preserv'd with religious care," Gray found an English past made palpably, even exquisitely, present through the queen's conspicuous absence from it. In Gray's reverie that sorrowful absence became the condition of communion with another time, indeed bringing time itself under the auspices of contemporary space.[21]

This may be a proprietary effect, but it is also a mystical one: Gray himself marked the "religious care" with which Mary's belongings had been "preserv'd" at Hardwick Hall. Indeed, the queen's Catholic faith (hinted at in the "oratory") quietly undergirds a modern poet's experience of her archaic prison; the charismatic objects in the "Gallery" now emptied of its tragic occupant recall the sacred relics that cannot be objects of adoration in a forward-thrusting Protestant culture. For Gray, the experience of history itself became a residual form of mysticism, the worship of objects permissible now that the act had been relieved of its potentially divisive religious charge.

No building better captures modern Britain's repudiation of Mary's Roman Catholic faith than Westminster Abbey. In Gray's day, Catholics could not, of course, hold office, inherit land or receive university degrees, but new guides to the Abbey appeared throughout the Georgian period, and all of them papered over its papist origins. Archaic royals, too, lay safely buried in the cathedral's maze of crypts, there to testify that British history had moved on, even as majestic monuments reclaimed their lives and times as the property of the present. Typically, Jodocus Crull's bestselling *Antiquities of St. Peter's* (1711) took its epigraph from Waller to commemorate an "Antique Pile" where "Royal Heads receive the Sacred Gold;/It gives them Crowns and does their Ashes keep,/There made like Gods, like Mortals there they sleep."[22]

In any scene that both evoked old royalty and confirmed its departure, Mary's tomb could only dominate. John Dart's massive *Westmonasterium* (1742) offered many dazzling fold-out reproductions of each of the Abbey's many chapels and tombs, concluding with a tour, in verse, of some of the most impressive sepulchres. Naturally, Dart lingered for pages beside that of "*Scotland's* bleeding *Queen*." Here a poignant "Marble Statue weeps," and the reader of 1742 was heartily encouraged to join it. Indeed, lamenting the "World of Grief" reserved for "unhappy *Mary*," such a reader was helpless but to mourn the "rud[e] Strokes of *Fate*" that kept an even more helpless queen "by thy rebellious Subjects long pursu'd" and eventually spurred her flight to "our unhospitable Land." But rather than share any sense of guilt for that failure of hospitality, let alone regret for the death of a certain kind of majesty, Dart lets Mary's tomb become a basin to catch the sovereign authority that drains away from her over the course of his poem:

> . . . thy fair Forehead waits the circling Gold;
> But thy stretch'd Hand no scepter'd Pow'r shall bear,
> Nor circling Gold shall bind thy Forehead fair;

> Nor shalt thou at *Eliza*'s Funeral moan,
> Nor fill the Regal Chair, nor mount the Throne:
> Thine is a melancholly Turn of *Fate*,
> A Pageantry of Death instead of *State*.[23]

With a "melancholy" Mary now safely expelled from Britain's political history, Dart's poem ends, in typically Georgian fashion, with a long reconstruction of the execution it is no longer objectionable to mourn. Symbols of coronation are emptied out, then twisted into the grotesque imagery of beheading: "Nor round thy Head refulgent Jewels beam,/But the dire Axe reflects a steely Gleam;/None from the *Onyx* mystick Ointments pour,/A dismal Unction thine! Of ruddy Gore." With such a deliciously viscous death so near, sex cannot be far behind. And indeed:

> Low groveling on the Earth thy Knees are spread,
> Thy lovely Neck unveil'd, th'unanointed Head
> Muffl'd, to wait the executing Blow,
> Then to the Crowd expos'd a publick Show;
> [. . .]
> What in the Rival could such Anger move,
> That *Pallas* thus should use the *Queen of Love*?
>
> (I: xxii)

Here the near pornography of the queen's long-ago exposure as "a publick Show" becomes acceptable through the pieties of a modern and private lament for her, the departure of all that Mary represented itself an object of desire. To mourn Mary was only to injure her again, and even to raise the erotic ghosts of the Elizabethan past in a more modern idiom of affront.

And then there was Fotheringay, that crumbling symbol of "the aggravated misfortunes of Royalty."[24] In his *History and Antiquities of . . . Fotheringay* (1787), John Nichols revisited the "concluding scene of [the] life" of a "fair and royal Unfortunate," even tendering his reader copies of Mary's last letters and a long account of her execution. He too finished with a long poem on the tomb at Westminster, one which does one better than Dart by denying that Mary is actually buried there. The "Verses on the Removal of What has been Inconsiderately Supposed the Tomb of Mary Queen of Scots, but is really the Shrine of St. Tibba," begin with their author wandering "through the long-drawn aisles of Peter's fame"; there, he tells us, he "sought for Mary's tomb, but sought in vain." But never fear: "murther'd" Mary can still be conjured in all her "shame and sorrow" (p. 79). Once this vividly imagined Mary has been vanquished by the "shafts of woe" pointed by Elizabeth Tudor's "female malice," she shows up for an execution that yet again comes across as a vaguely titillating rape. The modern speaker is naturally appalled: "'Tis base, 'tis foul: What scarce on maiden night!/Must ruffian hands those female cares supply?/Must insult thus disturb thy parting breath,/And, keener than the axe, embitter death?" (p. 81). These are the images that rise, more obeisant than genies, from Mary's supposedly empty tomb. The pages of the modern book in which they appear in turn simulate and even substantiate the unacknowl-edged rapture of the queen's demise, sharing it with a world of like-minded Britons.

Although their attachment to Mary was often mediated through the old buildings associated with her, the Georgians left those venerable forms to molder, in hot pursuit of their own desire to be affirmed by the course of past events. Mary herself could only fall sacrifice to these same desires; hence the ubiquitous spectacle of her degradation. Only thus could she support a his-torical fiction of modern British integrity and emotional wholeness; indeed, when we look back at Boswell's "strange satisfaction" with the room where Scotland's queen gave birth to the prince who would so soon replace her, we see an eerily familiar maternal sacrifice to modern fictions of identity.

THE ABDICATION

With Mary's sorrowful picture already positioned squarely before the eye of the Georgian mind, it was only a matter of time before British artists began to realize the saddest scenes from her life. Gavin Hamilton was the first: displayed at London's Royal Academy in 1776, his painting, *The Abdication* (Plate 5), was naturally an image of loss. It featured Mary giving up her crown at Lochleven, and although artists would evoke the same incident throughout the 1780s, Hamilton's *Abdication* remains uniquely revealing, for if we look closely enough we can see that its heroine perfectly mirrored the void at the heart of the informal society of artists, connoisseurs and critics whose overlapping interests made her their own.

As the Scottish historian William Robertson had put it in his influential *History of Scotland* (1759), for Mary to give up her crown had been to "consen[t] to her own bondage" – an illogical act whose meaning must consequently come from its interpreters.[25] Hamilton accordingly set the Queen of Scots off-center, so that the scene of renunciation is actually dominated by the men who are arranging it. Indeed, the only other woman present is barely visible, her face – and presumably her tears – well shielded. The result is an oddly emo-tionless tableau, the very bodies that compose it are disproportionate to themselves and weirdly torqued as if they themselves have been contorted by a certain lack of feeling. The lack is all the more perplexing since Hamilton himself had announced that "beauty in distress is what I mean to represent." What he did represent is the moment of power's reapportionment, for whereas the crown has left Mary's hand, her male companions firmly grip their own assorted instruments of authority, including a spear and the pen for signing the demission papers. Three of them, moreover, are cast in the role of spectators – a role emphasized by the framing of a soldier in the window. This is the only role that Mary cannot hope to play, and it is, we find, the decisive one.

Plate 5 The Abdication of Mary Queen of Scots, oil on canvas, 175.3 × 160.4 cm, by Gavin Hamilton. © Hunterian Art Gallery, University of Glasgow.

Demoted from a figure of sovereign authority to the object of most disobliging attention, Hamilton's Mary is also set apart from her spectators in another way. While they are mainly clad in classical dress, she wears a historical costume. The dress marks her *as* historical, in contrast to the nearly timeless abstraction of her observers.[26] Indeed, one of the painting's oddest features is that its ostensible subject does not really seem to belong in it. Hamilton's Mary is a curio, while her classicized captors' restraint and emotional control frame, distance and covertly dominate the historical relic she has become. So it is that an exceptionally awkward Queen of Scots resigns sovereign authority both thematically and formally. Her awkwardness means that, in sentimental and even aesthetic terms, the image of resignation is a failure. But, as a translation of Mary's fate into a thoroughly modern vocabulary, *The Abdication* is flawless.

The work, that is, had been commissioned by James Boswell in 1767. His own ancestor having fought on Mary's side at Carberry Hill, Boswell was personally interested in any and all objects related to "Queen Mary" – objects that not only aroused the "strange satisfaction" he felt in the birthing room at Edinburgh Castle but, equally important, connected him to other like-minded men. In Paris, for instance, the Principal at the Scots College showed him "Queen Mary's letters and testament, her prayer-book, &c., &c.," and by these he was "truly pleased, and thrown into reverend humour which kept off grief."[27]

Boswell's "grief" at that time happened to be over the recent death of his mother, and the objects concerned look very much like fetishes: that is, they stand for an absent figure of female authority in a way that permits her to be retrieved – and thereby dominated – symbolically. In Boswell's case, this solace entwined with Mary's erstwhile possessions' power to foster bonds with other, equally or more affluent men: in letters, he often begged his friend John Johnston of Grange to "mention Mary Queen of Scots and Lord Darnley, and many more of our favorite topics," and he instantly befriended a young Scotsman who visited him in London and happened to show a ring with Mary's face engraved on it.[28] More lasciviously, Boswell exchanged with other devotées such apocryphal items as "a real Petticoat of Mary Queen of Scots" and "a false Pego with which [Mary's Italian secretary] David Rizio [*sic*] was wont to tickle certain susceptible parts of that unfortunate Lady."[29]

When Boswell asked Hamilton to paint the Queen of Scots, he was in effect commissioning the biggest and best fetish object of all. The image of a lost mother at the moment of loss, Hamilton's *Abdication* could also provide Boswell with a passport to the established society of British connoisseurs – a society to which, as a mere Scot, Boswell would always be a bit of an outsider. He apparently got the idea for the painting from Robertson, whose *History of Scotland* had "carried [him] back in Imagination to the days of Scottish Grandeur; filled my mind with generous ideas of the valour of our Ancestors, and made me feel a pleasing sympathy for the beautifull accomplished Mary."[30] Mediated through another man's words, Mary's losses easily "filled" Boswell's mind; they did so, moreover in a manner eerily shadowed in Robertson's words themselves.

At the point in the *History of Scotland* that Mary's own subjects "persuad[e] or forc[e her] to resign the crown," that is, Robertson renders her desperation in the erotic terms familiar from so many Georgian visits to the scenes of her misfortunes:

> In this solitary state, without a counsellor or a friend, under the pressure of distress and the apprehension of danger, it was natural for a woman to hearken to almost any overtures. The confederates took advantage of her

condition and her fears. [. . .] Deference to their opinion, as well as concern for her own safety, obliged her to yield to every thing which was required, and to sign all the papers which Lindsay presented to her. [. . .] Mary, when she subscribed these deeds, was bathed in tears; and while she gave away, as it were with her own hands, the sceptre which she had swayed so long, she felt a pang of grief and indignation, one of the severest perhaps which can touch the human heart.[31]

Fraught with the imagery of violent seduction if not rape outright, Robertson's deliberately heart-rending version of Mary's surrender to masculine "opinion" and "papers" anticipated the way in which, in his own day, the mere image of that surrender would take on a life of its own, ultimately aligning him with Boswell and other modern "confederates."[32] This confederacy soon expanded, for when Boswell first "bespoke" his picture, he thought to guarantee it an air of "sacred solemnity" by having Hamilton model his queen on a miniature of Mary obtained from the Stuart secretary, Andrew Lumisden. The prized miniature, in its turn, was in reality a copy of a "fine painted picture" of a woman with chestnut hair and brown eyes which the enterprising engraver George Vertue had noticed in the hands of a London art dealer much earlier in the century. The portrait was eventually purchased by the confirmed bachelor Henry Boyle, Lord Carleton, who allowed Vertue to copy and sell it many times over, even to engrave it as the frontispiece of Samuel Jebb's 1725 *History* of Mary's life and reign.[33]

The Mary who finally appeared in Hamilton's painting, then, is not only a visibly strained redaction of a Stuart icon; she is really a copy of a copy, one of countless simulacra that had long been travelling back and forth among eighteenth-century British men. Her image's meaning lies not in its relationship to the historical Mary but rather in a sizeable coterie of modern connoisseurs. Hamilton himself seems to have been conscious of this when he announced that "beauty in distress is what I mean to represent and Mary's features I hope will not interfere with the representation."

For his part, Boswell felt decidedly anxious about *The Abdication*, and in the nine years it took Hamilton to complete it he paid frequent visits to the artist's studio in Rome. An early glimpse of the canvas revealed little more than a "confused" sketch. Happily, however, "by [Hamilton's] explanation [Boswell] understood it clearly and approved it much;" another day he went simply to watch Hamilton paint.[34] Such visits were bound to "interfere with the representation," but in so doing they show us how much representation's significance lay in the bond between artist and patron.

The financial transactions around *The Abdication* tell a similar story. Hamilton admired Boswell for "bespeaking a picture," for "it is only men of the greatest fortunes, like Lord Hopetoun, who do so."[35] And apparently to prove he could play in Lord Hopetoun's league, Boswell insisted on paying Hamilton two hundred pounds for the "Picture," even though Hamilton was willing to take one hundred and fifty, confident that he would more than make up the difference in proceeds from the prints. Boswell later confided to a friend that he felt "a little vain being the Patron of so a fine Picture from Scottish History; and, as times go, I may boast that I have *payed* it."[36] "Bespeaking" Mary's abdication was thus a way of consolidating identity and visibility as a "Patron," especially in relation to other potential patrons. Once more the Elizabethan appropriations of authority that structure Hamilton's canvas mirrored the Georgian jockeying that brought it into being.

As we might expect, when *The Abdication* was finally exhibited at the Royal Academy, Boswell made sure to view it in the company of Sir Joshua Reynolds, the premier artist of his generation. The master, alas, was politely disappointed: "I saw from Sir Joshua's manner of speaking before the picture was produced that he was not pleased with it," Boswell reported wistfully. Just as Boswell's own "bespeaking" commandeered the image of the Queen of Scots into another system of masculine privilege based on patronage and the display of wealth, so Reynolds' "speaking" again deprived Mary's image of independent meaning by subordinating it to a modern system of critical judgment and aesthetic taste. Ever eager for the approval of his peers and betters, Boswell of course immediately adopted Reynolds's response: "Indeed I was disappointed when I now saw it for the first time. All the figures were well but the Queen herself, who had neither beauty in a high degree, nor grace in any degree."[37]

Hamilton's painting does look awkward, even grotesque. There is a violence in its composition that comes of forcing Mary into a modern version of the Elizabethan cabals that had doomed her in the first place. But there is also a truth in this violence, for the very incongruity, even failure, of the canvas is an especially apt expression of the covertly exploitative modern cult of Mary Queen of Scots. In any case, Hamilton inaugurated an entirely new phase in the history of Mary's visual image, one no longer dominated by the forged miniatures and sundry frontispieces of the early and middle eighteenth century. After *The Abdication* the most popular depictions of the queen were narrative, dramatic, and – in keeping with the well-bred herding instincts of many eighteenth-century Britons – visible to groups of observers at a time.[38]

Hamilton's painting was imitated twice before the end of the 1780s, both times by Scottish history painters. Alexander Runciman's 1782 *Mary Queen of Scots Forced to Sign her Abdication* (Plate 6) is especially instructive, and not only because its savage strokes make such a very different impression from Hamilton's more inhibited, even crabbed, tableau. By admitting agitation into the visual field, and by infusing it with the artist's own physical tumult and nervousness, Runciman's pen and ink wash actually provides an antidote to Hamilton's canvas. If Hamilton awkwardly transferred authority to possessors and spectators, Runciman moves Mary to the center of the scene, and gives full attention to the waiting-woman Hamilton had left veiled. The very roughness and deficiency of Runciman's work place it in the truly dynamic emotional field that is so notably absent from Hamilton's remote and stilted canvas.

Plate 6 Mary Queen of Scots Forced to Sign her Abdication, by Alexander Runciman.
Courtesy of the National Gallery of Scotland.

Even more telling, however, is Boswell's idol Samuel Johnson's involvement with Hamilton's canvas. When Boswell "bespoke" his painting, he first asked the author of the book that had inspired it, William Robertson, to provide an inscription. Robertson came up with two rather sterile sentences, neither of which suited. Boswell then turned to Johnson, who had already written a glowing review of William Tytler's recently published vindication of Mary's character in light of the casket letters.[39] Johnson sent a "short and striking" inscription which Boswell rejected, on the grounds that it alluded to Mary's "hard fate" – her execution – but not to the matter at hand: "My picture," Boswell insisted, "is a representation of a particular scene in her history; her being forced to resign her crown." Johnson must "give me an inscription suited to that particular scene."[40]

If in the image of Mary's "abdication" Boswell saw an opportunity to court and possibly coerce the favor of the most illustrious men of his day, at least one of them seems to have seen something more in it – something, even, akin to another murder of the Queen of Scots. His second inscription confirmed as much: "Mary Queen of Scots, terrified and overpowered by insults, menaces and clamours of her rebellious subjects, sets her hand, with fear and confusion, to a resignation of the kingdom." Johnson's new inscription resembles the scene at hand almost as little as the first one did: Hamilton's Mary looks neither "terrified" nor "overpowered," and she is not signing anything, let alone with "fear and confusion." Moreover, the "rebellious subjects" at hand are neither insulting, menacing, nor clamoring. They are too detached for that. What then can we make of Johnson's *méconnaissance*? Why does his response to Hamilton's canvas take as its object a scene that does not even exist?

One answer to this question lies in the words that reinvest the canvas with an emotion that isn't there: "terrified," "overpowered," "fear," "confusion." Such words suggest a sympathetic attachment to Mary, one of an order which resists obsession with her as a mere object of exchange. Indeed, simply by refusing to attach the euphemism of "abdication" to a forced "resignation," Johnson treated the image of the queen's loss at Lochleven as, at last, no object at all. Instead, his inscription shows that he understood, even felt, the fatal role that the symbols and signs which reduced her to a thing – and thus potentially to nothing – had played both in Mary's own tragedy and in the patriarchal farce so recently re-enacted by the artists, critics and collectors of Georgian Britain. Johnson sees what Hamilton only suggests in the writing pen to the left of the canvas's center – that it was the will to freeze her in symbolic form (through "insults, menaces and clamours") that once stripped Mary of her sovereignty, and that does so again as she becomes a sacrifice to the modern frenzy of renown.

This is the same Johnson who would later reprimand the Keeper of the Advocate's Library in Edinburgh for his countrymen having "let your Queen remain twenty years in captivity and then be put to death."[41] He appears to have made no distinction between Scots present and past; both appeared, to him, equally guilty. Indeed, he seems to have felt especially close to Mary, perpetually aware of how her predicament could be re-enacted in the present. When his dear friend Hester Thrale was about to leave England with her Italian lover, Johnson tried to convince her that "only some phantoms of imagination" could "seduce [her] to Italy." Though he knew his "counsel [to be] vain," Johnson nonetheless "eased [his] heart" by reminding Thrale of Mary Stuart's fateful flight from Scotland into England:

> When Queen Mary took the resolution of sheltering herself in England, the Archbishop of St. Andrew's attempting to dissuade her, attended on her journey and when they came to the irremeable stream that separated the two kingdoms, walked by her side into the water, in the middle of which he seized her bridle, and with earnestness proportioned to her danger and his own affection, pressed her to return. The Queen went forward. – If the parallel reaches thus far, may it go no further. The tears stand in my eyes.[42]

These tears are very different from those, say, that the "T" family shed upon a waxwork Mary, or that antiquarian poetasters sprinkled over the many scenes of her travails. In clouding a vision that can only diminish its object, Johnson's tears open the heart, admitting Mary into the present instead of eliminating her from it. As those tears rise and "stand," time stops: movement "forward" is arrested in the sudden lacuna of sorrow that means the "parallel" can "go no further." Johnson seems to have known that it is precisely by acknowledging its difference from the past – its own limits and deficiencies – that the present truly coincides with it. So, when her archbishop wades into the water after Mary, the eighteenth-century man of letters plausibly lets himself into the picture of her life. Like his inscription for Hamilton's *Abdication*, Johnson's willingness to acknowledge his own involvement in a history of loss reminds us that the Georgian culture of sensibility did not invariably reproduce the barbarism of the past. In its interstices, reunion with Mary took on a poignancy and immediacy it could not have had before.

When Johnson's letter to Thrale was published soon after his death, a correspondent to *The Gentleman's Magazine* immediately disparaged this allusion to "Queen Mary," noting that no official history of the queen's life had ever touched upon the watery scene it evoked: "Where is the historian who mentions these romantic circumstances?"[43] But this absence is the point. Johnson's "parallel" is generated as much from within the recesses of feeling as from the filled sphere of common knowledge, shared reference object and fellow feeling. Indeed, the boundary between these seems to have been, for him, as "irremeable" as the stream that only Mary Queen of Scots could cross.

SO INTERESTING A CHARACTER

If Georgian historians never mentioned the "romantic circumstances" that meant so much to Johnson, then what exactly *did* they have to say about "Queen Mary?" A great deal, as it turns out, which is not surprising considering that Georgian historiography may be seen as the verbal equivalent of a national monument – as an attempt to create a shared and ultimately self-congratulatory impression of the past. For modern historians, this impression had to be sensible in two ways. First, it ought not to be distorted by religious zeal and political passion. New British histories prided themselves on their use of common sense and shared standards of evidence, especially as these diffused the violent partisan fervor that had surcharged the past, dispelling the murk of intrigue which shrouded the ever-questionable activities of, especially, the Elizabethans.

The first historians to write both for a popular audience and for the presumably unified body of Great Britain had to be sensible in a more physical sense as well. Adam Smith very typically opined that the "historicall stile" should concern itself with those objects which "interest us greatly by the Sympatheticall affections they raise in us."[44] Concerned to bind itself to its living readers, the new tribe of British historians thus "raise[d]" whatever "Sympatheticall affections" it could. Besides fostering a collectivity that understood itself and its past in both narrative and affectionate terms, a history of sensibility promised to widen the circle of available readers that included more and more women. And of all historical figures, it was Mary Queen of Scots who held out the most irresistible of emotional bribes. As early as 1739, a biography of "that Excellent Princess Queen Elizabeth" appended a "Life of Mary Stuart" because Mary's story alone boasted "something so interesting in the whole course of it, and so very mournful in the catastrophe" that it necessarily won admission to the modern heart.[45]

"So interesting" a character automatically riveted readers of sensibility to narratives about the national past. But she could also disrupt the progressive flow of historical narrative, as well as that of moral judgment. For just that reason, Hume – whose *History of England* was by far the most influential of its kind – struggled to maintain a skeptical distance from "the most amiable of women." In private life Hume once even bellowed into the ear of one of her defenders that "Queen Mary was a whore."[46] But since it was impossible to leave her trials and tribulations out of any account of England's history, Hume sought some way to exploit the emotions sure to be aroused by someone so "unfortunate in her life."

It seems to have occurred to the Scottish historian that, just as sensibility could soften and civilize, so might the sad sight of Mary's sufferings chasten its witnesses. In Hume's account of the "melancholy scene" of her execution, he thus claims that as their "attention [. . .] was fixed on the melancholy scene before them," her spectators' "zeal and flattery alike gave place to present pity and admiration of the expiring princess."[47] Here the same tableau that P.T. would render into wax transforms partisan, disruptive and even barbarous emotions like "zeal and flattery" into the unifying, civilizing, comfortingly "present" sentiments of "pity and admiration." In turn, Hume used the execution scene not just to demonstrate how Mary affected her Elizabethan spectators but also to school his own Georgian readers. For he meant those readers to take a balanced – a modern, enlightened, sensible – view of the Queen of Scots herself. Thus, even as most of the *History* acknowledges the many blots upon Mary's reputation, it is only by making her suffering present to his readers that Hume felt he could teach them "to form a just idea of her character" (IV: 251).

Mary also became an attractive, if unreliable, vehicle of collective apprehension – and modern self-congratulation – in Robertson's *History of Scotland*, a book that Hume recommended to one of his closest female friends precisely for its "highly lamentable and tragical portrait" of Mary's life.[48] Robertson purveyed the story of his country's past to "every British subject" as an "object of curiosity" that ought to be especially captivating now that, happily, Scotland and England were one.[49] And what better bribe to "curiosity" than the Queen of Scots? As Robertson's biographer Dugald Stewart observed in 1801:

> All [Robertson's] prepossessions (if he had any on this subject) must have been in favour of the Queen; for, it was chiefly from the powerful interest

excited by her story, that he could hope for popularity with the multitude; and, it was only by the romantic pictures which her name presents to the fancy, that he could accommodate to the refinement of modern taste, the annals of a period, where perfidy, cruelty, and bigotry, appear in all their horrors. [. . .] Indeed, without the aid of so interesting a character, the affairs of Scotland, during the period he treats of, could not have derived, even from his hand, a sufficient importance and dignity to engage the curiosity of the present day.[50]

More an eighteenth-century lady helplessly stranded outside her own time than a sixteenth-century queen, in Stewart's view Mary wooed the "modern taste" for "interesting" objects of curiosity. "So interesting a character" naturally aided Robertson in his campaign to seduce "the multitude" into a unified view of Britain's past.

To enlist her, though, carried perils of its own, for at the same time that Mary's involving charms marked her as a refugee from a modern culture of sensibility, they opened a potential chasm in the very narrative she was meant to domesticate and modernize. Their source was finally her sorrow, and as Robertson had ample occasion to observe, the queen's sufferings:

> exceed, both in degree and in duration, those tragical distresses which fancy has feigned to excite sorrow and commiseration; and while we survey them, we are apt altogether to forget her frailties, we think of her faults with less indignation, and approve of our tears as if they were shed for a person who had attained much nearer to pure virtue.[51]

It would seem that the excesses of "sorrow" Mary both endured and provoked not only undermine sorrow's socializing function: sympathetic investment in the Queen of Scots is apt to evolve into a form of "forget[ting]." And what is forgotten is not only the queen's "frailties" but also our own as self-congratulating moral judges of the modern age. This in turn leads us to falsely value our tears, in a way that disarranges the economy of meaning in which they properly belong. It also induces us to take as the object of emotion someone ("a person who had attained much nearer to pure virtue") who does not exist. Mary, in other words, equals both excess and privation – an excess of suffering and hence a privation of being, both of the subject and of the object. Just as she did in the other avenues of sensibility we have explored, she here uncovers the void at the heart of the sentimental method so crucial to eighteenth-century historiography. The most useful tool in the campaign to gain a common sensible view of the past, the Queen of Scots also threatens to overturn the stabilizing rhetorical techniques that had replaced the freewheeling and tirelessly inquisitive voices of the Stuart historians. Partly by provoking the treason of pity that had infiltrated so much of the literature about her in her own day, she could now turn modern versions of history into a romance of identification.

When in 1791 a teenage Jane Austen wrote her parody of eighteenth-century historiography, the diminutive *History of England*, she quite logically made that "bewitching princess" Mary Queen of Scots the heroine of the piece. Illustrated by her sister Cassandra with wry cameos of both Mary and Elizabeth, Austen's *History* miniaturizes and domesticates English history, abbreviating the life of every monarch it depicts and expressing far more interest in Henry VIII's "riding through the Streets of London with Anna Bullen" than in the broad canvas of political and religious upheaval that characterized his reign.[52] The centerpiece of English history so belittled can only be the "amiable" Mary, brought as she was to an "untimely, unmerited and scandalous death." Austen ostentatiously succumbs to Mary's legendary charms and sympathizes lavishly with her exorbitant sufferings. She thereby cheerfully sabotages her own postures of authority, betraying first her historian persona's thorough failure of impartiality and then the pretenses and pretensions that shaped so many Georgian ways of remaking the past. In her deliberately small way, Austen showed how heavily the sensible and self-approving "history of England" had come to depend on the one fiction of sensibility bound to turn it on its head – the sorrowful story of Mary Queen of Scots.

"Dozens of ugly Mary Queen of Scotts"

The women of Britain, 1725–1785

Jane Austen's droll postscript to a largely male-authored history of Britain arouses the suspicion that women of her day might have made their own investment in that "bewitching Princess," Mary Stuart. Austen herself flirted with the possibility: the narrator of her *History of England* joins forces with not only Mary's antiquarian defender John Whitaker, but also an otherwise unspecified "Mrs. Lefroy and Mrs. Knight" when she declares herself Mary's unconditional "friend."[1] Yet when we look to the many Georgian women who indeed do seem to have had Mary on their minds, we find something altogether more puzzling than a certain lack of objectivity about her. Or, rather, that is quite literally what we do find, for a significant number of these women seem to have been under the impression that it was actually possible to become the Queen of Scots.

Looking back on the fashion trends of the previous century, Austen's own contemporary, James Malcolm, noted that the most popular "Ladies Headdress in 1765 is said to have exactly resembled that of Mary Queen of Scots as represented in her portraits."[2] And in the middle of the eighteenth century the aesthete and dilettante Horace Walpole complained that the most Georgian of institutions, the masquerade, had become overrun with "dozens of ugly Mary Queen of Scotts." On one occasion, even "the Princess of Wales was one, covered with diamonds."[3] Meanwhile, both the aristocratic Mary Bellende and, presumably, the Irish actress Peg Woffington, sat for their portraits clad in sixteenth-century costumes meant to identify them as the tragic Stuart queen.

So many female impersonations of the Queen of Scots naturally express the general desire to make physical contact with the past that provoked, for instance, a mid-century rage for the Vandyke style. But there is a difference between the sentimental attempts to turn Mary into a doll – or a clutch of relics, or an estimable canvas – which we observed in Chapter 5, and many Georgian women's sense that they in some way *were* her. The ghost of inauthenticity which only haunts and reproves the former, fetishistic enterprise is here what makes the illusion of identity with Mary possible. What is more, whereas Georgians like Boswell and his cronies seem to have needed Mary's finally vacant image to feel visible and unique, the masquerade version of her is infinitely replicable: any number of "ugly Mary Queen of Scotts" could roam the assembly rooms of contemporary London, the Princess of Wales herself but one of them. The working-class poet Mary Leapor was no princess, for instance, but quite like one she failed to "spy" any "odds" between herself and the "Queen of *Scots.*"[4]

This epidemic of impersonations creates the impression that in Georgian Britain there were at once hundreds of Queen Marys about, and absolutely none at all. But from such a befuddling concoction of excess and anonymity, we can at least conclude that the "dozens" of women who all but became Mary may have seen, and used, her very differently from the way their male counterparts did. Indeed, their tendency to disappear into an embodied fantasy of the Queen of Scots suggests they may not have been "seeing" or "using" her at all. Besides the leading actresses (Anne Oldfield, George Anne Bellamy, Peg Woffington) who imitated Mary onstage, affluent and decidedly non-theatrical women like Bellende posed in period dress against backdrops that, at least in Bellende's case, were most remarkable for what they lacked, or, to put it positively, for the chasms that filled them. In Charles Jervas's portrait, oddly enough, no prop or detail of costume indicated that this was Mary; without such cues Mary Bellende could be anyone, herself and the Queen of Scots being but two of the possibilities.

At first, no such enigma seems to plague Hogarth's later portrait, reputedly of the Irish actress Woffington's sister Mary Cholmondeley dressed as the queen her sister had played on stage (Plate 7). Here certain signature accessories – chiefly a widow's cap and a cross – at least aim to conjure the historical Mary. The irony of Hogarth's portrait, though, is that opinion is divided as to whether its subject might not be Peg Woffington dressed as the character she played in Covent Garden or whether it is indeed Mary Cholmondeley, dressed either as Mary Queen of Scots or possibly as Peg Woffington dressed as Mary. Caught in so long a hall of mirrors, one can only conclude that the likeness is actually of the Queen of Scots herself.[5]

Even after the eighteenth century drew to a close, British women continued to see Mary as many women, not just one. The 22-year-old poet Mary Roberts's lengthy series of lyrics in Mary Stuart's voice was for example prefaced with the observation that while portraits of the Queen of Scots were not hard to come by, there were not "any two which greatly resemble each other. Nay, they so far differ as to have various coloured hair and eyebrows, Roman, Grecian and turned up noses; blue and hazel eyes and complexions of many different shades, dark and fair."[6] Yet these many versions of the queen seemed to make it more, not less, possible to glimpse oneself in her: in her poems, collectively titled *The Royal Exile*, Roberts assumed Mary's voice with confidence, filling hundreds of pages with the queen's sometimes wistful, sometimes lurid reveries before her doting father added a long historical introduction and trundled the lot off to a receptive London press.

A male friend took a similar interest in the work of the ageing Scotswoman Margaretta Wedderburn, whose *Mary Queen of Scots. An Historical Poem* appeared

Plate 7   Most Probably Peg Woffington as Mary Queen of Scots, by William Hogarth. © The Lord Egremont. Photograph courtesy of the Courtauld Institute of Art.

in 1811 with Wedderburn herself featured on the frontispiece. Wedderburn warned readers who expected to see "the usual vivacity naturally impressed upon the countenance of the once-lovely Margaretta" that they would "find it difficult to recognize" the face "which 'now the hue of sorrow wears.'" In fact, Wedderburn meant her portrait to be mistaken for the long sorrowing Mary's; in it, "the once-lovely Margaretta" even assumes Mary's widow's cap, partly to compensate readers for the fact that she had been able to find no accurate "likeness" of the queen herself with which to grace the first page of her book.[7]

By dressing as Mary Stuart, and even assuming her voice, certain Georgian women evidently folded themselves into an object of identification that they knew to be elusive, even phantasmic – neither quite present nor altogether real. After all, when Malcolm mentioned that "the Ladies Head-dress in 1765 is said to have exactly resembled that of Mary Queen of Scots as represented in her portraits," he most definitely was *not* claiming that the "Ladies" were miming Mary herself; rather, they were copying "portraits" of her. In this plethora of resemblances Mary herself tended to vanish, but so did the women who discovered that they could have been her. The queen's motto (*in my end is my beginning*) makes disappearances like these at least fitting, for it seems to predict that the oddly interchangeable women who recreated Mary in their words and next to their flesh would do so precisely by making the Queen of Scots anonymous as well.

Of this shared anonymity the most articulate example may be found in the washerwoman-turned-poet Mary Leapor's 1751 poem "The Consolation." Here, Leapor imagines her own death, the moment when "some kind friend [. . .] shall lay/This body in its destin'd clay." It is in the image of the "destin'd clay" – the grave – that our modern-day Mary finds connection with the Mary of old: though she pictures her own headstone as a "plain stone with chizel form'd" (and thus very different from the "lying marble" she has noticed in Westminster Abbey), it is nonetheless "inscribed with 'Natus Anno Dom/Here lies Mary in this tomb.'" And this inscription permits Leapor's speaker to conclude that "there's no odds that I can spy,/'Twixt Mary Queen of Scots and I." The "consolation" of the title lies in this reflection, and the Mary Queen of Scots it invokes could scarcely look less like the satisfyingly entombed monarch so voluptuously re-executed, say, in Dart's "Westminster Abbey."[8]

From one point of view, of course, the Mary Leapor who realizes that there are "no odds" between the Queen of Scots and herself merely denies that there is any difference between a working woman and a queen; the universal inevitabilities of death and dissatisfaction level them. But this commonplace only thinly veils a complex and oddly realistic engagement with the figure of Mary Stuart. What makes Leapor like – if not into – the Queen of Scots is not just a common mortality but also the fact that each has been absorbed into the signs which represent her. In sharing the same inscription ("Here lies Mary in this tomb"), queen and laundry maid inhabit the same place within language itself. Both rely on words in order to be recognized, even though those words can only announce their absence. In other words, they share the same unreality.

It is by embracing unreality as a condition of being, however, that Leapor becomes her own reader, and in time Mary's. Visibly indebted to the protocols of sensibility, this sense of self as both subject and object, disappearing body and malleable sign, creates a perversely immediate connection with the Stuart queen, even bringing her back to life in a present-day woman's conviction that she herself is as good as dead. So, let's say that a sense of not quite being did bind (Mary) Leapor not just to Mary Stuart, but to (Mary) Bellende, (Mary) Roberts and (Mary) Cholmondeley as well. Where on earth could it have come from?

Plate 8 Mary Queen of Scots, engraving by Shervin, from a painting by Zucchiro, in the possession of F. Tunberman Esq., in Hume's *History of England* (1788).

Plate 9 Elizabeth I, engraving, in Hume's *History of England* (1788).

FICTIONS OF FEMININITY

If Mary Leapor's "Consolation" is any indication, Mary Stuart's exceptional resonance for eighteenth-century British women owed something to her inherent fictionality – to her confinement in stories and images almost always managed by someone other than herself. But it also had something to do with what the Georgians saw as her exemplary femininity. Over the course of the eighteenth century, Britons grew more and more exercised over the "female character." They longed to agree about what it was, what its role in a peaceable and prosperous modern society should be, what kind of power it implied women should or did possess. Alexander Pope's cynical speculation that "most Women have no Characters at all" tripped continually over conduct books and sentimental novels which presented the high-strung female – "fine by defect and delicately weak" – as the figurehead of the new sensibility.[9]

The cult of vulnerable femininity that took shape in the middle of the eighteenth century was in great part a work of fiction, for it was both engendered and reflected by new literary heroines of sensibility like Samuel Richardson's Pamela Andrews and Clarissa Harlowe, or Henry Fielding's Amelia Booth. Ever in distress, these wildly popular heroines were often more desperately concerned to protect their reputations – their symbolic bodies – than they were their fleshly ones. And it is no accident that Richardson's Clarissa, who vindicates a reputation built in letters only by dying, was compared to Mary Queen of Scots by her would-be lover and eventual rapist, Lovelace.[10] Correspondingly, John Whitaker's three-volume *Mary Queen of Scots Vindicated* (1787) attributed Mary's scandalous elopement with Bothwell to the "amatorious poisons" with which the earl must surely have drugged her – to those "practices, which Lovelace actually uses upon Clarissa, STUPIFYING DRAUGHTS."[11]

So easily mistaken for Clarissa, the Mary of fragile reputation always struck Georgians more as a vulnerable woman than as an autonomous queen. "Formed with the qualities which we love, not with the talents that we admire," decided Robertson, Mary was "an agreeable woman rather than an illustrious queen."[12] Illustrations for Hume's magisterial *History of England* (1778, Plates 8 and 9) confirm the difference between the shrewd, successfully regnant Elizabeth Tudor and her imperilled cousin once-removed: while Mary's sweet, lace-draped likeness is framed by two diaphanous women, stern men flank Elizabeth's crowned and calculating one.

Mary's needlepoint, her elegant and touching letter-writing, her vulnerability to male predators and manmade sign systems and her poignantly frustrated maternal affections all anticipated the signal virtues of the new eighteenth-century lady – sisters, mothers and daughters now often charged with the softening and civilizing of a new British manhood. But, in Mary's case, queenly excesses and complexities often had to be pared away to make her "true" docility visible. When, for instance, George Ballard wanted to enroll the Queen of Scots among his illustrious "Ladies of Great Britain," he had to fight to overlook the uncertainties that clouded "her conduct in life." Ballard diverted Mary's notoriously strong erotic "inclinations" into devotion to the needle, insisting that "when she followed most her own inclinations, she would be employed amongst her women in needlework." And though the adulterous casket letters had been reprinted as recently as 1720, Ballard doggedly praised Mary's "stric[t] obedience and most obliging behaviour toward her husband" Darnley, her willingness to "observ[e] all the connubial duties with a peculiar sweetness of temper and incomparable address."[13]

Though far more skeptical than Ballard, Hume too conceded that "the beauties of her person and graces of her air combined to make [Mary] the most amiable of women," adding that "the charms of her address and conversation aided the impression, which her lovely figure made on the hearts of all beholders." Indeed, to him, Mary "seemed to partake only so much of the male virtues as to render her estimable, without relinquishing those soft graces, which compose the proper ornament of her sex."[14] Yet despite the "soft graces" and pleasing vulnerability to interpretation that made her a most interesting object in the culture of high sensibility, Hume's Mary, like Ballard's, is not an entirely convincing paragon of modern womanhood. The historian's seemingly approving catalogue of the "soft graces, which compose the popular ornament of her sex" denatures Mary's femininity as much as it exalts it: her "beauties" and "graces" artfully "combin[e] to make her the most amiable of women," while her "lovely figure" creates a decidedly aesthetic "impression." Not only does Mary herself seem unreal, but her all but explicit artifice betrays the "ornament[al]" nature of "proper" femininity itself, its true insubstantiality.

Mary's at best ambiguous and at worst scarlet sexual history continually threatened to expose her ladylike "beauties" and "graces" as mere masquerades. But if those qualities are not real, then neither are the ideals invested in them. For all her popularity, Mary therefore stood as an ironic icon of Georgian femininity. Even as she promised to gratify eighteenth-century Britons' desire to adulate the domestic woman of sensibility, the Queen of Scots remained the surest sign that, like the cultural power ascribed to her, such a woman was in reality nothing more than a pliable fiction. She was, in fact, nobody at all.[15]

THE REAL CAUSES OF ALL HER MISFORTUNES

Say, then, that it was the manmade tie of cultural invisibility, unto nonexistence, that bound Mary Leapor, Mary Bellende, Mary Cholmondeley, Mary Roberts and Georgian women of a hundred other names under the sign of Mary Stuart. To the extent that it reflected female complexity's disappearance into a self-consciously British fiction of femininity, that tie could prove especially binding for women who took up the pen. Then too, like anyone else in their line of work, British women writers were both materially concerned with the nature of fiction and conscious of their public role in the making of a distinctively British panoply of virtues – a role which included everything from the cultivation of the modern reader of sensibility to the forging of a proudly anglophone British literary tradition.

At least in the early stages of her long career, the popular novelist Eliza Haywood is not thought to have advanced either of these causes very far. Her first fiction was as racy as could be, its ebullient sentences giving rise to uninhibited and clever heroines whose quests for pleasure in turn pleased especially female readers throughout the early 1720s. But such tastes found themselves gravely chastened as a high culture of sensibility settled into place, and Haywood salvaged her literary reputation only by turning to long, didactic novels whose relatively vacant heroines bore little resemblance to the intrepid, enterprising vixens she had created in her youth. Haywood's literary life thus exemplifies the predicament of many British women of her day, whose cultural authority increasingly depended on the disguise, if not repudiation, of desire.

In 1725, however, Haywood published a long biography of Mary Queen of Scots, a rambunctious *tour de force* that eerily rehearses the dilemmas which beset female authority as the culture of sensibility usurped its name. Promising to leak the "Secret History" of Mary Stuart's "Life and the Real Causes of All Her Misfortunes," Haywood's *Mary Stuart, Queen of Scots* exposed a growing sentimental obsession with Mary's "Misfortunes" to the old frisson of sexual suggestion. At the same time, in designating her book a "Secret History," Haywood aligned her *Mary Stuart* at least as much with the scandalous memoirs popular in the free-wheeling days of the Stuarts as with the kind of sober and self-congratulating historiography Georgians like Hume would eventually render *de rigeur*. Finally, as a translation of the French Catholic economist Pierre de Boisguillebert's *Marie Stuart, Reyne d'Escosse* (1675), *Mary Stuart* held court on the cusp between male and female, English and French, and even Protestant and Catholic literary voices.

Its refusal to fit into any single category naturally identified Haywood's *Mary Stuart* with the multifoliate and elusive queen of Stuart and Elizabethan times. But even this was not a perfect alignment, for Haywood's biography was also very much in tune with its own times, making its debut in the middle of a decade that had already spawned several reprints of Mary's letters (usually apocryphal), a *faux* memoir of her imprisonment and death, three new biographies, and a four-volume folio collection of manuscripts pertaining to her. There could not have been a better time to bring Mary back to life.

For her part, Haywood carried off the task with a peculiarly female dexterity. It was not one that has been readily appreciated by literary critics: *Mary Stuart* was, for example, dismissed by Haywood's rebarbative but influential biographer, George Frisbie Whicher, as barely "distinguishable from her fiction." And it was misread by him as a "translation of fifteen or sixteen French biographies of the romantic Mary," not just one. Whicher also misconstrued the success of Haywood's translation which, according to him, "enjoyed but a languid sale" and yet somehow "passed into a second edition, which continued to be advertised as late as 1743."[16] In fact, Haywood's rendering of Mary's life remained the most popular of its kind until Hume's far higher-minded *History of England* replaced it; an edited version was even attached to an influential 1754 biography of Elizabeth Tudor as if to confirm Haywood's disingenuous vow "that this which now offers itself to [the reader's] Perusal, is not a *Romance*, but a *True-History*."[17]

Romance it might be, true history perhaps; but Haywood's work was foremost itself a misreading, and it is in her compulsive failures to translate Boisguillebert's *Marie Stuart* accurately that we encounter the Mary Queen of Scots who privately made herself known to so many Georgian women. While at first Haywood's heroine would not seem to exist except as the ghost of another's language, she turns out to be a most rebellious one. It is her rebellions, inseparable from the translator's deviations from her "original," which make Haywood's "Secret History" a perfect example of how Georgian women maintained themselves, and Mary, in their culture's — indeed their language's — gaps and vacancies, which is to say in the recesses that the Queen of Scots had fashioned for them.

Haywood's first error of translation was to designate *Mary Stuart* a "Secret History." In doing so, she traded the genre Boisguillebert had assigned to Mary's story — that of the "histoire très-veritable" — for a type of women's writing that had been especially popular in Britain in the last days of (nominally) Stuart rule. Under Anne, secret histories gave women writers access to political expression: pretending to expose courtly intrigues — often sexual ones — female-authored secret histories seldom told the truth. What they did do was reunite politics with Eros in a way that Mary Queen of Scots herself might have found highly congenial.[18] Through its subtitle alone, Haywood's *Mary Stuart* thus claims kinship with this subgenre of women's writing, so recently declined, and beyond that with the enigmatic and erotically powerful Mary whom we ourselves have glimpsed in the queen's own letters, in the defense she delivered at her treason trial, and even between the lines of contemporary reports of encounters with her. At the same time, Haywood's Mary also strongly resembles the headstrong, highly sexualized heroines of the popular amatory fictions that, like the scandalous memoirs, had been pioneered by Stuart-era women like Aphra Behn. These too were about to disappear from the literary landscape, but Haywood's Mary still partakes of their splendors. A "Lady of [. . .] Spirit," she revels in all the "Ardors and Impatiencies of a violent Affection" for more than one of the men in her life. But "the darling Passion" of her "Soul" is *"Ambition"*: "She burn'd with a Desire of Rule!" (p. 6).

Haywood's Mary's frankly sexual desire for love and power identifies her not just with women's secret histories and with Haywood's fictive heroines but also with the secret historian herself. This identification is reinforced throughout *Mary Stuart* because Haywood's Mary is above all a woman writer of the most "fertile Invention," one who, according to Haywood, left behind innumerable "elegant Pieces" and "Odes [that] discover a certain Sublimity of Sentiment, a vivacity of Wit, and Strength of Judgement, which few of our Male Poets since can equal" (p. 3). If they are exaggerated here, Mary's literary accomplishments nonetheless make her virtually one with the shamelessly prolific Haywood. The modern British writer confirms this identification by altering Mary's own letters as she reproduces them, ostensibly verbatim, in her own text.

This identification, though, cannot be fully appreciated as long as we merely count the ways in which Haywood made Mary like herself. In fact, the female translator only becomes visible in the infinitely translated, infinitely misapprehended Queen of Scots when we more squarely confront Haywood's failure to understand her original, Boisguillebert's *Marie Stuart*. For it is finally, if ironically, in Haywood's consciously feminine misprisions of Boisguillebert's "histoire très-veritable" that the Queen of Scots most fully materializes for us, Haywood's own readers.

As a translator, Haywood was to some extent volunteering a national service. By bringing the work of other nations into her own language, she was filling and fortifying the English tongue – a symbolic system which, like the story of the nation's past, was fast growing into yet another proof of Britain's unity and excellence in modernity. Yet as she embellished certain parts of Boisguillebert's text and depleted others, Haywood was, however playfully, denying the English its due. Indeed, her looseness with her French original finally strikes us less as a subversion – of a male-authored text by a woman writer, say, or of French by English – than as a teasing seduction, one that places Haywood in formal alliance with the notoriously seductive Queen of Scots.

Reading Haywood's "Secret History" of her life, it is impossible to forget that the French-speaking, secret letter-loving Mary once cast herself as an alien to English laws and conventions of expression – some of which, like the Bond of Association, were even invented to destroy her. In turn, the language Haywood herself finally seems to be seducing – leading astray – is not French but English, ever more the badge of proper Britishness. Haywood clearly saw Mary's most bitter enemy to be the symbolic constructions of others. Far more diligently than Boisguillebert, she traces the queen's progressive alienation from both the inimical and the amiable fictions that usurped her in her own lifetime, often noting the queen's tragic failure to "defend her *Fame* from the Appearances of Ill." As a result, Haywood tersely remarks, "her Authority had never been more limited." The victim of the rumor and propaganda ever aiming to limit and at last replace her, Haywood's Mary finds it harder and harder to recognize herself: by the time she is about to lose her crown, she (in a phrase unique to Haywood) "appear'd so cover'd with Dust and Tears, that her Face was hardly to be known" (p. 110).

What obscures Haywood's Mary is not just the slanders forged by the "Malice of her Enemies" (p. 19), but also her own burgeoning iconography of misfortune. Haywood interrupts Boisguillebert to persuade "any one" who happens to be reading to:

> form an Idea to himself of a young Princess of two and twenty years of Age, surrounded on all sides with Malecontents, Traitors, and People of a different Religion, and far from taxing her with imprudence, they will

pity the cruel necessity she was in, and conclude, that from the Time of her leaving *France*, her Life had been a continu'd Series of Misfortunes, in which she had only the Liberty to chuse which she wou'd fall into.

(p. 102)

This choiceless Mary hardly chimes with the queen of violent affections and ambitions we meet elsewhere in Haywood's "Secret History." Her failure to do so may be what persuaded Haywood's critics to believe that she had translated dozens of French authorities instead of one. Yet, as Haywood hints that the "real Cause" of Mary's "Misfortunes" was precisely the English compulsion to make symbolic use of her – thereby to eliminate her independent and self-determining meanings – she also seems to ask her readers to witness precisely the conflict between an autonomous and openly longing Mary and the pathetic creature forced by the English to "fall into" one pre-ordained system of meaning after another. Haywood's Mary has no choice but to end her life entirely, even bizarrely, alienated from the woman she knows herself to be, "thinking that she should have been beheaded after the *French* manner, that is, kneeling; but at last stretching her Neck upon the Block" (p. 240). When an English axe replaces the French sword Mary had requested, our attention is drawn to the fact that it is a symbol of Englishness which both shatters her body and forever quenches her desire.

Until this bloody end, Haywood's Mary stays secretly ambitious and wishful, her burning "Desire for Rule" only forced under cover as the myth of misfortune closes in around her. Significantly, Mary's "Desire for Rule" survives the longest in her relationship to language. Haywood amplifies Mary's mastery of "the Grounds of the *Latin*, *Italian*, *French*, and *Scotch* Tongues," noting that:

> there are at this day to be seen, among other curious Manuscripts, some Odes in *French* of her own composing; which, allowing for the alternation which Time makes in all the living Languages, discover a certain Sublimity of Sentiment, a Vivacity of Wit, and Strength of Judgment, which few of our Male Poets since can equal. And if the best Picture we can have of the Soul of any Person, is in their Works, as sure it is, we may judge by those elegant Pieces she has left behind her, that she had all the different Excellencies of those Nations whose Languages she was Mistress of – the Gaiety and Politeness of the *French*! – the *Latian* Solidity and Depth of Thought! – the *Italian* Majesty and Softness mix'd! – and the natural Wisdom of her native Country!

(p. 84)

Boisguillebert's resumé of Mary's accomplishments was infinitely more brief, mentioning only her French verses. In fact, the French historian confined the queen to one language, whereas Haywood gives her free play at the intersection of many. It is finally as a writer – one very much akin to a translator – that Haywood most fully escapes the constraints of any single system of meaning.

More striking still, Haywood hesitates to treat the many languages at Mary's command as so many vowels and consonants. They are instead extensions of non-verbal, even pre-verbal, qualities – "Solidity and Depth," for example, "Gaiety and Politeness," "Majesty and Softness." Partly to compensate for her loss of political power, Haywood's Mary Stuart thus cultivates a unique relationship to language, one that mischievously exposes its plurality and wealth of alternatives and the inability of any one tongue to be all and all, even as it apprehends the depth and glory of the world beyond words to which Mary may nonetheless give access. By appreciating – even participating in – the way Mary used language, Haywood's own words forge a unique intimacy, if not an identity, with their referent, the Queen of Scots.

Although the one language Haywood's Mary does not seem to speak is English, it is through her declared mastery of rival languages that Haywood's mistranslations of Boisguillebert conjure a Queen of Scots at once old and new, one who rules at last in the cracks and fissures between different languages. Haywood's Mary survives in what language finally leaves out – in what we might almost call reality. In turn, Haywood's commitment to what words may not say alters her relationship with what they may say in her own language, English. For, to the extent that she is identified with the francophone Mary, the translator must herself be outside English. This continual blurring of distinction between what is properly one's language and what is not is what makes Haywood's own English seem peculiarly foreign.[19]

It is also what makes us feel that "Mary Stuart" has somehow seduced Eliza Haywood into becoming part of her; indeed, both *Mary Stuart*'s author and its heroine feel most fully present in our own failure to track them down. Haywood intimates that an older and more complex Mary – a Mary who seems, eerily, of a piece with the historical Queen of Scots – survived *in* women's language, and so, to the extent that we speak ourselves into being, she survived in the women themselves. The "real Cause of all her Misfortunes" may have been Mary's too-unsettling claims upon the psychological and linguistic structures that made Britain and Britons, or it might have been those structures themselves. Most likely, though, it is the complicity between the two that "caused" her persistence in female fantasy. Haywood's apprehension that this is true is reluctantly tragic; embedded in the sad story of all Mary's misfortunes is a narrative of female desire always on the verge of comic fulfillment. As the eighteenth century wore on, that comic potential faded away. Sixty years after Haywood's *Mary Stuart*, only its absence was available to shape the work of the gothic novelist Sophia Lee.

THE RECESS

Ellinor and Matilda, the twin heroines of Lee's epistolary novel of sensibility, *The Recess* (1783–1785), have been brought up in deepest secrecy. The only home they have ever known is the "Recess" of Lee's title – an amazingly well-appointed cave that lies hidden beneath a ruined monastery in the middle of Elizabethan England. The only parent they have ever known is their surrogate mother, one Mrs. Marlow, who as the novel begins has told them nothing about who they are or why they are being reared so oddly. But one day, "being deprived of [. . .] books," Ellinor and Matilda wander through hitherto unexplored recesses of the recess in search of "whole-length pictures" from which, "to amuse a part of our melancholy leisure," they might "invent tales." They come upon one which "represented a lady in the flower of youth, drest in mourning, and seeming in every feature to be mark'd by sorrow; a black veil half-shaded a coronet she wept over." Rushing in to fill the void of linguistic privation, this image exerts an almost supernatural influence upon the twins. But instead of provoking words, Matilda recalls, it "seemed to call forth a thousand melting sensations; the tears rushed involuntarily into our eyes, and clasping, we wept upon the bosoms of each other."[20]

Pathos's influx into the abyss of "seeming" tells us what any Georgian would have guessed immediately: the full-length picture is of none other than Mary Queen of Scots. Indeed, it bears a striking resemblance to Gavin Hamilton's *Abdication*, and, though they do not as yet know the identity of the "lady in the flower of youth," Lee's Elizabethan heroines respond to the spectacle of lost female authority like good, sentimental eighteenth-century Britons: they sob convulsively. As happened when P.T.'s family viewed his wax-work replica of Mary's execution, the twins' tears make the scene of their own sorrow more visible and impressive than that of Mary's.

But in one crucial respect our heroines' unconscious response to the queen's likeness is unique. For before long Ellinor and Matilda learn that the lady who "seem[s] in every feature to be mark'd with sorrow" is their own mother. On her deathbed, Mrs. Marlow tells them as much, adding that Mary, a threat to the Tudor state, is now in captivity somewhere aboveground. "'Your mother lives,'" she rather brutally reassures the twins, "'but not for you.'" The fruit of a secret marriage to the Duke of Norfolk, Mary's daughters have been hidden outside history, the better to protect them from the insecure, vindictive Elizabeth and her bloodthirsty ministers. More exactly, they have been secreted deep in history's recesses of "seeming" and feeling. The remaining 900 pages of Lee's "Tale of Other Times" chart their efforts to deliver themselves from these recesses. But *The Recess*'s own status as fiction, not history, would seem to supply proof positive of their failure to do so.

In point of fact, Mary's daughters do manage to leave their womblike, tomblike cavern for Elizabeth's court, the enclave of fiction for the public space of recorded history. Fearful of discovery, Ellinor and Matilda stay in disguise and so remain undocumented; still, both become involved with actual historical persons. Matilda falls in love with, and marries, one of Elizabeth's favorites, the Earl of Leicester. Ellinor makes a bad marriage to a sadistic noble much her senior but falls in love with Elizabeth's other darling, the Earl of Essex. Along with several *rapprochements* with the Tudor queen herself, their erotic lives keep the twins in what we might call the negative space of history's tableau.

From the start, Mary's daughters confirm that tableau's contours without actually appearing in it. And over the course of Lee's novel they lose all hope of ever doing so. After Essex's death, Ellinor – who has flirted with madness since her mother's execution – expires in anguish before his portrait. Matilda fares little better. Though she leaves England for the South Seas and bears a daughter she adores, she lives to see the girl die of poison in an English prison, the indirect victim of Matilda's half-brother, James I. Told in the form of a long letter from Matilda to a French and female friend, *The Recess* ends with Mary's sole surviving daughter looking forward to the oblivion of her own grave.

Expunged from public record, the only written evidence of their relationship to the Queen of Scots shredded by Elizabeth herself, Lee's heroines would seem to inherit chiefly their mother's displacement from national politics to private affection, from circumstantially evident, recorded history to intangible fiction, from life to death. Apparently inspired by the legend that Mary had given birth to stillborn twins during her captivity at Lochleven, Lee imagines a female alternative to the royal Stuart line that extended from Mary through her son, James VI/I, and his male descendants. Perpetuated through this alternative line, Lee's Mary is thus also perpetuated through recessive cultural strains. She survives in women's stories, doubled and redoubled narratives of loss and longing whose feminine endings, in death and disappointment, are also, in the end, unreal.

That unreality makes it tempting to read Lee's novel as Jane Spencer has, as an elegy for women's erasure from history, their exile to some paltry underworld of fantasy and romance.[21] From this point of view, Mary is also history's victim, and her daughters' predicament merely extends their mother's by a few miserable years. But precisely because *The Recess* is built out of self-consciously female language (Matilda's, Ellinor's, Mrs. Marlow's, Sophia Lee's), around the figure of Mary Queen of Scots, its fictionality is no sure sign that this "Tale" isn't history. That is, their desire to "invent tales" marks Lee's unacknowledged princesses as fledgling women writers; the fact that Lee's "Tale" is actually told through their letters confirms that in one way or another they manage to fledge.

What is more, female authorship links Ellinor and Matilda both to Lee herself and to the Queen of Scots, that compulsive epistolary artist who was of course known to eighteenth-century Britons partly through the revival of the casket letters controversy. Since the true status of Mary's alleged love letters had stayed uncertain despite the best efforts of Georgian historians from Hume to Tytler, Mary's own place in the historical record is dubious; in part because of the mysteries that clouded her acts of authorship, she became, especially in the eighteenth century, the very point at which fact shades into its own fabulous otherwise. *The Recess* lives on the same cusp. And in this novel, the difficulty of telling fact from fiction is bound up with the fused fantasies of female authorship and a recovered maternal bond.[22]

"CHASMS IN THE STORY"

Reading *The Recess*, late Georgian literary critics were instantly affronted by the many equivocations Lee's female pen had fostered: "Fiction is indeed too lavishly employed to heighten and embellish some well-known and distinguished facts in the English history," carped *The Monthly Review*. "We say *too lavishly*, because the mind is ever divided and distracted when the fact so little accords with the fiction, and Romance and History are at perpetual variance with one another."[23] *The Gentleman's Magazine* likewise regretted that "we cannot entirely approve the custom of interweaving fictitious incident with historic truth."[24]

Lee had announced her intention to preserve this "custom" in her advertisement to *The Recess*. There she insists that "the line of which [her heroines] came has been marked by an eminent historian," Hume himself. Her own "Tale," Lee claims, "agree[s] in the outline" with what her reviewers regarded as "well-known and distinguished facts in the English history." Lee tenders this tale primarily to "the hearts of both sexes [that] nature has enriched with sensibility," whereas Hume had done so only secondarily and reluctantly. But the real difference between her story and Hume's infinitely more reputable history lay not in the fact that *The Recess* is a work of imagination but rather in its unflinching admission of the gnawing forces of time and emotion.

As Lee puts it, "the depredations of time have left chasms in the story, which sometimes only heightens the pathos." Her "inviolable respect for truth," she tells us, "would not permit me to attempt connecting these, even where they appeared faulty." Sources equally of fantasy and "pathos," such "chasms" take the form sometimes of a paratactic literary structure, sometimes of language so fraught with "melancholy" that it fails to move forward, and sometimes of physical gaps on the page. But regardless of the form they take, it is in these "chasms" that the "truth" of Lee's account is hiding. In contrast to the connected "great chain of events" that Hume and Robertson thought they were reconstructing in their histories of England and Scotland, *The Recess* is shaped, and verified, by what just isn't there.[25] Posing as a sixteenth-century manuscript, Lee's novel actually treasures its constitutive "chasms" both as reality's traces and as loops through which Mary herself might slip from past to present.

With what's missing already acknowledged as integral to its structure, *The Recess* begins with an adult Matilda's "heart exhausted by afflictions," her "eyes [. . .] no longer [able to] supply tears to lament [her] losses." Depleted on the first page of *The Recess*, Matilda on the last "turns [her] every thought toward" an even deeper aporia – "toward that grave on the verge of which I suffer" (I: 1). Itself predicated on the absence of another, the epistolary form perfectly suits Lee's conception of experience as a system of recesses, seeming "chasms" that are actually the wellsprings of "a thousand melting sensations." They are also the wellsprings of words, for Matilda's gaping sorrows generate more than a thousand pages of prose before Matilda puts down her pen to await "the nameless grave where [her reader] shall have interred my ashes" (III: 356). This "nameless grave" cannot but remind us of the "tomb" of "plain stone" that Mary Leapor felt that she shared with Mary Stuart. The recesses in *The Recess* are as perversely fertile as that earlier female plot; they stand as performative images of connection between women – between Lee and other Georgian women writers, between Matilda and her French reader of sensibility, between Matilda and Ellinor, between the twins and their missing mother, indeed, between Mary Queen of Scots and Sophia Lee.

Because Mary's absence is the condition of all of these relations, *The Recess* chronicles a uniquely female history of involvement with her. We have seen that as early as the 1720s this involvement had begun to unfold not through the progressive clarification of innately ambiguous historical information but rather through a process of displacement. Just so, Mary proliferates between the covers of Lee's novel very much as she did among the women of eighteenth-century Britain. A dead ringer for the queen, Matilda names her own daughter Mary. Both her life and Ellinor's replicate elements of Mary's – the queen's hysteria, her melancholy, her misplaced passions, her captivity, even her penchant for letter-writing all are revived in her daughters. The very name of the twins' foster mother, Mrs. Marlow, echoes Mary's. The world of *The Recess* thus mirrors a Georgian Britain likewise overrun with Queens of Scots, and as we saw, these eighteenth-century masqueraders, literary and living, were actually bound together by the alienation from the dominant symbolic order that they shared with Mary. That alienation is also dramatized in the novel's preoccupation with how Mary might survive in the literal and psychic lives of women who are themselves consigned not just to a bodily death but to a symbolic one as well.

As if to demonstrate one way Mary might indeed survive when this is so, Lee's text yokes linguistic with physical being, the transmission of written signs with that of feeling. From the start, Matilda describes her story as "a memorial which calls back to being all the sad images buried in my bosom" (I: 2), and that story unfolds as a kind of ghost narrative, one in which human characters and written ones become equally unstable "images" of one another. Lee's novel thus turns out to be involved with a history which can only convey itself through paratactic "images," or at least through visibly deficient words which approach that condition.

The recess of Lee's title supplies a natural matrix for all the settings in the novel. Matilda and Ellinor not only grow up there; compulsively, involuntarily and sometimes even unconsciously, they also return again and again to this hollow gallery of evocative and oddly nurturing images. Repetition undermines conventional trajectories of growth and change. Indeed, the twins' own faces apparently do not alter over time so much as they cling to an alternative, atemporal image system, for their exact resemblance to their parents – Matilda's to Mary and Ellinor's to Norfolk – makes present and future mere copies of the past. Such refusals of sequentiality render Lee's own, alternative history a kind of sub-history, one involved far more with the timeless life of dreams than with that of documented and sequential actions. Because they make the twins themselves into potential victims of Tudor *ressentiment*, the faces that signify the presence of an alternative system of meaning must themselves be made to seem absent. Shielded from scrutiny, the resemblance to their parents that should establish the twins in a documented family line pushes them out of the linear, volitional and potentially didactic plot lines that ought to be available to them and buries them in a spectral vocabulary that must be misread by historically real others if they are to survive. Making her way through adolescence in Elizabeth's court, Matilda struggles so hard to "guard from others [the] secret my very features betrayed" (I: 163) that she becomes "more like a spectre than myself." In her own long, fragmentary letter to Matilda, Ellinor confirms that "seen without being known, we were all an illusion" (II: 165).

"SHE CARRIED MY VERY SOUL WITH HER"

Their ghostliness is of course exactly what marks Ellinor and Matilda as Mary's own. And it is around Mary's absence and the perpetual longing to be with her that Ellinor and Matilda become who they are (not). Mary proleptically haunts her daughters from the first time that, as children, they stumble across the portrait that "call[s] forth a thousand melting sensations" (I: 9). Knowable only as "part of one great mystery," this "inanimate canvas," we recall, reduced the twins to "a thousand melting sensations" that could not be put into words, afflicting them with a sense of personal unreality so profound that they came to feel "like links struck from the chain of creation" (I: 14).

Their subterranean encounter with Mary's portrait leaves her daughters with an unassuageable desire to know more about the queen. But in order to do so, they must imagine themselves within the peculiar grammar of "chasms" Lee says that she, as editor, labored to preserve. Matilda therefore, fittingly, first learns about her own mother within the same non-didactic, non-narrative and ultimately non-verbal, realms: "'I would describe the Queen of Scots to you,'" Mrs. Marlow promises during the deathbed "relation" that tells Matilda who she is, "'had not nature drawn a truer picture of her than I can give. – Look in the glass, Matilda, and you will see her perfect image'" (I: 57). The moral is transparent: neither Mary nor Matilda can be known except through reflected "image[s]."

Not long after hearing the queen's sad story (and thus their own), the twins leave the recess. While living above ground, they learn that their mother is locked up in a nearby castle. They at once set off to see "that Queen whose matchless beauty was her least ornament; to behold her graces withered by eighteen years' confinement; to share in her afflictions and prove how dearly the children, who had never known her, could love their mother" (I: 194). At least for Ellinor and Matilda, loving what one has never known is the essence of "relation" to Mary. And thus "shar[ing] in her affections" is inseparable both

from "beholding" her at an aesthetic distance and from proving personal existence and the resources of the self.

Sadly, though, the twins are not "permitted to realize [the] visions" that
include not only Mary but themselves as seen by her. Instead, rather like
modern tourists, they must pay to watch the queen in pieces, glimpsing her
only "through a grated window." Once "conducted" there, they find Mary
gravely "changed" from the portrait they know:

> and yet how lovely! Damp rooms had weakened her limbs – her charming
> arms were thrown round the necks of two maids, without whose assistance
> she could not move. – A pale resignation sat on her still beautiful features;
> her regal mien could not be eclipsed by a habit of plain purple, nor her fine
> hair by the veil which touched her forehead. – Her beads and cross were her
> only ornaments, but her unaffected piety, and patient sufferance, mingled
> the Saint with the Queen, and gave her charms beyond humanity.
>
> (I: 194–195)

Clearly, Mary's dependency on the maids "without whose assistance she
could not move" makes her an allegorical figure of female dispossession; her
"patient sufferance" crowns her as a very Georgian sort of queen, "regal" only
in the loss of self-sovereignty and political authority. Yet the scene before us
(and before Lee's heroines) is not just an allegory. Mary's meaning is not
defined strictly through static correspondence to a set of extratextual meanings. Rather it comes of the broken and yet still compelling bonds that tie her
to her female spectators – spectators very much in the mediated yet immediate position of eighteenth-century readers.

As one version of such a reader, Matilda is absorbed entirely into the sublime
object of her contemplation. It would at first seem that there is nothing whatever to be gained from this absorption except for a profound loss, for the truly
feeling subject of the alternative sort of history that Mary embodies both
vision and visibility must remain unrealized. Yet it is precisely this unrealiz-
ability that permits Mary's very real revival. In turn, it is only their invisibility
to Mary that makes the twins visible to themselves:

> We wept – we incoherently exclaimed – and striking ourselves eagerly
> against the bars, seemed to hope some supernatural strength would break
> them. More afflicted at seeing her thus, than not seeing her at all, I neither
> could behold her for my tears, or resolve to lose a look by indulging them.
> [. . . O]ur hands, which we had thrust, in supplication, through the bars,
> caught her attention. – She raised her fine eyes . . . to the window – I
> would have spoke, but my lips denied all utterance. Alas! that blessed –
> that benignant glance, was the first, the last, the only one we ever received
> from a mother. – When she withdrew her eyes, she carried my very soul
> with her.
>
> (I: 196–197)

Matilda's words are extraordinarily moving, and this is partly because they capture such a devastating paralysis, reminiscent of the tears that stood in Johnson's eyes at the thought of Hester Thrale's imitating the Queen of Scots. Here, Matilda's eyes can neither "behold" nor "resolve to lose a look"; her "lips den[y] all utterance" until her body becomes an obstacle to its own articulation. Matilda's death – the departure of her "soul" with the "benignant glance" that does not even see her – discovers the origins of adult female subjectivity not in a moment of distinction from the object that affects it (naturally, the mother) nor in a moment of connection with other, like-minded and like-spirited selves (Matilda's with Ellinor), but in the extinction of what we usually think of as the historical self. Told in terms of others' relations to the Queen of Scots, Lee's version of Mary's life makes transient subjectivity the ironic condition of the queen's reproduction. Matilda herself both shares in the "sorrow" that Lee's fellow Georgians felt at "seeing the Queen" and reveals what was ironically at stake in experiencing it.

What was at stake was a believable fiction of personal specificity. We saw that Matilda cannot easily be told from Mary and that her sorrowful bond with her mother the queen is inseparable from a sense of her own reality, or unreality: it is also the condition of relationship to her sister. Ellinor's own story is built around a similar sense of loss. But in Ellinor's case, this loss is perversely recovered, and it is recovered in a form most relevant to the text of *The Recess* itself. Just before her own death of erotic grief, that is, Ellinor writes her story to Matilda; her manuscript (posthumously received) is reproduced in pieces connected only by asterisks and thus it not only fuses historical and psychological destiny but also transposes them into the field of letters that they both share. A labyrinth of literal recesses, the page in turn becomes a charismatic image of the atomizing losses that at once produce and are engendered by history; it remakes written words into an alternative species of "historical" evidence, one that illuminates and sustains the past by means of what is missing. Visibly bound to the myth of Mary Queen of Scots, Ellinor's letter moves beyond language's conventional gestures to perpetuate Mary's legacy, a legacy of life in death as well as death in life.

When we turn back to Matilda, we find a similar – and similarly literary – answer to the question of what sort of legacy the modern female subject charged with reproducing some version of the past might possibly inherit from the Queen of Scots. Throughout the last years of her mother's life, Matilda fantasizes about both becoming "the instrument of [the queen's] deliverance" (I: 164) and being "received to her arms" (I: 81). Rescuing Mary would both guarantee the recognition that Matilda craves and give the queen's daughter visibility in the realm of historical fact. When Mary dies before Matilda can touch her, the daughter naturally feels that it is she who has been annihilated. When she was told of Mary's beheading, Matilda remembers, "a sensation, to which fainting is ease, condensed every faculty, and nature [. . .] struck on my heart at the thought of my mother, with a pang perhaps equal to that with which she bore me. The radiant sun of Love seemed to dip into a sea of blood, and sink there forever."

As language gives way to "sensation," Matilda's very body seems to vanish – its "every faculty" and very "nature" are "condensed" and the daughter is absorbed in a "pain perhaps equal to what with which [the mother]" bore her. In this moment, Matilda seems to give birth both to her mother and to herself; hence the eroticism of her description. As the "radiant sun of Love" sets in a sea of blood, however, the bonds of love and those of non-being become those of cruelty as well. And thus, "unable to reduce the torrent of [her] ideas into language," Matilda is overtaken by a "horrible transport": "How multiplied, how complicate, how various, how new, were then my feelings! feelings which ever return with the remembrance! feelings which opened a vein in my character as well as my heart – all sense of gentleness vanished" (II: 53).

Perhaps because the queen is already dead to her own daughter ("your mother lives but not for you"), Mary's execution strikes Matilda differently from the way it touched, say, the spectators at her execution in Hume's *History of England*, or P.T.'s weeping family in *The Gentleman's Magazine*. What civilized them robs Lee's heroine of "all sense of gentleness" and leaves her without "character." When Matilda feels a "pang perhaps equal with which [Mary] bore me," her identification with the Queen of Scots cannot be distinguished from identification against her. Matilda therefore imagines that "even at the moment she laid that beauteous head, so many hearts were born to worship, on the block, every agony of death was doubled, by the knowledge her daughter brought her there. – Why did I not perish in the Recess by lightning? Why did not the ocean entomb me? Why, why, oh God, was I permitted to survive my innocence?" (II: 54).

These are reflections that Mary herself might have entertained, and they bind mother and daughter, queen and female subject, with the cord of cruellest love. The daughter's irrational guilt over the death of her mother in itself betrays what *The Recess* as a whole apprehends – the absence of the mother queen is the condition of her daughter's presence, but that presence must henceforth recognize itself as absence. Matilda's aggression is more than guilty fantasy. It is the most appropriate of responses to the knowledge of what it means to be Mary's daughter.

If Lee's exploration of the female bond with Mary ended here, we would have to conclude that the queen's legacy to her daughters is the negative one of oblivion, and that identification with her means killing both Mary and the self who identifies with her. But Matilda's relation to Mary does not end here, in the whirlpool of the daughter's own guilty and furious mind. Instead, Matilda moves from being her mother's daughter-killer to becoming Mary's reader. Handed the written records of the execution, including Elizabethan hagiographies of the sort we have ourselves encountered, Matilda sees "friends and enemies unite in the eulogium of the Royal Martyr," and thinks: "What magnanimity, what sweetness, what sanctitude did they assign her!"

These decidedly cosmetic eulogia distance Mary from Matilda, but in so doing they also bring her closer. In essence, they put Matilda in the place of the future female reader, whose place she here also takes, even as she calls upon the "Spirit of the royal Mary! oh thou most injured!" (II: 56). We are in turn reminded that the whole of *The Recess* is ostensibly addressed to a reader, one who like Mary is both female and French. At the novel's end, Matilda seals her letters in a "casket" for the benefit of this reader and looks forward to the "nameless grave" where her own ashes will be interred (III: 356). Caught like its author's body between competing modes of evidence, her letter seeks a similar fate, its power to disclose and perpetuate identity finally and ironically dependent on its own burial.

Addressed to the "dear and lovely friend" whose "sensibility," Matilda expects, will "lead" her to "retrace" the places she has described (III: 356), Matilda's last sentences anticipate her story's preservation through repetition in the heart and body of its reader. As a literal (burial) plot fuses with the literary one that will be carried on in the heart of another woman, Matilda's own private "casket" letter becomes a mirroring – thereby in its own terms a perpetuating – image of the letters, poems and other literary evidence of her life and character that Mary Queen of Scots allegedly left behind, in the infamous casket whose fictionality had haunted so much eighteenth-century historiography. *The Recess* vindicates the casket letters not by grappling with the question of their truth or falsehood, but rather by absorbing that unanswerable question into its own textual body.

The Recess was published just four years before the French Revolution, and so Lee's novel brings us to the end of one chapter of Mary Stuart's story. It is hard to imagine a more fitting conclusion. Known only through refraction and relationship, Lee's highly idealized, even sanctified, Queen of Scots belongs very much within the sentimental tradition: she lives and does not live, and the story of her life is that of her death. But Lee's novel is also about the transmission of ambivalent love through time; above all, it shows how this transmission (to which ambivalence itself is key) may take place in history's recesses. Those recesses exist precisely so that there will be room for the historical subject herself, and it is Mary of all historical figures who most permits them.

Obviously, *The Recess* amounts in many ways to a critique of Georgian rules of engagement with the maternal figure of Mary Stuart. It traces instead a counter-history of the Queen of Scots, one that goes back to her Catholic advocate John Leslie's plea for her readers to pity "a most careful tender mother with all" – to imagine, even feel, themselves as part of her. In tracing Mary's image from its inception forward, we have seen how threatening such involvement could seem, and how hard the makers of a modern Britain worked to suppress it. As not for the bulk of their more culturally privileged counterparts, for many Georgian women Mary's inherent ambiguities and impostures posed no obstacle to retrieving her; nor did these qualities threaten the possibility of true feeling with her. Instead, the queen's vulnerability to the impositions and desires of others testified to the privation built into all forms of sovereign femininity. Lee saw that this shared unreality finally provided the only grounds of being for the individual woman. But she also recognized it as the matrix of community among women of vastly different "Times," and orders of reality.

7 Guilt and vindication
1789–1837

In 1820, it appears, the people of Britain suffered a dire case of *déjà vu*, its catalyst the parliamentary proceedings that commenced one August Thursday
against the queen of England, Scotland and Wales. Charged with adultery – a
crime in the king's consort tantamount to treason – the queen stood, at the
very least, to lose her title if convicted. The Catholics among the nation's
peers had been barred from her hearing, and a secret tribunal appointed to
examine a trove of incriminating documents housed in a mysterious green bag.
Eager to enhance the picture of wronged majesty, the queen for her part arrived
at the House of Lords tricked out in the oddest of costumes: she wore a black
gauze gown with a high ruff, her naturally fair hair hidden beneath a brunette
wig and her face obscured by a snow white veil. True, the royal defendant was
foreign-born and had only recently returned to England from Italy, where she
had allegedly disported herself in the arms of a Mediterranean lover.
Nevertheless, hundreds of upright British women, working-class radicals and
opponents to the Tory party then in power all massed in the streets below,
rowdy with indignation on her behalf.

More than one of her accusers swore that she ought to pay for her indiscretions with her life, but happily Caroline of Brunswick escaped the fate that had
befallen her obvious role model, Mary Queen of Scots, almost 250 years before.
Pressured by the tide of popular affection for her – and against her long-
estranged husband, that philanderer in his own right, George IV – Parliament
settled on an acquittal. One disgusted baron, Thomas Erskine, even publicly
claimed that the evidence against Caroline had been manipulated in order to
relieve George of the irrepressible wife whose love of pleasure and recognition
had made her a thorn in his side from the earliest days of their marriage.
Vindicated, if not exactly proven innocent, Caroline kept the queenly title she
treasured; no doubt in the hearts of many an unenfranchised Briton she was
never in much danger of losing it.[1]

In Caroline's ordeal even the dullest ear will detect many echoes of the
trials for adultery and treason that had framed Mary Stuart's unhappy sojourn
in England so long ago. The green bag with its cargo of damning evidence
recalls the casket letters of old, and while there is no denying the cabalistic
character of the proceedings against both queens, it is also unlikely that either

was entirely guiltless of the charges brought against her. In the estimation of one onlooker, Caroline, like Mary, towered "full six foot high," and she exaggerated her resemblance to the Queen of Scots by assuming not only a sixteenth-century neckline but even Mary's signature hairpiece and veil of mourning.[2]

Albeit of natural causes, Caroline, like Mary, would be dead a year after what amounted to her treason trial. But no superficial resemblance linked the two queens so closely as the stubborn conundrum of desire that lay at the heart of both their predicaments. Mary in her time, like Caroline in hers, had brought a sexualized woman's desire to be queen into contact with a people's consequently divided desire for her. In the eyes of Caroline's contemporaries, the trials of both women seemed to raise the question of how far a kingdom which wishes to be united can tolerate the authority – cultural in Caroline's day, political in Mary's – of a woman who wants something for herself, and who arouses a mixed and often untoward measure of longing in return.

In Caroline's case, the conflict between those who condemned her for her romantic passions and those to whom her reputation simply did not matter was a very public one, and so easy enough to chart: on her side were the cultural subalterns who glimpsed in the king's drive to be rid of his wife their own exclusion from political representation. Lining up against the "Queenites" were those, usually in positions of wealth and influence, who wanted nothing more than to see a scandalous and self-willed woman out of the way. Caroline's trial gave a symbolic shape to long-simmering social tensions between the empowered and disempowered, visible and invisible, conservative and radical fractions of Britain's population. The sudden obviousness that Britain was far from one happy family – that the things which various groups within it wanted were at once too different and too much the same – gave the lie for good to eighteenth-century fantasies of affectionate concord.[3]

In many ways, these impasses of desire also shaped the new interest in Mary Queen of Scots that erupted in Britain around the time of Caroline's trial – an interest which Caroline herself seems to have exploited, and which far outlived her own celebrity. As late as 1831, a scepter would be dredged up from Scotland's desolate Loch Leven, not far from where a captive Mary had lost her crown. "Fitted with ivory, and mounted with silver, upon which latter the letters and the words 'Mary Queen of Scots' [were] almost wholly legible," the scepter was but one in a long line of Marian memorabilia to have appeared of late.[4] The Scottish poet Robert Burns treasured a snuffbox with a miniature portrait of Mary set into the lid, swearing that "the symbols of Religion shall only be more sacred,"[5] and even a humble Airdrie grocer could boast a pomander that had presumably belonged to her.[6]

The scepter would have surfaced on its own, no doubt, but it speaks loudest when placed alongside the "queenite" quandaries of the day. In Mary, many Britons were beginning to see yet another royal woman who had been excluded from her right – a woman, in the view of the ingenue poet Mary Roberts, "opposed, afflicted and calumniated almost beyond any other instance that history records." Even abundant evidence of sexual "guilt" could not make the Queen of Scots look less injured in the eyes of those who saw themselves as similarly deprived. In their turn, Caroline's enemies were liable to spy their own queen's lapses reflected in Mary's: "We have lived to see a queen as prodigal and accommodating in her choice of favourites as the Queen of Scots," complained Hugh Campbell, in his preface to an exceptionally indecorous 1824 edition of Mary's *Love Letters* to Bothwell. "For if Mary had her Chatelar, her Rizzio, and her Bothwell; report says, that Caroline had her S——, her M——, and her Bergami; whilst, in each case, the Lazzaroni triumphed, and decency and virtue hung their heads."[7]

As had Caroline, a Mary suddenly more sexualized than she had seemed in ages provoked a difference of opinion that was partly social and political, and therefore easily demarcated: she pitted British "haves" eager to believe – and reluctant to forgive – the most sordid ancient "report" about her against the "have nots" who even across the centuries saw their own wants in hers and made excuses accordingly. At the same time, however, Mary had something Caroline did not: an inherent unknowability that had only compounded as time had passed. By the early nineteenth century any definite version of her was finally, and conspicuously, the creature of private imaginations and intimate desires.

Hugh Campbell may again be called as something of a witness. Campbell justified his aversion to Mary's "prodigal and accommodating" nature with reference to her shameless letters to Bothwell. Since the erotic epistles that Mary's enemy Buchanan had first printed were quite possibly also forged by him, this was a risky business to begin with. Campbell at first seemed to have gotten around the problem by professing to have discovered the "long-missing originals" of still other, more condemning epistles – documents which he held to "possess more internal marks of originality" than the casket letters themselves. But while Campbell even touted these new letters as more "feminine" in character than any previously taken for Mary's, they had in fact been forged by him. As he himself well knew, the Queen of Scots whom he set up as a rebuke to "decency" was thus less a certified nymphomaniac – hence menace to domestic order – than a figment of Campbell's own imagination. Even more perplexing, Campbell did not expect the *Love Letters* to interfere a whit with readerly prepossession in favor of the "unfortunate Mary." He had already perceived that "sympathy" was "characteristic of our national feelings, which are generally biased to the side of the unfortunate, forgetting vices in their woe."[8]

Morally and socially grounded indictments like Campbell's eventually cancel themselves out, humbled on the one hand by their authors' awareness of the enormous power of "sympathy," unto identification, and on the other by Mary's own noticeably phantasmic attributes. But Campbell's implosive summary of who the Queen of Scots had been also marks a definite mutation in the Georgian compulsion to cast her as defenseless virtue in eternal and unmerited distress. While sentimental attachment to the woman Burns called "the greatly injured, lovely Scottish queen" persisted well after the turn of the century, it no longer required a feeble and innocent object in order to exist. On the contrary, it was as if, often within a single woman or man, the Georgian need to take her part came face to face with an equally strong need to acknowledge the Queen of Scots's own powerful, if thwarted, desires. The result was something we could call Mary's vindication. This may well have been the vindication of an imaginary object, and a project ever tending toward internal contradiction. But if Campbell's reflections upon "our national feelings" are any clue, making peace with the Queen of Scots's mistakes – and so with the magnitude of her supposed desires – was essential if modern Britain's romance with itself was to survive the crises of faith that beset it around the tumultuous time of Caroline and her husband George IV.

THE PRIVILEGE OF SAYING *"JE LE VEUX"*

George IV had been appointed Britain's regent in 1811, George III having long suffered from porphyria; he became king upon his father's death in 1820, and remained so until his own demise in 1830. But his devotion to his mistresses, not to mention a nasty and capricious temper, made him dismally unpopular in a country ever more disposed to venerate the domestic virtues above all others. That disposition had roots in the last decades of the eighteenth century, when George III's bouts of mental illness had left the country without a reliable public metaphor for paternal authority, and when in 1789 the French Revolution reflected violent social protest at home. Stimulated by the French citizenry's demands for *liberté*, *égalité* and *fraternité*, Britons unwilling to accept their own lack of social and political privilege found loud and angry voices that would begin to subside only with such liberalizing measures as the Catholic Emancipation Act of 1829 and the First Reform Bill of 1832.

Since to many the nation had begun to feel like a once stable patriarchal household under siege, it is unsurprising that agitation over the status of women should have spiked upwards in the stormy years following the French Revolution. It was during this time that the domestic wife and mother – self-sacrificing, long-suffering, sheltered from the public fray – became the repository of belief in what female cultural authority should resemble.[9] Never was feminine modesty at a higher premium; but then again never were more examples of its violation cited. Meanwhile, conservative entrenchment first against French republicanism and later against the Napoleonic menace manifested itself symbolically in the repudiation of what the popular historian Anna Jameson called "the true feminine idea of empire, viz. the privilege of saying *je le veux*."[10]

For the British conservatives who managed to remain in power during George III's twilight years, and even through the regency and reign of George IV, the exorbitantly desirous woman could symbolize either the foreign tyranny that patriotic Britons had long withstood or the terrors of an ungovernable mob. Many concurring voices were female themselves: "Women, in possession of power, are so sensible of their inherent weakness, that they are always in extremes," Jameson warned. "Hence among the most arbitrary governments are those of women."[11] In the 1790s such radicals as Mary Wollstonecraft found reasons of their own to reprove other women's appetites for pleasure and sway. Wollstonecraft had decided that the fantasy of being treated as a queen was what made women vulnerable to men already too willing to see them as merely physical beings: "Inheriting, in a lineal descent from the first fair defect in nature, the sovereignty of beauty, they have, to maintain their power, resigned the natural rights, which the exercise of reason might have procured them, and chosen rather to be short-lived queens," Wollstonecraft somewhat choppily lamented in her revolutionary *Vindication of the Rights of Woman* (1792).[12] It was on the canvas of such assumptions that she and fellow travelers like Mary Hays began to paint an all-too-convincing portrait of patriarchal Britain as a women's prison.

Convinced that modern women lacked recognition and political power in part because of their enslavement to the "sovereignty of beauty," and thereupon to their own carnality, Mary Wollstonecraft naturally noticed the popular conviction that the short-lived queen Mary Stuart had lost her birthright through the vagaries of her own libido. Indeed, the nineteen-year captivity that followed the queen's humiliation at Lochleven offered an allegory of female subjection so compelling that Wollstonecraft absorbed its iconography into the novel of protest she left unfinished at her death, *Maria; or, The Wrongs of Woman* (1798). Separated from her child, Wollstonecraft's eponymous heroine manages to produce only a fragmented narrative of her life and errors while her respectable English husband keeps her locked up in a middle-class madhouse. Wollstonecraft's theme is the conspiracy between woman's unruly desire and the conditions of her captivity: her Maria succumbs to the charms of a personable fellow inmate, the ominously christened Darnford, and so after her release she only enters upon a life of legal and social woes, her reputation ruined and her estrangement from her daughter permanent.[13]

Wollstonecraft's Maria Venables is nothing if not a Mary Stuart for the Jacobin era, a frustrated mother and compulsive lover who makes it clear that if in more quiescent days the Queen of Scots had been the occasion for self-congratulating sorrow, widespread *ressentiment* had at last cast her as an icon of political grief. The questions she now raised almost always had something to do with the ratio between female entitlement and female desire – with the fate of queenship in a post-revolutionary world. Writers and artists who would have delicately skirted the subject before thus took pleasure in recounting Mary's alleged crimes of passion, and restored the veil of guilt that had for centuries hinted at both sexual indulgence and the abuse of royal prerogative. Prominent history painters like William Allan and John Opie captured her life's more illicit episodes on canvas while images of Mary at her most libidinous proliferated in material culture, for example as the selling feature of a

Plate 10 Joseph Stromier long-case clock with painted dial (1840).

popular chiming clock (Plate 10).[14] Forgers like Campbell and the equally enterprising William Ireland, meanwhile, manufactured evidence of the torrid romances that the Queen of Scots had supposedly conducted with her besotted subjects and foreign-born hangers-on. Thanks only in part to a revival of interest in the history of Scotland, the years of her personal rule were almost always the ones by which she was remembered, their general appeal rivalled only by the myth of Mary's desire for her cousin Elizabeth's English crown.

As we have already had occasion to notice, the queenly longings that now took center stage could bear more than one meaning. For a feminist like Mary Wollstonecraft they spelled self-imprisonment and, at last, a slow and terrible death for the women who harbored them. For moneyed armchair moralists like Campbell the same wild wishes, if ever coupled with the power to gratify them, could only threaten the masculine privilege that held British society together. Campbell, as a matter of fact, put Mary's alleged extramarital escapades with Bothwell on a par with those of a farmer's wife recently "executed for instigating her partner in adultery to destroy her husband" (p. 6). As far as Campbell was concerned, both the sixteenth-century queen and the nineteenth-century farm wife confirmed his suspicion that it is "not only possible but probable" that a woman "could be so infatuated with a man as to urge him to sue for and obtain a divorce from his lawful wife, and afterwards to force that wretched dupe of her lust to destroy her own husband and assume his rights" (p. 6).[15] And yet, strange bedfellows though they make, both Wollstonecraft and Campbell fully recognized the popular urge to sympathize with such an obviously revolutionary woman. Wollstonecraft, who shared Mary's name, even felt that sympathy herself, and lived in constant struggle with the female legacy of frustrated passion and political exclusion that seemed to have come down to British women through the Queen of Scots.

For every Briton who made Mary out to be the feminine *je le veux* incarnate, there was one to pity her. Anna Jameson, for instance, clearly agreed with her most conservative contemporaries that "the power which belongs to us as a sex is not properly or naturally that of the sceptre."[16] But she pardoned Mary's lawless passions in light of the queen's "unexampled misfortunes." Authorized by the "mass of contradictory evidence" that would keep the "real" Mary forever an enigma, the historian echoed romantic artists eager to temper the ghost of queenly criminality with the wrenching spectacle of Mary's excessive punishment – poets as eminent as William Wordsworth, who addressed a poignant sonnet to her, and James Hogg, who produced considerably more than that (all sad), while no less a novelist than Sir Walter Scott built a bestseller around the queen's travails at Lochleven. On the London stage, adaptations of Scott and English-language versions of Friedrich Schiller's torrid tragedy *Maria Stuart* (1800) kept company with gothic extravaganzas like John St. John's *Mary Queen of Scots* (1798), Jane Deverell's *Mary Queen of Scots* (1798) and John Grahame's *Mary Stewart Queen of Scots* (1801). Schiller let a captive (if yet defiant) Mary be both affronted and exalted when one of her most ardent devotées tried to rape her. But when it came to the Queen of Scots it clearly did not take a German pen to blend pathos with baroque sexuality, confessions of guilt with the possibility of a higher purity.

On the contrary, the need to reconcile a Mary flagrantly guilty of experiencing and arousing passion with a too harshly punished one was finally British in the extreme. Its inherent contradictions provided a Regency-era analogue to Elizabethan conflicts and Stuart ambivalences alike, even as the delicate myths of high sentimental culture were exposed to present-day anxieties about foreign invasion and exorbitant female desire. The Queen of Scots had, of course, always stood for certain recurrent threats to Britain's evolving political and psychological coherence – for absolute female authority, Roman Catholicism, and France. Now those threats had to be domesticated if what they threatened was to prevail. Just so, when we listen to what nineteenth-century Britons had to say about Mary, it seems that taming the specter of her longings was often a means of engaging the feminine *je le veux* itself, or at least of making contemporary projections and phantasms of female desire somehow palatable. And, as we might expect, contemporary encounters with Mary usually reflected the degree of similarity between their author and the Queen of Scots. So, for example, many women leapt to Mary's defense, ironically aware that their faith in her was groundless but nonetheless conscious of its potential not only to validate their own inadmissible wishes but also to unite them with other women in a like state of economic or political deprivation. On the other hand, male protagonists often faced destruction at the hands of their own infatuation with an enticing but incalculable Queen of Scots. For men and women alike, though, to vindicate Mary was in the end to vindicate their own desires for recognition and symbolic power. Their fantasies about her thus converged, at first only secretly in ruminations like those of Campbell and Jameson, but at last openly in the imagination of Sir Walter Scott.

The Abbot, Scott's popular novel about the end of Mary's personal rule in Scotland, appeared in 1820, the year of Queen Caroline's trial. Scott himself attended the trial, having years before inserted a rhymed "tribute" to Caroline's "beauty afflicted" into a longer poem of his. He also kept a portrait of that no less afflicted beauty Mary Stuart's severed head in his drawing room at Abbotsford, where he was fond of discussing with his female acquaintants the interesting fact "that there are *no* absolutely undoubted originals of Queen Mary," only "innumerable copies," which leave their spectral subject "as unfortunate in this as in other particulars of her life."[17] Yet, while Scott may have been an aficionado of troubled queens, he was not an unembarrassed one. Eight years after *The Abbot* was published, he confessed to his son-in-law that the novel had been almost impossible to write "because my opinion [about Mary] in point of fact is contrary both to the popular feeling and to my own."[18] This division of sentiment stranded the Scottish novelist halfway between the two forms of attachment to Mary – one mediated by fear, the other by faith – that were most readily available in his day. Set in the last days of Mary's personal rule, *The Abbot* dramatizes his dilemma. Scott's captive Queen of Scots proves dangerously captivating in her turn, and she seduces both the faith of the Catholic girl who attends her and the highly flammable imagination of the Scottish youth whom her Protestant captors have appointed to be her page. But if we are to savor the way Scott sifted these two very timely genres of longing for Mary Queen of Scots together, we need to know just how they were practiced while *The Abbot* was taking shape in its author's unconscious mind.

MASCULINE EFFUSIONS

When Scott's hot-blooded young protagonist Roland Graeme first meets Mary Stuart, he finds himself instantly transfixed by her face. Scott himself clearly shared the fascination, for he arrested his narrative for several paragraphs in order to catalogue:

> that brow, so truly open and regal – those eye-brows, so regularly grace-
> ful, which yet were saved from the charge of regular insipidity by the
> beautiful effect of the hazel eyes which they overarched, and which seem
> to utter a thousand histories – the nose, with all its Grecian precision of
> outline – the mouth, so well proportioned, so sweetly formed, as if
> designed to speak nothing but what was delightful to hear – the dimpled
> chin, the stately swanlike neck.[19]

Who would not be enthralled by the physiognomy of "a thousand histories," or indeed by any one of the features which together "form a countenance, the like of which we know not to have existed in any other character moving in that high class of life"? If the same "countenance" is also nothing "like" the historical Mary's, it hardly seems to matter at first.

In time, we learn that Mary's beauty veils, and furthers, the most subversive of ambitions, which is in fact to bend history to the bow of her own desires. Almost at once, the queen casts her spell over Roland, hoping he will help her escape from Lochleven. Her flight could change the plot of Scotland's story – the "true" story that begins with the triumph of Mary's Protestant nobles over her and ends with her country's incorporation into the prosperous, mainly Protestant, Britain that Scott knew and heartily approved. On the other hand, we ourselves know that the historical Mary did get herself spirited away from her island prison, and to no ultimate avail. The more pressing danger that her face's thousand histories pose is a cognitive and affective one, for as it indeed mirrors no queen who ever lived, that face erases all sense of distance, be it crit-ical or historical, between Mary's beholder and her. This is a peril Scott's reader confronts along with his hero: "Who is there," Scott wonders:

> that has not her countenance before him, familiar as that of the mistress of
> his youth, or the favourite daughter of his advanced age? Even those who
> feel themselves compelled to believe all, or much of what her enemies laid
> to her charge, cannot think without a sigh upon a countenance expressive
> of anything rather than the foul crimes with which she was charged when
> living, and which still continue to shade, if not to blacken her memory.
> (II: 179–180)

Mary's uncanny familiarity bids to seduce author, reader and protagonist alike into pardoning her many "foul crimes," whereupon all stand to lose their own ambitions, concerns and even beliefs in hers. To be sure, the probability of such a thing happening in Scott's day seems to have been almost as high as he imagined it to have been in Mary's. By 1820, the ardent youth immolated by his desire for the Queen of Scots had become a stock literary figure, one pioneered both by continentals like Schiller (whose *Maria Stuart* Britons quickly adopted as their own) and by native Englishmen like William Ireland, who assumed the voice of one of the historical Mary's most obsessive devotées.

Schiller's Mortimer is an impressionable young Catholic convert who falls in love with the Queen of Scots even before meeting her, having come across her bewitching portrait in far- (but not far enough-) off France. His father is one of Maria's English jailors, and Maria herself is now years past her indiscretions with Bothwell, though still obsessed with them, as well as with her own role in Darnley's murder, to which she eventually confesses. Mortimer swears eternal devotion to her nonetheless and the queen, no puling whipping-girl of fate, is quick to take advantage of his perfervid reverence. She supplies Mortimer with a fresh copy of her portrait and dispatches him to the Tudor court where he is to rally other Englishmen to her side. With the help of one of Elizabeth's shadier nobles, Leicester, Mortimer manages to persuade Elizabeth to agree to a kind of amazonian summit with Maria. When the two queens meet, however, Maria refuses to humble herself before her Tudor rival, whose answering indignation eventually spurs her to sign Maria's death warrant. Mortimer for his part is rather differently inflamed by the spectacle of Maria's pride. His fanatical love turns to sexual savagery and he tries to rape his own queenly idol. She withstands his advances and, not much later, Mortimer's effort to rescue her fails. He falls on his own sword while Maria heads for the scaffold in a blaze of glory.

The Elizabethans would have been incensed, the Georgians shocked, by Schiller's proud and guilty heroine. But in *Maria Stuart* the queen's titanic desire fuels the most extreme ardor for her. For Mortimer this ardor spells death: "My heart is torn with torments," he gasps, "and/Enraptured with the joy of looking at you." Later he recognizes that "the beauty that with god-like power reigns" in Maria's "alluring form" not only "makes [him] dare and undertake all things," but also "drives [him] toward the ax the headsman swings."[20] And indeed, before the fourth act is over, Mortimer has stabbed himself. Having failed to set Maria free, he vows to "set an example by my love," and his last words are a plea for "holy Maria" to "pray for me/And take me with you to your life above" (p. 92).

It was in Mortimer's suicidal effusions that British audiences seem to have glimpsed some shadow of their own involvement with the queen who, of all in British history, most embodied sexual guilt and unassuaged political desire. Like Mortimer, they developed a perverse reverence that at last let them transcend their own anxiety about her. This development, it seems, was possible because Schiller's play made Mary Stuart's inner life and longings sharply visible, thence revealing the exact scope of a guilt which, while certainly of note, at least seemed not to extend to actual treason against Elizabeth and England.[21] The play's earliest English translator, for example, found it downright offensive at first, complaining that Maria's "guilt in conniving at the murder of her husband departs too much from the character required of a heroine; she thus abases herself in the eyes of spectators."[22]

But while Maria at first appeared "burthened with much extrinsic impurity," her "fiery ordeal" over the course of the play was seen to:

> develop the metal from the substances with which it is mixed; with every process, her innate worth becomes more and more conspicuous, till at length quite freed from the fortuitous excrescences which deformed her, she enforces that respect, which was perhaps before due to the virtuous part of her character.

(p. vi)

Schiller's play brought its viewers to the very point of "respect," unto reverence, that Mortimer models. Unlike Mortimer, though, a British spectator could hope to retreat from the abyss of total incorporation into Maria's guilty desires. By degrees "our pity is increased by her consciousness, and sincere repentance of her former guilt; and our minds receive the most religious impression;" "with every new indignity which is offered her, she gains upon our affections" until, with her eleventh-hour confession of certain crimes against men, the "mind of the spectator is put out of doubt as to the points of her guilt" (p. xii). Once Maria has been humiliated, the internal architecture of her true guilt thereby exposed, public terror of a desirous and guilty queen melts away, for moderns as it did for Mortimer, but without the same fatal consequences.

True to his name, Schiller's Mortimer never actually drew breath. Pierre de Chastelard did, however: the smitten Huguenot poet once followed Mary from France to Scotland, where he was beheaded for twice hiding under her bed. Centuries later, William Ireland's *Effusions of Love from Chatelar to Mary, Queen of Scotland* (1805) promised an account of his "suffering," as "written by himself in the form of fragments." In fact a forger to the core, Ireland claimed to have discovered these "fragments" in post-Revolutionary Paris, and brought them home to an appreciative Britain. The most famous of them, in which a lovesick Chatelar strums the lute while a leering Mary strategically drops Petrarch's love poetry beside a bouquet of passion flowers, even inspired Joseph Henry Fradelle's "Mary Queen of Scots and her Secretary Chatelar" (1830; Plate 11). When Fradelle's image turned up on a popular clock face a few years later, the need to make Mary's queenly libido fit for English parlors found total fulfillment at last.

Though the historical Chastelard was probably a political operative, Ireland's Chatelar seems to have no end beyond his love for the Queen of Scots, unless it was to appeal to the early nineteenth-century marketplace. In his *Effusions* autobiographical fragments afloat in seas of asterisks alternate with engorged lyrics to a Renaissance *belle dame sans merci*, all courting a popular taste that ran to exhibitions of male masochism and lurid myths of female domination.

Plate 11   Mary Queen of Scots and her Secretary Chatelar, stipple engraving by A. Duncan, after Henry Joseph Fradelle. Courtesy of the National Gallery of Scotland.

Ireland's preface presents the Queen of Scots as a woman "so irresistibly seductive, as to inspire with love every object that came within the vortex of her transcendent charms."[23] Chatelar himself becomes but one of the "numerous individuals that were sacrificed at the shrine of [her] beauty" (pp. i–ii). Just as Schiller's Mortimer first falls in love with Maria's portrait, so Chatelar steals the "amber beads" of Mary's rosary; dreaming that "her lips too have kissed them," he "scent[s] their fragrance, and [. . .] suck[s] their sweets" until they become beads of "inspiration" (p. 27). Despite such sublimities, Ireland's reader senses instantly that his goddess queen will eventually demand Chatelar's complete annihilation. Oblivious to this, Chatelar himself twice hides under the queen's bed, the better to feast his eyes upon the queen's ravishing form unveiled. Mary for her part seems to return his desire, prohibited only by rank and reputation from acting upon it. Chatelar's high-flown diary of obsessive love at last breaks off when, anxious to protect her name, the queen finally sentences him to death.

Ireland's was a Mary very much for his times – powerful, sexualized, preternaturally beautiful, and a warning to all men tempted to love her. Chatelar himself, we learn, looked up at Mary's empty window from his scaffold and "pathetically upbraided her, as the most cruel although the loveliest of women," his only consolation his ability to "repea[t] some lines out of the works of *Ronsard*, which were very applicable to his situation" (p. 53). Ireland ends with a list of "the victims of the shrine of [Mary's] beauty" (p. 62), including her enamored (and duly butchered) Italian secretary David Rizzio, whose own effusions Ireland promises to publish in the future, should those of Chatelar be well-received.

Although they recount the history of one man's death of love for a royal *femme fatale*, Chatelar's "fragments" are really organized by a febrile fantasy about Mary's own capricious desire, first for Chatelar, then for her own good name, and finally for her lover's demise. At the same time, the book of Chatelar's *Effusions* represents its present-day editor's own attempt to master the threat of female desire. Indeed, Ireland offered that book to his readers as a sign of Britain's power to withstand eruptions of passion like the ones now consuming the country that Mary herself had adored. His preface spins a long lie about how he rescued poor Chatelar's effusions from post-Revolutionary Paris and "the very unsettled state of political affairs in that capital, and the jarring factions, which almost hourly succeeded each other." A well-connected revolutionary (hence guillotined, it seems) supposedly gave Ireland access to the manuscripts, but even then the British visitor's "conduct was observed with the utmost scrutiny" until "his frequent attendances at length weaned his conductor, added to which the more weighty persuasion of British gold, which the editor threw into the scale." Only hereafter, Ireland confides, was he "at full liberty to make such transcripts as appeared to him of an interesting nature and cast" (p. iv).

Though it seems designed merely to authenticate Ireland's *Effusions*, this romance of their transcription really confirms the "weighty persuasion of British gold" and the infallible exercise of British "liberty." The historical Chastelard was French, but Ireland took care to make his Chatelar a Scot who goes off to the Wars of Religion very much on the Protestant side. Ireland's imaginary Chatelar is, in other words, a Briton through and through, and while his longing for just one languishing look from Mary makes him fatally vulnerable to her, and so at last destroys him, the national pride and principle that he represents are fully vindicated. In the end, Ireland's ersatz *Effusions* prove not the unconquerable force of female desire but rather the heft and stability of Britain in 1805 as it strained to glimpse its own integrity and permanence in the chaotic light cast by Mary's beloved France.

FEMININE INFUSIONS

Mortimer and Chatelar offered two effusive models for Scott's adolescent hero, Roland Græme. Like them, the hero of *The Abbot* feels himself drawn inexorably to "the beautiful and unfortunate Mary Stuart" (II: 163); like them he is entranced by the "smile expressive at once of favour and authority," that darts from behind a "transparent white veil," which "could be drawn at pleasure over the face and person" (II: 200). But Roland's enchantment is finally far less absolute than theirs, and once the queen has given up her crown he goes on to acquire power and property in a Scotland no longer obliged to gratify woman's "pleasure," or respect her *je le veux*.

Despite the resolution of his plot, however, Scott himself remained imaginatively committed to Mary's beauty and complexity, sympathetic to the need to love her even when she herself was clearly too inscrutable to be trusted: "It is in vain to say that the portraits which exist of this remarkable woman are not like each other," Scott mused, as he contemplated the enigmatic face that threatened to engage too many of his hero's affections:

> for, amidst their discrepancy, each possesses general features which the eye at once acknowledges as peculiar to the vision which our imagination has raised while we read her history for the first time, and which has been impressed upon it by the numerous prints and pictures we have seen. Indeed we cannot look on the worst of them, however deficient in point of execution, without saying that it is meant for Queen Mary; and no small instance it is of the power of beauty, that her charms should have remained the subject not merely of admiration, but of warm and chivalrous interest, after the lapse of such a length of time. We know that by far the most acute of those who, in latter days, have adopted the unfavourable view of Mary's character, longed, like the executioner before his dreadful task was performed, to kiss the fair hand of her on whom he was about to perform so horrible a duty.
>
> (*The Abbot*, II: 181)

Scott here paints a Mary who lives outside history – an always in part imaginary Mary whom even her killers long to love. Though Scott availed himself of the language of chivalry, and confirmed the perils of "admiration" for her, his "interest" in this Mary's infinitely variable face – a face often discerned precisely through what is "deficient" in its representations – was something, we know, he shared mainly with his female friends. Indeed, as his words recall the eighteenth-century women who found themselves in Mary's absence from her own image, Scott seems to have ventured some way down the path that they had trodden.

He was not alone. When the French Revolution brought a hot-blooded Queen of Scots back into view, British women answered with a flood of biographies, poems, travelogues and novels that expressed their own feelings about her. Ranging from sympathy to shame on Mary's behalf, these feelings were never simple, but the women who had them were at least free of the histrionics of a Mortimer or Chatelar. Like Wollstonecraft's Maria Venables, their Mary had lost her power, not gained it, through the pursuit of her heart's desire, and as they came to terms with her legacy of loss, they fell in more deeply with their literary mothers than with many of their more privileged contemporaries.

They were also on amazingly intimate terms with one another. In 1822, the "very young female" Mary Roberts acknowledged Scott as "the Enchanter" who had retrieved Mary's name from "obscurity" with "the power of his art," raising her "fair form from the realms of the dead./With a halo of beauty surrounding her head."[24] But Roberts actually dedicated her two-volume poem in Mary's voice, *The Royal Exile*, to the evangelical abolitionist Hannah More who, like the Queen of Scots, Roberts felt had "not escaped either affliction or calumny" (I: ix). Proceeds from the volume were even to go to the Aged Female Society, an organization "designed to alleviate the sufferings of deserving females, afflicted with the bereavements, the infirmities, and the too frequent neglects of old age, [. . .] tottering on the brink of the grave," and yearly "removed from the lists and the visits of their attentive benefactors" (I: ix–x).

Roberts set *The Royal Exile* against the background of these female difficulties. Suffering from similar infirmities of powerlessness and social invisibility, her Queen of Scots is first seen alone in the desolate Scottish landscape, clad "in sable vest,/While to her palpitating breast/The holy cross is warmly prest" (I: 151–152). But instead of venerating the image of the queen as Mortimer would have done, or like Chatelar stealing her cross to nibble and suck, Roberts looks out through Mary's eyes: "A heavenly throne, a heavenly crown/She sees, and knows them for her own:/She sees, and wrapp'd in ecstasy,/Forgets that she has yet to die" (I: 152). The transcendence that heroes like Chatelar and Mortimer sought through their infatuation with Mary is here something that the Queen of Scots achieves for herself. She does so in what Roberts clearly regarded as a peculiarly womanly way, through the admission of all she has lost.

Among the lost, Roberts's royal exile must number her daughter, whose name – Matilda – recalls the heroine of Sophia Lee's novel *The Recess*. Matilda is missing partly because she is fictitious; nonetheless, it is to her that the mother addresses a full fifteen verse epistles. The poems start out in tones of watery piety, but they gradually escalate to tortured and more than vaguely erotic fantasies, revealing an inner world of demons, ghosts and vampires who drink their mother's blood. As it strays ever farther and more luridly afield from the "Domestic Occurrences" that were the proper province of the female pen – and, it must be said, from anything that ever befell the Queen of Scots – the royal exile's operatic voice becomes indistinguishable from that of Mary Roberts. Indeed, just as Mary speaks (and sees) because of what she wants, so does Mary Roberts's poetic achievement originate in the Stuart queen's exile from her own world. Roberts herself tells us that she was inspired to write after rambling among the deserted ruins where it is possible to "breathe where [Mary] breathed" and "tread where she trod," but where at last no one can "find/Thy form in the shade and thy voice in the wind" (I: 7).

Mary Roberts was not the only modern woman to haunt the places where Mary Queen of Scots was no more. Here is Mary Douglas, the orphaned and chronically melancholy Scottish heroine of Susan Ferrier's novel *Marriage* (1818), wandering through the streets of Edinburgh:

Visions of olden times floated o'er her mind, as she gazed on its rocky bat-
tlements, and traversed the lonely arcades of its deserted palace. And this
was once a gay court! thought she, as she listened to the dreary echo of her
own footsteps; and this very ground on which I now stand, was trod by the
hapless Mary Stuart! Her eye beheld the same objects that mine now rests
upon; her hand has touched the draperies I now hold in mine. These frail
memorials remain; but what remains of Scotland's Queen but a blighted
name![25]

What did remain, not just of Scotland's queen, but of the female desire for
freedom and influence that she (and more lately Caroline of Brunswick) had
come to epitomize? Real-life women asked the same question, and, like
Roberts, found the answer in the recesses of their own fancy. When, just after
the French Revolution, the Jacobin Helen Maria Williams visited the Orleans
maison de ville where Mary's first husband François II had died, she fell into a
long reverie over the "unfortunate Mary," who "seems to have felt a sad presage
of her future calamities" – "calamities which make me forget every weakness
of Mary."[26]

A similar suspension of disbelief, again precipitated by the loss – and
losses – of a queen, shapes Ann Radcliffe's *Journey through Holland, &c* (1795),
whose final pages take the gothic novelist to one of "the unfortunate Mary's"
last English prisons, Hardwick Hall. When Radcliffe followed, "not without
emotion, the walk which Mary had so often trodden," she found that the
queen's "feelings upon entering this solemn shade came involuntarily to the
mind; the noise of horses' feet and many voices from the court; her proud yet
gentle and melancholy look, as [. . .] she passed slowly up the hall." Like
Roberts, Radcliffe saw Mary's "proud" face only by hearing through her ears;
the result was evidently an access of imaginative power that propelled the
modern novelist to the one apartment which "bears memorials of [Mary's]
imprisonment, the bed, tapestry and chairs having been worked by herself."
The furniture, Radcliffe concedes, "is known by other proofs, than its appearance, to remain as she left it." These "other proofs" are not things, but rather
"the veneration and tenderness" which rise in the modern woman at the sight
of so many "antiquities, and the plainly told tale of the sufferings they witnessed."[27]

Radcliffe's sense of Mary's presence, that is, is a matter of faith, flowering in
her own dark consciousness that time has passed, taking away far more than it
has given. The ability to find vestiges of Mary's royalty in the fading traces of
its wreckage was a talent Radcliffe perhaps learned from Sophia Lee, whose
girls' school in Bath she had attended. Infused with the language of religious
veneration and holy faith, Radcliffe's tour of Mary's apartments even stops
before "a spacious recess" – "a bed of state, used by Mary, the curtains of gold
tissue, but in so tattered a condition, that its original texture can scarcely be
perceived." At last, as the heroines of Lee's *Recess* had also done, Radcliffe
comes upon a portrait of Mary, this one "in black, taken a short time before her

death, her countenance much faded, deeply marked by indignation and grief, and reduced as if to the spectre of herself, frowning with suspicion, upon all who approached it, the black eyes looking out from their corners, thin lips, somewhat aquiline nose and beautiful chin" (p. 375).

The haughty visage here at last revealed (Plate 1) is remarkably strong, even domineering; it is an emblem of female beauty, complexity, authority and desire. But, like Roberts, Ferrier and Williams, Radcliffe perceived Mary's power only once she recognized a present reality of deprivation and loss. All four women seem to have understood how deeply their sense of a vital and demanding Queen of Scots was finally rooted in illusion – in what at last is not there. Since imagination itself thrives on what the given world fails to supply, many of them managed to turn Mary's absence into a source of individual vision and even of female imaginative community. But in the real world, the queen – like any woman empowered to pursue the *je le veux* – must remain a "departed shade." That, at least, was the conclusion that the obscure and sickly Scottish poet Margaretta Wedderburn reached in 1811. Her own long poem, *Mary Queen of Scots*, shrank from painting its heroine at her execution, for "any portrait I could now produce/Would come far short of what my feelings are."[28] For a description of the closing scene, "in colours lively, delicate and just," Wedderburn referred her readers to the Georgian historian William Robertson.

Robertson's *History of Scotland* was a bit long in the tooth by now, but it still would do, in part because Mary's present-day biographers – especially the female ones – tended to emphasize her years of personal rule over those of her English captivity. Often for the sake of their many female readers women historians were naturally most interested in the nature of Mary's power; indeed, eschewing the obliquity of poets and storytellers they went straight to the question of how she had lost it. Typically, they looked beneath her lust for Bothwell and resentment of Darnley to a single, fatal paradox: Mary's misplacement of faith coupled with the false conviction of her own omnipotence. Epitomized in her Catholic zeal, these two habits of fantasy had presumably left the otherwise resourceful Queen of Scots vulnerable to any number of coercive others – her nefarious French uncles, Murray, Darnley, Bothwell, even an Elizabeth herself manipulated by her own ministers.

In Elizabeth Benger's highly readable *Memoirs of the Life of Mary Queen of Scots* (1823) the curious may learn the exact number of Mary's "perukes" and whence they came, the style of dresses Mary wore and precisely when she traded "the white crape garb, which at the French Court procured her the appellation of the 'Reine Blanche,' for a sable suit."[29] An appendix even supplies menus from Holyrood House and, like Benger's prose, Mary is herself committed to the interests of other women. She takes young girls under her wing to educate them and makes many a heroic "effort to gratify a female friend" (II: 291), even as she displays no mean literary talent, her ladylike poems being "of a higher cast, which breathed of taste and feeling" (II: 107).

Countering these suitably feminine virtues, though, is the fatal love of saying *je le veux*. A "creature of impulse" (II: 312), Benger's Mary mixes unpredictable, even despotic passions with a deeper hedonism. Most pleasurable of all is the "pride of royalty," so much "the ruling passion of her soul" (II: 464) that when her son is born, the queen first sees not a child but a chance to "realise the dreams of ambition that had so long floated in her fancy." But Benger's Mary also exhibits a fatal "mixture of credulity and suspicion peculiar to her character" (II: 326), one which extends even to "the delusive persuasion, that her subjects might be reclaimed to the faith of their fathers" (II: 187), and which finally leaves her the dupe of her own worst enemies.

While it proved fatal for Mary, this misplacement of faith also permitted Benger to vindicate Mary's imagination and love of power, attributing her fall – and with it the permanent division of woman from queen – to something other than the *je le veux* itself. Something at least equally transgressive was afoot in Mary Hays's *Female Biography* of 1803. This encyclopedia of famous women began with Ababassa and ended with Zenobia, aspiring in between to "give an account [. . .] of every woman who, either by her virtues, her talents, or the peculiarities of her fortune, has rendered herself, illustrious or distinguished."[30] Mary Queen of Scots, unfortunately, belongs in the category of those most distinguished by "the peculiarities of her fortune." But so do most queens, an irony Hays would underscore when her digest of the *Biography*, *Memoirs of Queens*, appeared in 1821. This later work displays the cameos of five queens, of whom four – Marie Antoinette, Caroline of Brunswick, Anne Boleyn and Mary Stuart – lived and died demanding much and receiving little. Only Elizabeth Tudor (the one unmarried woman among them) escaped misery. Precisely by offering unhappy evidence of what it means to be a queen, Hays's *Memoirs* was intended "for the honour and advantage of my sex," its goal to assert "the moral rights and inherent advancement of women."[31]

On the surface, such advancement depends, as it did for Mary Wollstonecraft, on their giving up the wish to be a queen. Like Benger's, Hays's Mary is buffetted by her own "lively passions and sanguine spirit" (p. 151) and she too is the too credulous victim of her own subjects' lies and innuendo. In Hays's view, these subjects were fired foremost by resentment of the politics of "favour" that the too loving and too trusting Mary could not help but practice. The essence and expression of Mary's authority, "favour" is also the outward and visible sign of desire and the power to fulfill it. Hays unfolds the problem of Mary's favor – the problem of her at last politically untenable desire – in a footnote. She recalls Robertson's contempt for Mary's habit of "bestow[ing] her favour" on "beauty and gracefulness of person, polished manners and courtly address" and points out that it is not "peculiar to *woman* to be dazzled by the qualities enumerated by the grave historian. When do *men*, it may be asked, where their taste and passions are concerned, turn from personal graces and captivating manners, to distinguish the endowments of the mind, or recompense the virtues of the heart?" (*FB*, p. 48).

As she vindicates favor, Hays vindicates the prerogatives of female fancy. She also arouses our suspicion that she herself secretly favored the Queen of Scots.

Other footnotes rehearse recent arguments "alleged in [Mary's] vindication" (*FB*, p. 278), or take on the age-old schism between the malingering image of Mary as "model of perfection" ("held up" by "the Catholics") and the ever-ascendant one of the queen as a "monster of wickedness" ("represented" by "the Calvinists"). Hays poses a timely question about this duel of images: "Why, it may be asked, do we see the same division, and the same prejudices, for nearly two centuries after these [religious] fervours have receded, and a general indifference has taken place of the enthusiasm and violence which they produced?" (*FB*, pp. 278–279).

One might answer that it is because secular "fervours" to do with sex and class had taken their place. But for Hays it is a matter of favor: over time the caricatures "penned by her avowed and open enemies" have been "favoured" by the Protestants who seized British history's reins, while "those composed by the opposite party, whose credit and popularity were ruined and sunk, either remained unpublished, or were suppressed by the arm of power, or were written in languages to which the people were strangers" (*FB*, p. 279). Hays's rumination on "favour" thus turns into a skirmish with the politics of representation, a recognition of a dominating and indeed repressive fiction's power to mold both the perception and the experience of history.

Such reflections lie buried in Hays's footnotes, beyond and beneath the pale of her official narration. But there they replace a fable of overweening – and justly punished – female desire with a covert (if fragmentary) vindication of it. In the end, Hays's Queen of Scots altogether ceases to be the *femme fatale* of frightened patriarchal fantasy. Retaining her own right to favor and be favored, she is instead a *femme vitale* for all women. And, like the female poets of her day, Hays offers those women not only a reason to resist the fictions of history but an alternative, and finally timeless, focus of belief.

UNQUEENED QUEEN: *THE ABBOT*

Sir Walter Scott's problem was that he could see Hays's point, and this kept him uneasy as he sketched his own prose portrait of the Queen of Scots. The novel in which that portrait hung, *The Abbot*, was itself bound to the plot of history, a plot which had in essence eliminated Mary and much of what she had stood for. But Scott's sympathy with Mary – and with the imaginary alternative to history that she embodies – is also what allowed his "unqueened queen" (p. 250) to *be* Mary Stuart for more than a narrow band of nineteenth-century Britons. As Scott's headstrong hero Roland Graeme comes of age during Mary's captivity at Lochleven, *The Abbot* reflects and at last profitably sustains a contemporary paradox of desire. In its pages, fear of Mary oscillates with imaginative faith in her to produce the sort of compromise of imagination capable of sustaining the Queen of Scots through Scott's own divided historical moment.[32]

Fittingly, Scott's novel's very setting is one of strife – strife between the

Catholic factions bent on restoring Mary to her throne and the reformed Protestant forces equally determined to keep her captive, and strife therefore between a sensuous, imagistic, and even quasi-mystical past under the sway of female desire and a constitutional present in fact dominated by coalitions of Protestant men.[33] Scott famously cast his lot with the latter, and so with a progressive view of British history. However, *The Abbot* remains radically ambivalent toward the transition from ancient to modern authority. Predictably, its ambivalence is concentrated in the riddling person of the captive Mary Queen of Scots, whom Scott presents as at once defenseless and manipulative, satiric and pathetic, domineering and dominated. While Mary's inconsistencies keep her from commanding perfect sympathy, they also install in her the seductive authority of archaic, feminocentric and even Roman Catholic practices and pieties. In turn, figured in Roland Graeme's fascination with her, subliminal attachment to what she represents challenges *The Abbot*'s own narrative premises. Scott's Queen of Scots, that is, is more than a character. She is an actual presence that seduces the formally progressive structure of a modern British novel. Roland himself is a bit of a mystery, a foundling adopted in childhood by the wife of a Protestant nobleman. He grows up in the "Debateable Lands," along the border between Scotland and England, where controversy over the Queen of Scots raged hottest. Here, his adoptive mother, Lady Avenel, fosters his belief in his own noble birth, but after his swift temper and native hauteur lead to his dismissal from the Avenel household, he finds his way to the poor and devoutly Catholic grandmother who shares his blood.

In the nineteenth century this grandmother, Magdalena Graeme, would have been a decrepit relict, eligible for little more than membership in Roberts's Aged Female Society. But in Mary Stuart's day she is a political activist, up to her neck in plots to restore the Queen of Scots to the throne she has just lost. Magdalena pledges Roland to assist a young girl, Catherine Seyton, in the cause. Roland's immediate attraction to convent-bred Catherine mirrors his attraction to the Catholic faith, an attraction reinforced by his foster father Avenel's own brother, the abbot of Scott's title. But the Church's fundamentally female allure must compete with the persuasions of assorted Protestant politicians, and eventually the eye of Mary's ambitious half-brother, Murray, lights on Roland as a possible agent in his own campaign to keep her off her throne forever. Murray installs Roland as a page in Mary's otherwise all-female household, and the remainder of the novel traces Roland's conflicting impulses toward and away from the Queen of Scots, who not only enchants him more often than not but also holds all the faith of Catherine Seyton. After the captive queen is forced to surrender her crown, Roland makes up his mind that he is a Protestant. He stands firm, unswayed even by the discovery that his father is actually the abbot. Eventually the abbot's death leaves his son heir to the Avenel estate. Now both landed and firm in Protestant piety, Roland marries Catherine and, "spite of their differing faiths," they become a model of religious reconciliation – under Protestant dominance, of course.

The Abbot has a respectable plot, obviously, one that drives forward relentlessly to Mary's abdication and the establishment of Protestant rule in Scotland. But its foundation, like that of Lee's *Recess*, is a pattern of repetition and return, of recovery and the uncovering of compulsively maintained ambivalence. By placing a character of modern invention *vis à vis* certain historical personae, moreover, Scott's novel necessarily explores historical romance's erotic and affective claims on those who experience it. As relics of Mary Stuart had done for Chatelar, for Mortimer, and even for the reverent Ann Radcliffe alone in Hardwicke Hall, these claims devolve from Catholic mysticism. Scott's novel is strewn with charismatic objects and newly desecrated buildings, all of which are visibly metamorphosing into secular objects. Roland's own rosary beads are eventually melted down and refashioned as shoe buckles; broken crosses and shattered figures of saints elicit contradictory emotions in which "strong resentment [. . .] mingled with an expression of ecstatic devotion" (I: 176).

The objects of Catholic "devotion" scattered throughout Scott's novel create an atmosphere of animism, "wood or stone" dangerously worshipped as "things holy in themselves" (II: 21). Severed from the requirements of rational and consensual examination, surcharged with a despotic meaning in and of themselves, these seductive forms betoken enslavement to "the chains of antiquated superstition and spiritual tyranny" (I: 283). Their charm is appreciated most deeply by women – by Roland's grandmother; by an antiquated female friend of hers; by Catherine; and of course by the Queen of Scots, who defies all efforts to convert her, and first appears veiled, a rosary in her hand.[34] So while Roland's attraction to the Catholic faith draws him to a vanishing past and to the enchantment of sensuous shapes, it also subjects him to archaic female authority, as embodied in Mary.

From this point of view, the Queen of Scots – who supposedly gave birth a second time at Lochleven – looks very much like Roland's missing mother. She is not, but each of Roland's surrogate mothers certainly mirrors the queen whose baby son James now "reigns in her stead." Even Roland's beloved, the devout Catherine Seyton, adopts Mary's veil, embroidery and penchant for masquerade. In turn Roland himself is always in danger of being made irrelevant to an enveloping female world of illusion and passion. Mary herself teasingly notes that her page is "all our male attendance" and assigns him the redundant task of guarding her from her intrusive captors. It is from his place on the periphery of common sense itself that Roland feels himself drawn to Mary, then repelled from her as Protestant skepticism takes hold.

Rooted in illusion and "pleasure," the scope and nature of Mary's authority is ambiguous from the start. Her rebel courtiers accuse her of having failed to "rule herself" and at the same time try to present her imprisonment as a matter of choice. Such ambiguities of agency, along with Mary's own "vacillation" between claims of "divine warrant" for her rule, satiric raillery and uncontainable tears, keep her allure oddly reflexive, never certainly originating outside those who feel it, and accurately recapitulating her old hold on the

Elizabethans. And it is on Mary's own propensity to favor and love – thus to defy the boundaries of self – that her angry subjects pin Scotland's recent "tragedy of losses, disasters, civil dissentions, and foreign wars," of which "the like is not to be found in our chronicles" (II: 250). Scott's vision of a dangerous "princess so distressed and so beautiful" – and so very dangerous – itself recommends that modern readers not confuse love with political action. As compensation, though, those readers are allowed to retain vestiges of this older alliance with Mary in the private and implicitly apolitical act of subjecting themselves to the book that tells her story.

Scott dramatizes this conciliatory transfer of erotic authority from the public stage of history to the private page of historical fiction when Mary resigns her crown. In a scene that was to dominate the many artistic renderings and 160 stage adaptations of *The Abbot* that were to appear before 1875, Mary, nearly broken by the importunities of her male subjects, is about to sign the papers that will "unqueen" her. But when she is informed that she must also "declare I give away my crown of free will," (II: 242), she refuses to "put [her] name to such an untruth." Immediately, the demission's chief author, the Earl of Lindesey, "snatched hold of the Queen's arm with his own gauntletted hand. He pressed it, in the rudeness of his passion, more closely perhaps than he himself was aware of," and only "quitted his hold" at the insistence of the other nobles, "disguising the confusion which he really felt at having indulged his passion to such extent, under a sullen and contemptuous smile."

We might ask why the indulgence of his passion is so confusing to Lindesey: is it because what he feels is itself untoward, an expression not of anger but of desire? Mary herself does not interpret it quite so perversely. But she does interpret it:

> The Queen immediately began, with an expression of pain, to bare the arm which he had grasped, by drawing up the sleeve of her gown, and it appeared that his grasp had left the purple marks of his iron fingers upon her flesh. "My lord," she said, "as a knight and gentleman, you might have spared my frail arm so severe a proof that you have the greater strength on your side, and are resolved to use it. But I thank you for it – it is the most decisive token of the terms on which this day's business is to rest. – I draw you to witness, both lords and ladies," she said, shewing the marks of the grasp on her arm, "that I subscribe these instruments in obedience to the sign manual of my Lord of Lindesay, which you may see imprinted on mine arm."
>
> (II: 243)

Signing the papers then with a "hasty indifference, as if they had been matters of slight consequence or mere formality," Mary for the first time inspires "obeisance" and "reverence" in her rebel subjects, including Lindesey himself, who kneels to "pay that devotion [. . .], which I would not have paid to the power thou hast long undeservedly wielded." Lindesey's exorbitant "passion," like Mary['s] guilt, is now domesticated: he "kneel[s]," he insists, to Mary Stuart, not to the Queen" (II: 245). But Mary responds as if she still *were* a queen: "The Queen and Mary Stuart pity thee alike" (II: 245).

While Lindesey means only to announce the transfer of authority and erotic power from "Queen" to private woman ("Mary Stuart"), Mary's own interpretation of "the purple marks of [his] iron fingers" in the language of "proofs" and "decisive token" insists upon a different realm of meaning. Her bruises testify to desiring woman's forcible ejection from a new arrangement of power, betraying the brutality that brings this shift about. As she herself says, these "imprinted" marks compose a "sign manual" – not a system of meaning but instead a key as to how we might read the official history of Scotland which is, as it were, introduced by the demission papers. While the bruises can be no more physically present in Scott's text than the body of Mary Queen of Scots herself, they teach us to attend to certain disturbances throughout Scott's narrative, and to recognize them as indelible and still essential traces of this older history.

These disturbances are most visible in the prose portraits of the Queen of Scots that have already claimed our attention. Richard Westall, one of his illustrators, complained that Scott was always "difficult to paint from" because he "embodied [his] own ideas and presented them to the mind so completely, that little is left for the pencil to perform." As one twentieth-century reader has noticed, this pictorial property does not sit well with language's other function, which is to give a rational and consciously mediated version of history.[35] Just so, Scott's verbal cameos of Mary are charged with despotic and even anti-linguistic immediacy. Her face's "thousand histories," her "countenance, the like of which we know not to have existed," her complicity with "the vision which our imagination has raised" all raise questions that can only be answered subjectively. In the end, there seems to be no objective Mary for Scott to write about, only the projection of a "familiar" image that originates nowhere. Like her bruises, the queen's "countenance" precedes language ("the mention of [her] name") and compels us to perceive her as something more, and less, than a historical figure – as, in essence, the very image of desire. Her face's inherent "discrepancy" is that of desire, and its persistence in a narrative meant to endorse the world that replaced hers is the persistence of the desire for her and her world to survive, perhaps outside time itself, and certainly outside history. Ironically, it is this "sentiment" (as Scott called it), far more than his official "opinion" that she was best out of the way that assured his Mary's afterlife, breeding agreement that it was he, of all British writers, who had most truly conveyed her essence.

Not long after, the poet John Heneage Jesse dedicated his 1829 *Mary Queen of Scots and Other Poems* to Scott, the sections of *The Abbot* in which Mary appears were extracted from it and printed together as a "reading book," designed for "use in the schools, in the belief that the perusal of such an interesting narrative [. . .] must necessarily foster a taste for good reading and good literature." The resulting primer put Mary at the gateway to the English language, even as it removed the Marian matrix of Scott's novel from the context of history. In so doing, *Readings from the Abbot* signalled that it was precisely because Scott had lost the battle against his own ambivalence that the dream of a truly queenly Mary – loving, dreaming, seeking – managed to survive history's long rebuke to her. As the editor of the *Readings* acknowledged, "Mary Queen of Scots is here printed to the life. And though the novelist has had recourse to his imagination for minor facts and details, the pleasure in its great features must be considered as true to history."[36]

Part IV

Victorian Mary

Talked of poor Mary of Scots' execution, which M. said Elizabeth delayed too
long, for that her Ministers had been urging it. [. . .] Talked of poor Mary. "She
was a bad woman," said Lord M., "she was a silly, idle, coquettish French girl."
I pitied her.

Diary of Queen Victoria (Friday, 12 July 1839)

Two years after her coronation, Great Britain's 20-year-old queen, Victoria,
found herself at a rare point of disagreement with her urbane and influential
prime minister, Lord Melbourne. The difference of opinion centered on "poor
Mary of Scots," the memory of whose untimely end seems to have given
Melbourne a certain satisfaction. The queen, however, would much rather
have "talked of [Mary's] unhappiness, and the roughness of the Scotch towards
her," particularly that "of her brother Moray, whom Lord M. admires."[1]

The gap between Melbourne's wish for "a bad woman" to have been
beheaded sooner and Victoria's poignant and succinct "I pitied her" sustains an
ancient schism of desire, one that had kept the Queen of Scots alive for centuries. But because it opens between a female monarch and her own "urging"
minister, Victoria's difference with Melbourne also has an unusually disquiet-
ing immediacy: as the queen herself seems to have realized, it eerily
recapitulates Mary's struggles with her own advisors, not to mention those –
less often acknowledged – of her cousin Elizabeth.

Can it be that we have arrived at the middle of the nineteenth century only
to feel that we could be back in Mary Stuart's day? Before her death in 1901,
Victoria was destined to become the most widely beloved – and longest
ruling – queen in Britain's history, the symbol both of its triumph over domestic crisis and of its new imperial power; as an obsessive wife and devoted
mother, she would also come to exemplify a fully realized nation's highest
ideals of womanhood. Yet it would seem that even she was eager to join the
ranks of British women, from the wayward Caroline of Brunswick to the
obscure laundress Mary Leapor, whose sense of vulnerability made them wish
to identify themselves with Mary Queen of Scots.

For Victoria, it was a desire that did not diminish with time. She might have been a fraction of Mary's height, and bound for a resplendent future that could not have been more different from that queen's turbulent, doomed regnancy, but she was also a monarch and a mother at the same time, and after the death of her cherished husband Albert, the veil of mourning would becomingly drape her public image, much as it had Mary's.[2] Whenever she visited her romantic holiday home in Scotland, Victoria thus faithfully marked those features of the landscape where the Stuart queen had suffered,[3] and always she prided herself on being (however remotely) "lineally descended from Queen Mary."[4] Victoria's subjects in their turn obligingly saw the shadow of that tragic royal mother in her. At one of her last public appearances, everyone admired "the face of the Great Lady, [. . .] seamed with lines wrought there by a long life of public care, and by private sorrows, numerous and grievous." It was a face that brought the Queen of Scots to mind, along with those of "other queens who had lived a life of more brilliant gaiety; but to whom had been denied, in their last moments, the crowning consolations of public regard and private affections."[5]

So many mirrorings of Mary Stuart at her saddest! They seem by and large to have flattered Victoria, drawing the sentimental to her side; but less than a year after the ominous *tête à tête* with Lord Melbourne, an attempt was made on her life too. It happened on Constitution Hill, where a disgruntled young waiter from a local inn opened fire just as the queen drove by. Luckily, Victoria escaped injury, but the incident made it clear that, for all that they had welcomed her to the throne, at least some Britons had not altogether outgrown their desire to be rid of queens, even those as demurely removed from actual politics as Victoria soon shaped up to be.[6] Students of Victoria's reign will hasten to note that such impudence was only to be expected: precisely because she stood at the head not just of England, or even of Great Britain, but of the British Empire itself, Victoria's reputation for domestic piety made her a potentially embarrassing contradiction. Hence, as literary critics are fond of observing, behind every paean to her feminine purity lurks some covert assassination of the queenly character; twisted caricatures of female sovereignty abound in Victorian fiction, from Lewis Carroll's Red Queen to H. Rider Haggard's Ayesha, the terrifying "she who must be obeyed."[7]

For its part, though, the attack on Constitution Hill had as much to do with the past as with the present and future. It took place on 10 June, an old Jacobite holiday when, according to Victoria's (and Mary's) biographer, Agnes Strickland, "the loyal affections of our island were divided between the royal names of Stuart and Brunswick."[8] Stranger still, the queen's assailant seems not to have recognized whom he was shooting: he suffered, it was ruled, from "the delirium of physical insanity which produces delusions in regard to person, time and place."[9]

Victoria's subjects made the most of an awkward situation. They sent the would-be assassin, one Edward Oxford, to a mental asylum in lieu of the gallows, and vowed that in future 10 June would be consecrated to "our queen's preservation from imminent danger" rather than to the still disconcerting memory of the Stuarts. But 10 June must also for us mark a demonstration of the Victorian aptitude for a kind of historical "delirium," one whose roots may well be residual terror of female prerogative and one whose manifestation is in any case a slippage between the vanished past and present reality. It was a state of mind that Queen Victoria clearly triggered and, in her lifelong flirtation with the specter of "poor Mary of Scots," evidently came close to experiencing herself.

The two chapters which follow understand the Victorian proclivity for such delirious slippages in time, and the fearful wishes motivating them, as interlocking conditions of what nineteenth-century Britons termed their "fascination" with Mary Stuart. It was a fascination which far outstripped interest in Victoria's politically successful precursor Elizabeth. Between 1820 and 1892 the Royal Academy alone displayed fifty-six new scenes from Mary's life. Special exhibitions were mounted from London to Glasgow, and in 1887 the tercentenary of her death was lavishly commemorated at Peterborough. Schiller and Scott were recycled *ad infinitum*, but that did not keep eight new Mary Stuart tragedies from the stage between 1839 and 1880, with more to come before Victoria's reign drew to a close. Even history primers, normally inclined to take the moral high ground with licentious monarchs, temporized when it came to the Queen of Scots and gave her more than her fair share of pages.[10]

What sort of woman was realized between the covers of the books, inside the picture frames, and once the curtain rose? As if to reflect Victoria's own image in the mirror of history, many canvasses captured a lady of ethereal loveliness, one who – when not occupied with her needle or the feeding of her doves – was usually to be found enduring some distress with every flounce, rosette and sausage curl in place (Plate 12). Here, as in literary settings like Agnes Strickland's popular *Life of Mary Queen of Scots* (1844), Mary provided an "unparalleled instance of feminine forbearance and generosity" (II: 301). She seemed thereby designed to give notice that the more demanding (and more psychologically convincing) Stuart queen of Walter Scott and his contemporaries had vanished with the advent of new and chastened images of what it means to be a crowned head and a woman in the same lifetime. At the same time, however, the visage that Mary presented to the Victorians frequently lacked any such sentimental flourishes. Often it proved layered and irregular, so richly and so variously shaded as to verge on the hallucinatory.

Reborn in the decadent, self-serving Blanche Ingram of Charlotte Brontë's *Jane Eyre* (1847), her waxen image confused with that of Lord Byron in Charles Dickens's *The Old Curiosity Shop* (1841), and apotheosized in the vampire goddess of Algernon Charles Swinburne's late-century trilogy of tragedies about her, this other Mary seemed to invade and antagonize the cult of regal femininity which allowed imperial Britain to feel a measure of affection for itself. The perversion of Victoria, she was morally and often sexually ambiguous. She was also instinctively theatrical, and transgressive on a scale not seen since the days of George Buchanan and his "poisoning witch." She preyed on the dreams of the

Plate 12 Mary Queen of Scots in Captivity, by John Callcott Horsley (1871). Courtesy of Mrs Jean B. Ambrose of Naples, Florida.

innocent, and she planted the blasphemous suspicion that Victoria was a perversion of *her*. To the historian this Mary Stuart might be a "bad woman disguised in the livery of a martyr," to the novelist an erotically charged mother keen to seduce her own daughter, to the playwright a sapphist of sorts who donned men's clothes before setting out to reclaim her kingdom. She failed, of course, as she did to seduce her daughter or to convince a modern skeptic that she was a martyr indeed. But through such failures, a fantastic and forbidden Mary became real and even essential to a number of Victorians. Through her the past itself seemed to become the present.

It is with this second Queen of Scots, particularly as she tended to invade the first, that the next two chapters are concerned. As they trace two dimensions of this Mary's realization in Victorian culture, those chapters revolve around five literary portraits of the Queen of Scots, the most visible of their day. Mary's general popularity certainly owed something to the enduring cult of Sir Walter Scott, as well as to the Scottish romanticism that grew out of that cult. It also coincides with the new interest in the Stuart line that accompanied serious agitation for a more autonomous Scotland, breeding such otherwise unaccountable phenomena as the *poseur* Sobrieski brothers, *fin de siècle* nostalgia for Charles I, and in the first years of the twentieth century a claimant who actually called herself Mary IV of Scots.[11] But the portraits we will examine here were framed less by contemporary politics and the vagaries of popular taste than by the history of conflicted desire for Mary Stuart which from the start had underwritten modern Britons' history of imagining themselves, at once nourishing that history and threatening to turn it back upon itself.

From this point of view, Chapter 8 explores the linked fantasies of sovereign femininity and buried, alternative selfhood so often released by the woman Swinburne called "the queen of snakes and Scots"; Chapter 9 considers Mary in her most explicitly motherly guise, as the unlikely guardian of certain Victorians' sense of the reality and continuing presence of their collective past. Both chapters understand a transgressive Mary both as a conciliatory, even integrating figure, and as interwoven with popular affection for Victoria herself, even as they respect Victoria's longing to feel directly "descended" from the Stuart queen. Obviously shared by many of her subjects, this longing was perhaps fully admissible only once Britannia ruled the world, and so at last and indisputably itself. If the forms it took sometimes verged on the delusional, the Victorian involvement with Mary Queen of Scots nonetheless rehearses and completes the psychological labor of three centuries. For, under Victoria, it is possible to say, the queenly mother of Scots became what a critical mass of Britons, Scottish and English, were at last able to want her to be: for better or for worse, she became a part of them.

8 Victoria's other woman

The people we call the Victorians were in reality a miscellaneous crew, but they did share two interesting contradictions: at the most confident, prosperous and expansive moment in their collective history they lived under a queen who exemplified modest retirement and the sanctity of the home. Yet many were fascinated by a different queen, one who at once foreshadowed the perils of being like Victoria and stood for everything that she was not.

Victoria came to the throne after seven years of uninspiring rule by her dim-witted uncle William IV.[1] Sorely disappointed by its last two kings, Britain was ready for a female monarch in a way it had never been before. Indeed, even in the days of George IV, the popular fancy that queens were dangerous incarnations of unbridled female desire had begun to evaporate, while the pastel virtue of female self-denial ascended to become a mode of royalty in its own right. The shift was hinted at when the exemplary daughter of George and Caroline of Brunswick, the Princess Charlotte Augusta of Wales, died in childbed in 1816. All Britain wept. By the time of Caroline's own funeral five years later, many managed to believe that a paragon of womanly virtue had departed the earth, one who "had lived a Christian heroine and a martyr."[2]

Victoria stepped into this new mold of queenship at the age of eighteen, and there she stayed for the duration of a long life publicly devoted to the objects of her private affection — to her many children, to her husband Albert, and after Albert's death to his memory. It was above all through their living queen that the Victorians perfected their own peculiar myth of gynecocracy, one bourgeois, not courtly, in its inspiration and notoriously exacting in its expectations of female self-effacement. The rules of Victorian queenship are stipulated nowhere more clearly than in John Ruskin's "Of Queen's Gardens" (1871), which firmly established woman's "true place of power" in the home. "So far as [woman] rules," Ruskin proclaimed, "all must be right, or nothing is. She must be enduringly, incorruptibly good, [. . .] wise not for self-development but for self-renunciation."[3]

Of the age that gave us Dr. Jekyll and Mr. Hyde, it is only to be expected that Ruskin's self-sacrificing goddess of the hearth would find her own voracious double on the streets and in the boudoir. Mary Stuart often played

opposite Victoria in just such a drama. At the same time, though, representations of the Queen of Scots were themselves split between the image of Mary
as a "bad woman disguised in the livery of a martyr" and that of her as a
paragon of middle-class "purity" notable for the "moral influence she exercised
in her household."[4] This schism might of course be traced back to the
Elizabethans, but in the nineteenth century it could no longer be reduced to
ideological opposition. While Protestant Victorians scarcely folded the
Catholics among them to their breasts, by the nineteenth century rival religious and political passions had been diverted into the less clearcut arena of
conflicted feelings about female authority, and indeed about femininity itself.
Britons' infamous crisis of faith in most inherited institutions of knowledge
and belief meant that that fervor found at least one new object in ideals of
womanhood. Many writers therefore used Mary not to push religious and
political agendas, but to explore emotionally charged questions about who
women really are and what they truly want.

Under any circumstances, Victorian artists would have had trouble believ-
ably clothing a woman once suspected of adultery, murder and treason in the
garb of a nineteenth-century angel of the house. Under the present ones, they
perforce held Mary Stuart in a kind of double vision, one in which she sometimes appeared to be, as Roy Strong puts it, "a symbol to the repressed
womanhood of mid-Victorian England."[5] But even as the Queen of Scots
seemed to resist regnant models of female virtue, certain continuities appeared
among seemingly competing views of her, and these may in turn be traced to
the influential form of Victoria's own pity for Mary – her apparent longing for
contact with a punished and abandoned version of her more successful self.
Victoria may well have incorporated herself into her society's narrow and self-
serving picture of proper femininity. But for her subjects she often also
modelled desire for another woman, and ultimately for a more complex and
plausible version of femininity itself, embodied in Mary.[6]

Indeed, as in Victoria's own case, it was often the most proper of women's
explicit desire for connection with another woman that brought Mary into the
present. After her *Life of Mary Queen of Scots* appeared in 1844, the popular historian Agnes Strickland was felt to have "vindicat[ed]" the Queen of Scots
"with a lover's enthusiasm and a woman's generosity,"[7] and aristocrats such as
Mary Lowther Ferguson followed in the footsteps of Georgian ladies like Mary
Bellende by having themselves painted as Mary Stuart. Ferguson, personally,
went further, intending "her" portrait by Julius Jacob, for the eyes of another
woman, Lady Londonderry. At the other end of the social spectrum, meanwhile, the working-class poet Ellen Johnston conjured a rapturous vision in
which Johnston, "our present queen" Victoria and Mary Queen of Scots all
communed.[8]

Johnston and Ferguson were not alone in imagining Mary as part of com-
munity of women: works like William Walker's fanciful *Journal of Her
Captivity* (1840) played up her baroque negotiations with Elizabeth and
Bess of Hardwicke, and she was frequently supposed to have won Elizabeth's

Plate 13 The Execution of Mary Queen of Scots, by Ford Madox Brown (1840). Courtesy of the Whitworth Art Gallery, University of Manchester.

permanent enmity when she relayed a rumor, spread by Hardwicke, that the Tudor queen's womb had been sewn shut.[9] Historical paintings such as Ford Madox Brown's surreal depiction of Mary's execution (Plate 13) made her female disciples as much a part of the event as the queen herself, even anticipating Mary's severed head in the profile of one of her fainting ladies-in-waiting. Indeed, the Victorians were perfectly riveted on the Marys – Mary Seton, Mary Beton, Mary Fleming and Mary Livingston – who as her ladies-in-waiting had been so intimate with Mary Stuart from Fontainebleau to Fotheringay. A fifth Mary (Carmichael) could even be summoned as needed. Mary Stuart's vexed involvement with Mary Beton therefore drives Swinburne's trilogy about the Queen of Scots, and Mary Seton is frankly in love with the queen in Michael Field's closet drama *The Tragic Mary* (1890); Mary Livingstone pronounces herself Mary Stuart's "husband" in Maurice Hewlett's lurid historical novel *The Queen's Quair* (1904); and W.D.S. Moncrieff's no less febrile "historical drama" of 1872 has Mary Beton offering Mary Seton a ring that the queen once gave her, in exchange for a kiss.[10] Small wonder that *A Room of One's Own*, Virginia Woolf's classic 1929 commentary on (by and large) the lives and lots of female Victorians, should have named its exemplary women after three of the "Maries."

In defiance of her father's generation, Woolf's point was of course that the grinding realities of economic dependence and patriarchal contempt, masked as adoration, had long barred British women from the life of imagination. As we might expect, few Victorian impressions of either Mary or the Maries revealed quite this order of social consciousness, preferring instead to indulge thinly veiled fantasies of what amounted to erotic love among women. Likewise, in anticipation of Woolf, to imagine Mary first as a woman whose concerns overlapped with those of other women was sometimes to encounter her in a state of misery created by men and ameliorated by female supporters. Occasionally it was even to see her as women's champion. But more often it was to stumble upon a species of feeling for her that defied political or even rational analysis.

The popular term for this feeling was "fascination," and wherever Mary's name appeared, it was not likely to be far behind. The Scottish folklorist Andrew Lang concluded his famously inconclusive study of the casket letters, *The Mystery of Mary Stuart*, with the observation that that mystery "must always fascinate,"[11] and when the Russian prince Alexander Labanoff's esteemed (and still definitive) edition of her letters was translated in 1844, an English reviewer found "the fascinations of Queen Mary" proved in a "living lover [. . .] whose love kindles long after the object of his passion has breathed the breath of life."[12] Magazines as diverse as *Punch* and *The Academy* ruled Mary a creature of eternal "fascination" – "a sphinx, a myth, a mystery."[13] One historian demanded outright to know "the secret of the fascination that snared the hearts of mankind,"[14] and in an essay titled – what else? – "The Lady of Riddles," the Queen of Scots yet again materialized as a creature of "fascination," her beauty "a thing more felt than seen, a thing curiously indefinable and, therefore, insidious, haunting, like a fever in the blood the brain is unable to reach or cope with."[15]

For the Victorians, male and female alike, "fascination" seems to have borne directly upon a conception of femininity as a quality at once erotically enticing and utterly mysterious, as far as could be from the Ruskinian ideal of female self-abnegation. Perhaps most remarkable, though, is the affinity – even conspiracy – that fascination creates between its subject and its object, who remains by definition unknowable. The Queen of Scots, for example, holds fascination, but she also creates it, and what she creates is both "in the blood" and "unable to [be] reach[ed]," at once a quality of the imaginary woman within and a "historical feature" without.

Many Victorians pictured fascination as a kind of compact between some secret compartment within the one who is fascinated (a place "the brain is unable to reach or cope with") and his, or her, at least equally secretive object ("a sphinx, a myth, a mystery"). As Sarah Kofman once suggested in her classic study of the enduring myth of the enigma of woman, the source of that enigma is often found to be woman's own veiled narcissism.[16] We have already seen that Scott and his generation had returned the legend of Mary's narcissism to view, even linking it to her womanhood. The Victorians took this equation a step further: for them, the extent to which the Queen of Scots stood as Victoria's enigmatic and fascinating other woman was the extent to which she permitted those fascinated by her to love culturally and historically alienated parts of themselves.

Not every Victorian who openly indulged a fascination with Mary Stuart took advantage of this possibility, of course, but at least four of them very conspicuously did, and they numbered not just among celebrities of the British fringe but even among the most ardent acolytes of the mainstream cult of holy and true womanhood. Their attachment to Mary naturally presented itself in the language of unreality – of art, dream and waking fantasy. Nonetheless, that attachment visibly sustained and at last fulfilled a very real kind of desire, at once self-reflexive and self-alienating, whose avatars include pity as well as fascination. It is in fact useful to recall that the Elizabethans repressed their pity for Mary precisely because it forced an encounter with self-difference. What pity was to them fascination became for the Victorians – a means of loving not only an alien queen, but also the exiles within themselves.

A LOVER'S ENTHUSIASM

The specters of royal women had hovered around Agnes Strickland from her girlhood: her youngest sister, Catherine Parr Strickland, bore the same name as Henry VIII's last wife; and her own first publication was a "Monody upon the Death of the Princess Charlotte of Wales." Presented at court in 1840, Strickland soon thereafter finished her two-volume *Queen Victoria from Birth to Bridal* – an adulatory work, by and large, but also one whose hints at Victoria's ambivalence toward her bridegroom led to its suppression.[17] Also in 1840, Strickland and her sister Elizabeth published their copious *Lives of the Queens of England*, which Strickland followed single-handedly with her *Lives of the Queens of Scotland and English Princesses* (1851). This last work leaves the impression that all of Mary Stuart's female predecessors were but rungs in the ladder to her. But then Strickland could hardly have felt otherwise, having already translated, edited and published Mary's letters back in 1842; she dedicated the final product – all three volumes of it – to the Scottish historical novelist Jane Porter.

Strickland's *Life of Mary Queen of Scots* (1844) thus feels inevitable, the most conspicuous symptom of a lifelong obsession. Its internal qualities confirm this diagnosis, for while Strickland's general interest in the lives and lots of queens always involved her in intense collaborations with other women, both historical and living, her fascination with Mary Stuart yielded close to a thousand pages of the most intimate appreciation. The florid style in which Strickland expressed her "extraordinary devotion to Mary Queen of Scots" could irritate her contemporaries, one of whom dismissed it as "weak" and attributed its enormous "popularity" – especially with female readers – to a surplus of "trivial gossip and domestic details."[18]

Strickland's goddess, though, was in these details: every page of her *Life* brims with nuances of dress, quotations from Mary's own letters, intricate descriptions of the physical world the queen inhabited, and the most minute inspections of her imagined face. Embellished with long passages from the French poets who had worshipped Mary and embroidered with sentimental excursions on the queen's apparently limitless and always "feminine" virtues, Strickland's *Life* was at once the most textured and the least critical treatment of the Queen of Scots to appear in nineteenth-century Britain. The depth, quality and generosity of its perceptions are those of the lover, as readers instantly recognized.

What might it mean for a nineteenth-century woman – unmarried, Protestant, English and middle class – to feel what those readers called "a lover's enthusiasm" for the likes of Mary? And how could she have felt such a thing for someone she had never met? The question is even more perplexing when we consider that Strickland, a self-appointed guardian of female propriety throughout her long literary career, was also an indefatigable researcher, and thus acutely aware of Mary's ill repute. Yet, to hear Agnes Strickland tell it, Mary Stuart had been the very mold and mirror of sovereign woman, fitted to nineteenth-century standards. Queens, she always held, invariably provide "the most touching examples of all that is lovely, holy, and enduring in Womanhood," but even among them there is "not one more mournfully preeminent than MARY STUART."[19] Mary is the queen of queens to Strickland's mind; in her *Life* she is "true woman," endowed with the most pious "charities and instincts of woman's nature."[20] She is (once) living proof of what woman most truly and deeply is, and neither murder nor adultery, nor indeed any trace of malice or self-interest, lurks in her repertoire.

From this point of view the most striking feature of Strickland's *Life* – its wealth of luminous and absorbing detail – is also its most symptomatic, for no chapter unfolds without an exhausting campaign to disprove some evidence that its heroine fell, at times even criminally, short of Strickland's female ideal. Strickland's Mary is, for example, a slavish mother. The historian goes to enormous lengths to show how tirelessly the queen "beguiled her deep-seated melancholy, with maternal hopes and cares" (I: 355); hence she must have been innocent of such nefarious designs as the attempt to poison her own son with which, Strickland later admits, her enemies had charged her (I: 438). Likewise, when Mary is not thinking of her child, she is a virtuoso of needlepoint whose every embroidered nosegay begs to be catalogued. As Strickland obliges, and dozens of "specimens of feminine taste and industry" pile up before our eyes, the reader of the *Life* can only agree: surely Mary's "pastimes and propensities took so elegant and innocent a turn" that she "was unlikely to have embarked in projects of a bloody and barbarous nature, which emanate from restless minds, unaccustomed to the peaceful and sedative labours of the needle" (II: 408).

Such accumulations of detail reveal the female historian's desire to immerse herself all but physically in Mary Stuart's mind, her heart and her world, while yet vindicating an almost willfully idealized vision of her. These are the typical wishes of a lover, yet in Strickland's case they are informed by something more. For by gathering every possible nuance of Mary's world, no matter how widely flung, Strickland gained access to her own shaping power, the prerogative far more of the artist – the entitled, even despotic liar – than of the slavish and self-effacing historian of fact.

Of course, with Mary, there were relatively few undisputed facts in the first place. In preparing the *Life*, Strickland sifted through thousands of documents, and throughout she found the queen's image stunningly incoherent – not one image, indeed, but many, each the idol of a different desire. What might have humbled a less ardent biographer only made Strickland more confident of her own intimacy with her subject. The fragmentation that followed upon Mary's failure to control the way she was seen emboldened the modern historian to eschew historical record for the evidences of art, and at last to trust most the resources of her own shaping imagination.

Consider the story of Mary's physical shattering at Fotheringay. The headsman, Strickland reminds us, first:

> struck her a cruel but ineffectual blow. Agitated alike by the courage of the royal victim, and the sobs and groans of the sympathizing spectators, he missed his aim and inflicted a deep wound on the side of the skull. She neither screamed nor stirred, but her sufferings were too sadly testified by the convulsion of her features, when, after the third blow, the butcherwork was accomplished, and the severed head, streaming with blood, was held up to the gaze of the people. [. . .] The silence, the tears and groans of the witnesses of the tragedy, proclaimed the feelings with which it had been regarded.
>
> (II: 456)

Needless to say, Strickland leaves out the wig that the execution's first chronicler, Robert Wyngfield, had belabored to such gleefully disparaging ends. A tactful footnote concedes that "when the executioner took up the head, it fell out of the coif and dressings," but no hairpiece is involved, and instead of betraying the horrifying fact that she was no longer young, Mary's natural hair appears as but one more index of her long-suffering virtue, "perfectly gray, being polled very short, which the Earl of Shrewsbury said had been done in his house for the convenience of applying fomentations to relieve her severe headaches" (II: 456).

Out of a scene of disintegration in which even Mary's surface seems to part ways with the rest of her, Strickland creates an order of a different magnitude, one in which scattered features of the tableau – "feelings," "tears and groans," "convulsions" – draw together to "proclaim" and "testify" to the queen's surpassing integrity. "The butcher work" of the Elizabethan is finally no match for the art work of the Victorian, who by the end of the passage commands even the implications of the axe. Hence it is fitting that the minute Mary's head has been divided from her body (and, at least as important, her hair from its dressings), we are directed from something Strickland never did see to something she tells us she did: to a death portrait of the Queen of Scots. Unlike Mary's severed head, this fantastic image asserts plenitude and completion, from its "placid lips, and sealed eyebrows" to its "radiated diadem – the martyr's crown with which it has been adorned."

By admiring this "terrifically fine work of art," Strickland relaxes the "convulsion" of "features" that was the scaffold's legacy, replacing Mary's shattered visage with her own coherent vision of an original female sublimity. This act also permits another sort of integration, albeit delusional: that of the sixteenth-century queen with her nineteenth-century beholder. "It is impossible," Strickland declares, "to contemplate the ineffable composure of the [portrait's] features, without feeling that it verifies its own authenticity, by bringing Mary Stuart's countenance before us at the blessed season" of her death (II: 457). Here, even mutilated and illegible flesh resolves into self-authenticating, self-interpreting art, the strewn hallucinations of the past into present certitude.

Accomplished, finally, by female hands and female eyes, this ideal of integration is one that Strickland traces throughout her *Life*, primarily by exploring Mary's many bonds with other women. We always knew that the Queen of Scots showered her female devotées with gifts and affection; now we learn that she even gave them jobs, subsidizing whole communities of seamstresses, and planning to establish "domestic manufactures" in France, "in the hope of its affording, as it does, after the lapse of nearly three centuries, employment to thousands and tens of thousands of females" (I: 97).

Thanks in part to a degree of concern for other women that seems to make her all but a Victorian, "we never find [Mary] deserted by her own sex under any circumstance" (II: 79–80). Even in the darkest hours of her English captivity, she could always find "some tender-hearted woman, wife, sister, daughter, or domestic [. . .] to compassionate her, supply her wants, and perform all tender feminine offices for her, in her loneliness and destitution, for never was she forsaken by her own sex" (II: 409). On the one occasion women *en masse* turned against Mary, during the Bothwell scandal, Strickland refuses to concede that "any argument of [Mary's] guilt was derivable from the unfeminine conduct of those who could thus violate the charities and instincts of woman's nature." As far as the Victorian woman is concerned, "none but females of the vilest class were capable of acting a part like this; for when were modest maids or virtuous matrons ever known to lift up their voices in the public streets?" (II: 13).

When indeed? Mary's only other female detractors are women of the highest classes, and this leaves the many in the middle to join in confirmation that the queen was herself the epitome of womanly virtue. "With the exceptions of Queen Elizabeth, Catherine de Medici and the Countess of Shrewsbury, Mary had no female enemies," Strickland insists.

> No female witnesses from her household came forward to bear testimony against her. [. . .] None of the ladies of her court, whether of the reformed religion or of the old faith [. . .] lifted up her voice to impute blame to her. [. . . Mary's gentlewomen] clave to her in adversity, through good report and evil report; they shared her prisons, they waited upon her on the scaffold, and forsook not her mangled remains till they had seen them consigned to a long denied tomb.
>
> (I: 1)

Strickland justifies her own belief in Mary's sanctity through the evidence of other women's – gentlewomen's, middling women's – loyalty to her. Oddly enough, the further she pursues it, the less the historian's point seems to be that Mary was the essence of feminine perfection. More significant is that what made her so is the converging body of female perceptions of her. In just this way, the queen's "mangled remains" achieve coherence less because they were eventually pieced together again ("consigned to a long denied tomb") than because they were "seen," by women, to have been so.

It is the record of female witness to Mary, often creative, often silent, that retrieves her as a mended whole into the Victorian present. Strickland, the retriever, recalls, for example, that after Darnley's death Mary formed a fast friendship with his mother, the traces of which survive in lace that the Countess of Lennox tatted for the queen, as well as in letters between the two bound with "floss silk [. . .] and sealed down so that no one could open the letter without cutting through the silken bond that secured it" (II: 328). Together lace and silk provide the modern woman with "no light or inconclusive testimony" that Darnley's mother was "satisfied of Mary's innocence in the death of her son." They are wordless tokens of faith and female community that transcend even the ravages of time and too "cutting" inquiry.

The lace and silk are also works of art, and they return us to the question of Strickland's own art – of her power to create coherent and believable form out of the reservoir of desire she felt she shared with countless other women present and past. For all that the *Life*'s official portrait renders Mary as the soul of female charity, maternal devotion and exquisite taste and tenderness, another, even more desirable, woman reveals herself through that portrait – a longing artist who is the far side of Agnes Strickland as much as she is Mary Stuart.

Strickland observes that Mary's own art of embroidery, so similar to her own literary technique, began in incoherence, occasioned by the shattering and dispersal of other sources of power and self-completion. While in captivity, that is, Mary "preserved her overcharged heart from breaking, and her brain from frenzied excitement, by occupying those hands which had been accustomed to wield the sceptre and grasp the orb of empire, in composing and tracing with the needle allegorical illustrations of her misfortunes" (II: 214). Female art encodes its own origins in frenzy, dejection and failure, and Mary was but the first to substitute its consolations for the "injurious" loss of "regal authority" (I: 89). In turn, the achievement of Strickland's *Life* was to make such motives and implications again visible in the works of the female hand. The biography's subtext thus reveals the image – and the shaping power – of female desire not just for community and self-coherence but at last for unbounded and long denied "regal authority" itself. As her own art betrays the frustration of that desire, Strickland's Mary is less a testament to the vague holiness of true womanhood than a way for the female historian to regain contact with her own power to do what only queens of old and "holy" things can do – create coherence and compel belief.

Fittingly, Strickland's account of Mary's life ends at Westminster Abbey, where Strickland observes in the queen's effigy "a genuine and most satisfactory likeness of the beautiful and unfortunate mother of our royal line, corresponding in features, contour, and expression with her best-authenticated portraits" (II: 466). For Strickland, an image others have found almost certainly unrealistic verifies itself, to become a source of wholeness and satisfaction. Above all, the effigy achieves harmony and completion through Strickland's own absorption into the imagined, indeed idealized, face of the lost "mother" it depicts. "Nothing," Strickland holds, "can be more graceful and majestic than the form, or more lovely and intellectual than the face, which indicates every noble and benevolent quality that could adorn the character of queen or woman." If it is only through the illusion of completion that the incomplete woman of the present day apprehends this resplendent mother, queen and woman in one, these words are at last also their own proof. Strickland's discovery of coherence in fragmentation, of plenitude in loss, and indeed of everything in "nothing," makes it impossible to doubt the prediction of Mary's modern female lover and figurative daughter: that "the living shall never cease with full hands to strew lilies, violets, and roses on her tomb" (II: 466).

QUEEN OF SNAKES AND SCOTS

Algernon Charles Swinburne was not one to strew lilies, violets, or roses on anybody's tomb, least of all that of Mary Queen of Scots. As a matter of fact, he would have regarded such a gesture as an insult to her memory. Instead, the star pupil in the school of fleshly poetry that tweaked Victorian pieties throughout the last third of the nineteenth century professed to admire the very traits that the queen's enemies, from Buchanan and Knox onward, had ascribed to her.

Outrageously enough, Swinburne held that the lustful, headstrong sovereign whom Buchanan had first painted in his *Detection* was actually "an acceptable and respectable type of royal womanhood."[21] By forcing them to revalue the violence at the core of Mary's being, Swinburne aimed, with comparable violence, to convince his upright Victorian readers – who eventually included those of the *Encyclopedia Britannica* itself – that "the brightest and the bravest creature of her kind" ("Character," p. 424) had been the most "cruelly libelled" not by the vitriolic pens that had so often been taken up against her in the past but rather by the "laudations" of her defenders ("Character," p. 427).

In a flagrant rebuke to the Agnes Stricklands (and indeed the Queen Victorias) of the world, Swinburne applauded what he perceived to have been Mary's uninhibited pursuit of her own pleasure, her indefatigable "assertion of prerogative" ("Character," p. 439). And he sneered at the "unparalleled instance of feminine forbearance and generosity'" ("Character," p. 432) that we find on the surface of Strickland's *Life*, or in sanctimonious apologias like John Hosack's chivalrous *Mary Queen of Scots and Her Accusers* (1867). Victoria's "poor Mary," declared Swinburne's contentious 1882 essay on the subject, was nothing more than a "watery thing of tears and terrors held up to our compassion by the relentless if unconscious animosity of the implacable counsel for her defence" ("Character," p. 433). Such a "creature" was a "sarcasm implied on womanhood," and any supposedly reverent portrait of her was, in Swinburne's book, more "savage" than "the most sweeping satire of a Thackeray or a Pope" ("Character," p. 432).

Swinburne spent much of his life rescuing the Queen of Scots from the hounds of love, the better to twist "in the grip of Mary Stuart" by himself.[22] Through three unperformable plays (one of them the length of five tragedies), two influential essays and numerous private letters, he pursued the least "watery" Mary Stuart that nineteenth-century Britain was to know. His personal "queen of snakes and Scots"[23] was "an imperial and royal creature, in the good and bad or natural and artificial sense of the words." "Naturally self willed and framed to be self-seeking," she was "good" exactly insofar as she obeyed a "natural" passion ("Character," p. 441). And as Swinburne used the Queen of Scots to mock manufactured ideals of female power, he had the effrontery to redefine the masculine subject of modern Britain as well.

Agnes Strickland had been the strong-featured leader of an entire troupe of female historians whose lives' purpose seemed to be to light the candles in the Victorian cult of true womanhood. By contrast, the delicate, high-strung, Swinburne, with his floating aureole of fire-red hair and his enduring nostalgia for the floggings of his public school days, belonged very much to the Victorian avant-garde. His lurid, sensuous poetry placed him somewhere between the pre-Raphaelites of mid-century and the aesthetes and decadents who came into their own at the *fin de siècle*. As numerous commentators have noticed, both of these communities of male artists and male writers, while often obsessed with the most minute pricks of sensation and (especially female) fleshly being, were even more engrossed in one another. And their work – much of it phantasmagorical and escapist in nature – often subliminally seeks to eradicate the very woman whose engulfing charms its authors seemed to crave.[24]

Maneuvers such as these are usually attributed to the threat to male pre-eminence posed by women novelists' domination of the nineteenth-century literary market, or to increasingly effective movements for women's social and economic empowerment, or of course to Victoria's secretly intimidating regnancy. Swinburne's own adolescent fantasies certainly alluded to this last threat: as a schoolboy he wrote several burlesques that portrayed Mary's mother-in-law Catherine de'Medici as a shameless dominatrix and gave Victoria herself a prostitute sister (surely a shadow Mary Queen of Scots) who plots to usurp her throne.[25] Known – and, by polite Victorians, regularly reviled – for poetry that strove always for the condition of the sensuous body and observed no morality beyond that dictated by desire, Swinburne loaded all of his writing with mythically powerful, even destructive women – avatars of Medusa, Lamia and Salome – who dined with gusto on men's hearts. Small wonder that the Queen of Scots who held sway in the three tragedies that Swinburne considered to constitute his *magnum opus* should have turned out to be a vampire goddess of the first magnitude.

But Swinburne's actual investment in Mary Queen of Scots is not easily, or indeed appropriately, reduced to a symptom of masculine anxiety. For one thing, it was virtually inbred. Both a genetic heritage and a political one, it had shaped his childhood, and it was what allowed him very literally to feel part of a past he idealized. Swinburne's father had been born and raised in France and though no Gallic blood actually ran in the family, the younger Swinburne fiercely guarded the delusion that he, like Mary, was in fact French. More importantly, Swinburne saw his ancestors as having been "Catholic and Jacobite rebels and exiles." His was, he often reminded his friends, a "family which in every Catholic rebellion from the days of my own Queen Mary to those of Charles Edward had given their blood like water and their land like dust for the Stuarts." The matrix of his childhood fantasies of identity, revolt and heroic masculinity, this bodily link to Mary's cause was one that Swinburne cultivated, indeed flaunted, throughout his adult life. He hastened to remind his friend Theodore Opitz that "among the first to welcome [Mary] into this inhospitable country was the head of my family." Hence, Swinburne pointed out, he was "naturally inclined" to take a "favourable, just and rea-sonable view" of the Queen of Scots.[26]

In an effort to realize this view, Swinburne spent much of his creative life restoring queenship's rebellious body to it: he finished his play *Chastelard* (1865) before he turned thirty, following it first with the epic *Bothwell* (1874), then, in 1881, with the turgid closet drama *Mary Stuart*. The plays sold well even though they never saw the stage, and Swinburne's essay on "The Character of Mary Queen of Scots" circulated widely in an 1882 issue of the *Fortnightly Review*. Most impressive of all, the poet's 1883 contribution to the *Encyclopedia Britannica* remained definitive well into the twentieth century: no mean feat considering that its running diatribe against those who imagined

Mary as a coquette of "dastardly imbecility, [. . .] heartless irresolution, and [. . .] brainless inconsistency" ("Mary Queen of Scots," p. 385) violates the tepid conventions that normally govern encyclopedia entries.[27]

But then to Swinburne Mary was herself a lawbreaker. Fearless and unrepentant, she had died an "alien" and indeed a sworn enemy to all English laws. She even broke the rules of gender difference. Swinburne loved to speculate about what might have been "had she been born the man that she fain would have been born" ("Character," p. 430), and at the very least, Mary fused typically masculine and feminine characteristics to stand as "the most fearless, the most keen-sighted, the most ready-witted, the most high-gifted, high-spirited of women; gallant and generous, skilful and practical."[28] Swinburne lavished praise on the "statesmanlike yet feminine dexterity" ("Mary Queen of Scots," p. 386) of a queen who "steered her skilful and dauntless way with the tact of a woman and the courage of a man" (p. 378) and had indeed often "uttered her wish to be a man" (p. 389).

Obviously, to reconceive Mary as an androgyne was to expand the possibilities for masculine as well as feminine subjectivity. It was also to present customarily gendered forms of feeling, action, and even authority, as mere inventions. And in more respects than this, Swinburne's transgressive Mary had been made, not born, into what she was. The poet liked to remind his readers that Mary had been educated in a French court that was little better than a "flying squadron of high-born harlots." Her childhood "recreations," Swinburne noted, with not a little envy, "were divided between the alcoves of Sodom and the playground of Alcidama" ("Character," p. 425). Arguments from acculturation were the closest Swinburne ever came to extenuating Mary's presumed faults. And he saw the Queen of Scots as the product not just of French dissipation but also of the concoction of radical (and hence appealing) differences from the present that he called, simply, the past. To Swinburne, Mary was a "representative of the past – of monarchy and Catholicism."[29] She was a triply deviant "creature of the sixteenth century, a Catholic and a queen" ("Character," p. 425).

Swinburne's "trilogy of *Mary Stuart*" was a massive paean to this "creature" of a world that currently was not, and Swinburne conceived it as "an epic or historic whole."[30] It was, as such, a model of submission to the material dictates of the "past" whose "representative" Mary was. Throughout his three plays, Swinburne held himself excruciatingly accountable to historical material, whose weight came to exemplify the wonderful physical density and libidinal energy that he identified with the past and which he strove to assimilate into his own poetic language. The overwhelming bulk of the 600-page *Bothwell* alone registers Swinburne's desire to transpose historical substance into modern words, as do the transcripts from the treason trial at Fotheringay that *Mary Stuart* incorporated verbatim.

The case of *Bothwell* is especially revealing. Even Swinburne's friend Edmund Gosse found it a "huge chronicle [. . .] unsuited to the rapid habits of our time" and predicted that it would "always be a book to be dipped into or quoted from rather than to study from end to end."[31] Swinburne's own experience of writing *Bothwell* was apparently nightmarish precisely because he wanted its characters to be "living likenesses" of real people.[32] He saw its historical context as the "great battle between past and future, death and life, tradition and revolution," and the play's propensity to "dilat[e] in bulk and material at every step" was born of the author's own compulsion "to omit no detail, drop no link in the chain," until he had "wrung it from the clutch of historic fact." Writing *Mary Stuart* was likewise a matter of finding a body for Swinburne's own phrases and figments of imagination – of setting down a "skeleton of acts" and then "getting the bare bones clothed with flesh and sinews."[33]

As it follows Mary from her first days in hostile Scotland through her collisions with Knox, Darnley and Bothwell, to an English scaffold, Swinburne's trilogy thus fuses the words and wishes of a modern poet with both the sensuous matter and the enticing otherness of the past.[34] The author's desire for such a fusion reverberates with his longing to assimilate masculine and feminine characteristics. And all of these wishes converge in a quest, ironically reminiscent of Strickland's, to become one with Mary Queen of Scots. Refracted through all three of the Mary Stuart plays but articulated most fully in the first, it is this desire above all that perversely links the aggressively *outré* Swinburne with the most staid and sentimental of his contemporaries.

SHUTTING UP MEN'S LIPS: SWINBURNE'S *CHASTELARD*

Chastelard was the first part of Swinburne's Mary Stuart trilogy, and the only one his readers have ever been able to finish. He wrote it during a long stay in Paris, at a time when he was, as he put it, "not yet emancipated from servitude to college rule."[35] To his mind, the young Queen of Scots's doomed involvement with the adolescent French poet who eventually went to the scaffold for breaking into her bedroom was likewise the "last episode of the heroine's girlhood," offering moreover "the last tragic glimpse of [Mary's] easy years in France among young lovers and singers who could not hold their own in a strange country and changing time."[36] The play, in other words, rediscovers Swinburne's own immaturity in his heroine, who likewise mirrors his struggle to achieve a voice in an alien linguistic climate.

Questions of voice actually suffuse Swinburne's play. Its literary source, for example, lay in the vituperative pages of Mary's enemy John Knox's *History of the Reformation in Scotland*. There, after discovering the besotted "Chattelett" hiding in her bedchamber, Mary "bursts forth in a womanly affection" to beg her half-brother Murray "that as he loved her, he should slay Chattelett, and let him never speak word." When Murray begs Mary not to make him "secretly slave of your own commandment," the dialect of the queen's "womanly affection" is firmly pitted against the tongues of men.[37] It was, Swinburne later confessed, "upon this hint I spake" ("Character," p. 438). Perversely enough, it would seem that his own tongue had been unbridled by the historical (or at least the historically phantasmic) Mary's apparent determination to "shut up men's lips."

After he had finished *Chastelard*, Swinburne refused to accuse himself "of any voluntary infraction of recorded fact, or any conscious violation of historical chronology" ("Character," p. 438). But, in point of fact, the Victorian poet did considerable violence to both chronology and fact, inventing a pivotal infatuation with Chastelard for Mary's lady-in-waiting Mary Beton (now Beaton) and moving the entire Chastelard episode forward in time to coincide with the queen's marriage to Darnley. To take Swinburne at his word is to assume that his "infraction[s]" against the plot that history, or at least Knox, had scripted were simply *in*voluntary and *un*conscious. His Mary is similarly driven by impulses other than the ones she thinks she has. In particular, her spoken reluctance to have Chastelard put to death vies with her far less conscious determination to end his life. Mary's internally compromised authority is therefore linked to the voice of the Victorian male writer both as its troubled twin and as its *raison d'être*.

What is more, though the closest *Chastelard* ever came to performance was Swinburne's reading of it for a group of friends at an "aesthetic tea" he held in 1865, the play's rough, literally sensational verbal texture did physically affect many Victorian readers.[38] One reviewer declared that its "language will offend [. . .] those who have taste," and another denounced the play as a "forcing house of sensual appetite."[39] Ironically, it was through just such scandalous, physically jolting uses of words that Swinburne showcased his own often rarefied French poetry and forged bonds with erudite French writers he admired, from the play's dedicatee, Victor Hugo, to Mary's contemporary Ronsard, whose poetry is mentioned throughout and at last (as in William Ireland's *Effusions*) accompanies Chastelard to the scaffold.[40]

How remarkable that a play with so many linguistic ambitions – to unite with the exalted and often alien tongues of others, to shock modern sensibilities, to tell the truth and yet defy it, to realize the past – should center on a queen who, as in Knox's *History of the Reformation*, "shut[s] up men's lips!" Yet in Swinburne's plot, Mary guarantees masculine prerogatives of speech only by removing them. She compliments herself that her face alone:

> can yet make faith in men
> And break their brains with beauty: for a word,
> An eyelid's twitch, an eye's turn, tie them fast
> And make their souls cleave to me.
>
> (p. 81)

An epigraph from an Elizabethan travelogue identifies Swinburne's heroine with "fulle cruele and evele Wommen of Nature" who "zif they beholden ony man thei slen him anon with the beholdynge" (p. 6). But while typically this sort of *femme fatale* merely silences men with the sight of her, an actual language is woven into the flesh of Swinburne's man-absorbing queen. Her "word" is as rivetting as her "eye's turn," and when the fascinated Chastelard delivers the first of his many arias on Mary's enchanting body, he skips quickly from her "fair eyes," "smooth temples," and "flesh of lifting throat" to acknowledge that it is really "the speech and shape and hand and foot of heart" – all conjoined – "that I would die of – yes, her name that turns/My face to fire being written" (p. 20). The Maries likewise find that "the side of her that [. . .] snares in such wise all the sense of men" is Mary's "cunning speech – /The soft and rapid shudder of her breath/In talking" (p. 16).

As one of her namesakes points out, they may well "praise [Mary] in too lover-like a wise/For women that praise women" (p. 17). But for her male and female acolytes alike, the man-eating, body-centered words identified with Mary are also old ones. All three of Swinburne's epigraphs come from sixteenth-century texts, whose original spelling he retains. Mary's primary bond with the poet Chastelard is through the old French poetry that they exchange, and the verse she inspires him to write is deliberately archaic. So throughout *Chastelard*, the bodily power that Mary possesses is inseparable from the lure of a kind of mother tongue, one that belongs in the past but that she alone can bring into the present. Sometimes this is the French tongue that Swinburne mistook for his own natal language; more often it is a more primitive language still, one in which the speaker and the spoken are assimilated to one another. If that assimilation erodes distinct identities and threatens to pack male "lips full of earth" (p. 65) – if it bears fruit inevitably in the death of those, like Chastelard, who lust after it – it nonetheless also promises Chastelard's latter-day incarnation, the striving poet Swinburne, a fusion of another order, with the historical past, the physically actual and the sexually and symbolically opposite.

Some of Swinburne's contemporaries indeed felt that the very text of *Chastelard* had managed to merge with the primal woman, Mary, herself. "No one has succeeded in fascinating the spectator so fully as Swinburne," Gosse declared. "In the magic mirror of his verse we see [Mary's] splendid supple body, her long pale throat and pale bright breasts, her heavy scented hair, hot amorous eyes and lips, and all the wicked music of her words." Once Swinburne's "verse" had become a "magic mirror," there was no need or reason to distinguish it from what it simulated, indeed assimilated to itself – a queen so "false, cruel, light of love, [. . .] so fair that every man who saw her loved her, but died, having embraced her."[41]

In *Chastelard*, it is of course the title character who mimics the poet's own desire to be absorbed into an archaic, if not originary, female body. Not unlike Agnes Strickland's, Chastelard's verbal reconstructions of Mary are as minutely detailed as any pre-Raphaelite canvas, lingering on the "soft small stir beneath her eyes" and the "quivering of her blood" as he "feel[s] her hand's heat still in mine" (p. 34). He longs both to feel Mary "in all my breath and blood" and to leave "in the blue sweet of each particular vein/Some special print of me" (p. 137). His is ultimately a fantasy of being entirely devoured by Mary: he imagines that "her sweet lips and life/Will smell of my spilt blood" (p. 64); she is a vampire who "reddens at the heart with blood of men" (p. 128), and Chastelard longs for her to "leave her lips/Deep in my neck" (p. 131). In wanting her "lips," he seems to want her voice – something he can only possess by giving his to her. Swinburne's "queen of snakes and Scots" turns out to share this very fantasy. In the play's most startling scene, she sits alone before her mirror, enticing her own "fair face" to "be friends with me" (p. 67). Believing that she needs male devotion to realize that friendship, she longs for a man who will "do as much for me/As give me but a little of his blood/To fill my beauty from" (p. 68). This wish is instantly granted by Chastelard, who not only arrives on the scene to fulfill his own desire for incorporation into her but seems to Mary to come forward from her glass, as if he were in fact she.

Such syntheses of female authority and functionally infantile male subjectivity guarantee that Mary's own death will occur in Chastelard's, at least metaphorically. And in her last visit to this human "blurred glass" (p. 57) just before his beheading, she predicts that she too "shall die somehow sadly" (p. 142). Chastelard's response is to try to imagine himself Mary's killer as much as she is his; he begs the queen to "stretch your throat out that I may kiss all round/Where mine shall be cut through," and even to "suppose my mouth/The axe-edge to bite so sweet a throat in twain" (p. 143). Masochist and sadist become one another to permit long-craved, if unorthodox, re-alignments of gender identity and sexual impulse.

Though Swinburne's play is named after its male protagonist, Mary is surrounded by women (Mary Seton, Mary Beaton, Mary Carmichael and Mary Livingstone) who share her name, whose voices and perceptions frame the play, and whose longings mirror the queen's own. Of these women, Mary Beaton swiftly distinguishes herself as Mary Stuart's true shadow self. Infatuated with Chastelard, Mary Beaton sings love songs he has written for Mary to make him equally love's subject and its object. In turn, her complex identification with Chastelard merges with her own desire to be Mary Stuart: under cover of darkness, Mary Beaton even lets Chastelard kiss her under the delusion that she is the queen. For her part, the queen often seems to love Mary Beaton more than any of the men who surround her, even "swear[ing] she were no paramour for any man,/So well I love her" (p. 42).

By masochistically mirroring both Mary and Chastelard, the aptly named Mary Beaton assimilates the two to one another. And it is finally her pain – the pain of being in the end the displaced other of both of them – that accomplishes the work of assimilation, of grafting male language onto the female body ("my lips are beaten") in a way that will authenticate the one and perpetuate the other. It is at last Mary Beaton who fulfills Swinburne's own poetic and personal wishes for union with Mary Queen of Scots. And fittingly it is Mary Beaton's lust to avenge Chastelard's death that follows Mary Stuart through the two remaining plays in Swinburne's trilogy: *Bothwell* ends with Mary Beaton's sinister promise that "I will never leave you till you die,"[42] and at the end of *Mary Stuart*, Elizabeth finally decides to sign Mary Stuart's death warrant when Mary Beaton, ordinarily "dumb as death," arranges for the Tudor queen to receive a letter that her Stuart cousin had impulsively written, full of malignant gossip about Elizabeth's female parts (p. 184).

If Swinburne's Chastelard experiences the ecstatic triumph of synthesis with Mary Stuart, Mary Beaton is the condition of its possibility. It is finally thanks to her that Swinburne's play completes multiple acts of assimilation – body to word as we have seen, but also life to death, and, above all, male to female. *Chastelard* is well-stocked with androgynous characters – Mary recalls her first husband's "pale little mouth that clung on mine" (p. 68), Chastelard envisions Mary's face floating in a sea of men's helmets (p. 71), Darnley's hair is "a mermaid's yellow" (p. 9), Elizabeth Tudor is "maiden-tongued, male-faced" (p. 19) and Mary herself wishes "I had been a man" (p. 48). And in turn, Swinburne's obsession with Mary Queen of Scots may be traced to the desire for the forbidden woman within himself – an excruciating desire he pursued through a radical reordering of linguistic possibility. Though it seems to leave him outside the Victorian mainstream with its tirelessly resounded themes of unadulterated and "true" womanhood, this longing actually lodged him very firmly among them, for his fantasy of assimilation expresses a desire he shared even with the upstanding Agnes Strickland – a desire to know all the dimensions and boundaries of self, and so the possibility of complete self-utterance. In later life, the playwright even began to sound like the most conservative critic of his age. He dismissed Chastelard as a "suicidal young monomaniac" ("Character," p. 438), formally declaring that the play which bore his name was "never meant to be more than a mere love-play." But of course it wasn't. As Strickland also knew, attempts to test the self's boundaries never are.

A PASSIONATE DESIRE FOR ACCESS

Swinburne's self-seeking, man-devouring Mary Queen of Scots was not without her admirers. The *fin de siècle* poet Michael Field even decided that her "majesty of intellect," her "conscious[ness] of the burthen of her own beauty," and above all the devotion of her "every power of spirit and sense to the reception or excitement of desire" all proved her creator, Swinburne, "a great poet of our time."[43] She also usefully countered the other queen whom Strickland had recently put through "the process of canonisation" – "a creature," wrote Michael Field, "perfect in action and forbearance from the day of her first communion to her bowing down upon the block" (p. vii).

Yet instead of regaling Swinburne's "queen of snakes and Scots" as true Mary and true woman, Michael Field deemed desire's fluctuation between competing images of the queen the very secret of her survival in British imaginations. "The wife of Darnley and of Bothwell will be various to various natures throughout the ages," Michael Field decided. "For like Helen she never grows old." What is more, Mary's enigmatic variation liberated the modern from the harness of his own particular place and time, authorizing him to "transcribe his sense of the facts of her life, to justify the vision of her as it has come to himself, and yet be reverently conscious of the splendid and passionate qualities of former presentment" (p. vii).

The author of these astonishingly apt sentiments was himself one of the most fascinating figures on the Victorian literary scene, not least because he did not exist. A persona shared by two female poets, Katherine Bradley and Edith Cooper, Michael Field produced several volumes of classically inflected, often sapphic, poetry throughout the last two decades of Victoria's rule, as well as numerous closet tragedies centered on reckless, self-willed heroines like Marianne and Lucrezia Borgia. Aunt and niece, Cooper and Bradley set up house together and were apparently lovers into the bargain.

This lack of orthodoxy at home predicts that Bradley and Cooper would have cast their lot with Swinburne's transgressive temptress. But in fact, "Michael Field" found both confirmation of personal "vision" and connection with the "former presentments" of others in the perpetual "mysteries of [Mary's] nature." Only as long as no single version of Mary prevailed, and these "mysteries" thus stayed unsolved, could "he" be confident that "my impressions from contact with a personality the facts of which present perpetual change have not been embarrassed or irrelevant." Because only a mystery permits the illusion of total immersion in its object, such impressions "have grown from a vision almost to a conviction as I have explored and wrought" (p. vii).

The authorial psyche that wrought a convincing Queen of Scots out of its own depths was a fiction, a conspiracy, and at best a close dance with someone who was herself not quite there. Michael Field, that is, was fully as shadowy – and, as two women instead of one, fully as divided – as the half-phantasmic queen that "he" at once explored and created. In the play that brings her to life, "the tragic Mary" is herself perennially divided between competing models of femininity, achieving her one moment of psychological coherence and political efficacy whilst dressed as a man. She thus measures the degree to which the quintessentially Victorian question of who woman is and what she wants drove nineteenth-century fantasies about the Queen of Scots. And Michael Field's convincing answer to that question – that woman is many women and that what she wants are multiple versions of herself – does not fall terribly far from Swinburne's answer, or from Strickland's, or even from the one implied in Victoria's pity for a "silly, idle, coquettish French girl." If anything, it marks the spot where all of them converged.

Before writing *The Tragic Mary*, Michael Field had been to Edinburgh, a city which "fascinates us to herself" because "it is [. . .] the repository of the Queen's tragedy." There:

> in the apartments of Holyrood we can touch the very silks that Queen
> Mary handled; the mirror of scolloped edge [. . .] that without contradiction reflected her features, still hangs in her chamber: the flushed tatters
> of her curtains are before us. And beholding these things we are seized
> with a passionate desire of access, an eagerness of approach: we cannot

pause to wonder, or debate, or condemn; an impulse transports us: we are started on an inevitable quest.

(p. v)

The impulsive yet "inevitable quest" for "Queen Mary" that begins in the mirror she also touched reaches back in time through the many women – Agnes Strickland, Ann Radcliffe, Sophia Lee – who shared a "passionate desire of access" to Mary. This is a desire which must be its own completion, for like the love of a reflected image, Michael Field does not see that it is ever to be fulfilled. As did Strickland's *Life*, the preface to *The Tragic Mary* thus ends in Westminster Abbey, where "the Queen herself lies sculptured, [. . .] waiting with serenity of patience a judgment other than that of men." Until then, all knowledge of Mary must remain "but conjectures, and the real woman of magical nature must remain undiscovered and triumphant" (p. viii).

Here, Mary figures "woman" as she truly and deeply – and by definition secretly – is. Bradley and Cooper sought to protect Mary's fascinating enigma by discovering her reality in it. They wished, for instance, "that the crayon of Holbein might have given expression" to her face, "the self-betrayal of personality." Yet they supposed that the master would have painted a face actually more enigmatic than any of the countless extant; its unrivalled accuracy would lie, precisely, in its having captured Mary's inherent mystery. A true portrait of the queen, thus, would have "brought out in each subtle crease of the flesh, by its shadows and smiles, such experience as could not travel to the lips or eyes" (p. vi). It would have traced the ravines of Mary's own mysterious longings, and thereby those of her beholder. Such a portrait can not of course exist in paint. But *The Tragic Mary* attempts to create something like it in language.

In many ways, the result is an allegory of lesbian desire. Michael Field's play certainly represents all of Mary's heterosexual entanglements as repressive and deceitful at best, violent and even destructive at worst. It also idealizes her female followers' devotion to her. Beginning with the offstage stabbing of Rizzio and an overweening Bothwell's vow to win the pregnant queen, it ends after Mary has lost almost every source of the authority she once prized to become the pawn and prisoner of her own lords. The latter have plotted from the beginning to sequester her in the domestic prison of "high-set Stirling" where "she can rock/Her bairnie's cradle, sing the lullaby,/Or strain her bowstring on the garden pot:/While with their sovereign-king her faithful nobles/Do the man's work and govern" (p. 15).

Because Mary intends to be much more than a flower-tending cradle-rocker, a subliminal war rages between the sexes throughout the play. It is a war that maps onto religious schism. Perhaps to emphasize her deviance, or possibly to encode their own, Bradley and Cooper made Mary the most conspicuously Catholic Queen of Scots that we find among the Victorians.[44] But while Mary is "ciphered Catholic" from birth (p. 219), her male tormentors (who eventually force her to forswear her own faith) are rabidly Protestant, and as such they "wrec[k] her like an abbey" (p. 200). As in Scott's *Abbot*, it is Protestant passion, unresponsive to beauty and rapacious to the core, that kills women and secures men's power. Protestant men prefer "the lands" that once belonged to "fat priests" to women; one even brags that those lands are his as their own "buxom dames,/Put to rank purpose by idolatry" and boasts that "with them I ease my lust" (p. 46).

If the Protestant desires that shaped Great Britain's future degraded women, the Roman Catholicism of the past unites them with each other in communities of love. Mary's voluminous entourage of ladies-in-waiting wholly adores her. Her women sleep with her, twice nurse her back from the edge of the grave, sing and sew with her, and throughout the play enjoy intimate physical contact with her. Their choral voice longs for the return of the days, before the intrusion of Mary's desires for men and men's for her power, when the queen "would sit,/Peruse, and sort [her] jewels by the hour/Making such pretty presents and bequests/As set us weeping" (p. 71).

Whereas Mary's lords look to the day they will "mince [the queen] up,/And toss her from the terrace" (p. 15), her women love her to such distraction that one of them must leave the room whenever the subject of Mary and men rears its ugly head: after all, "when a woman sets her heart upon a woman she is inexorable in jealousy" (p. 69). When the ambitious Bothwell wants to marry Mary, ostensibly to her advantage, his wife agrees to a divorce because her love for the queen far surpasses her affection for her husband. And another of Mary's female devotées, Mary Fleming, insists that though she is herself married, "that mars not my constancy – a man needs so little of one's nature. It suffices him if one's complexion be fair. But there is not a balmy nook in one's soul undiscovered of her; she desists not from divining till she hath access to the honey-cells. [. . .] I will love her to my life's end." Such words work to define "the tragic Mary" at least as much in terms of female love for the Queen of Scots as in terms of the manipulative fictions of male adulation that she also, unfortunately, craves. And their urgency tempts us to see *The Tragic Mary* as a fable of lesbian longing whose moral is that female sovereignty is tenable only in relation to the love of other women, or in the refusal to submit to traditional heterosexual arrangements. Mary's own marriage to Darnley puts her on what threatens to be her deathbed, while her misguided union with Bothwell strips her of sovereignty.

Yet the nature of Mary Fleming's love suggests that Michael Field was ultimately writing something more interior and indefinable than strict allegory. For one thing, the waiting-woman's rapture when Mary gains "access" to her – her joy at being discovered – makes the Queen of Scots the mirror of the modern woman, driven, we saw, by a "passionate desire for access" to the "real woman of magical nature." So, just as we limit ourselves when we try to interpret Mary simply as an image – as one kind of woman or another, depending on who is representing her – so we flatten *The Tragic Mary* when we disengage it from the craving for mutual access, for intimate and mutually creative knowledge within and between all kinds of women, that motivated Cooper and Bradley's play and infuses its every line.

Because, "the tragic Mary" is the unknowable object of both desire and knowledge, she is to Michael Field's mind, Woman. Michael Field's early twentieth-century "biographer," Mary Sturgeon, was drawn to *The Tragic Mary* because its heroine was "no male apprehension of femininity as sheer sex-impulse." Instead, in *The Tragic Mary*, "femininity" is a "complex and subtle power" of which Mary is herself the "chief victim."[45] Treated as a "power" rather than as an essence – as a principle of relation rather than as an entity – femininity makes the subject into her own object.

What does a woman want? An answer to the question that that residual Victorian Freud was to pose so appositely hides in Michael Field's Mary, amalgam that she is of every wish that woman might conceivably have. Her impulses range from her craving for love ("I must be beloved" [p. 64]) to the will *to* love that makes her "aggressive and audacious in desire/As any unsunned girl" (p. 141). Mary's fierce maternal instincts counter a bloody thirst for the throne of another woman. Even as "a cry for empire pierces up [her] heart" (p. 58), the queen's lust to conquer crosses swords with the longing for erotic subjection that drives her into her subject Bothwell's arms. Meanwhile, many of her pleasures are humbly domestic, displayed whenever she deftly, if improbably, scrambles eggs onstage or takes up her embroidery. As a self-differing and undecidable woman, she is the work of "the lavish side of God,/Before the thought of judgment crippled Him,/When He was soft, creative, fostering, free" (p. 179).

All might yet be well if Mary's profusion of desires did not include the longing to fulfill those of men, particularly Bothwell and his alter ego, Mary's outwardly cynical secretary Maitland of Lethington. The queen's own enslavement to their romantic vision of her slowly undermines her equally potent desire for absolute sovereignty. Her marriage to Bothwell visibly "wither[s]" her authority (p. 200), abetted by her persistent willingness to "let love be terror," and by her need for erotic surrender. Hence eventually Mary's rebels force her into flight and hiding. But in so doing they also drive her inward, into a confrontation with her own mixed desires that leads her to redefine sovereignty in psychological rather than political terms. In the last act, a fugitive Mary "slips/Into her boyish hose and doughty cloak/To disappear forever" (p. 232). And she makes quite a convincing man: "Your change of vesture," Bothwell himself later tells her, "might/Win manhood to adopt you" (p. 235).

Here at last male masquerade seems to solve the tragic problems of feminine masochism and vulnerability. But in the end, Mary finds she cannot sustain the man's part: she cannot "shed my people's blood." Back in "a countrywoman's dress," she lets herself be taken into captivity, where she sits "dazed" and "confused," unable to "hold/Firm converse with myself" (p. 243). Mary regains herself in male dress because it was in that guise that she lost her way and, having lost herself, she lost "grief" and found "freedom": "Myself's own mystery closes round my soul/Once more, and I am healed" (p. 233). Just so, upon her return to female dress she clings to exactly the enigma that has brought her to this moment of dissociation. Still loving Bothwell, she now understands that her own essence is self-contemplating erotic paradox: "How vile was our false wedding, vile the banns,/The ritual," she muses. But how "dear the rape, the ride along/The High Street with my king at bridle rein;/So should Queen Mary flaunt upon a banner/Subject subjecting" (p. 259).

Discovered through the loss of her most recognizable self, Mary's desire to be "subject subjecting" recalls the Elizabethans' failure to learn how to be subject and object at the same time. Their solution to what presented itself as both a political and a psychological dilemma was to kill the woman they perceived to be its source, literally detaching her from the terrifying libidinal body that at once offered itself to them and made them long to yield to her. As we have seen, that act had to be repeated symbolically for centuries thereafter if the fiction of Britain – and of a certain state of mind equipped to believe in it – was to prevail.

But in *The Tragic Mary* Michael Field offers a different, if more enigmatic possibility, one no longer overwhelming. On the contrary, Mary ends the play in a delirium of tragic joy, one that she invites us to share. She has lost everything, yet muses:

> I have still myself
> To set within myself and crown, the true
> Religion to give faith to, also to love
> To weep for through the long captivity
> Of unenjoying years, and the whole earth
> To gain, when I have repossessed my soul.
>
> (p. 260)

These words allow Mary to attain herself as long as she differs from herself. They are the last of the play, and are deliberately inconclusive. Bradley and Cooper in the end refused to make their "tragic Mary" symbolize any single kind of woman, any single relationship between a woman and her others. Her meaning and her power to survive – her sovereignty – lie in the infolding of multiple, contradictory and inevitably frustrated desires. This infinite, infolding in turn links the Queen of Scots psychologically with other women, future and past. Women even of classical times fill Mary's own thoughts as the shadows lengthen and she faces the long captivity that will end at the scaffold. Those women "come in multitudes," she tells Lethington near the end:

> There is no time in them; it is alike
> If they fell ages back, or yesterday;
> And Helen [. . .]
> Moves close to me; she clasps Theonoe
> About the neck, and through the lotus-flowers
> The women press together.
>
> (p. 215)

When Lethington dismisses Mary's imaginary Queen of Troy as "the phantom, not the live Helen," Mary shrugs, having meant only "she who was a queen" (p. 215). And queenship lies like femininity itself in the elusive space between phantom and woman. It is a space any historical woman can inhabit: Mary, Helen, Theonoe. "The women press together."

As the Queen of Scots herself would surely have done, "the tragic Mary" marvels at those who love "the poor image of oneself, the clay,/Not the live creature" (p. 216). "Secluded in herself" (p. 216), she realizes that the "multitudes" within her will at last be perpetuated not in the "poor image[s]" of her but rather in the shared, yet various, and seldom nameable, fantasies and desires that they create. No one could have been better suited than "Michael Field" to understand this kind of queen, one who is only herself when she is beside herself – when she is in effect her own other woman.

9   A "laboured illusion" vanishes

Transgressive though they were, neither Michael Field's tragic Mary nor Swinburne's "queen of snakes and Scots" looks entirely aberrant when seen against the background of the Victorians' fixation upon the past. In 1862, for example, James Anthony Froude brought out his succulent *History of England*, thereby scaling an exalted reputation with the English reading public. Yet the feature of Froude's twelve-volume *History* to attract the most attention was the one that made the popular historian's otherwise adoring readers the least comfortable. One magazine even went so far as to "hope that there are few living men or women who can read Mr. Froude's most deplorable performance without emotions of indignant disgust."[1]

The "deplorable performance" that turned the public taste for English history against itself was the historian's portrayal of Mary Queen of Scots, for Froude had painted Mary Stuart as a colossal fraud, and he had done so with a spiteful virtuosity that rivalled the meanest Elizabethans. Had humanity advanced no further? Froude's account of Mary's first moments in eternity might have been written by Robert Wyngfield, whose ruthless report on the events at Fotheringay launched our inquiry into the mystery of British desire for the Queen of Scots. Like Wyngfield, Froude insisted that after the headsman had done his worst, Mary Stuart's

> head hung by a shred of skin, which he divided without withdrawing the axe; and at once a metamorphosis was witnessed, strange as was ever wrought by wand of fabled enchanter. The coif fell off and the false plaits. The laboured illusion vanished. The lady who had knelt before the block was in the maturity of grace and loveliness. The executioner, when he raised the head, as usual, to shew it to the crowd, exposed the withered features of a grizzled, wrinkled old woman.[2]

As he brutally rehearsed English history's least graceful spectacle of division, Froude offended many sensibilities. But it was hard to turn away from him because, always in the most fluent of prose, he also indulged an age-old obsession with the question of whether Mary Stuart was, as it were, for real. It was a question that the queen's Elizabethan enemies had been the first to pose, hoping to heal the breach of their own desire with the knowledge that she was not what she appeared to be, and in recent years Britons had given the riddle of Mary's reality a spin all their own: their "fascination" with the Queen of Scots was after all a state of mind which obscured its object precisely so that the sense of knowing her might survive. Froude likewise played fast and loose with Mary Stuart, ascertaining her reality by exposing her "illusion," and cloaking his own discovery of her truth in the imagery of prestidigitation, of enchantment, metamorphosis and wand.

Known only at the moment of her cleaving – and even then but in the shape of her observer's harsh desire – Froude's Mary will want a closer look: for now it is enough to note the historian's craving for familiarity with the real Queen of Scots, a variant of Michael Field's "passionate desire for access" that he actually shared with many of his contemporaries. Spurred on by the need to believe in a coherent national history that could justify their own sense of temperate place in time, Britons had begun to undo the Elizabethans' violent estrangement of Mary Stuart. In keeping with a trend toward ever more liberal revisions of the national history, they struggled for a true view of what the Queen of Scots had been, hoping to absorb her story, for good or ill, into the one they took to be their own.

Broadly speaking, Mary Stuart was far from the only feature of their collective past that the Victorians befriended in their quest for a homelier, less ideologically inflamed version of that past. In the second half of the nineteenth century, perceived extremists like Mary's own Stuart progeny and their inflamed antagonists, the Puritans, also moved to more central and respectable addresses in history than they had ever known.[3] But Mary's case was a special one. For one thing, as Michael Field recognized, part of her original essence was multiform fantasy: to adopt her was by definition to embrace something at once more immediate and more remote than simple fact. Then too, her repudiation was ironically one condition of the sense of collective security that now made it possible to seek a sense of connection with her. However barbaric the means he chose to gratify it might have been, Froude's need to show what Mary really was ("a grizzled, wrinkled old woman"), at the same time that he lowered his own veil of "illusion," exemplifies the Victorian compromise with a difficult legacy of desire for the Queen of Scots. It was only by ascertaining and incorporating a Mary who yet remained as imaginary as she had always been that Froude and his contemporaries could hope to gain a sense of belonging to their own past.

We find traces of this paradox everywhere. As history's only female icon of English might, chaste Elizabeth Tudor is the figure we might expect to have governed imperial Britain's picture of its sixteenth-century self. But just as the empire's living figurehead, Victoria, seemed to resemble Mary more than she did Elizabeth, so when they considered the queenly cousins of long ago did many find it "impossible so much as to think of the story of the one without finding involved in it fatal tangles of the life of the other."[4] Protestant Britons were likewise keen to rewrite Mary's rocky relationship to her

Presbyterian adversary John Knox: along with William Gorham Wills's 1874 play, *Mary Stuart; or the Catholic Queen and the Protestant Reformer*, a full seven canvasses joined the two in a union far more peaceable than the one they had shared in life. Artists even, if fondly, hoped to make Mary's stormy marriage with the English Darnley look like one long and sadly interrupted effort at *rapprochement*.

Often cast in a conciliatory imagery itself meant to make the past seem of a piece with the present, these efforts to braid the Queen of Scots more smoothly into the national history were far-fetched enough. Others were just wonderfully preposterous. As an adult, the folklorist Andrew Lang published long and earnest meditations on the casket letters as well as on Mary's portraits and jewels; in a more frivolous boyhood he had written a historical romance claiming that Elizabeth had masqueraded as Darnley, only to be blown up in that guise at Kirk o'Field. According to the precocious schoolboy, Darnley went on to "personate" the Tudor queen for the rest of his life, and this alone was "why Elizabeth, who was Darnley, hated Mary so bitterly."[5] For all their loopiness, such fantasies did manage to marry Mary to the English monarchy at the same time that they comically defused antipathy between Mary and the historical Elizabeth. They thus reshaped the fundamentally erotic conflicts of the sixteenth century to fulfill a mounting desire for some securing domestic harmony between the rival goddesses of Great Britain's dawn.

In the interest of that harmony too, it often seemed clear that Mary would have to become less Catholic.[6] To the Protestant mainstream, Catholics themselves did not look quite as foreign as they once had, thanks to the recent Catholic Emancipation Act (1829), not to mention the Oxford Movement and related efforts to romanize the Church of England.[7] It seemed in turn easy to purge the Queen of Scots of her papist zeal. "To say that Mary was a devout Catholic," reckoned one well-meaning Protestant soul, "is to my mind to misunderstand the character of her actions."[8]

Obviously, the route to acceptance and a sense of familiarity with a once alien queen could take the most bizarre of turns. Hailing Mary Stuart as the chief icon in a new Catholicism, secularized and touristic, one commentator counted up the latterday "pilgrims" who "hasten to Scotland to pay their devotions at the shrine of beauty, of heroism, and of misfortune" ("Queen Mary," p. 612). These devotées "approach the spots consecrated to her memory, hallowed by her casual residence, with the feelings of those bound in the olden time for the Holy Land; and relics, real or imaginary, are treasured up [. . .] in the spirit rather of ancient devotion than of modern scepticism or indifference." Victorian "feeling" for Mary was, it seemed, a truly "*Catholic*" feeling; the Protestants evince it not less strongly than the followers of the Romish church, the Lutherans than those of the Greek persuasion." But it was also a truly hallucinatory feeling. What exactly were these present-day pilgrims expecting to see? What, for that matter, did they?

At once "real" and "imaginary" — an apparition from the past who proved that the stability, liberality and continuity of the present were no illusion – Mary Queen of Scots promised a secular object of unifying belief. If it remained uncertain exactly what sort of object she was, this was not necessarily for the worse. In his study of the imaginative process he calls "realization," Martin Meisel proposes that nineteenth-century evocations of the past were, dream-like, forever fantastically "assimilating the strange to the familiar" and the old to the new, their aim to quell anxiety about a present whose own moorings were more far-flung, arbitrary and provisional. Artists who rendered scenes from British history in cosy, pseudo-contemporary detail performed the same service in reverse.[9] With the surreal the unspoken condition of a shared sense of integrated historical reality, it stands to something like reason that it should have been the bending of an illusion that made Mary Stuart seem less distant to the Victorians.

Froude's drive to expose Mary's "laboured illusion" is an expression, however idiosyncratic, of his society's longing to repose belief in a strategically realized Queen of Scots and thus in its own powers of assimilation and comprehension. His own urgency happened to spring as much from maternal deprivation as from cultural imperative, and its nakedness – occasionally unto sadism – disturbed those who otherwise shared his childlike desire to feel grounded in place and time. At the same time, Froude's savage realism uncovered the dark primeval roots of a seemingly simple collective longing for genuine contact with a past embodied in Mary Stuart. No one could read him without acknowledging the infantile need to repudiate her that still shadowed even the most liberal gestures toward reconciliation, threatening to divide them from their own best intentions.

For this reason, Froude found a surprising double in the popular historical novelist Charlotte Mary Yonge. Not unlike Froude's, Yonge's life's work was to produce the illusion of a familiar and habitable past, and with the historian she completes our picture of Mary Stuart's role in a modern nation's achievement of a fiction of organized and coherent being. In Yonge's aptly titled *Unknown to History* (1882), a daughter's quest for her "real" mother – the Queen of Scots, of course – becomes an instrument to probe that fiction. An allegory of the widespread Victorian wish to assimilate Mary Stuart, the imaginary daughter's voyage of desire counters the "real" historian's wish to dispel a "laboured illusion" and brings our own search for Britain's unclaimed mother back to its irreducibly mysterious beginning.

MARY AND THE MIRROR OF HISTORY

Both Yonge and Froude wrote out of a unique cultural condition. For, under Victoria, the middle-class market for histories of England and for historical novels boomed, British history was introduced into school curricula, and both amateur and professional historical societies proliferated: knowing its past had become Britain's favorite way of making its own acquaintance in the present.[10] The Victorian cult of history was not monolithic, or even necessarily monotheistic; popular sects split off from elite and professional ones, while high priests as opposite as Thomas Carlyle and T.B. Macaulay competed for ascendancy. But in general the Victorians tended to fulfill their desire for historical affirmation through the illusion of sensuous immersion in the past – in its plots and personalities, in every nook and cranny of "the olden time." Historians striving to reconcile "the splendour and picturesqueness of the past" with "the new impulses of modern life" agreed that the best mediator was realistic narrative with an immense and absorbing cast of characters. As practiced by everyone from major figures like Macaulay and his Roman Catholic counterpart John Lingard, to relative bit players like Charles Dickens, Victorian history-writing was not merely narcissistic but self-consciously "psychological,"[11] its aim, as one of its recent students puts it, to resurrect "living reality" from "dead facts" by activating the mind's power to make even absent things feel real.[12]

In our own highly suspicious day, the Victorian project of realizing the nation's past has sometimes looked like little more than an underhanded device for inculcating a myth of national superiority, while high "History" appears to have excluded all truths but those of male Britons of the middle classes and above. Women are counted as one great casualty in the formation of modern institutions of historical knowledge and thought. Literal and metaphorical violence to them, the critic Christina Crosby, for example argues, was required if "History" was to be equated with truth and if appeals to the past were to win the staggering authority they did,[13] and Victorian reappraisals of the Norman Conquest seem to have disparaged French influence on a native and purely Anglo-Saxon heritage.[14] By these lights, the francophone Queen of Scots ought to have been doubly barred from the chain of events leading up to the shining apogee of Victorian society.

And so, in the past, she had been – more or less. In the Victorian present, however, two negatives might make a positive, for public outcry against those who seemed to take pleasure in Mary's erasure from history suggests less a full scale determination to eliminate woman, French or otherwise, from the mirror of the past, than a far more pressing need to see the Queen of Scots as history's own reality, a condition of its psychological presence. At the very least, Mary's complex, involving story, her captivating personality, and above all her extraordinary sufferings, made the long ago feel immediate, hence real. Even John Knox's biographer, Thomas M'Crie, had to admit that the "enchanting" Mary "continues to this day to exercise such sway over the hearts of men that even grave and serious authors [. . .] cannot read of the tears which she shed without feeling an inclination to weep along with her."[15]

Thomas Carlyle was one of the first to complain. Of the contemporary clamor to know the history of Scotland, he carped:

> We ask, with breathless eagerness: How was it? How went it on? Let us
> understand it, let us see it, and know it! – In reply, is handed us a really

graceful and most dainty little Scandalous Chronicle (as for some Journal of Fashion) of two persons: Mary Stuart, a Beauty, but over-light-headed; and Henry Darnley, a Booby who had fine legs. How these two courted, billed and cooed, according to nature; then pouted, fretted, grew utterly enraged, and blew one another up with gunpowder; this, and not the History of Scotland, is what we good naturedly read.[16]

For Carlyle, Mary trivialized "History." But for the majority of Victorians, she clearly realized it. The elements of her life story, Lang found, were "wells [. . .] sunk, as it were, deep into human personality" so that "the inner characteristics of [her] age leapt upwards into the light."[17] Lang's contemporaries thus developed an insatiable appetite for editions of Mary's letters, for new biographies of her, even for versifications of her treason trial, and to them Mary *was* the past, one whose story was very far from the dainty *chronique scandaleuse* that Carlyle made it out to be. That the long-suffering Queen of Scots was history at its most accessible is nowhere more visible than in the widespread fascination with pictures of her execution, seven of which were exhibited over the course of the nineteenth century. The Victorians were not, of course, the first to feel an irresistible attraction to the closing moments of Mary's life: the Elizabethans had treated the final scene at Fotheringay as a struggle for symbolic mastery, while sentimental Georgians were drawn to it because it gave them the chance to spend as many tears as possible. But while the Georgians' visions of Mary at the scaffold usually dissolved into the images of her onlookers, their Victorian grandchildren were more likely to belabor the most graphic elements of the beheading in hopes of more deeply inhabiting that ever-receding moment in time.

Historians like Froude and Agnes Strickland merely led the parade to make Victorian readers believe that they were there. A handsomely illustrated sixpenny translation of Alexandre Dumas's popular biography of the Queen of Scots peddled details as particular as the dead queen's spleen ("in its ordinary condition"), veins ("slightly livid"), lungs ("yellowish in places") and brain ("one sixth larger than what is usually found in persons of the same sex and age.")[18] Other *exposés* of the royal execution dwelled upon the way the headsman's arm had "wandered" to bungle the beheading.[19] Or they reminded readers that Mary's hands had to be removed from the block before the first stroke. Then there was the tweaking of her wig to expose "the real [gray] hair beneath the false hair she had long worn." Even Mary's allegedly "blood red attire" was analyzed as "a woman's device to hide the splashes of gore that might have stained her raiment."[20]

Obviously, their fondness for detail made contemporary accounts of Mary's death far more gruesome than anything that had gone before. More textured and invasive than earlier historical accounts of Mary, these renderings were, in many ways, simply more "realistic" than their predecessors had been, Lang's "wells" sunk into the past. At the same time, though, they were also more fanciful; at the very least, they relied more on what one contemporary commentator called the historian's "inner consciousness," the "speculations of [his] closet."[21] Indeed, for all their address to the senses, few of the details brought forth in such abundance had much foundation in what we would consider fact. They thus exemplify a common rite within the Victorian cult of history, a slippage from objective article to private fiction, from disputable evidence to shared fantasy. Were we to interpret obsession with the Queen of Scots's execution as a displacement of aggression against the consciously loved Queen Victoria, such details would even mark the present's slide into the past.

The fact that these points of contact with the past were also sites of coercion and estrangement is betrayed by the guilty details themselves – by the "wander[ing]" of the axe, by the parting of Mary's wig from her "real hair," and of course by the separation of her head from her body. Amassing all possible particulars concerning the lost and rejected mother of the Stuart line might have looked like an easy way to enter history. But at the end of the day it was the disarming gap between what was real and what was phantasmic, between what is received and what is a formulation of desire, that was most likely to appear in the "mirror of history" that the Victorians held up to Mary.

THE LABOURED ILLUSION

No one was more familiar with that gap than J.A. Froude. The average reader sank into his lush, world-summoning prose with pleasure, but the popular historian attracted critical contempt for his cavalier treatment of material evidence. Throughout his *History of England* Froude never scrupled to mistranslate, misappropriate, and sometimes even misattribute the documents that were supposed to be the flesh and blood of his best-selling narrative of the national past. His habit of disfiguring evidence may have been born of a complicated grievance that he held against the sort of absolute authority he associated with the Roman Catholic Church.[22] But it was bred by a personal view of history as, in Froude's own phrase, "mythic" – as a random and incessantly shifting collection of facts meant less to register immutable truth than to create pliable, shareable psychological meaning. "It often seems to me as if history was like a child's box of letters with which we can spell any word we please," Froude ventured once. "We have only to pick out such letters as we want, arrange them as we like, and say nothing about those which do not suit our purpose."[23]

Froude's words brazenly subordinate objective fact to the despotism of present need and desire. The image of a child with blocks – an image of primitive "lik[ing]" and "purpose" – suggests less that history is arbitrary, or even that it is legendary than that it is uniquely real, rendered according to what the living, not necessarily consciously or politely, "please," "want" and "like." In turn, understanding historical realism as the fruit of a shocking collision between primal desire and symbolic order helps to explain how and why

Froude in effect defaced Mary Queen of Scots – his contemporaries' gateway to the reality of the past – throughout the last volumes of his *History of England*. It also elucidates his contemporaries' alarm at what he had done – an alarm that at last pushed some of them to call their wish to know the "real" Mary to account.

Froude's own childhood had primed him to confess the libidinal impulses that shape historical reflection. For one thing, his mother had died when he was two years old. This was of course far from rare in the nineteenth century. But whereas most Victorian families virtually canonized the dead, Froude's father would allow no portraits of his wife in the house, and her name was never mentioned: "I seem to remember her voice, but of her appearance I have no conception," the historian recalled in adulthood. Someone who had known his mother told him "that she was one of the most beautiful women that he had ever seen; but we had no likeness of her in the family, none at least that I ever saw."[24]

The mother's invisibility left the child's world anchorless, broken, unreal, and the child himself without access to his past: "Our early life remains with me in broken patches. Most of it is forgotten."[25] The chief principle of reality to intrude upon this shattered and phantasmic "life" was a horrific one supplied by an elder brother, Hurrell Froude, who subjected James Anthony to "funny tormenting" throughout his childhood: homosexual and sado-masochistic rituals that included scorching the future historian with hot cigars and nearly drowning him.[26] Only these painful conventions shaped and grounded the formless, aimless, dreamlike world that Froude's mother had left behind. In small, then, the historian's life seems to have recapitulated Britain's psychological history since the fragmented and fragmenting exit of Mary Queen of Scots almost 300 years before: on a grander scale, Mary was another mother who had left no definite likeness behind her, only a space to be wrested into shape by a thousand not seldom barbarous desires.

The Elizabethans had at any rate supplied history with a number of mothers who abandoned their children for the kiss of the axe, or eschewed maternity altogether; they were also well-stocked with male tormenters who had in effect shaped that same history. Froude was thus at home among them, and in adulthood he devoted a disproportion of his *History* to the second half of the sixteenth century. To him it was an age of lies and riddles, most of them, for his money, contrived by women and countered by men. Elizabeth herself was not especially compelling: little more than a "mistress" of relatively uninteresting forms of "chicanery," she had at least made it possible for "two nations" to "emanicipat[e] themselves from spiritual tyranny" (VIII: 227) and pursue what Froude considered legitimate (and truly British) objects of belief, chiefly "liberty." She had, in other words, made it possible for modern Britons to glimpse their most autonomous and efficacious selves in the mirror of her time.

On the other hand, Froude was fascinated by the most formidable threat to that possibility, Mary Queen of Scots. This Stuart "wild cat" (IX: 82, 130, 489), he found, was not only, as a Catholic, an automatic obstacle to individual religious freedom; she was so violently self-involved that she kept her potential subjects, present and future, from discerning their own reality through her. While "Elizabeth cared for English liberty," for example, "Mary Stuart was chiefly interested in herself" (VIII: 194). Mary's most pertinent difference from Elizabeth thus lay in her exceptional power to create false idols of belief: "Accomplished as the Queen of England often showed herself in the art of lying, her genius paled before the cynical proficiency of her rival" (XI: 91).

Mary's superior artistry, it seemed, sprang from the tidal force of her female desire for pleasure and sway: even in captivity, where she sat weaving "fresh plots and schemes" with other women, she remained "the same bold, restless, unscrupulous, ambitious woman" she ever was. "Hers," Froude assures us, "was the panther's nature – graceful, beautiful, malignant, and untamable. What," he wonders, "was to be done with her?" (XII: 269). Yet in the end, its openness made the question of "what was to be done with her?" a way for Froude to achieve contact with the woman behind the plots and schemes. His savage portrait of the Stuart "panther" accordingly instances a mind doing things with her in its own right, albeit so long after the fact that the exorbitance of what it did do seems almost ridiculously obvious.

In the simplest sense, what Froude "did with" Mary merely copied what her Protestant enemies had done. He realized her as an image of the "spasms" of his own loathing of female autonomy and self-love. At the same time, though, there had been more to Elizabethan caricatures of the Queen of Scots than met the eye, and Froude likewise harbored a certain grudging admiration for Mary Stuart. Virago or not, she remained "the keenest-witted woman living" (VIII: 225), not lacking "iron fortitude and intellectual address of the first degree" (VIII: 271).[27] In light of such genius, what upset the historian most was his belief that Mary had perverted her own boundless physical and intellectual energy into the "power of gratifying herself" (VIII: 211). It is both to expose and to reprimand that narcissism – the closed circle of Mary's own desire as it seemed to eliminate him – that Froude split and twisted every atom of evidence concerning her. His finished portrait of the queen as a pathetic charlatan stands as a concerted defense against the frustration of his desire for intimacy with a woman evidently adept at making his own autonomous reality invisible to him.

The irony is that the intellectually energetic Froude actually had everything in common with the Queen of Scots. As he conceived her, she was his truest, if least acknowledged, mirror. In his *History of England*, she is, for example, an artist of the first magnitude, her copious writing distinguished by "sustained and elaborate artifices" (XII: 306), and her defense at her treason trial conducted "in the grand style of which she was so accomplished a mistress" (XII: 304). In turn, Froude's fellow historian John Skelton described him as a "master of English prose," his Mary in particular a "masterpiece of graphic art" that had by the 1880s "stamped itself upon the popular imagination of our time."[28] Even Froude's loudest detractor, James Meline, was forced to admire his "art in imagery and diction."[29] It would thus appear that, in a latter-day variant upon George Buchanan's psychodrama 300 years before, Froude saw in a Mary of "sustained and elaborate artifices" a version of himself that he could not quite touch. She stands in his *History* as the mirror image which he felt he must shatter if he was to achieve his own end of make believe – if, like the best loved of their kind, the author and his story were to seem convincingly real.

The dénouement of Froude's *History* thus naturally arrives with the "scene" of Mary's execution "in all its dread reality." According to Froude, all of Mary's artful fantasies – all her "busy schemes, her dreams of vengeance, her visions of a revolution" – fell apart at Fotheringay. The scaffold was the last place Mary had a hope of reclaiming "victory" over England's political imagination and so, grounding the fiction of martyrdom in her own majestic body, she allegedly spent her last "busy" night contriving her costume and practicing her part, so that when she at last entered the hall of execution, she "seemed as if coming to take a part in some solemn pageant" (XII: 354–355; 357).

Until the end, it is Mary who rules the scene of her own death. But once she kneels at the scaffold, her campaign to make believe collapses. First, we learn that as her shoulders were "exposed, two scars became visible, one on either side." When one of her prosecutors points to them "with his white wand," it is revealed that they are the abcesses left by recent disease, and Froude's exposition of what follows is relentless in details, similarly realistic, which does nothing to speed the action but serves merely to funnel the then down to the now. At the scaffold, for example, "the hard wood seemed to hurt [Mary], for she placed her hands under her neck. The executioners gently removed them, lest they should deaden the blow." Whereupon:

> one of them holding her slightly, the other raised the axe and struck. The scene had been too trying even for the practiced headsman of the Tower. His arm wandered. The blow fell on the knot of the handkerchief and scarcely broke the skin. She neither spoke nor moved. He struck again, this time effectively.
>
> (XII: 361)

It is of course a moment later that Mary's head is held aloft, her wig falls off, and her "laboured illusion vanishe[s]," her true face at last revealed. In each of these violently cleft details, the real Mary Stuart is laid bare, and the slippage of her false coiffure formally announces the triumph of Froude's own reality principle over a myth of ravaged piety propagated for centuries.

Or does it? In spite of itself, this scene also betrays Froude's surprising pleasure, not always in something other than illusion. The wand produced belongs to Mary's enemies, not to her. Apparently a "scene" of disengagement from the Queen of Scots, her execution from this point of view emerges as something else – as a fantastic bonding with her that is possible only once that bond is repudiated consciously, its reality denied along with that of the other with whom it is shared. This process is one which the psychoanalyst Jessica Benjamin identifies as the basis of the sado-masochistic personality and traces to botched infantile separation from the mother.[30] And indeed, throughout the *History*, Froude's own prose confirms the intertwining of his symbolic practices and those he despisingly links to Mary, whom the modern author needs to kill again in order to reify his own art, and thereby his effectual and authoritative self. "Confident in imagination" (VIII: 194), Froude's Mary is his own parodic avatar, the true matrix of his ostensible realities.

Since Froude's make-believe actually depends on Mary's counter-fiction, his last words on the death of the queen can only undermine their own propositions about "reality:"

> A spectator, who was one of her warmest admirers, describes her bearing as infinitely transcending the power of the most accomplished actor to represent. The association of the stage was, perhaps, unconsciously suggested by what was in fact, notwithstanding the tremendous reality with which it closed, the most brilliant acting throughout. [. . .] Never did any human creature meet death more bravely; yet, in the midst of the admiration and pity which cannot be refused her, it is not to be forgotten that she was leaving the world with a lie upon her lips. She was a bad woman, disguised in the livery of a martyr.
>
> (XII: 362)

While "tremendous reality" would here seem to do away with Mary's "disguise," exposing her as a "bad woman" and no "martyr," it is in fact only through the Queen of Scots's "faultless" performance that Froude can come to know, or believe he knows − or make us believe he knows − where that "tremendous reality" begins and ends. However perversely, the historian thus regained and even absorbed the maternal figure who presided over all his labors to immerse himself and his readers in a familiar past. Which is why the scene of Mary's death ends not in rage but with a certain recognizing laughter, the echo of a childish ecstasy.

THE WAR-DANCE OF THE SAVAGE

A number of Froude's contemporaries caught this echo and were embarrassed, even appalled by it. One, James Meline, spent 300 pages castigating the general "perver[sion]" and "abuse" of Froude's talents.[31] But he found the execution scene the most alarming of all, for, "far from being painful to him," it evidently afforded the historian "the most exquisite delight." Meline saw that Froude's pleasure came not from contact with a past made almost sensuously present but rather from his talent for making it seem so. This was in turn a talent that aligned him more with the Elizabethans who had expelled Mary from history than with the Victorians who hoped to reclaim her to it: "We shudder as we see him warm up to his ghoullike task," Meline declared,

> travestie [Mary's] bearing, mock her words, inventory her garments, play the costumer, decree the historian into a man-milliner, and − falsifying her

motives – blasphemously challenge as dramatic affectation the last appeal of a poor soul to God, betray a revolting satisfaction in her suffering, positive delight in the discovery that she was no longer in the maturity of grace and loveliness, and, with a hideous leer, call on his readers to feast with him their gaze on the withered features of a wrinkled old woman.

(p. 312)

Meline saw that Froude's realistic portrait of Mary at the point of death at last revealed not the fact of a "wrinkled old woman" but the historian's own leering visage: if Froude seemed to have entered the past, he had not done so as himself. Rather, feminized into a "man-milliner," the artist bent on twisting Mary's death to fulfill his own desire for affirmation looked more like a sixteenth-century queen than a Victorian gentleman.

To make matters worse, it seemed that Froude had intruded not only into Mary's reality but into the "inner depths" of his readers' "consciousness" as well, invading the proverbial "blank page" upon which he "contrived to inscribe" the contents of his own fantasies (p. 23). On its own terms, Froude's art may have allowed a phantasmic union with a lost mother. But because it threatened to draw the aggregate of humane moderns not into liberal agreement about a queen that all of them could recognize, but rather into a brutal fantasy their ancestors had shared, that art made Froude seem, to Meline, a "social pariah" (p. 311). The editors of *Blackwood's* likewise declared that his "ill-suppressed exultation" in his own "horrible minuteness of detail" made "the epithet 'inhuman' [. . .] far too gentle and forbearing" to describe him.[32]

Meanwhile, *Blackwood's* solicited a Scottish woman, Margaret Oliphant, to review the Mary Stuart sections of Froude's *History of England*, and she too was outraged at a scene in which Froude's "insinuated sneer intrudes into the very presence of death itself." Like Meline's, Oliphant's revulsion began with his absorption of the Queen of Scots in a barbaric orgy of authorial self-confirmation: "He grins horribly a ghastly smile when the axe falls upon Mary's neck, and feels himself still at liberty to jeer when the dead face which had won so many hearts is held up, awful in the first distortion of slaughter" (p. 106). She went on to express her indignation on behalf of other Victorians, who as a group, she acknowledged, had very much at stake in now being with Mary rather than against her. Her "memory," Oliphant explained, "still retains the allegiance of an almost unanimous nation, and of enthusiastic partisans over all the world. Surely there is something more than unseemly, more than unjust, in so strange a treatment of such a subject" (p. 106). In other words, Froude's "strange [. . .] treatment" of Mary was, finally, taboo. What Froude had violated in his delirium of desecration and desire was a fragile myth of cohesive and civilized identity. For "an almost unanimous nation," Mary had become the matrix of a certain way of knowing the past, and of identifying it with the present. Froude's savage realism threatened just this matrix because he parodied and perverted the wish at its core – the wish not just to join with Mary but at last to see her torn away, exposed as an illusory object of desire.

But he also forced his readers to examine the nature of their own desire to work their way into the heart of her "reality." Oliphant herself spoke not just as one of an offended "nation" but also as a woman exceptionally eager to "enter into Mary's being." The "workings of Mary's mind," Oliphant charged, were "nothing to [Froude]" (p. 110). But they were everything to his Scottish critic, and in her effort to inhabit them she eventually came to terms with Mary's baffling difference from herself. Oliphant saw the Queen of Scots, though a "great actress," to have believed deeply both in certain "religious prejudices," and in a "popular delusion in respect of the rights of princes" (p. 111). Both of these were general convictions of her time, and "the woman availed herself [of them], as any modern actress" might. In turn, precisely because it *was* acting, there was "a different picture to be made" from her performance (p. 111). Oliphant saw Mary's masquerade as having secured the queen's "full faith" in her own "absolutism," in the "divine right [that was then] no tradition, but a reality" (p. 112). And if these "views are not our views" (p. 112), Oliphant was nonetheless profoundly sympathetic with – even invested in – the fact that Mary had them and was entitled to those then-realities. Like the queen's image and her reality, belief and disbelief in her could at last coexist.

As a matter of fact, Oliphant found Froude less believable than his sixteenth-century actress. "Mary Stuart," she concluded, "with all her sins on her head, [. . .] is more comprehensible than is the man who, three hundred years after her troublings have come to an end, is able to insult her dying, and throw a farce over the conclusion of such a tragedy as has seldom been witnessed by man" (p. 122). Oliphant was able to acknowledge the sins on Mary's head without diminishing her tragedy. This was to grasp the complexity of a great many other women too, for the Queen of Scots was really "as Helen, as Cleopatra, as all the other fair women who have disturbed the world, and yet been wept as its saints are seldom wept" (p. 106). If inadvertently, Froude's offenses permitted at least some of his contemporaries to make amends with a complex, even self-contradictory woman – to claim her even as they disbelieved her, and to comprehend her more fully than ever before as the creature both of their indelible guilt and of their enduring, essential desire.

THE DAUGHTER'S SEDUCTION

Charlotte Mary Yonge published her version of Mary Stuart's story in 1882, two decades after Froude's *History of England* made its debut. Yonge was fifty-nine that year, the Queen of Great Britain sixty-three, and in her novel *Unknown to History* Yonge gave the Queen of Scots "features that were aging" too.[33] In Yonge's novel, as in Froude's sneering strip-search of "a grizzled, wrinkled old woman," Mary's age certainly makes her seem more real. But it also makes her endlessly fascinating – to men, to boys and above all to the young English girl who turns out to be her daughter. When that girl and her playmates first lay eyes upon the queen, they find her face "worn and wearied, and bearing tokens of illness. The features were far from being regularly beautiful; there was a decided cast in one of the eyes." Nevertheless, "the extraordinary magic of her eye and lip, the queenly grace and dignity joined with a wonderful sweetness, impressed and each in measure felt the fascination" (pp. 40–41).

Yonge's story of the daughter's seduction by Mary Stuart's "extraordinary magic" raises the phantoms of "fascination" that are at once "unknown to history" and probably the source of its deepest meaning to us. At the time of its appearance, *Unknown to History* also exercised a popular compulsion to assimilate Mary Queen of Scots to the history of modern Britain as something other than a threat to its advancement. At the same time, however, Yonge's adolescent heroine proves painfully ambivalent toward her decidedly transgressive birth mother, and the story of her life thus also registers the difficulty of absorbing the Stuart queen into a single and perfectly linear narrative, either of personal or of collective identity. If Froude's *History* finally indulged the oldest form of involvement with Mary in the book, *Unknown to History* is best read as a history *of* British attachment to the Queen of Scots, one that interweaves dominant and recessive, aggressive and affectionate strains of an antique obsession. The remarkable result is that, while Froude's history sometimes awakened anxiety and guilt, Yonge's counter-history actually revised and gratified a nation's antique desire for union with what it once, and must yet, cast aside.

Yonge herself was one of the most phenomenally successful and prolific domestic novelists of her day, so widely esteemed as a national treasure that soldiers carried her sagas of contemporary English family life to the Crimean War. She was also the author of numerous popular histories, mostly meant for youth, and often staples of the British classroom.[34] By 1882, she had also written her share of "historical romances," many inspired by dreams, and all benignly regarded, by her, as "the shaping of the conceptions that the imagination must necessarily form when dwelling upon the records of history."[35]

Unfortunately, one Christabel Coleridge destroyed most of the records of Yonge's own life after publishing a hagiographic biography in the 1920s. But it does seem that Yonge's historical fictions were born of something older than her adult acquaintance with the records of history. Her twentieth-century readers have often felt that their "indiscriminate, passionately enthusiastic" temper reveals "the side of her genius that never quite outgrew adolescence."[36] As for *Unknown to History*, Yonge's own contemporaries allowed as how its readers, whom they expected to be mainly "boys and girls," would "like it and it will do them good."[37]

Yonge's novel is in fact steeped in the passionate enthusiasms that generate adult habits of knowledge and choice, only to be spurned by them in the end. Dreamlike, idolatrous, childish, it is of course this former, eventually repudiated, state of mind that gives deepest access to Mary Queen of Scots, and not unlike Froude Yonge found ways to cling to it. At the same time, however, by

developing her tale out of a teenaged girl's evolving and often anxious awareness that she is Mary's daughter, Yonge (like Sophia Lee before her) confronted
what it means to be uncontrollably entangled with Mary at the deepest and
oldest levels of consciousness. By the end of her novel, conscious commitment
to the kind of history that cannot pretend that it actually "knows" Mary has
thus made peace with a subliminal need to stay in love with the Queen of
Scots. Tutored by a largely female-authored (and, it must be said, an essentially
non-historical) tradition of involvement with Mary's maternal image, Yonge
was able to accept the schism between rationally acknowledged history and its
seductive unknowns as a condition of survival – Mary's mythic survival, naturally, but that of the love of her as well.

The central family in Yonge's *Unknown to History*, the Talbots, are an indus-
trious, pragmatic, determinedly Protestant clan. Their head, Richard Talbot,
is a naval captain and cousin to the Earl of Shrewsbury, Mary's "host" for
much of her English captivity. Such connections place the Talbots "on the
border" between a blood-based system of "feudal retainership that was about
to be extinguished" and the resourceful, independent, essentially middling
class that would soon replace it to make a new nation. The plainspoken and
wholly devoted mother of the family, Susan, is the chief representative of a
rising Protestant England that is also linked to the domestic realism of Yonge's
own day: even her "modern" kitchen has been converted from a priory refec-
tory. On the other hand, as in Scott's novel *The Abbot*, Mary Queen of Scots is
the living exemplar of a vanishing, feudal and Roman Catholic past. Family
opinion concerning her is accordingly divided. Susan maintains a healthy
skepticism about the royal captive, whom her son Humfrey denounces as "an
evil lady who slew her husband" (p. 43). But Richard Talbot and his daughter,
Cicely, are bewitched by the Stuart queen.

Cicely, it seems, is not a Talbot by blood. Saved by Richard Talbot from a
storm at sea, she arrives in infancy with little more than two brands on one of
her shoulderblades. The first of these is the letters "MR" entwined with a
crown above them, the second a cross-like figure that rises to a *fleur de lys*.
Trained by Froude to notice the twin scars that marred Mary's own shoul-
derblade at her execution, any Victorian would have recognized Cicely's tattoos
as signs that she is Mary's as yet wordless child. But the Talbots find them
inscrutable, legible only as "Popish marks" (p. 14), or possibly as evidence that
"they that parted from her meant to know her again." They name the castaway
after a daughter who has just died, and raise her as their child, only much later
managing to translate a mysterious "strip of writing" into confirmation that
she is indeed the daughter of the captive Queen of Scots and the Earl of
Bothwell, born secretly at Lochleven and smuggled to a convent after Mary's
flight to England.

By the time Cicely's heritage becomes known, she is well into her girlhood.
Her foster father has been appointed one of Mary's guards, and the Talbot
family has moved into the captive queen's field of influence. Upon realizing
that Cicely is her daughter, Mary for her part insists on keeping the girl by her

side. The queen's deft tongue and slippery physical charm, her passion for romantic legends, her artistic prowess with needle and thread, her love of twisting and untwisting plots, her sensuality and charisma all offer Cicely a new legacy of female invention and sensuality, a secret and intensely romantic narrative both of self and of relationship to the past. Unfolded always in the language of dream, this romance is above all a narcissistic one, both on Mary's side and on that of Cicely: Mary would teach Cicely to love and value herself as a royal princess in part because the queen sees herself in her.

Like Sophia Lee's twin heroines, who also discover their bond with Mary through the mirror of romantic narration, Cicely learns she is Mary's daughter via bedtime stories that the queen spins for her. She does so just as she enters puberty, and thus very much in the imagery of sexual awakening. On the first of the many nights she will ask the child to sleep with her, the queen embraces Cicely as "my sweet bed-fellow, my little Scot – one more loyal subject come to me in my bondage" (pp. 186–187). Seeing a "subject" and erotic captive even as she sees a daughter, Mary kisses and caresses the shoulder brands that Cicely herself cannot see: "The girl felt a pair of soft lips kiss each mark in turn" until "the covering was quickly and caressingly restored." Half-lover and half-mother, Mary tells Cicely her own "irresistibly pathetic" story, which is the romance of Cicely's own origins as well. From Mary, Cicely also learns that her real name is Bridget (or Bride) after the Scottish Catholic saint. "Be Cicely Talbot by day as ever," Mary croons. "Only at night be mine – my child, my Bride" (p. 186).

Mary Stuart rules the night side of Cicely's split identity, the eroticized realm of mystery, legend and love between women that threatens to engulf the "real," extroverted world of Protestant female service that Cicely's adoptive mother Susan Talbot exemplifies. Torn between the "veritable parent," whose excessive "endearments" entice but also discomfit her, and "the restrained manner of Susan," Cicely is also torn between two versions of herself; her conflict is resurrected in the tension between Yonge's own "natural" narrative style, cluttered with bourgeois realist detail, and the emptying undertow of fantasy and romance.

Structurally, *Unknown to History* labors to assimilate these two narrative heritages; psychologically, Cicely tries to do the same with her two mothers. It is unbelievably hard. Ashamed that she cannot wholly love the "mother that hath hungered for [her]" (p. 185), Cicely only reluctantly fulfills Mary's wish for her to "'lie on my weary bosom to still its ache and yearning, and let me feel that I have indeed a child'" (p. 186). Yet the daughter's too is a "dull feeling of aching and yearning" mixed with "a certain exultation" (p. 199). And who would not exult to find it gratified, the familiar fantasy that one's parents are not one's parents and that one is, as one always suspected, in fact of royal birth?

Cicely's actual "turmoil" in the face of this fantasy's apparent realization captures the ambivalence of Yonge's own era – its fearful fascination with the alternative selves and societies that Mary Stuart embodied. This should translate into ambivalence to what is, as Yonge's title has it, "unknown to history" – to what, historically speaking, failed to stay in some sense "real," surviving only in imagination after Britain's vaunted history of Protestant autonomy and progressive liberty began. But in *Unknown to History*, it is of course Mary Stuart who "really" existed. The Talbots stand for the future – the historical – Britain but it is they who are figments of imagination. This inversion means that, as in Froude, Mary Stuart might seduce and deceive, but she still carries the very principle of historical reality. She even protects it, if perversely, by confusing our sense of its difference from the imaginary.

Yonge played with such agility on the brink of this confusion because her own authorial inheritance was a dual one. Her paternal line, we might say, is the "records of history" that houses an entire garrison of facts about Mary Stuart, but her maternal legacy was a tradition of literary longing for the Queen of Scots sustained largely by women.[38] In this tradition, to date most fully expressed in Lee's *Recess*, daughterly desire for one glimpse of the mother's face engenders a vision of history which includes the experience of certain non-historical chasms of privation, reflection and wish. As they wed historical events to the recesses of desire unknown to them, such ties also bind *Unknown to History* to Agnes Strickland's *Life of Mary Queen of Scots*, that work so visibly shaped by its author's less than historiographical desire for the other woman who is also herself.

Yonge's brief preface suggests that *Unknown to History* was in fact "founded" on Strickland's *Life*. But when we turn to the parts of the *Life* to which Yonge herself directs us, we find the historian concluding that "the tradition that Mary was delivered of a daughter while in Lochleven [. . .] is not verified by the slightest evidence, and appears utterly devoid of truth."[39] Yonge thus only appears to have used Strickland's history to authenticate her own story. In fact, Strickland's role is to make ironic Yonge's own truth claims – to expose history to its own timeless unknowns.

If the British women in Yonge's literary family tree attach themselves to one another by believing the same lies, then that is how their involvement with the queen of lies, Mary Queen of Scots, must work as well. In Sophia Lee's novel, this involvement's most evocative trope was the recess that nourished Mary's fictive daughters. Yonge's version of the recess is also a cave, and like Lee's it is eerily domestic, furnished with "sheeted tables and statues standing up, all grand and ghostly on the floor" (p. 205). Yonge's "marvelous cavern" also descends from Strickland, who tells us that, during her English captivity, Mary:

> is said to have explored the dismal cavern at Poole's Hole, [. . .] and penetrated as far as the stalactical group which has, in memory of her, been distinguished by the name of Mary Queen of Scots's pillar – no very easy or agreeable exploit for a person of her towering height, every visitor having at times, to stoop nearly double, and scramble over a rough, wet, irregular path, among broken, tottering, or disjointed stones, at risk of [. . .] slipping down into the black murky stream that creeps sullenly below this perilous causeway.[40]

The "black murky stream" and "disjointed stones" embody the seductive perils of time travel, and especially of immersion in Mary's submerged, fragmented and compelling story. And yet the pillar counters those perils with the comforting symbols that we might find in an ordinary history book. Just so, even as it links a chasm in Yonge's story with its incarnations in Lee and Strickland, the cave at the heart of *Unknown to History* also ties female dream life to those crannies of Britain's political unconscious that did manage to manifest themselves in history.

Halfway through Yonge's novel, the Queen of Scots arranges an expedition to this prodigious cavern. She does so because Cicely wants to see the cave, and the queen is determined that "my daughter shall have her wish" (p. 207). So the cavern fulfills and synchronizes female wishes, both Mary's to please her daughter and her daughter's to be pleased. These are wishes for a kind of timelessness: Mary even promises that she and Cicely will "'play the part of the pale ghosts of the unburied dead'" (p. 214). But to be dead with Mary in the deepest cathedrals of the cave is also to be surrounded by public signs of the Queen of Scots, who "inscribe[s] her name on the farthest column that she had reached," as if to mark the buried universe of the cavern for use in the historical world above.

Just so, as Mary and her largely female party "penetrate further into the recesses of the cave," they find not a deeper connection with one another but instead a group of young men in disguise, including Mary's most famous devotée, the young Anthony Babington. All known to history, these acolytes "gaze on the true and lawful mistress of our hearts, the champion of our faith, in her martyrdom" (p. 218). The six vow allegiance to Mary by dividing a white handkerchief of hers among them, but when they swear Cicely to secrecy, she resists becoming one of them, fearing her own death and at last begging to be taken away. As male passions divide Mary symbolically and thus promise to bear her upward, out of the cave and into fatal history, it is Cicely who internalizes the division between history and desire.

Babington and his friends meanwhile indulge in an order of fantasy that did make itself known to history, to their and Mary's enormous detriment. These historically familiar deliriums are Yonge's concern too, and she traces them back to their childhood. Son of a Catholic mother, we learn, Babington even at eight "pressed forward with an eager devotion which made the queen smile and press her delicate hand in his curled locks" (p. 42). Unlike Cicely's filial trysts with her own mother, the nights that Babington bands with other over-heated youths to swear allegiance to Mary actually happened. Here they also pass "like a perpetual fairy tale" (p. 263), one that arrests everyone in a child's dream of maternal love, and replaces history with family romance. Babington's illusion even comes up with a literary lineage of its own; as Yonge points out, in his *Faerie Queene* Spenser too "beheld" Mary in "his false Duessa." Though Catholic, Babington and his fellow devotées actually mirror the Protestant poet as they absorb her "witching loveliness" in the "fitful torch light of the cavern" and fail to "recollect how that very obscurity might have assisted it" (p. 260).

Reflected in the carnival mirror of Spenser's allegory, Babington's infantile delusion offers one model for the imaginary Mary's incorporation into a knowable history; it is countered by the old-fashioned English skepticism of Cicely's foster brother, the Protestant Humfrey Talbot. From his own childhood, Humfrey resists Mary's attractions; it is only when Mary is stripped "of all the tokens of her royal rank" (p. 518) and told that she is "a dead woman in the eye of the law" (p. 516) that she touches the heart of the "stout lubberly Yorkshire lad" who is Britain's future, as Babington is its doomed, Catholic and courtly past. "Crowned in his eyes as the Queen of Sorrows" (p. 519), Mary at the eleventh hour becomes the admissible object of an authentic English love. If Babington embodies an Elizabethan hallucination of desire, Humfrey rehearses the Georgians' willingness to care for Mary only as long as she was lost.

But Cicely's achievement of what we might call a habitable love for her queenly mother charts a different course from either Humfrey's or Babington's, one on the whole less often documented than theirs. For one thing, it is born neither of political infatuation nor of a secretly savage sympathy, but rather of intense conflict. This conflict may be seen to take place either between Susan Talbot and Mary Queen of Scots or between the two sides of Cicely – English "Cis" and "Bride of Scotland." In either case, it is the mother–daughter bond that forces admission of that conflict and thereby holds the secret of complete reconciliation with Mary. The achievement of Yonge's novel is that this reconciliation founds a new kind of subject, whose birth takes place in Cicely.

On the surface, Cicely's two mothers could not be more different, but in Cicely's flowering mind the two women turn out to be deeply alike as well. Both have lost daughters, Mary to regain hers but incompletely, Susan to acquire a substitute in Cicely. Susan, too, is a queen of sorts, one who "in her quiet way [. . .] proved capable of ruling men and maids, farm and stable as well as house, servants and children" (p. 35). In turn, Yonge gives the historically French-speaking Queen of Scots a "thorough Scottish accent" (p. 31) and Mary's insatiable craving for fresh air makes her like a "modern English girl" (p. 394). Each of the rival mothers divides from herself into her own other, whom she can thus replace in the daughter's mind. That daughter, meanwhile, bears no convincing physical resemblance to either Susan or Mary. On the one hand, she displays such a "graceful bearing," reminiscent of Mary, that Susan looks on her "with wondering admiration, as something more her own and yet less her own than ever" (p. 475). But Mary is puzzled by Cicely too, acknowledging on the eve of her execution that she has "lived too long with thy mother" for the queen "to be thy mother," and lamenting that "I would have made a princess of her, but it passes my powers'" (p. 553). Mary's words point up the internal divagation that in fact constitutes Cicely, and as she brings it to her daughter's consciousness, that breach emerges as the condition of the queen's absorption and perpetuation through her.

Just so, instead of becoming Mary's "princess" – and so the heir to her title – Cicely becomes her daughter in a different sense, not just the recipient of her phantasmic love but also her companion through the trials of history. As she attends the Queen of Scots through her last and bitterest captivity, Cicely at first enjoys more adventures in romance than she has ever known before: Mary again lies down with her and tells her stories of France, trying as well to convert her to Catholicism. But as the romance of being with Mary begins to give way to the historically imposed pains of captivity, Cicely at last concludes that "the finding herself a princess, and sharing the captivity of a queen, had not proved so like a chapter of the *Morte d'Arthur*" as she had imagined. Indeed, "it was as unlike as was riding a white palfrey through a forest, guided by knights in armour, to the being packed with all the ladies into a heavy jolting conveyance, guarded before and behind by armed servants and yeomen" (p. 441).

As history and romance reflect each other's deficiencies, and as Mary's own dreams and schemes are trampled by the weight of that crammed, jostling, female reality, the attachment to her that once felt compulsive now becomes a matter of choice. Cicely's desire to save her mother likewise finds fulfillment neither in dream nor in historical action, but through an ironic compromise with a historically documented past. When Mary is sentenced to die for her part in the Babington Plot, Cicely turns herself over to Elizabeth Tudor as a hostage. History of course compels the Tudor queen to stand by her own warrant and Mary is beheaded anyway. Elizabeth allows "the Princess Bride of Scotland" to live on the condition that she disappear from the record, and so she does, surviving "in happy obscurity, 'Unknown to History'" (p. 589).

What might Cicely's survival mean? For one thing, it means that Mary will survive too, by some means other than the official bloodline that of course persisted through her son James. Stricken from the official record, this alternative line can be conveyed only in the ciphers of imagination and desire. Cicely virtually embodies this resolution, for the physical signs that she shares Mary's blood are themselves artificial, confined to tattoos and scribbled strips of paper. Indeed, Cicely fails to resemble the Queen of Scots in any of her "features" (p. 170). She grows into a "black-browed wench" whose "dark-avised face" contrasts starkly with Mary's legendary white hands. Larger-boned than Mary, her face round where the queen's is angular, her gray eyes lacking Mary's "fascinating beauty" (p. 103), Cicely is, frankly, "more border lassie than princess" (p. 136). Her similarity to the queen is limited to an "indefinable grace" that flowers into "certain queenly gestures, manners, habits of air and movement" only after a long exposure to the Queen of Scots has taught her the "pretty tricks of [Mary's] head and hands" (p. 234).

What is more, near the end of *Unknown to History*, Cicely marries her staunch adoptive brother Humfrey. The union seems to promise that, if Mary's female offspring could herself only be adopted into Protestant Britain, Cicely's children with Humfrey will at last embody an even more natural graft. But Cicely and Humfrey leave England for the Hague, where they prove unable to have children of their own. We learn that in the future they will be adopting orphans and raising them in an atmosphere of "perfect content, and peace, and trust" (p. 589).

Trust in what? In adoption, one imagines. *Unknown to History* is really a novel about adoption – of children, of manners, of mothers – and it is through Cicely's adoption by the Talbots that Mary Stuart's old threat of immersion and invasion is assimilated to modern Britain, much as the groundless elaborations of romance are assimilated to Yonge's historically grounded narrative. Then too, Yonge's living contemporaries wanted nothing more than to adopt the Queen of Scots into their own history, and their narcissistic fantasies about her, like Victoria's own, doubled as fantasies that they were Mary's children – that, in some forgotten infancy, *they* (in reality of other parentage) had been adopted by the Britain most familiar to them.

In turn, the adoption motif that shapes *Unknown to History* reminds us that that novel's resolutions and indeed its peace of mind are achieved only by imagining forms of continuity in which, as in an adoption, the most intimate bonds coexist with the knowledge that certain others simply do not. From this point of view, any chance of contact with the Queen of Scots depends on respect for the human capacity for substitution and other such acts of humble magic. Intimacy with her – and so a sense of genuine continuity with the past – will be possible only when the severing of connection with her is acknowledged as well. Yonge's Cicely Talbot both gains and embodies this knowledge.

In *Unknown to History*, as in Froude's *History of England*, Mary Stuart's labored illusion at last vanishes. Here, though, it does so less because it is exposed as a lie than because it is at last internalized as both the absence of the historical self (Cicely's condition after all) and that self's *sine qua non*. This is a resolution that could only have been achieved through an exploration of the daughter's bond with the mother of her own dreams, but it reaches back to the earliest English fantasies about the Queen of Scots – those of her would-be political sons. Yonge's novel charts Britain's history of imaginative engagement with Mary Stuart from that time forward, but instead of denying the gap between history and desire, her story, like her heroine, manages to incorporate it. Yonge thereby transformed a nation's archaic wish for its long-lost queen . . . and so at last fulfilled it.

Part V
Epilogue
Postmodern Mary

And secondly, dear Mary, let me stress:
there's nothing, barring Art, sublunar creatures
can use to comprehend your gorgeous features.
Leave History to Good Queen Bess.
> Joseph Brodsky, "Twenty Sonnets to
> Mary Queen of Scots"

The sort of historical narrative that posits beginnings, successive phases and provisional ends has fallen far out of fashion. But the reader will not, perhaps, be mortally offended if asked to imagine that, at least with respect to Mary Queen of Scots, the Victorians finished something the Elizabethans had begun. With them, anyway, this story stops. After the executioner bungled his stroke, Mary's severed head floated for centuries through England's dreamlife, estranged from the queen's body as ambiguously as longing for her was estranged from the desire for separation, autonomy and dominance that brought modern Britain into being. The Victorians were the first investigators of the unconscious, after all, and it was they who most fully admitted a subterranean and not altogether governable involvement with Mary Stuart; hence they seem to have comprehended her with a clarity and completeness often missing in earlier eras. Ironically enough, this power of comprehension came of acknowledging comprehension's limits: it came because Britons as different as Strickland, Swinburne and Yonge began to recognize Mary's own mysterious difference as part of what they themselves were.

The Victorian triumph of moral and historical imagination of course accompanied an achievement of a less lovely kind – that of general belief in the fiction of a fully actualized, and hence globally entitled, Great Britain. Before Victoria's reign, the myth of Mary Stuart had both frustrated and secretly sponsored an evolving fiction of national pre-eminence: the Great War would shatter that fiction not long after Victoria's death. The decades since often seem to have furnished little more than an asylum for imperial Britain to fall apart in; today the devolution of the Scottish parliament marks the United Kingdom's decomposition from within, even as economic and political incorporation into the European Community beckons from without. The self-difference and absorption into a larger whole that Mary Queen of Scots so terrifyingly embodied for the Elizabethans look suspiciously like realities now.

Mary's mysterious motto – *in my end is my beginning* – is here uncannily apposite. The same motto of course also hints that history itself is something other than the sequential narrative so blithely embraced above – that it may, even, be something besides a sequence of events agreed "really" to have happened. Just so, while Britain's history considered in both these senses – as the story of a developing modern nation and as a series of documented occurrences – has framed the present study, that is not really what this book has been "about." My subject has been much more a desecrated queen's powerful hold on individuals who might as easily as not have been her political children and grandchildren. Over time, what amounts to a persistent desire for a lost political mother has found its most literal expression in fantasies about her secret daughters – creatures of desire who manage to survive outside recorded history, but who at last propagate themselves only in stories, letters and contagious dreams. Yet, really, almost every Briton who writes about Mary seems in some way her secret child, driven by the often inadmissible wish to recover her. This motif is, as we've seen, tenacious and omnipresent in the fiction of Britain. Thus while that fiction's Mary Queen of Scots can reveal herself to us only in the reveries of individuals living in unique historical moments, those individuals' feelings for her seem to be of a different nature. After the philosopher Agnes Heller, we might call this other nature non-historical.[1] Mary Stuart's afterlife in our own century can illuminate this persistent habit of an other than conscious mind, one whose infantile, or at least preverbal, ingredients allow it to transcend the particularity of person and time.

For Mary refuses to go away. To this day tourists troop through her rooms at Holyrood House and hire motorboats to Lochleven Island. They buy admission to "her" house at Jedburgh, flock to her tomb in Westminster Abbey, and demand that her birthplace at Linlithgow be devoted to her memory alone.[2] Scottish women don period dress and hold seances on the anniversary of her death.[3] In 1992, Liz Lochhead's phantasmagorical play, *Mary Queen of Scots Got Her Head Chopped Off*, took first prize at the prestigious Edinburgh Fringe Festival, and in the 1996 season Schiller's *Maria Stuart* drew crowds to the National Theatre. They came to see, at long last, a French actress (Isabelle Huppert) in the title role; meanwhile, collectives of Scottish women artists exhibited work relating to Mary, one – Lys Hansen – filling an entire room with multimedia evocations of her execution whose touchstones range from medieval saints to Plato's *Phaedo*.

In this century there have been two major films about the Queen of Scots as well as a popular Broadway play; two more are in production today. Mary's poetry, apocryphal and authentic, can be purchased in any international airport, while biographies, fictional and factual alike, proliferate. After the death in 1997 of Diana, Princess of Wales, mourners reported visions of the princess's face superimposed on a portrait of Mary Stuart's grandson, the beheaded Charles I, in Kensington Palace. If rumors concerning Charles II's dalliances with Diana's ancestors prove true, then some of her blood once ran in Mary's veins. But even if it did not, the magnitude of recent mourning for a tall, fair, troubled near-Queen of England resonates eerily with an ancient grief for Mary. Again the best-loved queen, like perhaps the most lovable mother, turns out to be the one most lost, not only among too many images of her but also to herself, albeit in a way that makes her the least resistible of mirrors to almost everybody else.

In Mary Stuart, these guilty secrets of the private mind bleed visibly into the no purer concerns of the collective mind. For instance, if anything, Mary seems more at home than ever as nations modify old images of themselves as bounded and determinate entities. Her qualities of ambiguity and seductive otherness have themselves come to seem more the flesh than the shadow of collective identity. Meanwhile, the moral of the story of twentieth-century wars and their attendant atrocities seems to be that history itself – both human events and the interpretation of them – is a mere symptom of our most horrific urges. That is of course one of the more obvious lessons of Fotheringay, where law and bloodlust mingled souls, with faith and betrayal their indistinguishable attendants.

At Fotheringay too, Mary Stuart's divided body became the vector of opposing desires, one for the well-written narrative of Protestant history, but the other, more infantile, not to enter "history" at all. To uncover the story of the dead queen's representation in British fiction is to feel the violence of this opposition time and time again. But while in the past the desire for history prevailed, this century has seen a certain reversal. Not long after the death of Victoria, the "inevitable quest" for the Queen of Scots so vividly described by Michael Field forsook the road built by the dauntingly many words that had been written about her in the past. Instead, Britons began, concertedly, to seek Mary through the many visual images that had been made of her. In the space of four years, three hefty books had been consecrated to the mystery of the queen's painted face. Works like J.J. Foster's *True Portraiture of Mary Stuart* (1904), Lionel Cust's mammoth *Authentic Portraits of Mary Queen of Scots* (1903), and Andrew Lang's *Portraits and Jewels of Mary Stuart* (1906) all abandoned documentary apprehensions of the Queen of Scots, while the pages of *The Athenaeum* predicted that Mary would be ascertained only through an appreciation of the "wonderful resemblance" among "the different faces presented as hers."[4] Lang declared that even the remotest "likeness of Mary Stuart" gave him to know what she "was like," and, once provided with one, he happily assured his readers that he would "ask for no more! I understand Mary Stuart."[5]

If, in the twentieth century, this "Mary Stuart" became less recognizable as a historical being than as a recurrent image, she also helped many to re-interpret history itself as an almost mythic repetition of repeated ravishment, privation and loss. The Queen of Scots bore witness to an other than coherent and purposive history even in the midst of the war, so famous for having blasted not only Britain's confident illusion of itself but also the supporting fiction of what Paul Fussell once memorably described as "seamless, purposeful 'history,'" the sense of "a coherent stream of time running from past through present to future."[6]

In 1918, poems commemorating Mary's defeat at Langside offered themselves up for sale alongside displays of memorabilia from that battle. The end was to raise money for Scotland's War Relief Fund; after all, wondered a biographer in the preface to the poetry,

> What more direct and vivid method of carrying out such work could there be than to present to public view such treasures as well-authenticated portraits of Mary Stuart, letters written by her own hand, needlework done by her own fingers? Such stimulation deepens sentiment, engenders love of country and Empire, encourages national and Imperial unity, enlarges the true patriotism which surely leads to right victory.[7]

Mary and the charismatic objects she once touched promised to restore a shattered sense of long-established "national and imperial unity" – to defend Britain from the ravages of war and give its sense of meaningful continuity with its own past back to it.

As it turns out, this was a visibly suicidal mission. The ambiguous and congenitally incoherent Queen of Scots was an extremely unlikely catalyst of historical consolation, serving far better as a symbol of modern Britain's dissolution into something primordial and blind. More than anything else, she brought to mind the dark collapse of time, as the auctioned poetry about her in fact admitted in its opening lines: "Three hundred years and fifty gone!/Yet closer to you now than then." What brings the queen "closer" is what annihilates, not what preserves:

> Mary, our Queen, none shall forget
>   Your beauties or your iron woes,
> And when your crown with spines was set
>   To us you grew more dear for those.[8]

In 1918, to call Mary "our Queen" was less to gain command of history than to slip wishfully under its surface, moving backward even past the moment she was unqueened. It was an older, long-obliterated relationship to her that provided the matrix of a present reality. Mary thus awakened a desire less to repair a wounded view of history than to escape it altogether.

Just so, the rule in future was to glimpse Mary Stuart not as part of the panoramic tableau of a known, finished and wholly accessible story about the past but instead as history's vanishing point. In the late 1930s, the expatriate poet T.S. Eliot ended "East Coker," the second of his *Four Quartets*, with Mary's motto: "In my end is my beginning." Eliot's poem begins with an inversion of the same phrase: "In my beginning is my end." In between, Mary herself does not appear as a personality; all that remains of her is a "tattered arras woven with a silent motto" (I: 13). Silenced by time, she is the absent icon of a poem about the way "in succession/Houses rise and fall, crumble, are extended,/Are removed, destroyed, restored" (I: 23). With Mary's motto as his emblem, Eliot's speaker finally resigns himself to time, which he understands not as a history responsive to our efforts to mold and guide it but rather as an endless reiteration of amnesia and loss.

Mary's motto also snared the imagination of a Catholic novelist, Maurice Baring, whose 1931 novel, *In My End is My Beginning*, is told in the several voices of her four women-in-waiting. Instead of making Mary seem multi-dimensional, this quartering of perspective fragments its object, who is thus most present in the photograph of a moldering death mask that appears inside the front cover. Such visages remind us that, no matter how tightly its eye is trained on history, the twentieth-century camera can capture only the fact that something has evaded it. Celluloid likewise projects the image of its own unfulfilled desire: in John Ford's 1936 film version of Maxwell Anderson's *Mary of Scotland*, shadows swallow sets where Mary herself (played with notice-able uncertainty by Katharine Hepburn) is dwarfed and often engulfed by the spaces and objects around her – a giant globe, a looming ship, an empty throne. Adrift and ever vanishing into the mists of falsehood and dream, Hepburn's lonely Mary finally eludes the camera. "The film has no direc-tives," one critic complained, "no point of view, is entirely unclear as to its purpose."[9] Yet it was precisely by adopting no fixed "point of view" – by depicting, as a different critic put it, "the triumph of histrionics over history" and a heroine "less a woman than a symbol" – that Ford's film typifies this cen-tury's Mary, ever slipping beyond the horizon of history's eye to become at last the reflection of its desire.[10] It is in turn this elusive queen who must be the imaginary addressee of Joseph Brodsky's "Twenty Sonnets to Mary Queen of Scots." For, leaving "History to Good Queen Bess," Brodsky put Mary in the realm of art – a realm not itself wholly divorced from history, but, rather like Mary herself, best apprehended as "a body that has lost its head."

It would seem that, historically speaking, it has been British society's invis-ibles who have brought the history that has lost its head – the irrational and atemporal history of desire – the closest to consciousness. Often, they have been women, and it is striking that Mary's most revealing recent appearances in British fiction have through the agency of the female pen. Since British women today can hardly be described as excluded from, or unknown to, his-tory, their consciousness of Mary Stuart seems to originate in something deeper, older, darker than political exclusion – in a matter, finally, of spilled blood, of a hole in the bottom of the historical mind.

Margaret Drabble's novel *The Witch of Exmoor* (1996) is, for example, preoc-cupied with Britain's degeneration from the sceptered isle of the distant past – and from the splendid empire of the recent past – to the crumbling social man-sion of the present. This transformation's chief witness is an ageing sociologist,

Frieda Haxby, whose Britain has too much blood on its hands not to be now collapsing under the weight of the sins that brought it into being. Mary Queen of Scots, not unsurprisingly, gives those sins a local habitation and a name when, while attending an exhibition at the National Portrait Gallery, Frieda (with a psychoanalyst no less) discusses the "sibling slaughter" that made England what it was. The topic is prompted by portraits in which "Scottish Mary rests her hand beneath her right breast above her rosary, and victorious Elizabeth Gloriana dazzles in many poses with ruff and fan and jewels and brocade"; as Frieda watches, "rivalries, hatreds, treacheries gleam from their stiff bodies, their hard bold eyes." When the psychoanalyst glibly refers these portraits to "the murderous passions engendered by heritage and court," Frieda remembers for the first time that her own sister once tried to shake her off the top of a ladder.

Drabble's Frieda is much absorbed with queens, being the author of a lengthy biography of Christina of Sweden as well as an obvious connoisseur of sixteenth-century women like Mary Stuart and Lady Jane Grey, not to mention the Tudor sisters who did them (and each other) wrong. But a queen's meaning, for her, takes shape at the crossroads of history and some less conscious life. So through the ruthless grace of this life, Frieda seems to see her own face in that of Mary Queen of Scots. The bottom drops out of her own sense of historical specificity, and her mind, now gaping and dark, opens into a shared past.[11] Primal guilt is puzzling when the victim, like the culprit, seems to be oneself. But that is the delicacy of Frieda's psychic position.

A similar accident befalls Claudia, the heroine of Penelope Lively's 1986 novel *Moon Tiger*, who in its first pages is found struggling to learn history at school. "I was thirteen," Claudia recalls:

> At Miss Lavenham's Academy for Girls. In Lower Four B. Doing the Tudor Monarchs with Miss Lavenham herself. Miss Lavenham wrote names and dates on the board and we copied them down. We also, to her dictation, noted the principal characteristics of each reign. Henry VIII was condemned by his marital excesses, but was also not good as king. Queen Elizabeth was good; she fended off the Spaniards and ruled firmly. She also cut off the head of Mary Queen of Scots, who was a Catholic. Our pens scratched in the long summer afternoon. I put up my hand: "Please Miss Lavenham, did the Catholics think she was right to cut off Mary's head?" "No, Claudia, I don't expect they did." "Please, do Catholic people think so now?" Miss Lavenham took a breath: "Well, Claudia," she said kindly, "I suppose some of them might not. People do sometimes disagree. But there is no need for you to worry about that. Just put down what is on the board. Make your headings nice and clear in red ink . . ." And suddenly for me the uniform grey pond of history is rent; it is fractured into a thousand contending waves; I hear the babble of voices. I put my pen down and ponder; my headings are not nice and clear in red ink; I get 38% (Fail) in the end of term exams.[12]

The moral of Lively's fable would seem to be that "history" is not uniform but "rent" and "fractured," multiple and contradictory, different for Catholics to what it is for Protestants, different if you do not think it was "right to cut off Mary's head" to what it seems if you believe that "Queen Elizabeth was good" and that what happened upon her reign – Britain's first steps toward a moral and political state based on possessive individualism and a creed of private liberty – is also "good." But the sensuous and emotional texture of this incident takes us far beyond the worn question of what history is and whose picture of it prevails.

For what matters, at least as far as Lively's Claudia is concerned, is less history's relativity than the often involuntary fantasies and identifications that make that history internal, palpable, personal, real. Here the identification is between the infinitely splitting rivulets of blood flowing from Mary's severed head and an almost primitive writing consciousness, symbolized by the errant red pen of a British schoolgirl. This pen enters history ("I hear the babble of voices") only through art, which is to say by mistranscribing history ("my headings are not nice and clear in red ink") in a form that replicates, if it does not actually revive, the bloody, headless, unclear "Queen of Scots, who was a Catholic."

This unconscious involvement with Mary Stuart presents history as a layering of transpersonal memories and fierce, inchoate desires, of primal violences that force us to re-enact them, if only in the realm of Brodsky's "Art." Like the crude sketch of British history that gets Lively's Claudia "38% (Fail) in the end of term exams," the story thence told is textbook history with something missing. Accessible only through the gracious violence of art, Mary stands for, if not is, the something missing – the possibility of substitution – that once drove and defined modern British history, and which seems now to be surviving its collapse.

Lively's perception that Mary is the point at which our historical selves know their own obliteration returns with a vengeance in Liz Lochhead's *Mary Queen of Scots Got Her Head Chopped Off*. Through all of its many short hallucinatory scenes, Lochhead's 1992 play keeps for its chorus an "interesting, ragged ambiguous" raven who directs us to watch, among other things, a series of vignettes from Mary's life, each revolving around some brutality that Mary's Scottish subjects, or her prospective English ones, inflicted on her.[13] For her part, Lochhead's Mary speaks with a thick French accent that in the course of the play turns into a Scottish brogue. She slips in and out in the body of Elizabeth's waiting-woman, Marian, just as Elizabeth passes through the body of Mary's waiting-woman, Bessie. Such metamorphoses and mergings liberate the unconscious processes that both propelled and threatened to engulf many of the historical events that Lochhead also stages. So while on the surface Lochhead's play shows Mary repeatedly torn down and stamped out of Scotland's version of its own past, these very events achieve dimension and visibility because of something else, an unnameable persistency which the raven at last names as a "black hole, [a] jaggit slash, '*naethin*'" (p. 23).

Though Lochhead's raven speculates that this black slash was made during the Protestant Reformation, when the "Mother of God" was "torn [. . .] oot of the sky o' Scotland" (p. 23), its current residence is the female mind. It is a mind returned to its own childhood through an attachment to Mary. Midway through the play, that is, Lochhead's Elizabeth turns into an English girl who is obsessed with the Queen of Scots. Decapitated dolls litter her floor, while "in real time and like a child [she] cries for her dead mama" (p. 23). A little later, Mary and Elizabeth turn up as Mairn and Leezie, two Scottish beggar girls "in love with royalty and splendour" (p. 32), whose irrational love of Mary Stuart prepares the ground for the next gruesome episode of that queen's historical life.

Just before the curtain falls, historical event and fantastic identification at last meet in a ritual re-enactment of Mary's beheading. All of Lochhead's characters come forward, "stripped of all dignity and historicity, transformed to twentieth-century children" (p. 63). As these children "begin miming childhood games" and reciting primitive rhymes, a young girl, Marie, "appears, by herself, very prominent, an outsider" and "stands silent" until the others notice her, light upon her and humiliate her into "a sobbing shamed victim." Gradually, the children begin to re-enact Mary's execution, forcing Marie to pantomime kiss the axe and pardon the executioner. In jumprope rhymes they mock the pieties of Mary's death, chanting "Mary Queen of Scots got her head chopped off" over and over again. It is only a moment before these children stripped of historicity cluster "all around Marie/Mary [. . .] grab[bing] up at her throat in a tableau, just her head above their hands. Very still in the red light for a moment then black" (p. 67).

At once killed as she was in history and retrieved as she was in wish, reached for but never touched, Mary's severed head figures the timeless realm over which the Queen of Scots still presides. And this image, so up-to-date in its expression, is also archaic: even Spenser would have recognized it, and no one after him could altogether turn from the face so early shoved out of British history's sight. Here, in the last decade of the twentieth century, Lochhead retrieves the memory of that face as an instrument of cultural critique. In her hands Mary's metamorphoses expose the violence that makes modern history. And why shouldn't it? Mary Queen of Scots has always been for hire to such projects, as her cousin Elizabeth's propagandists were well aware. But specific as her applications at individual historical moments might be, Mary has always also been a door opening into what isn't exactly there, in history – into the non-historical experience of self-induced and eternally lamented loss. This experience recurs embedded in the most mundane of moments in time and material space – in a *tête à tête* at an art museum, a history lesson, a friendly game of jump-rope.

In his "Theses on the Philosophy of History," Walter Benjamin regretted that materialist interpretations of history have themselves lost the beauty of a certain "process of empathy whose origin is the indolence of the heart, *acedia*, which despairs of grasping and holding the genuine historical image as it flares up briefly."[14] Despite their differences, I would cast all of the apprehensions of Mary Queen of Scots that we have encountered not just as episodes in material history but also as symptoms of this finally immaterial – even anti-material – despair. More specifically, they are instances in which failure to recover the mirror of the lost mother becomes in itself her meaning, the sign of her presence in – and even as – us. Once this seems true, history can only shed its mask as an epic tale of consolidation and attainment. It drops its veil of knowability as well, to reveal the ravishing phantom of an unassuageable grief.

Notes

Introduction

1 Nathaniel Hawthorne, *The English Note-book*, ed. Randall Stewart (New York, 1962), p. 343.

2 Joseph Brodsky, "Twenty Sonnets to Mary Queen of Scots." In Joseph Brodsky, *Urania* (New York, 1991), p. 22.

3 The definitive modern biography of Mary Queen of Scots is Jenny Wormald, *Mary Queen of Scots: A Study in Failure* (London, 1988).

4 Michael Lynch offers a pertinent analysis of Mary's role in Scotland's struggles toward what became its political future in *Scotland: A New History* (London, 1991), pp. 203–225. For a still more general view of Mary's role in the formation of modern France, Scotland and England, see Lynch, ed., *Mary Stewart, Queen in Three Countries* (Oxford, 1988).

5 James Emerson Phillips, *Images of a Queen: Mary Stuart in Sixteenth-Century Literature* (Berkeley and Los Angeles, 1964).

6 See Jessica Benjamin, *The Bonds of Love: Psychoanalysis, Feminism, and the Problem of Domination* (New York, 1988); John Bowlby, *Attachment, Separation and Loss* (London, 1971); and Margaret Mahler, Fred Pine and Anni Bergman, *The Psychological Birth of the Human Infant* (New York, 1975).

7 Helen Hackett, *Virgin Mother, Maiden Queen* (Basingstoke, 1995).

8 The classic delineation of this process is to be found in Stephen Greenblatt, *Renaissance Self-Fashioning, from More to Shakespeare* (Chicago, 1980), but on some of its complexities and for a more direct probe of the doctrine of purity that it implies, see Peter Stallybrass, "Patriarchal Territories: The Body Enclosed." In *Rewriting the Renaissance: The Discourses of Sexual Difference in Early Modern Europe*, ed. Margaret W. Ferguson, Maureen Quilligan, and Nancy J. Vickers (Chicago, 1986), pp. 123–142.

9 John Leslie, *A Defence of the Honour of the most High, Mighty and Noble Princess Marie Queen of Scotland and Dowager of France* (London, 1569), p. 6.

10 An exceptionally helpful summary of the many aspects of Mary's maternity may be found in Karen Robertson, "The Body Natural of a Queen: Mary, James, *Horestes*." In *Renaissance and Reformation/Renaissance et Reforme* 26 (1990), p. 29.

11 Sophia Lee, *The Recess; or, A Tale of Other Times*. 3 vols. ([1783–5] 2nd edn, London, 1786), I: 19.

12 A powerful historical account of the odds against both Mary and Elizabeth: Wallace MacCaffery, *The Shaping of the Elizabethan Regime* (Princeton, 1968), especially pp. 145–247. On individual problems confronting a queen of Elizabeth's day, see *The Reign of Elizabeth I*, ed. Christopher Haigh (Hampshire and London, 1984).

13 Katherine Bradley and Edith Cooper ("Michael Field"), Preface to *The Tragic Mary* (London, 1890), p. v.

14 Sigmund Freud, *Totem and Taboo*, trans. James Strachey ([1913] New York, 1950), p. x.

15   Several portraits of Mary Stuart were made during her long stay in France, the two most complete and definitive by the Valois court painter François Clouet, who rendered her as Dauphine in 1559 and as his widow in the famous "deuil blanc" portrait of 1560–1561. In 1578, during her captivity at Sheffield Castle, Pierre Oudry produced the only image of her that remains from the last thirty years of her life. On the uncontrollable permutations of the Marian portraiture, see Lionel Cust, *Authentic Portraits of Mary Queen of Scots* (London, 1903) and Andrew Lang, *Portraits and Jewels of Mary Queen of Scots* (Glasgow, 1906).

16   Ernst Kantorowicz, *The King's Two Bodies: A Study in Political Theory* (Princeton, 1957).

17   Marie Axton, *The Queen's Two Bodies: Drama and the Elizabethan Succession* (London, 1977); Constance Jordan, "Woman's Rule in Sixteenth-Century British Political Thought." In *Renaissance Quarterly* XXI (1987), pp. 421–451. On the sexualized complexities of Elizabeth's solutions to some of the dilemmas of female sovereignty, see Susan Bassnett, *Elizabeth I: A Feminist Perspective* (Oxford, 1988); and Carole Levin, *"The Heart and Stomach of a King": Elizabeth I and the Politics of Sex and Power* (Philadelphia, 1994).

18   Jacqueline Rose, *States of Fantasy* (Oxford, 1996), p. 6.

19   Helen Smailes and Duncan Thomson, *The Queen's Image: A Celebration of Mary Queen of Scots* (Edinburgh, 1987). Besides Smailes and Thomson's, the only transhistorical survey of Mary's myth is Pearl Brandwein's mostly descriptive *Mary Queen of Scots in Nineteenth- and Twentieth-Century Drama: Poetic License with History* (Amsterdam, 1989).

20   Hawthorne, *Note-book*, p. 343.

Elizabethan Mary

1   Robert Wyngfield, *An Account of the Execution of Mary, the Late Queen of Scots* (1587), in *The Clarendon Historical Society's Reprints*, series II. 2 vols (Edinburgh, 1884–1886), I: 11.

1   "The finest she that ever was": Scotland, 1558–1568

1   James Emerson Phillips's *Images of a Queen* remains the pre-eminent authority on this material.

2   Elizabeth's renowned poem about Mary was published in 1589 in George Puttenham's *Arte of English Poesie*, ed. G.D. Willock and A. Walker (Cambridge, 1935), p. 247.

3   Thomas Randolph to William Cecil (21 February 1563). *Cal. State Papers, Scot.*, II: 229.

4   Randolph to Cecil (February 1563). *Cal. State Papers, Scot.*, II: 229; Nicholas White to Cecil (February 1569). *Cal. State Papers, Scot.*, IV: 300.

5   John Stubbs, *The Discoverie of a Gaping Gulph* (1579). In *The Gaping Gulf, with Letters and Other Relevant Documents*, ed. Lloyd E. Berry (Charlottesville, Va., 1968), p. 80.

6   John Knox, *The First Blast of the Trumpet Against the Monstrous Regiment of Women* (1558). In *The Works of John Knox*, ed. David Laing. 6 vols (New York, 1966), IV: 415.

7   Elizabeth's difficulties are taken up with particular clarity in Bassnett, *Elizabeth I*, Hackett, *Virgin Mother*, and Levin, *Heart and Stomach*.

8   In "Woman's Rule" (pp. 421–425), Constance Jordan unfolds the tenet of sixteenth-century political thought that held, in Britain anyway, that because woman was *"persona mixta"* – equal to man in her resemblance to God but socially and physically beneath him – she was unfit to govern.

9   In *The Queen's Two Bodies*, Marie Axton explains in detail the logic whereby "the body politic was supposed to be contained within the natural body of the queen" (p. 12), inevitably at the expense of that natural body. Louis Montrose analyzes the strategies Elizabeth used to abstract herself into a "medium through which power, authority and legitimace are passed between generations of men", in "The Elizabethan Subject and

the Spenserian Text," in *Literary Theory/Renaissance Texts*, ed. Patricia Parker and David Quint (Baltimore, 1989), pp. 189–310.

10 Susan Frye examines Elizabeth's following among London's emerging entrepreneurial class in *Elizabeth I* (Oxford, 1993), and Axton (*The Queen's Two Bodies*) her potentially treacherous support among lawyers in the Inns of Court. Philippa Berry shows how courtier poets like Spenser and Sidney absorbed Elizabeth into Petrarchan and neo-platonic poetics through which they could secure individual authority, in *Of Chastity and Power: Elizabethan Literature and the Unmarried Queen* (London, 1989).

11 See especially Richard Helgerson, *Forms of Nationhood: The Elizabethan Writing of England* (Chicago, 1992).

12 Roy Strong shows how representations of Elizabeth were rendered deliberately diffuse and ambiguous in order to reconcile her physical body with her political and spiritual identity. See *The Cult of Elizabeth* (London, 1977). Differently, John Archer and Lowell Gallagher examine the way Elizabeth's sovereign authority ultimately depended on the queen's self-concealment (Gallagher, *Medusa's Gaze: Conscience and Casuistry in the Renaissance* [Stanford, 1990]) or on the diffraction of her subjectivity among her courtiers (Archer, *Sovereignty and Intelligence: Spying and Court Culture in the English Renaissance* [Stanford, 1993]).

13 This is not to say that contemporary representations of Elizabeth were devoid of the imagery of fertility and even maternity, only that they were in the end disjunct from her actual physical state, and they ultimately depended on this very disjunction for their rhetorical force. See Frye, especially, for descriptions of Elizabeth's actual and canny remoteness.

14 Mortimer Levine, *The Early Elizabethan Succession Question, 1558–1568* (Stanford, 1966); and *Tudor Dynastic Problems, 1460–1568* (London, 1973).

15 A classic example of this latter argument appears in Edmund Plowden's "Treatise Proveing that [. . .] the Quene of Scotts [. . .] is not disabled by the law of England, to receave the crowne of Ingland by discente" (1567), which holds that "the quene of Scottes and her father were homagers to Inglande, and borne with the fee and sayniory of England." The counter-argument is made in the anonymous *Allegations Against the Svrmised title of the Qvine of Scotts* (1565). For a discussion of Plowden's argument for Mary's entitlement to the English throne, see Marie Axton, "The Influence of Edmund Plowden's Succession Treatise." In *Huntington Library Quarterly* 37 (1974), pp. 209–226.

16 Peter Stallybrass analyzes the Elizabethan drive toward national purity in "Patriarchal Territories," pp. 123–142. See also Claire McEachern, *The Poetics of English Nationhood, 1590–1612* (Cambridge, 1996).

17 Women's symbolic power in the Valois court is analyzed in Sheila ffollett, "Catherine de'Medici as Artemisia: Figuring the Powerful Widow." In *Rewriting the Renaissance*, ed. Ferguson, Quilligan and Vickers,(Chicago, 1986) pp. 227–241.

18 Mary was notably enamored of "the more picturesque rites of her religion;" She could be seen "carrying tapers at Candlemas; and washing the feet of the poor on Maundy Thursday." For other examples of Mary's extraordinarily concrete piety, and of the tendency of objects around her to acquire the aura of relics, see *Inventories of the Jewels and Dresses*, ed. Joseph Robertson (Edinburgh, 1843), p. lxiv.

19 Mary's "Chanson sur la mort imprevue de François II" turns on a conceit in which Mary professes to hold "au coeur et à l'oeil/Un portrait et image" of, one imagines, the dead king. But instead the "portrait et image" turns out to "figure mon deuil/En mon pale visage." In Le Roux de Lincy, ed., *Receuil des chants historiques français* (Paris, 1942), p. 226.

20 In the space of only a few letters Mary cast Elizabeth as her "sister and cousin," a lover who promises that "even the heart and all shall be yours," and as a child appealing to Elizabeth's "maternal good inclination" who later begs for "the honour of being your daughter." See Agnes Strickland, *Letters of Mary Queen of Scots*. 2 vols (London, 1874),

I: 84; I: 87; I: 90; and *Letters of Mary Stuart, Queen of Scotland*, ed. Alexander Labanoff, trans. William Turnbull (London, 1845), p. 177. Mary also vows to "love, honour and obey" Elizabeth (Labanoff, p. 178), and declares herself "not an enchanter, but your sister and natural cousin."

21 Adam Blackwood, *History of Mary Queen of Scots* ([1588] Edinburgh, 1834), p. 150.

22 James Melville, *Memoirs of James Melville, 1535–1617*, ed. A. Francis Steuart (New York, 1980), p. 94. Patricia Fumerton reads the episode of the miniatures as Elizabeth's canny and finally self-protective performance of her own interiority in *Cultural Aesthetics: Renaissance Literature and the Practice of Social Ornament* (Chicago, 1991), pp. 67–110.

23 *The Trial of Mary Queen of Scots*, ed. A. Francis Steuart (Edinburgh and London, 1923), p. 56.

24 Stallybrass analyzes this contradiction in "Patriarchal Territories," p. 130.

25 John Knox, *History of the Reformation in Scotland*, in *Works*, ed. Laing, II: 269.

26 *Inventories and Jewels*, p. lxiii. Gordon Kipling analyzes the anti-Catholic strains of Mary's entry into Edinburgh in *Enter the King: Theatre, Liturgy and Ritual in the Medieval Civic Triumph* (Oxford, 1997), pp. 353–355.

27 Melville, *Memoirs*, p. 92.

28 Cecil to Elizabeth, *Cal. State Papers, Scot.*, II: 80.

29 Thomas Craig, "Epithalamium," in *Epithalamia tria Mariana*, ed. Francis Wrangham (Cheshire, 1837), p. 47.

30 Melville, *Memoirs*, p. 101.

31 Blackwood, *History*, p. 24.

32 *Satirical Poems of the Time of the Reformation*, ed. James Cranstoun, 2 vols (Edinburgh and London, 1891–93), I: 74.

33 Randolph to Cecil (8 January 1563), *Cal. State Papers, Scot.*, II: 47.

34 George Buchanan, *The History of Scotland*. 2 vols ([1583] 3rd edn, London 1753), II: 124.

35 Knox, *Reformation*, II: 290.

36 Knox, *History*, II: 290.

37 Randolph to Cecil, *Cal. State Papers, Scot.*, II: 47. Mary's "Maries" were her four ladies-in-waiting, Mary Seton, Mary Beaton, Mary Livingstone and Mary Hamilton, immortalized in the Scottish ballad, "Mary Hamilton." See *The English and Scottish Popular Ballads*, ed. Francis James Child. 5 vols (New York, 1956), II: 385. The sensuous, promiscuous atmosphere of Mary's Scottish court, from equestrian events featuring horsemen dressed as women to elaborate court masques in which Mary herself often acted, is captured in *Inventories and Jewels*, pp. 34–37.

38 Randolph to Cecil (6 January 1563), *Cal. State Papers, Scot.*, II: 44.

39 Knox, *Reformation*, II: 288.

40 Randolph to Cecil, (21 February 1562), *Cal. State Papers, Scot.*, I: 664.

41 Leslie, *Defence*, p. 40.

42 Randolph to Cecil (16 December 1562), in *Works of John Knox*, VI: 147.

43 Buchanan, *Scotland*, II: 97.

44 Randolph to Cecil (17 September 1561), *Cal. State Papers, Scot.*, I: 551.

45 Gordon Donaldson, *The First Trial of Mary Queen of Scots* (London, 1969), p. 174.

46 See especially Phillips's discussion of the "semi-publicity" against Mary in *Images*, p. 55.

47 Peter Frarin, "Oration against the Unlawefull Insurrection of the Protestants" (London, 1565), sig Ev.51/Frarin, sig Eiiv.

48 Norfolk to Elizabeth (9 October 1567), in Donaldson, *First Trial*, pp. 106–141. See also J. Hosack, *Mary Queen of Scots and her Accusers* (Edinburgh, 1870–1874).

49 *Baptistes* (1577), Buchanan's religious drama about John the Baptist (whom he treated as a type of Thomas More) was aptly translated from Latin into English in 1642 as "Tyrannical Government Anatomised." Buchanan dedicated it to Mary's son, James.

His *Medea*, written much earlier, rehearsed an imagery of conspicuously feminine tyranny that would resurface in his famous *Detection*.

50 *The Book of Articles, or Comprehensive Indictment of Mary*, reproduced in Donaldson, *First Trial*, pp. 142–143. Presented to the English commission at Westminster by Mary's ambitious half-brother James, Earl of Moray (who stood to gain control of Scotland in Mary's absence and her son James's infancy), *The Book of Articles* included a short "Narrative" by the Earl of Lennox, but most of it was written by Buchanan, at Moray's behest.

51 Buchanan's *Detection* has a complex publication history, which is set forth in *George Buchanan: Quatercentenary Studies* 1906 (Glasgow, 1907), 439–445, and in R.H. Mahon, *The Indictment of Mary Queen of Scots* (Cambridge, 1923). The *Detection* was first published in Latin in 1571 with three of the casket letters; Thomas Wilson, one of Elizabeth's diplomats, translated them into Scots and included the rest of the letters and a translation of his own even more inflammatory *Action against Mary* (originally *Actio contra Mariam*). Another edition, also Scots, appeared the same year (1571). See Phillips, pp. 62–63.

52 "The Writings and the Letters found in the said Casket," in *A Detection of the Actions of Mary Queen of Scots* ([1571] London, 1721), p. 119. Future references, both to the letters and to the *Detection* are to this edition and will appear in the text.

53 Peter Hume Brown, *George Buchanan: Humanist and Reformer* (Edinburgh, 1890), p. 197. Phillips treats Buchanan as an aspiring, even ambitious, poet eager to break into the uppermost echelons of Elizabethan literary culture in "George Buchanan and the Sidney Circle." In *Huntington Library Quarterly* XII (1948), pp. 23–55.

54 Leslie, *Defence*, p. 4.

55 Jordan offers a provocative *précis* of the way in which Leslie's rejection of "written law" equals rejection of ahistorical directives in *Renaissance Feminism: Literary Texts and Political Models* (Ithaca, 1990), p. 244.

56 Leslie, *Defence*, p. 6.

57 Leslie, *A Discourse Containing a Perfect Account given to the Most Virtuous and Excellent Princess, Marie Queen of Scots, and Her Nobility*, (1571). In James Anderson, *Collections Relating to the History of Mary Queen of Scotland*. 4 vols (Edinburgh, 1727), III: 4.

58 Leslie, *Historie of Scotland*, trans. James Dalrymple. 2 vols ([1696] Edinburgh, 1888–1895), I: 2.

2   "The treason of pity": England, 1568–1603

1 Norfolk was tried and beheaded in 1572 for his apparent role in the Ridolfi conspiracy against Elizabeth in 1571.

2 Lacey Baldwin Smith, *Treason in Tudor England: Politics and Paranoia* (London, 1969).

3 George Whetstone, *The Censure of a Loyal Subject {. . .} upon Notable Traitors* ([1587] Amsterdam, 1973), p. G2v.

4 *Cal. State Papers, Scot.*, VIII: 104.

5 One nineteenth-century editor of Mary's letters, Agnes Strickland, dwelt at length on their physical properties – "obliterated words and confused sentences," and an "orthography" that requires "a particular study to copy it, much more to understand it" (*Letters*, I: xix). Compare G.B. Harrison's dismissal of Mary's "downhill schoolgirl hand" in *The Letters of Queen Elizabeth* (London, 1935), p. xiv.

6 *Cal. State Papers, Scot.*, IV: 70.

7 The verse goes, aptly enough, "Much suspected by me,/But nothing proved can be." *Cal. State Papers, Dom.*, VI: 76.

8 Babington to Mary, July 1586. Reproduced in Steuart, *Trial*, p. 29.

9 William Kempe, "A Dutifull Invective against the Most Haynous Treasons of Ballard and Babington . . . Together with the Horrible Attempts and Actions of the Queen of Scots" (1587). In *Fugitive Tracts Written in Verse*, nd, np.

10 Whetstone, *Censure*, p. G2v.

11 *Cal. State Papers, Scot.*, VI: 413.

12 William Cobbett, *Parliamentary History of England* (London, 1803), p. 1181.

13 In Steuart, *Trial*, pp. 15–16.

14 *Cal. State Papers, Scot.*, IV: 391.

15 John Pikeryng, *Horestes*, in *Three Tudor Classical Interludes*, ed. Marie Axton (Cambridge, 1982), p. 95. Future references will be indicated by line number and incorporated into the text.

16 Robert Semphill, "Ane Ballat declaring the Nobill and Gude inclinatioun of our King," in *Ballads*, p. 5. Semphill's ballads likened Mary to Clytemnestra, Delila and Medea, among others. They were so inflammatory that as late as 1801 the antiquarian and famous vegetarian Joseph Ritson vowed to ban these "false, scandalous and despicable libels" from his library rather than "suffer such an infamous and detestable piece of trash to pollute and infect my shelves." See *The Semphill Ballads* (Edinburgh, 1872), p. xxi.

17 Karen Robertson reads *Horestes* as a kind of prescient allegory of James VI's conflict between the male nobles who governed Scotland in Mary's absence and his filial relationship to her, one in which Horestes/James finally comes to see that "Execution of the mother [is] a necessary prerequisite of good government." Robertson, "The Body Natural," p. 32.

18 On the legality of the proceedings against Mary, see Steuart, *Trial*, pp. 91–113.

19 Job Throckmorton, in J.E. Neale, *Elizabeth I and Her Parliaments*. 2 vols (London, 1953), II: 110.

20 John Pikeryng, in Steuart, *Trial*, p. 46.

21 *Trial*, p. 54.

22 *Trial*, p. 48.

23 Elizabeth's "answer without an answer" is also known as her "answer answerless;" her speeches to Parliament following Mary's trial took two forms, since she revised them for publication after their delivery. See Neale, *Elizabeth I and Her Parliaments*, II: 122–144.

24 *Cal. State Papers, Scot.*, IX: 330–331. Phillips (*Images of a Queen*, p. 129) also quotes this epigram in his survey of pro-Marian responses to the execution.

25 For a general overview of Elizabeth's apparent belief that desire's economy is one of scarcity in later Tudor England, see Alison Plowden, *"Two Queens in One Isle": The Deadly Relationship of Elizabeth I and Mary Queen of Scots* (Sussex, 1984).

26 Verstegan's martyrologies are analyzed in A.G. Petti, "Richard Verstegan and Catholic Martyrologies of the Later Elizabethan Period." In *Recusant History* V (1959–1960), pp. 64–90.

27 Blackwood, *History*, p. 202.

28 "Necessity of the Sentence of Death" (1586). *Cal. State Papers, Scot.*, IX: 356.

29 The most detailed and persuasive of these readers is Gallagher, who identifies the many images of fracture and "surfeit" in Spenser's representation of Mary's trial to show that Spenser is really concerned to show the brutality with which "historical discourse" is fit into allegory (*Medusa's Gaze*, p. 233). Michael O'Connell likewise shows how Spenser's poem "fails" when the troublesome "specifics of the contemporary world" are mythologized. See O'Connell, *Mirror and Veil: The Historical Dimension of Spenser's* Faerie Queene (Chapel Hill, 1977), p. 129.

30 See especially O'Connell, pp. 129–140; and Kerby Neill, "*The Faerie Queene* and the Mary Stuart Controversy." In *ELH* 2 (1935), pp. 192–214.

31 Edmund Spenser, *The Faerie Queene*, ed. Thomas P. Roche ([1590, 1596] Harmondsworth, 1970), p. 33 (5.9.38). All future references will be to this edition and will appear in the text, with their Elizabethan spelling preserved.

32 Gallagher ingeniously holds that Duessa's silencing really only literalizes Mary's effectual silencing during her own trial (*Medusa's Gaze*, p. 26).

33 John Lyly, Prologue to *Endimion, or the Man in the Moon*, in *The Plays of John Lyly*, ed. Carter A. Daniel (London and Toronto, 1988), p. 149. Future references to *Endimion* will be to this edition and will appear in the text.

34 Berry, *Of Chastity and Power*, p. 167.

3 "A new and unexampled kind of tomb," 1603–1714

1 Giovanni Carlo Scaramelli to the Venetian Doge and Senate (22 May 1603). *Cal. State Papers, Venetian*, X: 33. Two years later, Scaramelli reported that James's daughter had been christened Mary, "after the king's mother" (X: 155).

2 Sir John Harington, *Nugae Antiquae* (1607), in *James I by His Contemporaries*, ed. Robert Ashton (London, 1969), p. 160.

3 The epitaph is reproduced in full in William Camden, *Annals, or the History of the Most Renowned and Victorious Princesse Elizabeth, Late Queene of England* (London, 1635), p. 385. This is the third edition of Camden's book, first published in Latin, in 1615, as *Annales rerum Anglicarum et hibernicarum regnane Elizabetha*.

4 John Gerard, *A Narrative of the Gunpowder Plot* (1604?), in *The Condition of the Catholics under James I*, ed. John Morris, s.j. (London, 1871), p. 21. The Catholic response to James's perceived neglect of Mary – and thus of them – was one of "great exasperation and exulceration of minds, mixed with grief and despairing, foreseeing that all would pass worse for Catholics under his reign than in Queen Elizabeth's time" (p. 78).

5 Henry Keepe, *Monumenta Westmonasteriensi; or, an Historical Account of the Original, Increase, and Present State of St. Peter's, or the Abby {sic} Church at Westminster* (London, 1682), p. 90. A Catholic sympathizer, Keepe added a poignant and succinct biography of Mary to his description of her monument, the longest of its kind in his extensive account of the Abbey. He saw her death as one that should have "purchase[d] relief for the oppressed Catholics" of England but did not (p. 35) and paints her as an exemplar of Roman piety, one who "shed [her] blood drop by drop" for the Church and one whose "life of forty-five years was one of unceasing sorrow and strife" (p. 34).

6 James I to Dean of Peterborough Cathedral, 28 September 1612. In *Letters of King James VI and I*, ed. G.P.V. Akrigg (Berkeley, 1984), p. 326.

7 10 October 1612. *Cal. State Papers Dom.*, IX: 90. Phillips (*Images*, p. 128) notes that the first drafts of Northampton's epitaph were so fervently devoted to Mary that they recall the martyrologies of the late sixteenth century.

8 To the extent that a royal's unburied body serves to perpetuate longing for it, the case of Mary Queen of Scots reprises that of the medieval king Richard II, whose corpse likewise resisted interment in interesting ways. Paul Strohm theorizes its consequently continuing availability to desire in "The Trouble with Richard: The Reburial of Richard II and Lancastrian Symbolic Strategy." In *Speculum* 71 (1996), pp. 89–111.

9 *Cal. State Papers, Venetian*, X: 9–10.

10 On Northampton's cultural importance as a leading connoisseur of the early seventeenth century, see Linda Levy Peck, "The Mentality of a Jacobean Grandee," in *The Mental World of the Jacobean Court*, ed. Peck (Cambridge, 1991), especially pp. 146–148.

11 William Drummond, *The History of Scotland, from the year 1423, until the Year 1542* (London, 1655), pp. 263–265.

12 See, for example, his political treatise of 1598, *Basilikon Doron*.

13 Robert Johnston, *The Historie of Scotland during the Minority of Kingdoms* (London, 1646), pp. 1, 9.

14 Akrigg, *Letters*, p. 78.

15 David Moysie, *Memoires of the Affairs of Scotland* (Edinburgh, 1655), p. 35.

16 Jonathan Goldberg, "Fatherly Authority: The Politics of Stuart Family Images," in *Rewriting the Renaissance*, ed. Ferguson, Quilligan and Vickers, p. 5.

17 Cited in W. McElvee, *The Wisest Fool in Christendom* (New York, 1958), p. 158.

18 James Harington, *Nugae Antiquae*, in Ashton, *Contemporaries*, p. 160.

19 Moysie, *Memoires*, p. 120. Once convinced, James supposedly "laid the death of his mother . . . deeply to heart" (p. 118).

20 Moysie, *Memoires*, p. 113. Typically, many clergy, especially the ministers of Edinburgh, "refused to pray but as they were moved by the spirit" (p. 115) and the spirit steadfastly refused to move them to pray for Mary.

21 Edward Peyton, *The Rise, Reign and Ruin of the House of Stuart* (London, 1652), pp. 3–13.

22 Bishop Wares, Funeral Sermon, in Ashton, *Contemporaries*, p. 19.

23 See Thomas Birch, *The Court and Times of James I*, 2 vols (London, 1849), I: 86; also *James I and Henry IV: An Essay in English Foreign Policy, 1693–1610* (Illinois, 1970), p. 10; and Peyton, *Rise, Reign and Ruin*, p. 22.

24 Peyton, *Rise, Reign and Ruin*, p. 15. Fascination with the Rizzio episode continued throughout the seventeenth century: certain "remarkable Passages" from Buchanan's *History of Scotland* were even compiled in 1699 to offer a new and especially salacious *Relation of the Death of David Rizzi*.

25 Anthony Weldon, *The Court and Character of King James* (1651), p. 164. The same speculation appears in Robert Vaughan, *Memorials of the Stuart Dynasty*, 2 vols (London, 1831), I: 177.

26 Sir Kenelm Digby, *A Late Discourse, . . . Touching the Cure of Wounds by the Powder of Sympathy* (London, 1660), p. 105. This notion was still in circulation in 1681, when the anonymous *Brief History of the Life of Mary Queen of Scots* notes that after the stabbing "Providence was pleas'd to prevent her *miscarriage*, yet the sight of so dismal a Tragedy could not but surprise herewith wonderfull Astonishment, insomuch that [. . .] King *James* retain'd an aversion to the sight of *naked weapons*, and attributed the same to the Impressions of this unparalleled violence" (p. 4). Isaac D'Israeli later rejected "the idle tale that James trembled at the mere view of a naked sword, which is quoted as an instance of the effects of sympathy over the infant in the womb from his mothers terror" as "probably not true, yet still serves the purpose of pusillanimous writers to show his excessive pusillanimity." *An Inquiry into the Literary and Political Character of James the First* (London, 1816), pp. 145–146.

27 Marie-Hélène Huet, *Monstrous Imagination* (Cambridge, Mass., 1993), p. 24.

28 Thomas Craig, *Right of Succession to the Kingdom of England* ([1603] London, 1703), pp. 293, 345.

29 Thomas Wenman, *The Legend of Mary Queen of Scots* (1601) in *The Legend of Mary Queen of Scots and Other Ancient Poems*, ed. John Fry (London, 1810), pp. 6–7.

30 Arthur Penrhyn Stanley, *Historical Memorials of Westminster Abbey*, 3 vols (New York, 1887), III: 260.

31 Camden *Annals*, p. 385.

32 This point of view is nimbly expounded in Richard Ollard, *The Image of the King: Charles I and Charles II* (London, 1979), p. 26.

33 Gilbert Burnet, *History of My Own Times* ([1705] London, 1883), p. 1.

34 Henry Keepe, *Genealogies of the High-born Prince and Princess, George and Anne of Denmark* (London, 1684), p. 87 and "Preface," n.p.

35 Murray Pittock, *The Invention of Scotland: The Stuart Myth and Scottish Identity, 1638 to the Present* (London, 1991), p. 7. Curiously, Pittock's study of the "fatal attraction" (p. 7) the Stuarts held, and their unique belief in their own myth barely mentions Mary, though if the Stuarts are indeed, as he holds, *the* "underground" myth in the emerging fiction of Britain, then Mary is the underground of the underground. See also Paul Kleber Monod, *Jacobitism and the English People, 1688–1788* (Cambridge, 1989).

36 Quoted in Eva Scott, *The King in Exile* (London, 1908), p. 162. Later, Jacobite ballads like "Speed Bonny Boat" sustained the same motif.

37 *Mercurius Politicus* (13 June 1650), p. 19.

38 Gilbert Burnet, *An Essay on the Memory of the Late Queen* (London, 1695), pp. 30–31, 60.

39 On Anne's efforts to pattern herself after Elizabeth, see Carol Barash, *English Women's Poetry, 1649–1714: Politics, Community and Linguistic Authority* (Oxford, 1996).

40 Susan Staves encapsulates Britain's shift from "religious and feudal myths" to "secular and democratic myths of authority" in *Players' Scepters: Fiction and Authority in the Restoration* (Lincoln, Neb., 1979), p. xiv.

41 Anon., *The Loyal Mourner for the Best of Princes* (London, 1716), p. 10.

42 Robert Chambers, *The Scottish Songs* (Edinburgh, 1829), pp. 562–563.

43 Charles Edward to James Francis Stuart, 18 June 1747, in *The Stuart Papers at Windsor*, ed. Alistair and Henriette Tayler (New York, 1939), p. 209.

44 Andrew Erskine to James Boswell in *Correspondence of James Boswell and John Johnston of Grange*, ed. Ralph S. Walker, 2 vols (London, 1960), I: 232; *Boswell to Johnston*, I: 41.

45 Francis Osborn, *Historical Memoires of the Reigns of Queen Elisabetha and King James* (London, 1673), p. 419.

46 See especially Nicolas Abraham, "Notes on the Phantom: A Complement to Freud's Metapsychology," in Nicolas Abraham and Maria Torok, *The Shell and the Kernel: Renewals of Psychoanalysis*, ed. and trans. Nicholas T. Rand (Chicago, 1994), pp. 171–176.

47 William Udall, "Preface", *Historie of the Life and Death of Mary Stuart, Queen of Scotland* (London, 1636), sig. A4v. Originally printed under the pseudonym John Stranguage, Udall's *Historie* is a condensation and creative transcription of the parts of Camden's *Annals* that deal with Mary.

48 "To the Reader," prefacing Buchanan, *Detection* (London, 1651), p. 122.

49 Hayden White, *The Content of the Form: Narrative Discourse and Historical Representation* (Baltimore, 1987), pp. 1–25.

50 Udall, *Historie*, sig. A2v; Sanderson, *A Compleat History of the Lives and Reigns of Mary Queen of Scotland and Her Son and Successor James the Sixth* (Edinburgh, 1656), p. 2.

51 John Stow, *The Annales or General Chronicle of England* (1631), np.

52 Camden, *Annals*, sig. A4v.

53 Sanderson, *Compleat History*, sig. A7v.

54 D.W. Woolf's probing discussion of Stuart historiography compares it to a biography of the state's body. See Woolf, *The Idea of History in Early Stuart England: Erudition, Ideology and "The Light of Truth," from the Accession of James I to the Civil Wars* (Toronto, 1990), p. 11.

55 Udall, *Historie*, p. 267.

56 John Evelyn, quoted in Strickland, preface to *Letters*, I: xx.

57 Camden, *Annals*, p. 661.

58 Details of Camden's negotiation with James may be found in Woolf, *Idea*, pp. 118–121; and in Phillips, *Images*, pp. 228–231. On the "contradiction in the informations" Camden gives in *Annals*, see his nineteenth-century editor, Richard Gough, "The Life of Mr. Camden," in Camden, *Britannia*, trans. Gough (London, 1806), I: xvi.

59 Udall, *Historie*, sig. A5r.

60 Thomas Morgan, *Allegations on Behalf of the High Princess, the Lady Mary, Now Queen of Scotland* (London, 1690), sig. A2r. Earlier in the century, John Gerard's *A Narrative of the Gunpowder Plot* had used Mary's allegedly unwitting involvement in the Babington Plot to "elucidate" the Gunpowder Plot.

61 Anon., Preface, *Brief History*, p.1.

62 "Did not some People remain too obstinate to adore that tribe, which is now scatter'd and ruin'd, there had not been liberty, or safety to put abroad such a Discovery as this; neither had there been any occasion to bring it to life again." "To the Reader," in *Detection* (1651), p. 1.

63 See the Beinecke Library's copy of *A Brief History of the Life of Mary Queen of Scots*.

64 On historiography as arbitration among different species of evidence, see White, *Content*; Woolf, *Idea*; and Leo Braudy, *Narrative Form in History and Fiction* (Princeton, 1970).

65 Sanderson, *Compleat History*, p. 47.

66 Johnston, *Historie*, sig. A5v.
67 Marie Madeleine de la Vergue de Lafayette, *The Princess of Cleve. The Most Famed Romance*, trans. "A Person of Quality" (London, 1688), p. 3.
68 Edmund Bohun, *The Character of Queen Elizabeth, or a Full and Clear Account of the Policies and the Methods of their government Both in Church and State* (London, 1693), p. 114.
69 Anon., *Brief History*, p. 18.
70 Sanderson, *Compleat History*, p. 121.
71 John Speed, *Great Britaine* (London, 1611), p. 857; Sanderson, *Compleat History*, p. 135; Camden, *Annals*, p. 160.
72 Sanderson, *Compleat History*, p. 125.
73 Udall, *Historie*, sig. A6v.
74 Sanderson, *Compleat History*, p. 3.

4 "False kindred": *The Island Queens* and *The Albion Queens*

1 John Banks, *The Island Queens* (London, 1684), p. 70. Future references to *The Island Queens* will be to this edition and will appear in the text.
2 Gerard Langbaine, *An Account of the English Dramatick Poets* (London, 1691), p. 8; David Erskine Baker, *Biographia Dramatica, or A Companion to the Playhouse*, 2 vols (London, 1812), II: 336. A recent commentator, James Sutherland, attribute's the play's suppression to anxieties about Catholic succession with Charles II's heir apparent, James II. See Sutherland, *English Literature of the Late Seventeenth Century* (Oxford, 1969), p. 77.
3 The virulence of anti-Catholic sentiment of the day is reflected in the popularity of Nathaniel Lee's dramas of 1679–1680, and in the Pope Joan plays of the same period.
4 Antoine de Montchréstien, *Tragedie de la reine d'Escosse* (1601), ed. C.N. Smith (London, 1972), p.105. Future references will appear in the text.
5 Colley Cibber, *An Apology for the Life of Mr. Colley Cibber* (London, 1740), p. 285.
6 Allardyce Nicholl, *Introduction to Dramatic Theory* (London, 1923), p. 109.
7 Eric Rothstein, *Restoration Tragedy: Form and the Process of Change* (Madison, 1967), pp. 96, 98. On Banks and the she tragedy see also David Wykes, "The Barbinade and the She-Tragedy: On Banks's *The Unfortunate Favourite*." In *Augustan Studies*, ed. Douglas Lane Patey and Timothy Keegan (Newark, Del., 1985), pp. 79–94.
8 Langbaine, *Account*, p. 7.
9 *Daily Courant* (22 February 1704). In *A Register of English Theatrical Documents*, ed. Judith Milhaus and Robert D. Hume, 3 vols (Carbondale, Ill., 1978), I: 328–329.
10 Langbaine, *Account*, p. 7.
11 Cibber, *Apology*, p. 285.
12 Cibber, *Apology*, p. 286.
13 "Biographical Notice" to *The Albion Queens*. In *Bell's British Theatre* (London, 1791), III: vi.
14 Baker, *Biographia Dramatica*, II: 336.
15 Baker, *Biographia Dramatica*, II: 336.
16 Banks, *The Albion Queens* ([1704] London, 1735), p. 8. Future references will be to this edition and will appear in the text.
17 Richard Bevis, "The World Well Lost." In *English Drama: Restoration and the Eighteenth Century* (London and New York, 1988), p. 69.
18 Sanderson, *Compleat History*, sig. A3v.
19 Lockhart to Carnmath, in David Daiches, *Scotland and the Union* (London 1977), p. 91.
20 Those Scots who opposed an "incorporating Union" feared a loss of the "Power to Manage their own Affairs by themselves," and ultimately a monstrous disproportion of resources and power that would leave them to starve while England, "like the head of a ricketty child, [. . .] by drawing to itself the nourishment that should be distributed in due proportion to the rest of the languishing body becomes so over-charged that

frenzy and death unavoidably ensue." Positive arguments for the union, on the other hand, saw it as "an Act that preserves us from Anarchy." See Daiches, *Scotland*, p. 89.

21 Sigmund Freud, *The Psychopathology of Everyday Life*, in *Basic Writings of Sigmund Freud*, trans. A.A. Brill (New York, 1938), p.104.

Georgian Mary

1 *The Gentleman's Magazine*, LIX (November 1789), p. 1100.

5 "The sorrow of seeing the queen,": 1714–1789

1 *The London Stage, 1660–1800*, ed. Arthur A. Scouten (Carbondale, Il., 1961); Sybil Rosenfeld, *Strolling Players and Drama in the Provinces* (Cambridge, 1939).

2 David Hume, *The History of England from the Invasion of Julius Caesar to the Revolution of 1688*, ed. William B. Todd, 6 vols ([1778] Indianapolis, 1983), IV: 132. All references to Hume's *History* are to this edition, which reproduces the 1788 edition, the first to contain all of Hume's corrections to the *History* (1754–1762).

3 *The Gentleman's Magazine* of 1787 (pp. 1178–1179) and 1790 (p. 450) printed summaries of the debates over the poems, and samples thereof.

4 *The Gentleman's Magazine* was an especially assiduous purveyor of Mariana. See, for instance, March 1779 (pp. 36–37); and April 1790 on the whereabouts of Mary's prayer book and a picture bearing "fatal vestiges of injured sovereignty" (p. 316); also November 1789 (pp. 1078–1079); as well as *The Projector* (July 1807), p. 12.

5 *Critical Review* IX (June 1760), p. 421.

6 James Boswell, *A Journal of a Tour to the Hebrides with Samuel Johnson, Ll.D.*, ed. Frederick A. Pottle and Charles A. Bennett ([1785] New York, 1961), pp. 23–24.

7 Linda Colley paints a most thorough and engaging picture of this transition in *Britons: Forging the Nation, 1707–1837* (New Haven, 1991).

8 Several studies of the eighteenth-century culture of sensibility survey these phenomena, among them G.J. Barker Benfield, *The Culture of Sensibility: Sex and Society in Eighteenth-Century Britain* (Chicago, 1992); and John Mullan, *Sentiment and Sociability: The Language of Feeling in the Eighteenth Century* (Oxford, 1988).

9 John Locke, *An Essay Concerning Human Understanding*, ed. Peter Nidditch ([1690] New York, 1975), II: xx.

10 *Memoirs of the Imprisonment and Death of Mary, Queen of Scots*, in *A Select Collection of Novels and Histories*, ed. Samuel Croxall, 6 vols (London, 1727), VI: 374.

11 Walter Goodall, *Examination of the Letters Said to be Written by Mary, Queen of Scots* (Edinburgh, 1754), p. xxviii.

12 Dugald Stewart, *Account of the Life and Writings of Dr. Robertson* ([1801] London, 1802), p. 39.

13 Jane Austen, *The History of England from the Reign of Henry the 4th to the Death of Charles the 1st*, ed. R.W. Chapman (Oxford, 1954), p. 14.

14 Goodall, *Examination*, p. 44.

15 My own essay, "'Mary Stuart's Fatal Box:' Sentimental History and the Revival of the Casket Letters Controversy," explores the details and implications of eighteenth-century Britain's fascination with the casket letters. In *The Age of Johnson* 7, ed. Paul J. Korshin (New York, 1996), pp. 427–473.

16 William Tytler, *An Inquiry Historical and Critical into the Evidence against Mary Queen of Scots*, 2 vols ([1759] London, 1790), I: 131–132.

17 Charles Ryskamp and Frederick A. Pottle, eds, *Boswell: The Ominous Years, 1774–6* (New York, 1963), p. 166.

18 Christine Gerrard explores many of these monuments in *The Patriot Opposition to Walpole* (Oxford, 1995), p. 102.

19 *The Gentleman's Magazine*, LVIII (1788), pp. 312–313.

20 James Boswell, *Correspondence of John Boswell and John Johnston of Grange*, ed. Ralph S. Walker, 2 vols (London, 1960), I: 49.
21 Thomas Gray to Dr. Wharton (4 December 1762). In *Letters of Thomas Gray*, ed. Duncan C. Tovey, 2 vols (London, 1904), II: 267–268.
22 Jodocus Crull, *The Antiquities of St. Peter's or the Abbey Church of Westminster* (London, 1711), n.p.
23 John Dart, "Westminster Abbey. A Poem." In *Westmonasterium, or The History and Antiquities of the Abbey Church of St. Peter's Westminster*, 2 vols (London, 1742), I: xx.
24 John Nichols, *History and Antiquities of the Town, College and Castle of Fotheringay* (1787), in *Bibliotheca Topographica Britanica* (London, 1790), IV: v.
25 William Robertson, *The History of Scotland During the Reigns of Queen Mary and King James VI* ([1759] New York, 1859), p. 176.
26 See also Duncan MacMillan, "Woman as Hero: Gavin Hamilton's Radical Alternative." In *Femininity and Masculinity in Eighteenth-Century Art and Culture*, ed. Gill Perry and Michael Rossington (Manchester, 1994), pp. 78–98.
27 Boswell, journal entry, 29 January 1766. In *Boswell on the Grand Tour*, ed. Pottle and Brady (New York, 1955), p. 275.
28 Boswell, *Correspondence*, ed. Walker, I: 41. The prominent Jacobite Andrew Erskine also praised Johnston for the expansive mind that "revolv'd the various misfortunes of the beautiful and unhappy Mary" (7 August, 1767), I: 231.
29 Andrew Erskine to Boswell, *Correspondence*, ed. Walker, I: 248.
30 Boswell, *Correspondence*, ed. Walker, I: 15.
31 Robertson, *History of Scotland*, pp. 176–177.
32 Hamilton generally tended to see art as a way to align himself with certain male patrons and beholders. For instance, of his famous *Achilles Lamenting the Death of Patroclus*, he assured his patron James Grant that "when I painted Patroclus I thought as much of pleasing you as greaving Achilles." In David G. Irwin, *Scottish Painters at Home and Abroad, 1700–1900* (London, 1975), p. 101.
33 These transactions are recorded in Cust, *Authentic Portraits*, pp. 133–136.
34 Charles N. Fifer, ed., *Correspondence of James Boswell, with Certain Members of the Club* (London, 1976), p. 63.
35 *Correspondence*, ed. Fifer, p. 64.
36 *Correspondence*, ed. Fifer, p. 56.
37 Boswell, journal entry (18 March 1776). In *Boswell*, ed. Ryskamp and Pottle, pp. 272–273.
38 A rich account of Hamilton's legacy may be found in Smailes and Thomson, *Queen's Image*, pp. 75–76.
39 Samuel Johnson, "Account of a Book, entitled, An Historical and Critical Enquiry into the Evidence [. . .] against *Mary* Queen of *Scots*" appeared in *The Gentleman's Magazine* in October, 1760.
40 Boswell to Johnson (30 August 1774). In *Letters of James Boswell*, ed. C.B. Tinker, 2 vols (Oxford, 1924), I: 204.
41 Pottle and Brady ed., *Tour*, pp. 23–24.
42 Samuel Johnson to Hester Thrale, 8 July 1784, in *Letters of Samuel Johnson*, ed. R.W. Chapman, 3 vols (Oxford, 1952), III: 971. Thrale had herself copied one of Mary's poems into her private journal. See *Thraliana*, ed. Katharine C. Alderson (Oxford, 1942), pp. 412–413 (1 December 1779).
43 *The Gentleman's Magazine* (May 1791), p. 467.
44 Adam Smith, *Lectures on Rhetoric and Belles Lettres*, ed. J.C. Bryce ([1771] Oxford, 1983), p. 90.
45 *Life of Mary Stuart*, in Anon., *History of the Life and Reign of that Excellent Princess Queen Elizabeth* (London, 1739), p. 315.
46 For this anecdote, see Robert Chambers, *Biographical Dictionary of Eminent Scotsmen*, 4 vols (Edinburgh, 1835), II: 453.

47 Hume, *History*, IV: 251.
48 Hume to the Comtesse de Boufflers (15 May 1761). In *Private Correspondence of David Hume with Several Distinguished Persons* (London, 1820), p. 3.
49 Robertson, *History of Scotland*, p. 9.
50 Stewart, *Account*, pp. 39–40.
51 Robertson, *History of Scotland*, p. 273.
52 Austen, *History of England*, p. 142.

6 "Dozens of ugly Mary Queen of Scotts": The women of Britain, 1725–1785

1 Austen, *History of England*, p. 141.
2 James Peller Malcolm, *Anecdotes of the Manners and Customs of London during the Eighteenth Century* (London, 1810), p. 204.
3 Horace Walpole. In *Letters of Horace Walpole*, ed. Lord Dove. 3 vols (London, 1833), I: 82.
4 Mary Leapor, "The Consolation." In *Poems upon Several Occasions*, 2 vols (London, 1748–1751), I: 41.
5 For the conclusion that the portrait is of Woffington see R.B. Beckett (1949), p. 198; but the Yale Center for British art holds that it is of Cholmondeley.
6 Preface to Mary Roberts, *The Royal Exile; or, Poetical Epistles of Mary Queen of Scots*, 2 vols (London, 1822), I: vii.
7 "Advertisement." In Margaretta Wedderburn, *Mary Queen of Scots. An Historical Poem, with Other Miscellaneous Pieces* (Edinburgh, 1811).
8 Leapor, "Consolation," I: 41.
9 Eighteenth-century constructions of femininity are delineated with notable verve in Nancy Armstrong, *Desire and Domestic Fiction: A Political History of the Novel* (New York, 1987) and Catherine Gallagher, *Nobody's Story: The Vanishing Acts of Women in the Marketplace, 1670–1820* (Berkeley, 1994).
10 Richardson's Lovelace writes that "neither the Queen of Carthage, nor the Queen of Scots, would have thought they had any reason to complain of cruelty, had they been used no worse than I have used the queen of my heart." In *Samuel Richardson, Clarissa or The History of a Young Lady*, ed. Angus Ross (Harmondsworth, 1985), p. 1143.
11 John Whitaker, *Mary Queen of Scots, Vindicated*, 3 vols ([1787] Edinburgh, 1788), II: 116.
12 Robertson, *History of Scotland*, p. 272.
13 George Ballard, *Memoirs of Several Ladies of Great Britain*, ed. Ruth Perry ([1752] Detroit, 1985), pp. 171, 169.
14 Hume, *History*, IV: 251.
15 Gallagher traces the female biography of "Nobody" in *Nobody's Story*.
16 George Frisbie Whicher, *The Life and Romances of Mrs. Eliza Haywood* (New York, 1915), p. 87.
17 Eliza Haywood, *Mary Stuart, Queen of Scots. Being the Secret History of Her Life and the Real Causes of All Her Misfortunes* (London, 1725), p. iii. Future references will be to this edition and will appear in the text.
18 On the seductive mechanisms built into these early schools of women's writing, see Ros Ballaster, *Seductive Forms: Women's Amatory Fiction from 1684 to 1740* (Oxford, 1992).
19 In his classic essay of that name, Walter Benjamin sets forth "the task of the translation" as that of becoming, in essence, foreign to his or her own language. See Benjamin, "The Task of the Translator." In Benjamin, *Illuminations*, trans. Harry Zohn (New York, 1969), pp. 69–82.
20 Sophia Lee, *The Recess; Or, A Tale of Other Times*, 3 vols ([1783–5] 2nd edn, London, 1786), II: 181. Because Lee made some changes between the first and second editions of *The Recess*, I am using the second. The first edition is available in an Arno Press reprint (New York, 1972), ed. Devendra P. Varma.

21 Jane Spencer, *The Rise of the Woman Novelist from Aphra Behn to Jane Austen* (Oxford, 1986), pp. 195–201. Margaret Anne Doody's consideration of the novel uses it to recover the place of female subjectivity in gothic and historical fiction in "Deserts, Ruins and Troubled Waters: Female Dreams in Fiction and the Development of the Gothic Novel." In *Genre* 10 (1977), pp. 144–188.

22 April Alliston, "The Value of a Literary Legacy: Retracing the Transmission of Value thorough Female Lines." In *Yale Journal of Criticism* 4 (1990), pp. 109–127. See also Alliston, *Virtue's Faults: Correspondences in Eighteenth-Century British and French Women's Fiction* (Stanford, 1996).

23 *Monthly Review* LXXV (1788) p. 134. Two years earlier the same magazine had complained that *"The Tale of other Times* is a romantic title." But "the Preface [. . .] soon broke the *charm* of the title and we were brought back to our sober senses by an assurance, that the ground we had before us was real and not imaginary; it was founded on fact, and not on fiction; and that what we took for romance was only a history." See *Monthly Review* LXVIII (January 1786), p. 455.

24 *The Gentleman's Magazine* LVI (1795), p. 327.

25 David Hume, *An Enquiry concerning Human Understanding*, in *Essays and Treatises on Several Subjects* (London, 1755), p. 294. On the chain as a favored figure in eighteenth-century historiography see Braudy, *Narrative Form*, p. 33.

7 Guilt and vindication, 1789–1837

 1 Caroline's trial is rendered in detail in Flora Fraser, *The Unruly Queen: The Life of Queen Caroline* (London, 1996), pp. 413–414.

 2 On the details of Caroline's costume, see Fraser, *Unruly Queen*, p. 419; and, in conjunction with eyewitness report, Lloyd Stryker, "The Trial of Queen Caroline," in *For the Defense: Thomas Erskine, the Most Enlightened Liberal of His Times, 1750–1823* (Garden City, NY, 1947).

 3 Political and cultural theories of Caroline's trial are set forth in Colley, *Britons* (pp. 265–268), and in Thomas W. Laqueur, "The Queen Caroline Affair: Politics as Art in the Reign of George IV." In *Journal of Modern History* 54 (1982), pp. 419–467.

 4 *The Gentleman's Magazine* (April 1831), p. 351.

 5 "In the moment of Poetic composition, the Box shall be my inspiring Genius. [. . .] When I would interest my fancy in the distresses incident to Humanity, I shall remember the unfortunate MARY," Burns wrote to Lady Winifred Maxwell Constable on 25 April 1791. In *Complete Letters of Robert Burns*, ed. J.A. Mackay (Ayrshire, 1987), p. 547. Burns also sent his poem "Queen Mary's Lament" to his friend Frances Anna Dunlop and her daughters, because "you know & with me, pity the amiable but unfortunate Mary Queen of Scots" (*Letters*, p. 187).

 6 *The Gentleman's Magazine* (May 1844), p. 525.

 7 Hugh Campbell, *Love Letters of Mary Queen of Scots to James Earl of Bothwell* (London, 1824), p. 6.

 8 Campbell, *Love Letters*, p. 8.

 9 On the emergent ideology of the domestic woman, see Mary Poovey, *The Proper Lady and the Woman Writer* (Chicago, 1984).

10 Anna Jameson, *Memoirs of Celebrated Female Sovereigns* (London, 1832), p. viii.

11 Jameson, *Female Sovereigns*, p. ix.

12 Mary Wollstonecraft, *A Vindication of the Rights of Woman* ([1792] New York, 1988), p. 55.

13 Gary Kelly also mentions this resemblance in *Revolutionary Feminism: The Mind and Career of Mary Wollstonecraft* (New York, 1922), p. 209.

14 These romantic manifestations of Mary's myth are discussed in Smailes and Thomson, *Queen's Image*, (Edinburgh, 1987) pp. 78–82.

15 To be fair, Campbell was not much less salacious on the topic of Elizabeth I: the

subtitle of his 1825 *Case of Mary Queen of Scots and Queen Elizabeth* promised to "embrac[e] the amorous life of the virgin queen."

16 Jameson, *Female Sovereigns*, p. 147.

17 Walter Scott, *The Journal of Sir Walter Scott*, ed. W.E.K. Anderson (Oxford, 1977), p. 3.

18 H.J.C. Grierson, ed., *Letters of Sir Walter Scott* (New York, 1932), X: 493.

19 Walter Scott, *The Abbot*, 2 vols (London, 1820), II: 180–181. Future references will be to this edition, and will appear in the text.

20 Friedrich Schiller, *Maria Stuart*, in *Maria Stuart and The Maid of Orleans: Two Historical Plays*, trans. Charles E. Passage (New York, 1961), p. 83.

21 English playwrights had recently experimented with ways to externalize Mary's inner life. John St. John's gothic tragedy of 1789, for example, kept its heroine locked away in a "mansion of despair" expressly contrived to render the queen's inner world visible, its "lawful gloom," in her own words, [. . .] congenial to my soul." St. John's play gave Mary's state of mind, even her dreams, the sort of name and habitation of interest to modern audiences frightened by conflagrations of desire such as the French had recently ignited, but morally and psychologically, Schiller's anatomy of one queen's guilty desire was far more nuanced than his. See John St. John, *Mary Queen of Scots* [1789], in *The Modern Theatre*, ed. Elizabeth Inchbald (London, 1811), p. 91.

22 "Preface," *Mary Stuart. A Tragedy*, trans. James Grahame (London, 1801), p. iv.

23 William Ireland, *Effusions of Love from Chatelar to Mary, Queen of Scotland* (London, 1805), p. i.

24 Roberts, *The Royal Exile*, II: 7.

25 Susan Ferrier, *Marriage* ([1818] Oxford, 1987), p. 207.

26 Helen Maria Williams, *Letters from France*, 2 vols ([1796] Oxford, 1989), I: 65–66.

27 Ann Radcliffe, *A Journey through Holland, &c* (London, 1795), p. 373.

28 Wedderburn, *Mary Queen of Scots*, p. 36.

29 Elizabeth Benger, *Memoirs of the Life of Mary Queen of Scots*, 2 vols (London, 1823), II: 131.

30 Mary Hays, *Female Biography: Memoirs of Illustrious and Celebrated Women of All Ages and Countries* (London, 1803), p. iii.

31 Mary Hays, "Preface." In *Memoirs of Queens* (London, 1821), p. v.

32 One testament to *The Abbot*'s enormous cultural power was the fact that, between 1820 and 1886, it was brought to the stage in 160 different productions. See *Scott Dramatized*, ed. H. Philip Bolton (London, 1992), pp. 375–393.

33 Judith Wilt's provocative, if brief, discussion of *The Abbot* casts the conflict underlying it in linguistic terms, with "the careful textual language of private religious judgment" pitted against "the performative significations of communal myth." See Wilt, *Secret Leaves: The Novels of Walter Scott* (Chicago, 1985), p. 84.

34 Quoted in Smailes and Thomson, *Queen's Image*, p. 65.

35 Wilt, *Secret Leaves*, p. 81. As Avrom Fleishman notes, it is its resistance to the "graph" ("writing") in "historiography" that distinguishes historical fiction generally, but this is doubly true of Scott. See Fleishman, *The English Historical Novel* (Baltimore, 1971).

36 *Mary Queen of Scots, Being Readings from the Abbot* (London, 1838), p. 5.

Victorian Mary

1 *The Girlhood of Queen Victoria. A Selection from her Majesty's Diaries Between the Years 1832 and 1840*, ed. Viscount Esher, 2 vols (London, 1912), I: 219.

2 Ira Nadel even suggests that Victoria "held an almost medieval view of her powers as a sovereign, believing that her royal authority was divinely authorized" – a point of view last held among female sovereigns by Mary Stuart. See Nadel, "Portraits of the Queen." In *Victorian Poetry* 25 (1987), p. 173.

3 In 1879, for instance, Victoria "passed near Loch Leven, with the ruined castle in which poor Queen Mary was confined (which we passed in 1842)." The year before, she viewed not only Inchmahone ("Queen Mary lived there once") but also "the "old Castle of Dunbar [. . .] to which Queen Mary was carried as a prisoner by Bothwell after the murder of Darnley," there to see a ""gipsy queen"" surrounded by "several women, very dark and rather handsome and well dressed" – spectral refractions of the Queen of Scots herself? See David Duff, *Victoria in the Highlands* (London, 1968), pp. 244, 345, 338.

4 "Queen Mary," in *Blackwood's* (November 1852), p. 616.

5 R. Storry Deans, *The Trials of Five Queens* (London, 1909), p. vi.

6 On the intimate relationship between Victoria's lack of influence over politics *strictu sensu* and her image as an exaltation of the middle-class wife, see Margaret Homans, ""To the Queen's Private Apartments': Royal Family Portraiture and the Construction of Victoria's Sovereign Obedience." In *Victorian Studies*, 37, no. 1 (Autumn 1993), pp. 1–45. It should also be noted that it took time for the Victorians to conceive of themselves as Victorians, and time as well for Victoria to flower into the very image of a united empire with Great Britain at the helm. See David Cannadine, "The Context, Performance and Meaning of Ritual: The British Monarchy and the 'Invention of Tradition,'" in *The Invention of Tradition*, ed. Eric Hobsbawm and Terence Ranger (Cambridge, 1983), pp. 117–140.

7 See especially Adrienne Auslander Munich's lively account of Victorian ambivalence about Victoria in "Queen Victoria, Empire and Excess." In *Tulsa Studies in Women's Literature* 6 (1987), pp. 265–280; and Munich, *Queen Victoria's Secrets* (New York, 1996).

8 Agnes Strickland, *Queen Victoria, from Birth to Bridal*, 2 vols (London, 1840), II: 252. For a more recent account of the assassination attempt, the first of five, see Cecil Woodham-Smith, *Queen Victoria: Her Life and Times*, 2 vols (London, 1972), I: 212–213.

9 Strickland, *Birth to Bridal*, p. 263.

10 In *History for Our Masters* (Somerset, 1970), Valerie Chancellor notes that despite incidental textbook potshots at Mary, exemplified in the *Pitman Reader's* determination that her execution was "one of the great blessings of English history," Victorians were actually more likely to disapprove of the unmarried Elizabeth, on whom the death of Mary was, according to one textbook editorialist, a "foul stain" (p. 77).

11 On the Victorian "cult of Scottishness" as manifest in newly erected statues of Scottish worthies and tartan crazes, see Pittock, *The Invention of Scotland*. Scotland's militant political resurgence toward the end of the nineteenth century is ably analyzed in G.F.A. Best, "Mid-Century Scottish Nationalism: Romantic and Radical," in *Ideas and Institutions of Victorian Britain*, ed. Robert Robson (London, 1967), pp. 143–179.

8 Victoria's other woman

1 On the coronation, following the demise of the king popularly known as "Silly Billy," see Munich, *Secrets*, p. 21.

2 *An Account of the Last Sufferings and Death of the Royal Martyr Caroline of Brunswick, the Injured Queen of England* (Newcastle-upon-Tyne, 1821), p. 3.

3 John Ruskin, "Of Queen's Gardens." In *Sesame and Lilies* ([1871] Chicago, 1900), p. 143.

4 James Anthony Froude, *The History of England*, 12 vols (London, 1862), XII: 360.

5 Roy Strong, *And When Did You Last See Your Father?* (London, 1978), p. 134.

6 Homans, "To the Queen's Private Chambers," p. 30.

7 "Queen Mary," in *Blackwood's* (November 1852), p. 615.

8 Ellen Johnston, "The Wrongs of Mary Queen of Scots." In *Autobiography, Poems and Songs of Ellen Johnston, the "Factory Girl"* (London, 1867), pp. 75–76.

9 Relayers of this myth ranged from Swinburne, discussed below, to the author of a review essay in *Fraser's Magazine* CLXV (September 1843), p. 259, to J.A. Froude, who advanced it in an 1882 issue of *Fraser's*.

10 W.D.S. Moncrieff, *Mary Queen of Scots. A Historical Drama in Three Acts* (Glasgow, 1872), p. 21.

11 Andrew Lang, *The Mystery of Mary Stuart* (London, 1901), p. vii.

12 *Blackwood's* LXXXVI (November 1859), p. 818.

13 *The Academy* (4 November 1905), p. 1146.

14 Deans, *Trials*, p. 194.

15 "The Lady of Riddles." In *The Academy* (14 September 1901), p. 206.

16 Sarah Kofman, *The Enigma of Woman: Woman in Freud's Writings*. Trans. Catherine Porter (Ithaca, NY, 1985), p. 53.

17 Victoria, evidently, rejected Strickland's efforts to render her in a complex way, declaring that it was "not true" that at her wedding she "was agitated and with difficulty restrained her feelings." When Strickland mentioned the "melancholy" she supposedly felt after the ceremony, Victoria corrected her: "Not melancholy – joy!" The book was soon suppressed; see Woodham, *Queen Victoria*, II: 203.

18 "Agnes Strickland," in *Dictionary of National Biography*, XIX: 50. It was, however, granted that "in her extracts from contemporary authorities [Strickland] amassed much valuable material, and her works contain pictures of the court, of society, and of domestic life not to be found elsewhere."

19 Agnes Strickland, *Lives of the Queens of Scotland and English Princesses*, 6 vols (New York, 1851), I: v.

20 Agnes Strickland, *The Life of Mary Queen of Scots*, 2 vols (London, 1844), II: 130. Future references will appear in the text.

21 Algernon Charles Swinburne, "The Character of Mary Queen of Scots" (1882). In *Complete Works of Swinburne*, ed. Edmund Gosse and Thomas James Wise, 6 vols (London, 1926), IV: 428. Future references to "Character" will appear in the text.

22 Swinburne, letter to Lord Houghton (1 June 1876). In *Letters of Algernon Charles Swinburne*, ed. Cecil Y. Lang, 6 vols (New Haven, 1959–1962), IV: 190.

23 Swinburne, *Chastelard*. In *Tragedies of Algernon Charles Swinburne*, 5 vols (London, 1905), II: 30. Future references to this play will appear in the text.

24 Recent exponents of this view, who point to grotesque fantasies like H. Rider Haggard's *She*, include Marilyn Woroner Fisch, Wayne Koestenbaum and Thais Morgan. See Fisch, "Swinburne's Divine Bitches: Agents of Destruction and Synthesis." In *Journal of Pre-Raphaelite Studies* 7 (1987), pp. 1–11; Koestenbaum, *Double Talk: The Erotics of Male Literary Collaboration* (New York, 1989); and Morgan, "Male Lesbian Bodies: The Construction of Alternative Masculinities in Courbet, Baudelaire and Swinburne." In *Genders* 15 (1992), pp. 37–53.

25 On the perversions of this set of juvenilia, see Jean Overton Fuller, *Swinburne: A Critical Biography* (London, 1968), pp. 446, 453.

26 Letter to Theodor Opitz (24 June 1879). In *Letters*, ed. Lang, IV: 64, 268.

27 Swinburne was himself flattered and slightly mystified that a "mere poet" would be asked to contribute to such a venerated organ of cultural authority, doubting "if the like compliment was ever paid before to one of our 'idle trade.'" Letter to Steadman (4 April 1882). In *Letters*, ed. Lang, p. 265.

28 Swinburne, "Mary Queen of Scots," reprinted from *Encyclopedia Britannica* (1883). In *Complete Works*, ed. Gosse and Wise, IV: 410.

29 Letter to Lord Houghton (12 July 1874). In *Letters*, ed. Lang, p. 307.

30 Or so Swinburne wrote to Alfred Austin, in *Letters*, ed. Lang, p. 305.

31 Edmund Gosse, *Swinburne* ([1875] Edinburgh, 1925), p. 46.

32 Quoted in Archibald Strong, *Four Studies* (Adelaide, 1932), p. 18.

33 Letter to John Morley (16 December 1872). In *Letters*, ed. Lang, pp. 211–212.

34 Swinburne was even anxious about the physical well-being of his texts pertaining to

Mary, down to the typeface of the Qs on the page. Letter to Andrew Chatto (26 July 1874). In *Letters*, ed. Lang, p. 320.

35 Swinburne, "Dedicatory Epistle" to *Works*, quoted in Strong, *Four Studies*, pp. 17–18.

36 Swinburne to Alfred Austin (10 July 1874). In *Letters*, ed. Lang, p. 305.

37 Knox, *Reformation*, II: 368.

38 For details of the tea see Donald Thomas, *Swinburne: The Poet in His World* (London, 1979), p. 87.

39 *The Spectator*, 2 December 1865; *Athenaeum*, 23 December 1865. Similar critical opinions were aired on *Mary Stuart*. The *Saturday Review*, for example, turned up its nose at the "rank flavour of Billingsgate" that its pages exuded (3 December 1881). This was a response that Swinburne wanted publicized.

40 Swinburne dedicated all three parts of the play to Hugo, and established other bonds with male contemporaries by sending a copy to Ford Madox Brown and leaving part of the manuscript in the house that he had shared with Theodore Watts. See *Letters*, ed. Lang, p. 238.

41 Gosse, *Swinburne*, p. 46.

42 *Mary Stuart*, in *Tragedies*, V: 196.

43 Michael Field, "Preface" to *The Tragic Mary* (London, 1890), p. vii. Future references to the preface and to the play will appear in the text.

44 While it happened some time after the play was finished, their conversion to Catholicism upon the devastating death of their Chow dog may do something to explain the fascination with Mary Stuart that spurred Bradley and Cooper to write *The Tragic Mary* in 1890.

45 Mary Sturgeon, *Michael Field* (London, 1922), pp. 153–154.

9 A "laboured illusion" vanishes

1 Editorial note to Margaret Oliphant, "Mr. Froude and Queen Mary." In *Blackwood's Magazine* (January 1870), p. 106.

2 Froude, *History*, XII: L361.

3 On the liberalization of Victorian historiography, see Timothy Reid, *The Victorians and the Stuart Heritage: Interpretations of a Discordant Past* (Cambridge, 1995).

4 Anon., "Elizabeth and Mary." In *Blackwood's* (April 1867), p. 389.

5 Quoted in Roger Green, *Andrew Lang: A Critical Biography* (Leicester, 1946), p. 19.

6 "Queen Mary," p. 614.

7 M'Crie, *The Life of John Knox* (Edinburgh, 1841). Knox, especially after Carlyle, became one of the great heroes of British history, partly to confirm its Protestant trajectory. On the Victorians' attitudes toward Catholicism, see "Popular Protestantism in Victorian Britain." In *Ideas and Institutions*, ed. Robson (London, 1967), pp. 115–142.

8 Deans, *Trials*, p. 96.

9 Martin Meisel, *Realizations: Narrative, Pictorial and Theatrical Arts in Nineteenth-Century England* (Princeton, 1983), p. 230.

10 On history as a "primary habit of mind" for the Victorians, and their tendency to regard the past as a mirror, see A. Dwight Culler, *The Victorian Mirror of History* (New Haven, 1985), p. 4.

11 Anon., "The New Spirit in History," in *Nineteenth Century* 38 (October 1895), p. 632.

12 Rosemary Jann, *The Art and Science of Victorian History* (Columbus, Ohio, 1985), p. xiii.

13 Christina Crosby, *The Ends of History: Victorians and the "Woman Question"* (London, 1991), pp. 6–7.

14 Clare Simmons, *Reversing the Conquest: History and Myth in Nineteenth-Century British Literature* (New Brunswick, NJ, 1990).

15 M'Crie, *Life of John Knox*, p. 203.

16 Thomas Carlyle, *The French Revolution*, 3 vols (London, 1837), XXVIII: 82–83; quoted in Culler, *Mirror*, p. 43.

17 Lang, *Mystery*, p. vii.
18 Alexandre Dumas, "Mary Queen of Scots." In *The Illustrated Literature of All Nations* (London, 1852), p. 38.
19 Froude, *History*, IX: 361.
20 "Mary Stuart and the Peterborough Exhibition." In *The Spectator* 60 (27 August 1887), p. 1148.
21 John Skelton, *Maitland of Lethington* (London, 1877), p. 277.
22 Jann proposes that Froude's nearly rabid reaction against Roman Catholic doctrine was the foundation of his historiography, and she traces his aberrant portrayal of Mary Queen of Scots to her faith; *Art and Science*, pp. 129–132.
23 James Anthony Froude, "The Science of History." In *Short Studies on Great Subjects* (London, 1899), I: 1.
24 Froude, "Autobiographical Essay," reprinted in Waldo Hilary Dunn, *James Anthony Froude: A Biography* (Oxford, 1961), p. 15.
25 Dunn, *Froude*, p. 16.
26 Froude's tormented childhood is elegantly summarized in Gertrude Himmelfarb, *Victorian Minds* (New York, 1968), pp. 236–238.
27 Swinburne praised Froude's "study" of her as "fascinating" in "Character," p. 428.
28 Skelton, *Maitland*, p. 204.
29 James Meline, *Mary Queen of Scots and Her Latest English Historian* (New York, 1873), pp. 1–2.
30 Benjamin, *Bonds of Love*, pp. 50–84.
31 Meline, *Latest*, p. 2.
32 Editorial preface, "Mr. Froude and Queen Mary," p. 106.
33 Charlotte Mary Yonge, *Unknown to History. A Story of the Captivity of Mary of Scotland* ([1882] London, 1901), p. 180. Future references will be to this edition and will appear in the text.
34 Both Yonge's volume on the history of France for E.A. Freeman's Historical Course for Schools and her *Landmarks of History* series were common classroom texts. Meanwhile, her *Aunt Charlotte's Stories* narrated episodes from Greek, German, French and American history, while her *Cameos from English History* appeared regularly from 1851 to 1898.
35 Yonge, "Preface," to *The Chaplet of Pearls* (London, 1868), p. v.
36 Alice Fairfax-Lucy, "The Other Miss Yonge." In *A Chaplet for Charlotte Yonge*, ed. Georgina Battiscombe and Margharita Laski (London, 1965), p. 90.
37 E. Purcell, "New Novels." In *The Academy* 21 (17 June 1882), p. 429.
38 Between Sophia Lee and Charlotte Yonge came two especially notable female-authored novels about Mary, Harriet Martineau's *The Wings of the Dove* (1862) and Emily Finch's *The Last Days of Mary Stuart* (1841).
39 Strickland, *Life*, II: 23. Strickland later insists that this "tradition" acquired its "delusive colour" from one of Mary's long illnesses, which was mistaken for pregnancy and childbirth (*Life*, II: 58).
40 Strickland, *Life*, II: 30.

Epilogue: postmodern Mary

1 Agnes Heller, *A Theory of History* (London, 1982).
2 *The Independent* (11 June 1997).
3 *The Guardian* (7 February 1994).
4 *Athenaeum* 4036 (4 March 1905), p. 278.
5 Andrew Lang, *Portraits and Jewels of Mary Stuart* (Glasgow, 1906), p. 8.
6 Paul Fussell, *The Great War and Modern Memory* (Oxford, 1975), p. 311.
7 Ludovic Maclellan Mann, *Mary Queen of Scots at Langside, 1568* (Glasgow, 1918), pp. 12–18.

8 Katherine Mann, "The Queen of Scots at Langside, 1568–1918." In Mann, *Langside*, p. 9.
9 Anon., *New Theatre* (September 1936), p. 21.
10 Otis Ferguson, *The New Republic* (19 August 1936), p. 47; *Hollywood Spectator* (1 August 1936), p. 8.
11 Margaret Drabble, *The Witch of Exmoor* (New York, 1996), pp. 73–74.
12 Penelope Lively, *Moon Tiger* ([1987] New York, 1988), pp. 14–15.
13 Liz Lochhead, *Mary Queen of Scots Got Her Head Chopped Off* (London, 1989), p. 11.
14 Walter Benjamin, "Theses on the Philosophy of History." In *Illuminations* (New York, 1968), trans. Zohn, p. 256.

Index